# GOD'S BEAUTY PARLOR

> Nostalgia Jewishness is a lullaby for old men
> gumming soaked white bread.
>
> J. GLADSTEIN, *modernist Yiddish poet*

## CONTRAVERSIONS

### JEWS AND OTHER DIFFERENCES

DANIEL BOYARIN,

CHANA KRONFELD, AND

NAOMI SEIDMAN, EDITORS

> The task of "The Science of Judaism"
> is to give Judaism a decent burial.
>
> MORITZ STEINSCHNEIDER,
> *founder of nineteenth-century*
> *philological Jewish Studies*

# GOD'S BEAUTY PARLOR

AND OTHER QUEER SPACES
IN AND AROUND THE BIBLE

STEPHEN D. MOORE

Stanford University Press • *Stanford, California*

Stanford University Press
Stanford, California

© 2001 by the Board of Trustees of the
Leland Stanford Junior University

Library of Congress Cataloging-in-Publication Data

Moore, Stephen D.
  God's beauty parlor : and other queer spaces in and around the Bible /
Stephen D. Moore.
    p. cm. — (Contraversions)
  Includes bibliographical references and indexes.
  ISBN 0-8047-4331-2 (alk. paper) — ISBN 0-8047-4332-0 (pbk. : alk. paper)
  1. Homosexuality—Biblical teaching. 2. Homosexuality—Religious aspects—Christianity. 3. Sex—Biblical teaching. 4. Masculinity of God—Biblical teaching. 5. Jesus Christ—Person and offices—Biblical teaching.
I. Title. II. Contraversions (Stanford, Calif.)
BS680.H67 .M66  2001
261.8'343—dc21                                                2001031183

Original printing 2001
Last figure below indicates year of this printing:
10  09  08  07  06  05  04  03  02  01

Typeset by James P. Brommer in 10/14.5 Minion
and Copperplate

*Ger and Pat,*
*this one's for you.*

## CONTENTS

LIST OF ILLUSTRATIONS *xi*
ACKNOWLEDGMENTS *xiii*

PROLOGUE / PLOT PREVIEW *1*

INTRODUCTION: THE YEAR OF QUEER *7*

### PART I: GOD'S BOUDOIR, GOD'S BEAUTY PARLOR . . .

**1** THE SONG OF SONGS IN THE HISTORY OF SEXUALITY *21*
Beautiful Brides, *22*; Scholarship Is Sexy, *29*; Allegory's Double Cross (Which Turns the Cross-Bearing Christian into a Christian Cross-Dresser), *39*; The Breast Pump, *50*; Allegory's Engine, *54*; Carnival Queens, *66*; After the Carnival (the Commentator Removes His Makeup), *74*; The New Allegorists, *82*

**2** ON THE FACE AND PHYSIQUE OF THE HISTORICAL JESUS *90*
The Tannery, *90*; The Beauty Parlor, *92*; The Asylum, *129*

**PART II: . . . GOD'S LOCKER ROOM, GOD'S WAR ROOM**

**3 SEX AND THE SINGLE APOSTLE** *133*
Of Men and Unmen, *135*; What's That Peculiar Thing Poking through the Tear in Saint Paul's Epistle to the Romans?, *146*; Things That Cannot Be Thought without Shame or Horror, *146*; The Locker Room, *169*

**4 REVOLTING REVELATIONS** *173*
War Book, I, *176*; War Book, II, *176*

IN LIEU OF A CONCLUSION: LINES INTENDED FOR A PUBLIC LAVATORY DOOR IN SAN YSIDRO, CALIFORNIA *201*

NOTES *207*
BIBLIOGRAPHY *279*
GENERAL INDEX *317*
INDEX OF ANCIENT AND MEDIEVAL SOURCES *331*

## ILLUSTRATIONS

1    Jacket illustration for John P. Meier, *A Marginal Jew*, vol. 2   *101*
2    Jacket illustration for John P. Meier, *A Marginal Jew*, vol. 1   *102*
3    Jacket illustration for E.P. Sanders, *The Historical Figure of Jesus*   *103*
4    Jacket illustration for John Dominic Crossan, *Jesus: A Revolutionary Biography*   *104*
5    Warner Sallman, *Head of Christ*, 1940   *109*
6    Warner Sallman, *Portrait of Jesus*, 1966   *112*
7    Warner Sallman, *The Lord Is My Shepherd*, 1943   *114*
8    Warner Sallman, *Christ Our Pilot*, 1950   *116*
9    James M. Murphy, *Christine on the Cross*, 1984   *157*

## ACKNOWLEDGMENTS

HATCHING AN IDEA for a book can be the work of a moment; enfleshing the idea and giving it wings is a labor of years. Bloated now, the four fledgling essays that make up this book are poised on the lip of the nest, ready to soar spectacularly, plummet disastrously, or flutter unsteadily over the void.

I might never have felt impelled to delve into the Song of Songs if Cheryl Exum and Fiona Black hadn't incited me to do so, and if their passion for it hadn't ignited my own. Later on, I traded Song of Songs papers with Roland Boer and David Carr. Initial incitements for the handsome Jesus essay, the ugly Paul essay, and the revolting Revelation essay stemmed from Fernando Segovia, David Clines, and David Jasper respectively, whether they realize it or not. And it was Janice Capel Anderson who first initiated me into the multidisciplinary field of masculinity studies.

Somebody undertaking an experimental project in biblical studies could hardly ask for more supportive and informative dialogue partners than Loveday Alexander, David Clines, Philip Davies, Cheryl Exum, and Barry Matlock, my former colleagues in the Department of Biblical Studies at the University of Sheffield—unless it be my present colleagues at Drew University Theological School, too numerous to acknowledge individually. Two in particular, however, have been unfailing sources of encouragement and inspiration to me, Virginia Burrus and Catherine Keller. Virginia is the most demanding reader I have ever had (well, next to Elizabeth Castelli, but certain of Elizabeth's pills have been too big for me to swallow whole, although my book would undoubtedly have been better had I managed to ingest more of them). Again and again Virginia declared, "You can do better than that," until eventually, somehow, I did. Catherine's support, too, has been very important to me, as has that of Daniel Boyarin, Amy-Jill Levine, Dale Martin, and Yvonne Sherwood. I write to please them, because their writing pleases me. I also feel a profound sense of gratitude to Marcia Ian, whose interest in my work has meant so much to me. A special word of thanks is also due to Elizabeth Clark.

I was fortunate to have among my graduate students at Sheffield gifted individuals whose creativity fanned the embers of my own—Andrew Dowsett, Ela Nutu, Simon Samuel, James Smith, Andrew Wilson, George Young, and especially Susan Graham. And now my Drew graduate students are challenging and inspiring me in turn—Marion Grau, Rob Seesengood, Eric Thurman. . . . My gratitude, too, to Vereene Parnell, for granting me admittance to her fascinating file on contemporary artistic representations of the crucifixion, to James Murphy for allowing me to reproduce his *Christine on the Cross*, and especially to Terry Todd for ushering me into the weird and wonderful world of Warner Sallman.

Numerous other colleagues and students in assorted institutions around Britain were dished up half-baked versions of various portions of this book at different times. For invitations and incisive input, I am especially grateful to Jimmy Dunn, Stephen Barton, and Loren Stuckenbruck at the University of Durham; to David Jasper, John Barclay, Joel Marcus, and John Riches at the University of Glasgow, along with the late lamented Robert Carroll; to Judy Lieu, Eddie Adams, Richard Burridge, Douglas Campbell, and Francis Watson at King's College London; to George Brooke, Philip Alexander, Kate Cooper, and Gerald Downing at the University of Manchester; and to Paul Fletcher at Lancaster, Hugh Pyper at Leeds, and John Schad at Loughborough. Since my return to the United States, Yale Divinity School has generously provided me with a similar forum (special thanks to Dale Martin, Harry Attridge, and Diana Swancutt), as has Vanderbilt Divinity School (special thanks to Amy-Jill Levine and Marianne Blickenstaff, as well as to Tina Pippin, my official dialogue partner on that occasion), and the Department of English at Rutgers University (special thanks to Marcia Ian and Barry Qualls). Various program units of the Society of Biblical Literature, too, provided outlets for portions of the book during its formative period, as did the American Society of Church History on one occasion (special thanks to Elizabeth Clark) and also the British New Testament Society, which supplied me with a wealth of constructive criticism in response to a plenary presentation (special thanks to Howard Marshall, Bruce Longenecker, and Brook Pearson).

The New Revised Standard Version is the English translation of the Bible most often favored in these pages, except when I venture my own translation or indicate that another has been used. For the Greek and Hebrew I am reliant on the twenty-seventh edition of the *Novum Testamentum Graece*; Rahlf's *Septuaginta*; and the fourth edition of the *Biblia Hebraica Stuttgartensia*.

Earlier drafts of various parts of the book—trial balloons, in some cases—appeared in the following books and journals, and are reprinted here in revised and extended form with the publishers' kind permission: *Church History*; David J. A. Clines and Stephen D. Moore, eds., *Auguries: The Jubilee Volume of the Sheffield Department of Biblical Studies* (Sheffield: Sheffield Academic Press, 1998); J. Cheryl Exum and Stephen D. Moore, eds., *Cultural Studies / Biblical Studies: The Third Sheffield Colloquium* (Sheffield: Sheffield Academic Press, 1998); Fernando F. Segovia, ed., "What Is John?" Vol. 2: *Literary and Social Readings of the Fourth Gospel* (Atlanta: Scholars Press, 1998); Ingrid Rosa Kitzberger, ed., *The Personal Voice in Biblical Interpretation* (New York: Routledge, 1998); and S. Brent Plate, ed., *The Apocalyptic Imagination: Aesthetics and Ethics at the End of the World* (Glasgow: Trinity St. Mungo Press, 1999).

I am grateful to Daniel Boyarin, Chana Kronfeld, and Naomi Seidman for graciously opening their series to a book that weighs in so heavily on the "Other Differences" side of the titular scale; to Peter Dreyer, my light-handed, eagle-eyed copy editor; and to the other superb professionals at Stanford University Press, not least its editorial director, Helen Tartar, and my production editor, Larry Goldsmith.

It is to Ger Shanahan and Pat Anderson, finally, friends and more from my Limerick and Galway days, that this book owes its ultimate raison d'être. This one's for you, lads, as they like to say in that part of the world, generally while raising a glass.

**GOD'S BEAUTY PARLOR**

_____

# PROLOGUE / PLOT PREVIEW

> There are many rooms in my Father's house...
>
> —JOHN 14:2 (JB)

THIS BOOK IS A SEQUEL, or possibly a prequel, to my previous book *God's Gym*. That book was composed of three freestanding but interlocking essays; this book rises to four. Like that book, this book too is obsessed with images of God and Jesus in and around the Bible, or rather the Bibles, Christian mainly, but also Jewish. The four essays in this book are staged in four distinct spaces—which, in another sense, are all the "same" space, since they are separated from one another (and from *God's Gym*) only by moveable partitions. The four spaces are God's boudoir, God's beauty parlor, God's locker room, and God's war room. And the action that unfolds across these four spaces—really, four stages—is not altogether innocent either of plot or character development.

I'm surprised to be able to report this. Certainly, it wasn't intentional. The essays were composed in countercanonical order, beginning with the essay on the Book of Revelation and culminating with the one on the Song of Songs—the opposite order to their present order in the book. The narrative linking the four essays (to which I shall shortly turn) only became apparent to me when I chanced to play them backwards.

Thematic links also exist between the four: *masculinity, homoeroticism, beauty*, and *violence*. These four themes are found in all four essays, although no one essay contains equal measures of each. Still further connections are provided by the common pool of theory and criticism from which the essays have imbibed. Queer theory provides a theoretical resource throughout (although particularly for the first three essays), as do masculinity studies (although particularly for the last three). The book leads off with an "autobiographical" introduction to queer theory, which segues (smoothly, I hope) into the first essay, "The Song of Songs in the History of Sexuality." Cultural studies and postcolonial studies also constitute significant resources for this book, particularly for the second, third, and final essays, while autobiographical (or personal) criticism is something that all four have internalized, but particularly the second and the last. And since I am not paid to do any of the above, but rather to be a professor of biblical studies, all four have consumed considerable quantities of critical biblical scholarship in addition (although not without occasionally affecting a Clintonesque refusal to inhale).

In truth, however, none of these corpulent corpora of theory and criticism have provided me with a "methodology" as such. Each of my four essays is ultimately reducible to a single syllogistic flourish. The flourish in each case entails the posing and answering of a central question: *Let us accept for the sake of argument that X happens to be the case. What flows from that proposition? What are its logical implications? its hidden ramifications? its probable consequences?*

What, then, are my propositions? They are four in number, naturally enough. And they center on sex and gender. But their real interest for me resides in their apparent innocuousness—their deceptive innocuousness, as we shall see: each of them turns out to be a rich site for ideological excavation. They can be crudely stated as follows:

Christianity and, to a lesser extent, Judaism have traditionally tended to enjoin on their male (no less than their female) adherents an affective relationship with their male deities.

Christians have almost always conceived of Christ—the "pre-Easter" as well as the "post-Easter" Christ—as conforming to cultural canons of physical attractiveness.

Paul's elliptical but incalculably influential pronouncements on homoeroticism are connected by diverse subterranean tunnels to other Greco-Roman discourses on sex and gender (the blandest proposition of all, perhaps: generations of Pauline scholars have descended into these ancient passageways; but have they really followed them through to the end?).

Messianic war is a prominent theme in that Christian arch-apocalypse, the Book of Revelation. (A hint as to where this might be leading: warfare was widely conceived of in antiquity as the quintessential performance of masculinity.)

But enough of propositions; it is time we turned to the plot.

The first essay fixates on the seductiveness of the Jewish God, the Christian God, and the Christian Christ, their apparent irresistibility even (or especially?) to religious persons of their own sex, who so often, it seems, have desired nothing more than to be swept up in the infinitely muscular divine arms and borne away to the infinitely mysterious divine bedchamber. To put it all too unsubtly (and no doubt riskily), the immodest aim of this first essay is to "out" the male religious Jew and Christian.

And what better place to stage this outing than on the verdant slopes of the Song of Songs, easily the most seductive text in any Bible, and the one in which Jewish and Christian commentators have traditionally frolicked with their Gods in and through the medium of allegory, Yahweh or Christ assuming the dashing role of the male lover in the Song, and Israel, the Church, or the soul assuming the buxom role of the female lover. The century that has recently drawn to a close tried to shut the book on the allegorical reading, preferring instead to read the Song literally, as ancient (human) love poetry. Whereas the literal reading is predicated on the assumption that the real subject matter of the Song is the mutual attraction between a man and a woman, the allegorical reading is predicated on the assumption that its real subject matter is, rather, the mutual attraction between two males: between a community or individual, on the one hand, classically conceived of as male, and a divine being, on the other hand, similarly conceived of as male. Allegorical readings of the Song thereby plunge the male allegorist into an intensely erotic relationship with the male God or male Christ. Allegory becomes a sanctioned space for the sublimated expression of homoerotic desire and for the adoption of a dizzying assortment of "queer" subject positions, as the male allegorist internalizes the femininity of the female protagonist of the Song, together with her ardent desire for her male lover. The significance of the allegorical interpretation of the Song for the reconsideration of male Jewish or Christian spirituality generally is that it thrusts out into the open a queer relationship that is ordinarily closeted. But the demise of the allegorical interpretation is no less significant. What are we to make of the fact that it apparently coincided with the invention and dissemination of heterosexuality?

Emboldened by the allegorical excesses analyzed in the first essay, the second essay shyly takes hold of Jesus' outstretched hand and lets itself be led away by him to feast its eyes greedily upon his handsome face and form. Christians have long demanded physical attractiveness in their Savior. Yet it has not always been so: the Church Fathers were no less desirous that he should be ugly. This curious fact (long gathering dust in the bottommost basement of the Church's collective memory) prompts an extended meditation on Jesus' place—and face—in the contemporary global culture industry, epitomized by the Hollywood film industry, with its trademark equation of looks with worth. The ultimate product of this global culture machine is an idealized heterosexual human couple, who are beautiful in accordance with an aesthetic code that is simultaneously white and Western, a new Adam and Eve. And it is in the image of this Adam, this Adonis, that Jesus is being remade, or made over, in the minds of millions of his adorers.

Intriguingly, whereas fewer and fewer people know what Jesus is supposed to have said, most remain reasonably confident that they at least know what he looked like—undeterred by the fact that no ancient document contains a description of his "earthly" form. In light of the latter consideration, one might reasonably expect that current scholarly reconstructions of the historical Jesus would accord no role whatsoever to his physical aspect—but one would be wrong. A large number of recent historical Jesus books beg to be read by their covers, which feature surprisingly specific images of the supposedly faceless Nazarene, images that almost invariably depict him as physically attractive. Might not the socially subversive Jesus sketched by leading contemporary Jesus scholars be sorely in need of a rather different face and form, less those of a Hollywood leading man than of the unprepossessing Man of Sorrows embraced by the patristic Church?

As the third essay commences, the stage lights dim, the orchestra strikes a sinister note, and the plot takes a darker turn. If the first two essays analyze the Jewish God, the Christian God, and the Christian Christ as *objects* of sexual desire primarily, the third essay singles out the Christian God and analyzes him as a *subject* of sexual desire. God's fantasy life is thus laid bare—and in the Epistle to the Romans, of all places.

This third essay attempts to decode the dense logic of Romans 1:18–3:31, using 1:26–27—Paul's infamous pronouncements on homoeroticism—as a cryptographic key. The God lightly concealed in these chapters turns out to be a Priapean personage who is the exact antithesis of the celibate Paul's public persona. In the fullness of time, this ithyphallic deity had the perfect orifice offered to him, and in a spirit of perfect submission. The crucified Jesus in his relationship to God perfectly models the submissiveness that should characterize the female's proper relationship to the male. This is the sexual substratum of Paul's soteriology.

Paradoxically, however, the Pauline Jesus' spectacular act of submission—his consummately "feminine" performance—is simultaneously a performance of "masculinity," through being a bravura display of self-mastery (the supreme index of masculinity in the intellectual milieux of the ancient Mediterranean world). Implicitly for Paul, Jesus is both a paragon and an enabler of masculinity, so that the salvation proffered to the audience of Romans amounts to the attainment of true manhood. Righteousness in Romans is essentially a masculine trait, therefore—the very mark of masculinity, indeed. What then is unrighteousness, sin? What else but loss of self-mastery, lack of masculinity—in a word, femininity. Sinfulness is essentially a feminine trait in Romans.

Although Paul implicitly presents Jesus' submission to God as a model of feminine submission in 1:18–3:31, Paul cannot permit Jesus to become mired in femininity. The redemption of femininity is accomplished through its transmutation into masculinity. The passage from sin to righteousness that Romans proclaims is not only christological through and through, it is also gendered through and through. And so the story that Romans tells is a saga of soteriological sex change: the Jesus of Romans is a woman forever in the process of becoming a man. But that is not the end of the story, as we shall see. In a sense it is not even the beginning.

In the fourth and final essay, the violence that seethed beneath the blue-veined surface of the Priapean protagonist of the third essay erupts fully, and the Christian God rampages across the stage, now become an apocalyptic battlefield. Starting from the observation that warfare was the quintessential performance of masculinity in the ancient Mediterranean world (whether literal war with an external enemy or metaphoric war with an internal enemy, one's unruly passions and desires), this essay explores the gender dynamics of the profuse martial imagery in the Book of Revelation. (Too) simply put, the argument runs as follows. Revelation can plausibly be said to be about the establishment of God's kingdom on earth. How is this kingdom to be established? Through the messianic war. And what is the messianic war? An activity that, on the symbolic level, is conducted exclusively by male subjects, and is constitutive of the masculinity of those subjects, since it is ultimately directed against the feminine.

Interwoven with this reading of Revelation, however, are several other threads, each of them blood red. The first concerns the ancient Jewish martyrological text, 4 Maccabees, itself a splatter text of the first order. The intricate interweaving of the martyrological and the martial in Revelation is not the least of its interests. But whereas Revelation is a muted celebration of martyrdom and masculinity, 4 Maccabees is a garish celebration of both. Superimposed upon Revelation, 4 Maccabees colors in its blanks with lurid hues.

The second thread is drawn from much further afield (the interest here lies in seeing just how far a reading can be stretched without breaking) and concerns the role of martyrs and martyrdom in modern Irish nationalism. The armed revolt of 1916 against British colonial rule succeeded only because the authorities unwittingly turned the captured rebel leaders into popular martyrs by executing them. But this Irish martyrology is itself framed by the ancient Irish war book the *Táin Bó Cuailnge*, every page of which is a paean to war, warriorhood, and masculinity (yet another splatter book, in fact). In colonial and postcolonial Ireland, the hero of the *Táin*, Cúchulainn, has functioned as a central symbol for the armed struggle for nationhood.

The purpose of the *Táin* in this essay, however, is to frame the Book of Revelation. Whereas Revelation is a muted celebration of war, the *Táin* is a garish celebration of war. Superimposed upon Revelation, the *Táin*, too, colors in its blanks with lurid hues. Revelation is a Christian war scroll. But the *Táin* is what this war scroll would look like fully unfurled. For the themes of masculinity and mass death are intimately intertwined in Revelation, which turns out to be a book about war making men making war making men . . . —some of whom also happen to be gods.

Stir in the steamy spectacle of men and gods making passionate love to each other, and you have most of the active ingredients of the present book as well.

# INTRODUCTION: THE YEAR OF QUEER

> Mulrennan spoke to him about universe and stars.
> Old man sat, listened, smoked, spat. Then said:—
> Ah, there must be terrible queer creatures
> at the latter end of the world.
>
> —JAMES JOYCE,
> *A Portrait of the Artist as a Young Man*

*San Diego, California, December 27, 1994.* An army of name-tagged academics is pouring into the lobby of the San Diego Marriott Hotel. The 110th Convention of the Modern Language Association is under way. With attendance figures regularly in excess of twelve thousand, making it the largest meeting of its kind in the humanities, this conference is to the average North American literary studies professional as the Joint Annual Meeting of the American Academy of Religion and the Society of Biblical Literature is to the average North American religious studies professional, which is to say unmissable. The MLA has long been an incubator for movements, methods, and trends that, when hatched, immediately begin to waddle under disciplinary fences into neighboring fields, where they are stalked, devoured, and digested by field hands bored with the dreary fare that their own disciplines dish out, or merely hungry for a more varied diet.

Sitting in the lobby of the Marriott, one of a tiny handful of biblical scholars at the 1994 MLA,[1] I wonder, not for the first time, whether I myself am not trying to tunnel under the fence in the opposite direction, to escape altogether from biblical studies, a discipline that, despite the deep affection I still feel for it, insists on burying me alive every now and then. I feel this sense of suffocation most acutely, and hear the earth raining down on my coffin most clearly, whenever I attend the annual meeting of the Studiorum Novi Testamenti Societas, the most prestigious learned society in the international field of New Testament studies, but also one of the muddier corners of that forbiddingly high-walled field. For so mired is the SNTS in nineteenth-century epistemological assumptions that I sometimes have to rub my eyes to reassure myself that a given presenter at a seminar or plenary session is not sporting muttonchop whiskers, a stovepipe hat, or a frock coat. And so far distant is the world of the SNTS from the world of the MLA that light from the latter, speeding toward the former this very instant at 186,000 miles per second, probably will not reach it before the MLA has ceased to exist altogether, having exploded or imploded during some future Orwellian or Atwoodian regime. Or merely fallen victim to some less dramatic demise of the sort to which any gigantic gaggle of intellectuals is perennially prone in an anti-intellectual culture. In such a culture, an association such as the MLA is ordinarily invisible—except for fleeting moments when it is sensationalized, certain of its more provocative paper titles, say, being seized upon with outraged delight by conservative news columnists in the cites in which the MLA encamps. (They especially relished Eve Kosofsky Sedgwick's "Jane Austen and the Masturbating Girl," to which I shall return below.)

The passage of ideas from literary studies to biblical studies has generally been plagued by weird temporal distortions. Illustrations of this are embarrassingly easy to come by. A two-minute rummage through my bookshelves turns up a typical example, whose author is a distinguished New Testament scholar. "Scholarly study of the Gospels entails several important tasks," he informs his implied audience of neophytes in an essay on early Christian images of Jesus, "which are achieved through the application of three methods: (1) source criticism, (2) form criticism, and (3) redaction criticism." Succinct definitions of these traditional methods then follow. The section ends with a statement that interests me (and depresses me, if the truth be told): "We now hear of new methods such as 'structuralism,' 'reader response' criticism, 'rhetorical' criticism, and 'social-scientific' criticism." This short announcement is punctuated by no fewer than four footnotes, the last of which contains a further interesting observation: "I have deliberately omitted 'deconstructionism.' It is more of an assumption than a method, resting on confusion and misunderstanding of what language and literature attempt to and in fact usually do accomplish."[2] Question: What year is this scholar writing in? 1977? (That, give or take a year or two, might appear to be the likely answer, but it is in fact incorrect.) 1987? Try 1997. This time-warp factor is what enables reader-response critics of the Bible, say, to seem like an exotic new species of scholar to the SNTS regular long after the last reader-response critic in the far distant galaxy that is literary studies has closed her book, and then her eyes, and gratefully slipped into the slumber from which there is no awakening.[3]

An exaggeration? Undoubtedly. Still, of the 774 sessions featured at the 1994 MLA meeting (each session containing an average of around three papers), not a single session—not a single paper, indeed (judging from the paper titles in the program, all of which I perused, although I didn't quite manage to attend all of them)—was devoted to reader-response criticism. What else gets literary critics of the Bible excited? Answer: narratology.[4] But of the 774 sessions, only one was devoted to narratology. Of course, I am not suggesting for a moment that the sober scholars of the SNTS, or their no less sober colleagues in the SOTS (Society for Old Testament Studies), laden down as they are with massive erudition in all matters ancient, should lumber after every fleeting fashion or fad that flashes across the sultry skies of the MLA. That sounds a little too much like the script for a Monty Python sketch. And anyway I'm not exactly quick on my own feet—I'm still stuck in 1994, after all, mired in a century now past—and a little short-sighted, too, liable to mistake a flash in the dark for a bolt from the blue.

I don't want to idealize or romanticize the MLA either. By and large, it's a sea of gray, like any other academic association. But within the vast monochrome expanse, unique forms of intellectual life do flourish. Whimsical forms, too. Consider the following creation, for instance, sighted in the Call for Papers for the 1999 MLA convention:

> *Victorian Breasts.* Functional versus ornamental breasts, erotic breasts, classed breasts, imperial and/or colonized breasts, nationalist breasts, aging breasts, beauty and the breast, medical breasts, and related topics considering representations of the breast in Victorian Britain. 1–2 page abstracts and vitae by 10 Mar. . . . [5]

So what is hot at the MLA in 1994? Well, the weather is warm for one thing. A midwinter conference in a subtropical venue tests the commitment of the conferencee like no other when he or she happens to hail from colder climes. By early afternoon on the first day, I'm already terribly torn between heading over to the book exhibit hall (over 175 publishers peddling their wares) and making a beeline for San Diego's famed Gaslight District instead—or even hopping on a bus to the Mexican border, a scant fifteen miles away. Duty triumphs over temptation (at least for now) and I trudge off resignedly to the book exhibit.

Perusal of the conference program on the plane to San Diego, coupled with hit-and-run visits to upwards of a dozen paper presentations during the course of the morning, has left me in no doubt: 1994 is the Year of Queer.[6] Here and there, if not yet everywhere, earnest young women and men, some clad in funereal black, their faces discreetly pierced, together with older women and men, some clad in conventional conference garb, have been reading papers with titles such as:

"The Queer Gaze"
"The Queerness of Collaboration"
"Queer Sexuality: From Tautology to Oxymoron"
"Queer Theory and the Problems of Identity"
"In the Nation's Closets"
"Obstructive Behavior: Dykes in the Mainstream of Critical Discourse"
"Lesbian and Gay Parenting in Academe"
"So Just When Can You Be a Lesbian in Cyberspace?"
"Monotheism as a Masquerade: Homosexuality, Effeminacy, and Other Graven Images"
"Sexual, Racial, and Religious Queerness in the Late Middle Ages"
"*Edward II*: Renaissance Sex, Queer Nationality"
"Queer Cousins: Balzac's Dissymmetries"
"Mark Twain and the Transvestite Novel"
"Transference as Queer Performativity in *The Turn of the Screw*"
"Queer Histories and Deviant Science: Rereading 1940's *Wonder Woman*"
"Out in Africa"
"Gays on the Contemporary Russian Literary Scene"
"The Construction of Russian Lesbian Identities"

"Latino Bodies, Queer Spaces"
and "Mucho Multi: La Queer y Coalition Building in Latina Drama"

in sessions with titles such as:

"Queer Space"
"Que(e)rying Sexuality"
"Que(e)rying the Millenium"
"Queer Culture, Pop Culture"
"Queer Emergences: A Graduate Student Showcase"
"The Epistemology of the Queer Classroom"
"Dissymmetries: Lesbian Theory, Gay Theory"
"Lesbian Studies, Feminist Studies, and the Limits of Alliance"
and "Russian Lesbian, Gay (and Queer?) Studies: The State of the
    (Emerging) Field."[7]

It's the same story at the book exhibit. Trend-setting publishers such as Routledge have managed, in a remarkably short space of time, to amass an impressive number of "queer" titles:

*Queer Looks*
*Queering the Pitch*
*Tilting the Tower: Lesbians/Teaching/Queer Subjects*
*The Lesbian and Gay Studies Reader*
*The Gay and Lesbian Liberation Movement*
*Inside/Out: Lesbian Theories, Gay Theories*
*Sexual Sameness: Textual Differences in Lesbian and Gay Writing*
*Lesbian Utopics*
*What a Lesbian Looks Like*
*Reclaiming Sodom*
*Modern Homosexualities*
*One Hundred Years of Homosexuality*
*My American History: Lesbian and Gay Life During the Reagan/Bush Years*
*Walking after Midnight: Gay Men's Life Stories*
*Growing Up Before Stonewall: Life Stories of Some Gay Men*
*Erotics and Politics: Gay Male Sexuality, Masculinity and Feminism*
*Homographesis: Essays in Gay Literary and Cultural Theory*

*Making Trouble: Essays on Gay History, Politics, and the University*
*Defiant Desire: Gay and Lesbian Lives in South Africa*
*Safety in Numbers: Safer Sex and Gay Men*
*Crossing the Stage: Controversies on Cross-Dressing*
*Vested Interests: Cross-Dressing and Cultural Anxiety*
*Male Impersonators*
*Straight Male Modern*
*Perversions*
*The Politics and Poetics of Camp*
and *Gender Outlaw*.[8]

"Queer theory" is currently the term of choice for this particular flurry of academic activity, a term coined, not by right-wing denouncers of the academy (who are going to have a ball with MLA '94 once they get wind of it, I realize as I peruse the program; the columns will write themselves: "Homosexuals are taking over our universities and corrupting the minds and morals of our youth . . . "), but by certain of the practitioners of lesbian and gay studies themselves. The term itself is rather queer, in fact. Lauren Berlant and Michael Warner remark: "We wonder whether *queer commentary* might not more accurately describe the things linked by the rubric, most of which are not theory."[9] The term made its public debut at a 1990 conference on queer theory at the University of California, Santa Cruz. The following year saw it emblazoned on the covers of *differences* and *Social Text*.[10] But what is the explanation for the subsequent explosion of interest in lesbian and gay studies among literary studies professionals—not *all* of whom, presumably, are lesbian or gay?

In order to fathom the mystery, we must first chart the contours of gender studies, the larger phenomenon of which queer theory is frequently said to be a part.[11] The standard story runs as follows. Gender studies should not be confused with feminist studies. Gender studies does encompass feminist theory and criticism, and women's studies generally, but it also encompasses men's studies or, as it is less commonly (but more aptly) termed, masculinity studies, which, in its more sophisticated manifestations (those that blush or blanch at the mere mention of Robert Bly's *Iron John*), culls critical strategies from feminist studies in order to examine how masculinity is culturally constructed or performed.[12] The (unisex) umbrella term "gender studies" also offers shelter to lesbian and gay studies, and its obstreperous offshoot, queer theory—or so it is often assumed. Sometimes it is said in addition that just as feminist studies, followed by masculinity studies, has succeeded in making *gender* a viable subject for academic work, queer theory has succeeded in making *sex* and *sexuality* viable subjects for academic work—but this particular division of labor is almost certainly a crude fabrication, as Judith Butler has pointed out. "Where would the feminist traditions in favor of enhancing sexual freedom fit in such a scheme," she asks rhetorically, "much less those that analyze the interrelation of gender and sexuality?"[13] The fact remains, of course, that queer theory *has* come to be commonly associated with the study of sex and sexuality to an extent that feminism has not. Is the secret of queer theory's immense popularity, even among "straight" professors and their students, thereby revealed at a stroke? Very likely. But there's more.

What *is* sex, anyway? Many things to many people, no doubt, but in recent academic textbooks, it is a term that is routinely contrasted with "gender." "Sex," in this rather chaste usage, denotes the complete set of anatomical or biological "givens" (most conspicuously those least often seen) that mark (most) human bodies as either male or female. "Gender," in contrast, denotes the cultural product of a complex set of symbolic practices that mark (most) human subjects as either masculine or feminine, beginning in contemporary Western culture at the moment when most newborn infants are swaddled in either blue or pink as the outward mark of a gendered identity that they will eventually be expected to internalize.

So far, so good, it might seem, *nature* on the one side, exemplified by "sex" (maleness or femaleness, biologically determined), and *culture* on the other side, exemplified by "gender" (masculinity or femininity, behaviorally determined). But now *sexuality* flounders in to muddy and disturb these clear and tranquil waters. For as Eve Kosofsky Sedgwick, author of the aforementioned "Jane Austen and the Masturbating Girl"[14] and doyenne of queer theory, has intimated, sexuality inhabits sex and gender simultaneously, deftly blurring the boundary between them and causing each to lose its identity in the other in a kind of epistemic ménage à trois. What contemporary culture refers to as "sexuality" "is virtually impossible to situate on a map delimited by the feminist-defined sex/gender distinction," argues Sedgwick.

> To the degree that it has a center or starting point in certain physical sites, acts, and rhythms associated (however contingently) with procreation or the potential for it, "sexuality" in this sense may seem to be

of a piece with "chromosomal sex": biologically necessary to species survival, tending toward the individually immanent, the socially immutable, the given. But to the extent that, as Freud argued and Foucault assumed, the distinctively sexual nature of human sexuality has to do precisely with its excess over or potential difference from the bare choreographies of procreation, "sexuality" might be the very opposite of what we originally referred to as (chromosomal-based) sex: it could occupy, instead, even more than "gender" the polar position of the relational, the social/symbolic, the constructed, the variable, the representational.[15]

Sedgwick's casual allusion to the assumptions of Michel Foucault is by no means incidental here. For the French philosopher-cum-historian's three-volume *History of Sexuality*—the introductory volume in particular—is frequently regarded as the charter document of the new gender studies, most especially of queer theory.[16] More than any other work before it, *The History of Sexuality* deftly unhooked sexuality from its presumed attachment to "nature" and left it dangling, naked and shivering, from the peg marked "culture" instead.

The definitive distinction for the concept of sexuality is that of heterosexuality versus homosexuality, just as the definitive distinction for (chromosomal) sex is that of male versus female, and for gender that of masculine versus feminine. Foucault famously locates the "invention" of the homosexual in the nineteenth century and the (then nascent) sciences of psychology and psychiatry.[17] (He actually assigns a precise age to the homosexual: an 1869 article by Karl Friedrich Otto Westphal on "contrary sexual sensations . . . can stand as [his] date of birth.")[18] As defined by earlier legal and religious codes, "sodomy was a category of forbidden acts; their perpetrator was nothing more than the juridical subject of them." In stark contrast, however, the nineteenth-century homosexual was

> a personage, a past, a case history, and a childhood. . . . Nothing that went into his total composition was unaffected by his sexuality. It was everywhere present in him: at the root of all his actions because it was their insidious and indefinitely active principle; written immodestly on his face and body because it was the secret that always gave itself away. It was consubstantial with him, less as a habitual sin than as a

singular nature. . . . Homosexuality appeared as one of the forms of sexuality when it was transposed from the practice of sodomy onto a kind of interior androgyny, a hermaphrodism of the soul. The sodomite had been a temporary aberration; the homosexual was now a species.[19]

Not surprisingly, Foucault's confident dating of the birth of the homosexual has not met with universal agreement, even among those who share his social constructionist assumption that homosexuality is not a transhistorical essence but a historical formation.[20] And it is not a case of alternative dates deviating from Foucault's by a year or two; rather, they range all the way from the Middle Ages to the early decades of the twentieth century.[21] Closer inspection reveals, however, that these various historians are not all engaged in the same language game. In contrast to a scholar such as Alan Bray, say, who argues in his book *Homosexuality in Renaissance England* that the so-called "molly houses" of late-seventeenth-century London constituted a fledgling homosexual subculture,[22] Foucault characteristically wants to know when the concept of homosexuality itself first became enshrined in a "discourse of knowledge." Discourses of knowledge conspire to produce that which they purport to describe (or so Foucault's fundamental Nietzscheanism powerfully predisposes him to believe), although never without resistance. And resistance itself put the finishing touches to the figure of the homosexual that nineteenth-century discourses of knowledge had painted over the earlier portrait of the sodomite, or so Foucault seems to imply:

> There is no question that the appearance in nineteenth-century psychiatry, jurisprudence, and literature of a whole series of discourses on the species and subspecies of homosexuality, inversion, pederasty, and "psychic hermaphrodism" made possible a strong advance of social controls into the area of "perversity"; but it also made possible the formation of a "reverse" discourse: homosexuality began to speak in its own behalf, to demand that its legitimacy or "naturality" be acknowledged, often in the same vocabulary, using the same categories by which it was medically disqualified.[23]

When homosexuality took its first shambling steps in the sexological laboratories of nineteenth-century Europe, however (lightning crackling above the castle, the villagers huddling fearfully below), it did so hand in hand with a nonidentical twin, heterosexuality. For the terms "homosexual(ity)" and "heterosexual(ity)" first saw the light of day simultaneously. This Foucault omits to mention—along with the fact that the Westphal article that he proffers as the homosexual's birth certificate uses neither term. Coincidentally, in 1869, the same year in which Westphal published his paper, Karl Maria Kertbeny gave birth to both these terms of destiny, "homosexual" and "heterosexual" (along with two further terms, "monosexual" and "heterogenit," which, unfortunately, were stillborn) in a letter to a fellow sexologist, Karl Heinrich Ulrichs. As it happened, both these sexological label-lovers were *defenders* of same-sex love, the paradox to which Foucault alludes in the previous quotation from *The History of Sexuality*, although not in reference to their work. The term "homosexual" took to the streets almost immediately, appearing publicly in an anonymous leaflet by Kertbeny mere months after he had created it, whereas its twin, "heterosexual," did not appear in print until 1880, again in a defense of homosexuality, this time by a zoologist.

But to speak of homosexuality and heterosexuality as twin products of a single act of creation may be misleading. If emphasis is placed instead on the fact that the term "homosexual(ity)" made its public debut *before* the term "heterosexual(ity)," a rather different myth of origins comes into view, one in which the creation of the former category enabled the subsequent creation of the latter. Or as Annamarie Jagose provocatively puts it, "since the term 'heterosexuality' is a back formation of 'homosexuality'—the former circulating only after the latter—heterosexuality is derivative of homosexuality."[24]

Indeed, Jonathan Katz argues compellingly in *The Invention of Heterosexuality* that the concept of heterosexuality "as we know it" is principally a twentieth-century product. He shows how the sexological term "heterosexuality" began life, not as the name of the normal and the good, but rather as the name of a *perversion*: the compulsion to seek sexual pleasure purely for its own sake and not as a means to procreate. As late as 1923, Merriam-Webster's authoritative *New International Dictionary* defined heterosexuality as a medical term denoting "morbid sexual passion for one of the opposite sex." Only in 1934 did Webster's "heterosexuality" attain its now familiar form, a "manifestation of sexual passion for one of the opposite sex; normal sexuality."[25] Freud is both the hero and the villain of Katz's sexological saga, the "real" inventor of heterosexuality. Freud's Promethean accomplishment, according to Katz, was the transformation of heterosexuality from an obscure late-Victorian sexual pathology into the gold standard of twentieth-century normality.[26]

Despite the best efforts of the sexual constructionists, however, many continue to object, whether on intellectual or intuitive grounds, that the invention of the terms or even the concepts "heterosexuality" and "homosexuality" should not be confused with that to which they refer: a fundamental polarity in sexual orientation that transcends the contingencies of culture and history. The rebuttal of this eminently commonsensical assumption, the mounting of a compelling counterargument that there is no transhistorical essence either of homosexuality or heterosexuality, is one of the more ambitious tasks that queer theory has taken on (to the extent that queer theory can be spoken of in the singular). This counterargument has profound political stakes, striking as it does at a central pillar of Western culture, what queer critics commonly refer to as "heteronormativity." For what is at issue "in the postfeminist appropriation of Foucault's history of sexuality is a radical questioning of the . . . hegemony of heterosexuality," as Naomi Schor puts it. And it is surely no accident that this questioning, this que(e)rying, "has been carried farthest by gay or gay-identified and lesbian theoreticians bent on disturbing, not to say dismantling, heterosexuality,"[27] which, so long as it is assumed to be natural, neutral, universal or God-given, remains the ultimate ideological formation.

What of me personally? Certainly, I am more than a little bent. But am I "bent on disturbing, not to say dismantling, heterosexuality"? In my own modest way, yes, if by heterosexuality we mean compulsory heterosexuality. And on dismantling masculinity as well while I'm at it, if by masculinity we mean hegemonic masculinity, the latter also being a major concern of this book. Why limit myself to one absurdly outsized target when I can have two? At least it will be doubly hard to miss.

But if queer theory tends to be so preoccupied with the heterosexual/homosexual opposition, can it cope adequately with cultures that possess neither concept? Do such cultures provide "logical" points of engagement for queer critique—ancient Mediterranean culture, say, to raise what for me is the most pressing example, the culture that numbers the New Testament among its products? I am confident that the latter culture, at least, does provide obvious points of insertion for queer interrogation. If life in contemporary Western culture (sexual life especially) is regulated by regimes of the normal, life in ancient Mediterranean culture (sexual life especially) was regulated by regimes of the natural, as we shall see, and the natural, no less than the normal, demands close critical scrutiny—all the more since "their" natural was the progenitor of "our" normal—and queer theory, although a critical sensibility more than a methodology, eminently equips us to scrutinize it.[28] (In the present work, as in so many others, "queer" is a supple cipher both for what *stands over against* the normal and the natural to oppose, and thereby define, them, and what *inheres within* the normal and the natural to subvert, and indeed pervert, them—this opposition and subversion privileging, but by no means being confined to, the mercurial sphere of the sexual.) Add to the normal-natural liaison the curious fact that the so-called "charter document" of queer theory, Foucault's *History of Sexuality*, while setting out initially to examine the modern invention of sexuality, is soon obliged to backtrack drastically, and ends up spending two of its three extant volumes in the Greco-Roman world and only one in the modern—and the suspicion soon arises that queer theory and the New Testament are already having an affair behind our backs. The details of this affair are a subject of speculation in the present book, especially in Chapter 3, "Sex and the Single Apostle."

Yet queer theory's reach in biblical studies need by no means be limited to the New Testament, nor to the Christian tradition, as the opening essay, "The Song of Songs in the History of Sexuality," is designed to show.

## PART I: GOD'S BOUDOIR, GOD'S BEAUTY PARLOR . . .

It remains for us to find how to obtain the beauty without which [the soul] cannot please him who is lovelier than all the sons of men [Ps. 44:3]. For it hears that "the king shall desire your beauty" [Ps. 44:12]. What great spiritual goods we have mentioned: gifts from the Word, goodwill, knowledge, virtue, wisdom! Yet we read that none of them is desired by the king, who is the Word, but it only says, "the king shall desire your beauty." The prophet says, "The Lord is king, he is clothed in beauty" [Ps. 92:1]. How can he but desire a like garment for his Bride, who is also his likeness? And the closer the likeness, the dearer she will be to him.

—BERNARD OF CLAIRVAUX,
*Sermons on the Song of Songs 85.10*

. . . that other, Immaculatus, from head to foot, sir, . . . he who was well known to celestine circles before he sped aloft, our handsome young spiritual physician that was to be, . . . that mothersmothered model, that goodlooker with not a flaw. . . .

—JAMES JOYCE,
*Finnegans Wake*

# 1 THE SONG OF SONGS IN THE HISTORY OF SEXUALITY

> Solomon produced this book by divine inspiration
> in the language of a woman. . . .
>
> —RASHI, *Commentary on the Song of Songs,*
> Prologue (trans. Marvin Pope)

"SO YOU ACTUALLY READ THE BIBLE?" I asked in wonder. We had begun to converse two hours into the flight to San Diego. She had interrupted her copious note-taking on an issue of *GQ* (which magazine she had earlier claimed from a mildly bewildered flight attendant who had offered her *Vogue*) to whip out and consult an issue of *GLQ*[1]—at which point I could restrain my curiosity no longer. She turned out to be an English professor, not entirely unexpectedly, and when I admitted what I did for a living (usually a guaranteed conversation-killer) she casually revealed that she still read the Bible regularly. (One expects a professor of biblical studies to crack the Bible occasionally—less and less, admittedly—but not a professor of English, at least not the kind who subscribes to *GLQ*.) "But only the *beautiful* books," she added, hefting my Bible in one hand (she had caught it peeping out of my briefcase, shy as always about appearing in public, and deftly yanked it out) and *GQ* in the other; "Genesis, Ruth, and John—but mostly the Song of Songs." And in response to my look of frank disbelief, she began to recite, in a tone redolent of Pentecostal summer camp, all the while hoisting *GQ* aloft with its bare-torsoed male-model cover spread:

I charge you, O daughters of Jerusalem, if ye find my beloved, that ye tell him, that I am sick of love.

What is thy beloved more than another beloved, O thou fairest among women? What is thy beloved more than another beloved, that thou dost so charge us?

My beloved is white and ruddy, the chiefest among ten thousand. His head is as the most fine gold, his locks are bushy, and black as a raven. His eyes are as the eyes of doves by the rivers of waters, washed with milk, and fitly set. His cheeks are as a bed of spices, as sweet flowers; his lips like lilies, dropping sweet smelling myrrh. His hands are as gold rings set with the beryl; his belly is as bright ivory overlaid with sapphires. His legs are as pillars of marble, set upon sockets of fine gold; his countenance is as Lebanon, excellent as the cedars. His mouth is most sweet; yea, he is altogether lovely. This is my beloved, and this is my friend, O daughters of Jerusalem. . . .

**Beautiful Brides**

The arduous task of queering the Song of Songs, a text that is ostensibly an unequivocal celebration of male-female sexual love, was accomplished over many centuries by the Fathers and Doctors of the Church (as well as by Jewish sages of blessed memory, although they were hampered by a modesty and restraint to which their Christian cousins were seldom subject). Night after night in their cells, by flickering candlelight, they queered the Song of Solomon, strenuously enquiring after its spiritual meaning and confidently setting it forth. And as they did so, their austere cells were transformed into lavish theaters.

These performances are seldom seen or heard any more. Literal readings of the Song of Songs, which take its lyrical language of love and lust to mean precisely what it seems to be saying—*I want your body and I want it now*—have become commonplace in the past century or so, largely displacing the allegorical readings of the Song that proliferated and predominated in preceding centuries.[2] The literal readings purport to reveal what the allegorical readings sought to conceal. The allegorical readings can themselves be read as discourses of sexual repression. But it is as discourses of sexual *expres-*

*sion*—and of "deviant" sexual expression, at that—that I shall be reading them here. That which must under no circumstances be mentioned in the allegorical readings—the fact that the Song is suffused with erotic desire, that its cheeks are flushed with it, its pages moist with it—everywhere comes to expression in these readings.

Consider Origen of Alexandria (ca. 185–253), for example, whose commentary and homilies on the Song set the stage for so much that would follow. Actually, Origen not only sets the stage; he himself takes to the stage, amid rapturous applause, in his celebrated role as the "Bride" of the Song, played opposite the "Bridegroom," who is Christ. The following soliloquy is representative of many that punctuate Origen's exegetical performance:

> For there is a certain spiritual embrace, and O that the Bridegroom's more perfect embrace may enfold my Bride! Then I too shall be able to say what is written in this same book: *His left hand is under my head, and His right hand will embrace me* [Song 2:6].... And if He will condescend to make my soul His Bride too and come to her, how fair must she then be to draw Him down from heaven to herself, to cause Him to come down to earth, so that He may visit His beloved one! With what beauty must she be adorned, with what love must she burn that He may say to her the things which He said to the perfect Bride, about thy neck, thine eyes, thy cheeks, thy hands, thy shoulders, thy feet![3]

Christendom had to wait almost a thousand years for an artiste able to match Origen's rendition of the Bride's role. Indeed, Bernard of Clairvaux (1091?–1153) not only matched it, he outdid Origen in effusiveness. Listen to Bernard as he warms up:

> Of what use to me the wordy effusions of the prophets? Rather let him who is the most handsome of the sons of men, let him kiss me with the kiss of his mouth [Song 1:1].... [E]ven the very beauty of the angels can only leave me wearied. For my Jesus utterly surpasses these in his majesty and splendor. Therefore I ask of him what I ask of neither man nor angel: that he kiss me with the kiss of his mouth.

Now listen to this declaration of passion:

It is simply that I am in love. . . . It is desire that drives me on, not reason. . . . I ask, I crave, I implore: let him kiss me with the kiss of his mouth. Don't you see that by his grace I have been for many years now careful to lead a chaste and sober life, I concentrate on spiritual studies, resist vices, pray often. . . . As far as I can judge I have lived among the brethren without quarrel. I have been submissive to authority, responding to the beck and call of my superior. . . . With sweat on my brow I eat my bread. Yet in all these practices there is evidence only of my fidelity, nothing of enjoyment. . . . If therefore he is to find my holocaust acceptable, let him kiss me, I entreat, with the kiss of his mouth.[4]

And for a gender-bending finale:

While the bride is conversing about the Bridegroom, he, as I have said, suddenly appears, yields to her desire by giving her a kiss. . . . The filling up of her breasts is a proof of this. For so great is the potency of that holy kiss, that no sooner has the bride received it than she conceives and her breasts grow rounded with the fruitfulness of conception, bearing witness, as it were, with this milky abundance. Men with an urge to frequent prayer will have experience of what I say. Often enough when we approach the altar to pray our hearts are dry and lukewarm. But if we persevere, there comes an unexpected infusion of grace, our breast expands, as it were, and our interior is filled with an overflowing love; and if somebody should press upon it then, this milk of sweet fecundity would gush forth in streaming richness.[5]

How eerie it is to hear Bernard's voice again after all these years. I've aged, of course, and even he sounds different than he did when he first accosted me twenty-five years ago in Mount Melleray Abbey, in the Knockmealdown mountains of County Waterford. He was required reading in the novitiate, as were the other Cistercian Fathers.

But I cannot hold Bernard wholly responsible for that curious interlude in my life. It was Thomas Merton's *Elected Silence* that first seduced me, that convinced me that I had to become a monk. Merton's autobiography cost me two years of my own life. But they were memorable years, all told, and are the sole reason that I am sitting here writing this now, writing at all, being a biblical scholar, if that indeed is what I am. Merton's idyllic descriptions of Cistercian life drew me like a moth to a flame, the fierce flame of Christ's love, as I thought of it then. A single example will have to suffice. Listen to Merton emote on the occasion of his first visit to a Cistercian monastery—an effusion that told *me* exactly what to feel upon my own first visit to Mount Melleray, so that the ghost of Merton took possession of me and caused me to cast myself with abandon into the abyss of which he writes:

> The cloister was cold and dimly lit, and the smell of damp wool astounded me by its unearthliness. And I saw the monks. There was one, right there, by the door; he had knelt, or rather thrown himself down, before a *pietà* in the cloister corner, and he had buried his head in the huge sleeves of his cowl there at the feet of the dead Christ, the Christ who lay in the arms of Mary, letting fall one arm and a pierced hand in the limpness of death. It was a picture so fierce that it scared me; the abjection, the dereliction of this seemingly shattered monk at the feet of the broken Christ. I stepped into the cloister as if into an abyss.[6]

In the darkness of the abyss, aberrations occur. You yourself are a past master of the art of aberration, Bernard, of tightrope-walking above the abyss, you who did not hesitate to attribute even the voluptuous words of the female lover of the Song to the Blessed Virgin herself, casting her in the role of the Bride, mouthing the words for her, heedless of her blushes, when she hesitated to voice them herself, whispering them into the ear of her Son, now become her Bridegroom, and limp in her arms no longer. (Thankfully that prostrate monk still has his head buried in the sleeves of his cowl, and does not notice.) But I'm getting ahead of myself. We're not scheduled to view your pornographic *pietà*, Bernard, until much later.

Even Bernard would be hard-pressed, however, to hold his hard-won place as Christendom's most extravagant interpreter of the celebrated role of the Bride in the face of the stiff competition that was to follow—Denis the Carthusian (1402?–1471), for example, known, not for nothing, as the Ecstatic Doctor. The immoderation of Denis's interpretation merits a lengthy quotation:

> And so the contemplative soul once cleansed, set alight with a holy love, . . . with all its heart seeking its Bridegroom, . . . the Bridegroom above all nature and beyond the highest beauty, . . . bursts forth into a

sweet and love-laden cry: *May he kiss me with the kiss of his mouth*—he, that is, the most tender Bridegroom, who alone satisfies me. . . . He sets on fire my innermost will and my highest loves so that I may love his unlimited goodness with complete purity, constancy and intensity; so that I may taste his sweetness, an unfathomable, limitless and measureless stream; so that I may rest in his most pure embrace, so that I may be carried away, transformed and absorbed into him and all enraptured, be plunged into the most joyful, vast ocean of his happiness.

But how, oh you poor silly little soul, . . . how can you have the presumption, the boldness, even the least self-assurance to ask a kiss of him, of whom the heavens, the earth, the seas are all in awe, before whom the highest of the supreme spirits tremble, beneath whom bow the foundations of the globe? Again, if it would seem presumptuous to ask a kiss, I shall not say of the most glorious Virgin Mary, the mother of Christ, but even of the glorious virgin Queen Catherine or of Saint Ursula, how much the more so it seems to ask a kiss of the Holy of Holies, the all-powerful King before whom the whole world is like a tiny speck of dust? . . .

THE SOUL'S REPLY: Why do you call me back from the sight of my bridegroom? Why do you hold me back from his embrace? . . . Do you not know that the eagerness of love is not to be restrained by commonplace decencies? . . . Did he not himself create me so as to receive that happy kiss of his mouth in the homeland of the Blessed, to see him as he is, to enjoy endlessly his goodness and his sweetness, for the most complete fulfilment, for ever far from all disturbing distractions? He who pours his love into me, he also sets that love aflame and encourages it, and it is he who provokes and inflames me to beg for the kiss of his mouth. . . . He gave himself up to death so that I might become one with him for eternity and that I might be kissed by him. Behold, my heart is like wine that has no vent, like new wineskins it is ready to burst, I must speak that I may find relief. I will speak, therefore, to the Bridegroom and little by little I will recover my breath; and now, provoked by an explosion of desire I will say for the first time, *May he kiss me with the kiss of his mouth*; and a second time, *May he kiss me with the kiss of his mouth*; and a third time I repeat, *May he kiss me with the kiss of his mouth.*[7]

Denis was the first expositor to actually sing the role of the Bride, and in a shrill soprano, accompanied by startling contortions of face and body (at one point even falling off the stage).

Divas such as Denis would soon be exposed as hopeless hams, however, by the elegant interpretation of the role enacted by the Mystical Doctor, St. John of the Cross (1542–91). Here is a choice snippet from his performance, sung again, but with real feeling this time, and a seemly economy of gesture:

There He gave me His breast;
There he taught me a sweet and living knowledge;
And I gave myself to Him,
Keeping nothing back;
There I promised to be His bride.[8]

What are we to make of these intensely erotic readings of the "Spiritual Song"? In the past century or so, as was noted earlier, literal readings of the Song have all but displaced the allegorical readings. But whereas the enabling assumption of the literal readings is that the Song concerns the mutual attraction between a man and a woman, the enabling assumption of the allegorical readings is that the Song concerns the mutual attraction between two males: between a community or individual, on the one hand, classically conceived as male,[9] and a divine being, on the other hand, also conceived as male.

To put it another way, for classical Jewish and Christian commentators, the Song simply could not be what it seemed. That would have been unthinkable. Yet allegorizing it only had the effect of turning it into something yet more unthinkable: not just the torrid expression of a sizzling sexual relationship between a horny young woman and her hunky young man, hidden away among the books of Holy Scripture like a sex manual in a monastery library or a rabbinic House of Study, but the expression of an erotic relationship between two *male* lovers instead.

The allegorical interpretations of the Song sprang from disinclination, discomfort, or downright disgust on the part of pious male exegetes at the prospect of being thrust into an encounter with its female protagonist,[10] intimate knowledge of whose body or libidinal life is served up in every stich. Origen again sets the tone:

>HIS LEFT HAND IS UNDER MY HEAD, AND HIS RIGHT HAND SHALL EMBRACE ME [Song 2:6]. The picture before us in this drama of love is that of the Bride hastening to consummate her union with the Bridegroom. But turn with all speed to the life-giving Spirit and, eschewing physical terms, consider carefully what is the left hand of the Word of God, what the right; also what His Bride's head is—the head, that is to say, of the perfect soul or of the Church; and do not suffer an interpretation that has to do with the flesh and the passions to carry you away. (*Commentary on the Song of Songs* 3.9)

Subsequent allegorists of the Song, Jewish as well as Christian, also whisk us away, like nervous nannies, every time the bride and groom look as though they are getting ready to engage in a clinch.[11] Is it possible any longer to read with a straight face the staggering profusion of delicious nonsense occasioned by this discomfort? "*The meeting of your thighs.* . . . This refers to the coming together of Jews and Gentiles in the one Church of Christ. . . . *Your two breasts* are the two Testaments, from which the children begotten in Christ draw milk for their growth," and so on ad nauseam.[12]

With exquisite irony, however, the austere expositor's attempt to evade the perilous embrace of the Song's female lover through allegory plunges him instead into the arms of another lover, a *male* lover, no less—God or Christ. ("Each soul living in charity is an individual Bride of Christ," croons Denis, "and so our Lord and Saviour holds her close to him with the arms of love.")[13] With astonishing ease, the male expositor is seduced by the Song into whispering Shulamith's white-hot words of passion into the ear of the divine male personage in whose muscular arms he has eagerly taken refuge. ("Join with the Bride in saying what she says," urges Origen, "so that you may hear also what she heard" [*Homilies on the Song of Songs* 1.1].) Allegorical exegesis of the Song thereby becomes a sanctioned space—a stage, indeed—for some decidedly queer performances.[14] Finding himself upon this stage, the monk or rabbi (for the restraint I earlier ascribed to the latter is only relative, as it happens), however respectable or repressed he might be in "real" life, is possessed by a divine madness. Throwing off his religious garb and all his inhibitions with it, he paints his nails, decks himself out in flamboyant costumes, and camps it up with abandon. "I am the beautiful Bride in sooth," purrs Origen, sashaying across the stage, "and I show not my naked face to any save Thee only, whom I kissed tenderly but now" (*Homilies on the Song of Songs* 1.8).

## Scholarship Is Sexy

Some say that it was Rabbi Akiba (d. 135 C.E.) who first gazed upon the beautiful body of the male lover in the Song of Songs and beheld the body of God.[15] And Akiba was consumed with chaste desire for the owner of this exquisite body. He exclaimed in awe: "All the ages are not worth the day on which the Song of Songs was given to Israel!"[16] And he further announced:

> Before all the Nations of the World I shall hold forth on the beauties and splendor of Him Who Spake and the World Came to Be! For, lo, the Nations of the World keep asking Israel, "What is thy Beloved more than another beloved, that thou dost so adjure us" (Song 5:9), that for His sake you die, for his sake you let yourselves be slain, as it is said, "Therefore do the maidens (ʿlmwt) love Thee" (Song 1:3)—they love Thee to the point of death (ʿad mwt)!—and it is written, "Nay, but for Thy sake are we killed," etc. (Ps 44:23). Look you! you're attractive, look you! you're brave. Come, merge with us!
>
> But Israel replies to the Nations of the World: Have you any notion of Him? Let us tell you a little bit of His Glory: "My Beloved is white and ruddy," etc. (Song 5:10 ff.).
>
> And when the Nations of the World hear but a little bit of the Glory of Him Who Spake and the World Came to Be, they say to Israel, Let us go along with you, as it is said, "Whither is thy Beloved gone, O thou fairest among women? Whither hath thy Beloved turned Him, that we may seek him with Thee?" (Song 6:1).
>
> But Israel replies to the Nations of the World: You have no part of Him; on the contrary, "My Beloved is mine, and I am His" (Song 2:16), "I am my Beloved's and my Beloved is mine," etc. (Song 6:3).[17]

All of this has an uncannily familiar ring to me, as the father of a five-year-old girl, who, even as I struggle to compose these lines, is tugging at my sleeve and insisting, "I want you to play with me, Daddy, and I want you to play with me now!" And once I submit to this imperious summons, as I must, the stipulated game will almost certainly be Pretend. "Let's play Pretend. Let's pretend that I'm a beautiful princess, the most beautiful princess in the whole world, and you're a handsome prince, the most handsome prince in the whole world. . . . " But it's a relatively short step from that to this: "Let's play Pretend. Let's pretend that we're a beautiful girl, the most beautiful girl in the whole world, and that our god is a handsome god, the most handsome god in the entire universe, and that the other nations are other girls who are all madly jealous of us and want to share our handsome god with us, or even to steal him away...." Now pretend that this absorbing game is being played, not by a gaggle of girls in the four-to-seven age range, but by a company of venerable scholar-sages, and the incomparable queerness of the allegorical reading of the Song of Songs begins to become apparent.

For Rabbi Akiba is not the only one tugging at our sleeves. According to *Song of Songs Rabbah* 6.12 § 1, Rabbi Hiyya, commenting on Song 6:12 ("my fancy set me in a chariot beside my prince"), compared Israel's deliverance from Egypt to the situation of a princess who chanced to be laboring in a field when a king happened by. Perceiving that she was no common wench, he had her placed beside him in his carriage. "Her companions thereupon began to gaze at her in astonishment, saying, 'Yesterday you were gathering sheaves and today you sit in a carriage with the king!'"[18] Salvation history as a rags-to-riches fairy tale, with Israel in the role of a Jewish Cinderella? Allegory as children's fantasy? What is it about the Song of Songs that sends so many of its interpreters back to the nursery?

Even nonallegorical expositors of the Song are not impervious to its demands to play elaborate games of make-believe. The nineteenth-century German scholar Franz Delitzsch, for instance, saw Song 6:10 ("Who is this that appears like the dawn, fair as the moon, bright as the sun, majestic as the stars in procession?") as the beginning of what, for him, was the "First Scene of the Fifth Act" of the Song, a scene he fondly entitled "Shulamith, the Attractively Fair but Humble Princess," imagining that this stunning but modest beauty had just stepped forth from the recesses of the royal garden, causing the daughters of Jerusalem, who are bowled over by her appearance, to exclaim, "Who is this," etc.[19] This Shulamith is but "a rustic maiden," writes Delitzsch; "in body and soul she is born to be a princess, but in reality she is but the daughter of a humble family." Solomon, captivated by "her beauty and by the purity of her soul," "raises this child to the rank of queen."[20] And they live happily ever after.

And yet, for the rabbis at least, the interpretation of the Song was not all sweetness and light. The Hadrianic persecution of Jews in the early second century C.E. was inscribed in blood in the Song in interpretations attributed to Akiba of certain of its verses. And when Akiba himself was martyred, 1:4e ("rightly do they love you") was applied to him, the Song he had loved aptly becoming his crypt.²¹ On occasion, therefore, the hermeneutical playground in which the allegorical interpretation of the Song was staged could be bounded by barbed wire, elevated machine-gun posts, and storm troopers with snarling guard dogs.

Of this early martyrological turn in Song of Songs interpretation Daniel Boyarin has recently written:

> Rabbi Akiva is privy to a vision.... This vision, moreover, renders him, and by metaphorical extension the whole martyred people of Israel, brides of God—female, desiring subjects who render their desire in graphic description of the body of the desired divine male. Precisely because the desired object is male, within the normative heterosexuality of the text, the desiring subject is gendered female, whatever her sex. In other words, the martyr is the bride of God here, as in the stories of the archetypical fourth-century [Christian] virgin martyrs, Eulalia or Agnes.²²

And yet there is a more sinister aspect to this figure of the martyr bride. "'What is thy Beloved more than another beloved, that thou dost so adjure us' (Song 5:9), that for His sake you die, for his sake you let yourselves be slain, as it is said, 'Therefore do the maidens (ʿlmwt) love Thee' (Song 1:3)—they love Thee to the point of death (ʿad mwt)!" Willingness to do anything and everything for love, for one's beloved, that perennial romantic topos, receives a peculiar twist here—is, indeed, peculiarly, not to say perversely, twisted—since the Beloved in this instance is now ultimately responsible for the death-dealing trauma inflicted upon the body of his lover through his (human) instruments of torture and destruction. Through willing embrace of this torment, she is required to demonstrate the depths of her desire for him—essentially an S/M scenario coupling absolute power, on the one hand, with abject submission, on the other, and thereby transforming the anteroom of the World to Come into an S/M dungeon equipped with all the implements of intimately intermingled pain and pleasure (a place not without its attractions for me personally, if the truth be told, although I'm not sure that I would want to encounter my God there, at least not if he's the one wielding the whip).

In time the romance between God and Israel that had so enthralled Rabbi

Akiba was fully fleshed out in the *Targum of the Song of Songs*,[23] a romance extending from the creation of the cosmos to its eschatological climax and expressed through the Scriptures and the Oral Torah: God ta(l)king Israel to orgasm.

Scholars and scholarship loom large in the *Targum of the Song of Songs* and in the cognate midrashic commentaries on the Song,[24] as in rabbinic literature generally. And what the targum and the midrashim have to say concerning scholars and scholarship is calculated to give comfort even to a contemporary scholar such as myself, hunched hour after hour over a hot computer, steadily going blind as I stare into its glare, my body gradually turning to mush under the awful weight of endlessly deferred physical exercise. The message of the targum and the midrashim is as simple as it is seductive: *Scholarship is sexy.*

Listen, for example, to the *Targum of the Song of Songs* 5:12: "[God's] eyes are constantly directed towards Jerusalem." Why? Because "of those who sit [assembled] in the Sanhedrin, engaged in the study of the Law," together with those who sit "in the House of Study."[25] *God can't take his eyes off the sage.* Or consider the targum of Song 4:1: "Now on that day King Solomon sacrificed upon the altar a thousand burnt offerings, and his offering was accepted with favour by the Lord; whereupon the Bath-Qol [lit. 'daughter of the voice (of God)'] proceeded from heaven and said: 'How comely art thou, O Assembly of Israel, and how comely are those leaders of the Assembly, and those scholars sitting in the Sanhedrin.'"

*Song of Songs Rabbah* 1.15 § 2 is still more complimentary, interpreting Shulamith's stunning eyes as a transparent reference to the Sanhedrin: "THINE EYES ARE AS DOVES. THINE EYES: these refer to the Sanhedrin who are the eyes of the congregation." *Israel has beautiful eyes.* And it seems that beautiful eyes are a woman's greatest asset: "BEHIND (*MIBAʿAD*) THY VEIL (*LEẒAMMATHEK*). R. Levi said: If the eyes of a bride are unprepossessing, one must survey her whole body, but if her eyes are beautiful, one need not look at the rest of her body" (4.1 § 3). This rule of thumb is reliable, apparently, for it turns out that Israel's charms are by no means limited to her eyes. Rabbi Levi continues: "When a woman ties up (*meẓametheth*) her hair behind, this is a great ornament to her. So when the great Sanhedrin sat behind the Temple, this was an ornament to the Temple" (4.1 § 3). *Israel has fabulous hair.* Or consider *Song of Songs Rabbah* on Song 4:5: "THY TWO BREASTS: these are Moses and Aaron. Just as the breasts are the beauty and the ornament of a woman, so Moses and Aaron were the beauty and ornament of Israel. Just as the breasts are the charm of a woman, so Moses and Aaron were the charm of Israel. Just as the breasts are the glory and pride of a woman, so Moses and Aaron were the glory and pride of Israel" (4.5 § 1). *Israel has terrific breasts.*[26] The overall message is plain (even if Israel is not). It is not the beautiful women and girls of Israel who set God's male hormones raging; rather, he only has eyes for the scholar. (He has something of a one-track mind, actually: "LET ME SEE THY COUNTENANCE: this signifies study.... FOR SWEET IS THY VOICE: this signifies study..." [*Song of Songs Rabbah* 2.14 § 5].) It is too little to say that the sage passively adopts a "feminine" subject position in relation to God's infatuated gaze; he actually camps it up.

Consider some further examples, such as the *Targum of the Song of Songs* 4:9: "Fixed upon the tablet of My heart is thy love, O My sister, Assembly of Israel, likened [in the Song] to the modest bride! Fixed upon the tablet of My heart is the love of the least of thy scholars!" Or the targum of Song 4:8: "And He continued: 'With Me shall dwell the Assembly of Israel, likened to the modest maiden.'" Or of Song 4:10: "How beautiful unto Me is thy affection, O My sister, Assembly of Israel, likened to the modest bride!"[27] The sage as virginal bride puts words of tender passion in God's mouth, and blushes demurely as they drip off his tongue.

But the bride's own mouth is itself an object of fixation for God. Consider the *Targum of the Song of Songs* 4:11, for example: "And during the hour in which the priests pray in the court of the Temple, their lips drip liquid honey as from the comb." *The sensuality of prayer.* God laps up the words of his priests, thrusting his tongue hungrily into their gorgeous mouths ("how beautiful are the Priests and Levites, who bring Thy offerings" [*Targum of the Song of Songs* 4:2]). He also laps up the words of his scholars, as *Song of Songs Rabbah* 4.11 § 2 implies: "Even if one only reads the Scripture with proper modulation and intonation, it may be said of him HONEY AND MILK ARE UNDER THY TONGUE." Compare the targum of Song 5:13: "and as for the lips of His scholars engaged in the Law, they distil taste on every side, while the word issuing from their mouths is as choice myrrh"; or *Song of Songs Rabbah* on the same verse: "HIS LIPS ARE AS LILIES: this is the scholar who is fluent in his Mishnah" (5.13 § 1). *The sensuality of scholarship.* And the pleasure is mutual; God enjoys the oral ministrations of his bride, and bestows luscious kisses of his own in return: "The words of His palate are sweet as honey" (*Targum of the Song of Songs* 5:16). Marvin Pope notes "the prominence accorded Torah, or rather the Oral Torah, as the symbol of God's love for Israel and the means by which rabbinic leadership retains God's providential interest even while they are in exile."[28] The Oral Torah: the divine tongue and lips. Or is it the scholar's tongue and lips instead? What is certain is that the scholar knows how to use his mouth. And that's what keeps God interested in him.

Some of the other things that turn God on are a good deal queerer than mere French kissing, however, such as inhaling the fragrance of foreskins—and not live, healthy foreskins, but dead, decaying foreskins:

> When Abraham our ancestor circumcised himself and his sons and the members of his household, he made their foreskins into a heap, and the sun shone on them and they bred worms, and the odour of them ascended to the Holy One, blessed be He, like the odour of the incense and the perfume of the handful of frankincense which was cast on the fire-offerings. And the Holy One, blessed be He, said: "When the descendants of this man commit transgressions and evil deeds, I will remember this odour in their favour." (*Song of Songs Rabbah* 4.6 § 1)

Returning to the scholars, we discover that it is not only the activity of scholarship itself but the way in which scholarly findings are presented that is intensely sensual. "Rabbi Johanan said: 'If one discourses on the Torah in public and his words do not give as much pleasure to his hearers as a bride gives pleasure to the beholders when sitting in her bridal chamber, it were better that he had not delivered them.'" Resh Lakish manages to go one better: "If one discourses on the Torah and his words do not give as much pleasure to his hearers as a bride to her husband when she enters the bridal chamber, it were better that he had not delivered them" (*Song of Songs Rabbah* 4.11 § 1). *The scholar as love machine.*

"O Assembly of Israel, thou fairest among peoples," sighs God in the *Targum of the Song of Songs* 5:9. The enjoyment of his wife's beauty is a husband's due, after all, or so the sages assume: "Rabbi Hunyi said in the name of Rabbi Meir: 'Why were the matriarchs so long barren? In order that their husbands might enjoy their beauty. For when a woman conceives, she becomes clumsy and stout. The proof is that so long as Sarah was barren she sat in her house like a bride in her bridal chamber, but when she became pregnant her charm faded; and so it says, *In pain thou shalt bring forth children* (Gen. III, 16)'"

(*Song of Songs Rabbah* 2.14 § 8). She lost her looks, poor cow, and so her husband lost interest in her (Rabbi Hunyi and Rabbi Meir sigh in unison; they have Sarahs of their own sitting at home), but not before she had presented him with a son to enjoy instead, not a bad exchange all told (the rabbis nod their heads sagely and fondly turn their thoughts to their sons).

The bride had better not lose her looks, then.[29] But what is the secret of her beauty? The targum of Song 1:15 supplies the first clue: "When the Children of Israel did the will of their King, He did praise them in the company of the holy angels, saying, 'How beautiful are thy actions, O beloved daughter, Assembly of Israel, in the hour when thou doest My will, engaging in the dictates of My Law!'" Now consider the targum of Song 6:4: "The Eternal spoke: 'How beautiful art thou, My love, at the time when thou are desirous of doing My will!'" Next the targum of Song 6:9: "Now at that time the Assembly of Israel, resembling a perfect dove, was serving her Sovereign Lord with one heart, and cleaving to the Law, busy with the practice of its ordinances with a perfect heart. . . . " Finally—and most important—the targum of Song 4:7: "And whilst the Israelites performed the will of the Lord of the Universe, He would praise them in the heavens on high, and say: 'Thou art all beautiful, O Assembly of Israel, there is no blemish in thee.'"[30] *Israel's compliance is what makes her beautiful*[31]—above all her willingness to perform textual acts at God's bidding. For supreme intimacy with the deity takes the form of Torah study. Listen to *Song of Songs Rabbah* 5.11 § 1: "HIS HEAD IS AS THE MOST FINE GOLD. HIS HEAD is the Torah. . . . MOST FINE GOLD: this refers to the words of the Torah. . . . HIS LOCKS ARE CURLED. This refers to the ruled lines (in the Scroll). AND BLACK AS A RAVEN: this refers to the letters." And *Song of Songs Rabbah* 7.3 § 2 adds: "THY BELLY IS LIKE A HEAP OF WHEAT. This refers to the book of Leviticus. Just as the belly is in the middle between the heart above and the legs below, so the book of Leviticus has two books before it and two after it" (cf. 5.14 § 2). Intimate knowledge of this incomparable body of literature is a source of unending gratification for the scholar. For the Torah scroll is also God's phallus, the ultimate symbol of his authority. The scholar must permit the scroll to penetrate him; he must allow it inside him, internalize it completely. For when Israel or the scholar *refuses* the scroll, she or he is beaten into submission: "And when it became manifest to the Lord that they were righteous, and engaged in the study of the Law, the Lord said: 'I will no longer smite them, nor will I make an end of them'" (*Targum of the Song of Songs* 6:12). And Israel is never more beautiful to her Lord than when, smitten with love, she accepts her beating humbly, even taking pleasure in it: "How beautiful art thou, O Assembly of Israel, at the time when . . . I chasten thee with afflictions for thy misdeeds, and thou receivest them lovingly, they appearing in thy sight as delights" (ibid. 7:7).[32]

The beauty of the bride, then, to the extent that it is an effect of her compliance, is in the eye of the divine beholder. Listen to *Song of Songs Rabbah* 5.11 § 5: "LOCKS BLACK LIKE A RAVEN: these are the scholars; they look repulsive and black in this world, but in the time to come, *The appearance of them will be like torches, they [will] run to and fro like the lightnings* (Nah. II, 5)." The scholar's brilliant beauty smolders beneath his veil. The theme also makes an appearance in the Babylonian Talmud. There Song 5:15, "his countenance as the Lebanon, excellent as cedars," is somehow made to say, "He who blackens his face for the sake of the study of Torah in this world, the Holy One (blessed be He) will make his luster shine in the next" (*b. Sanhedrin* 100a). The rabbinic House of Study as a beauty parlor? Torah study as a mudpack treatment? (The rabbis do swap notes on beauty treatments on occasion: "The sensual Ahasuerus said, *Six months with oil of myrrh*, etc. [Est. II, 12]. Rabbi Judah ben Ezekiel said: 'Oil of myrrh means oil of boxwood'; Rabbi Jannai said: 'It is oil of unripe olives which removes hair and makes the skin smooth . . . '" [*Song of Songs Rabbah* 4.8 § 1].)

But what does *Israel* see in *God* that impels her to undergo this most grueling of makeovers, unremitting study of Torah? What does Israel see in God that makes her positively ill with love? (The targum of Song 5:8 has the Assembly of Israel plead, "I adjure you, O prophets, by the decree of Heaven, if our love should appear unto you, tell Him that I am sick from love of Him.") Admittedly, he *is* beautiful—"The Assembly of Israel replies to the Sovereign of the Universe, and says: 'How beautiful is Thy Holy Presence at the time that Thou dwellest in our midst'" (*Targum of the Song of Songs* 1:16)—but is there more? The answer soon emerges: "Then the Assembly of Israel began to think of the praise of the Lord of the Universe and said: 'That God do I desire to serve who, day by day, is enveloped in a robe white as snow,[33] occupied with the twenty-four books of the Law, and the words of the Prophets and the Writings, and by night with the six Orders of the Mishnah, and the splendour of whose countenance radiates as fire'" (ibid. 5:10).[34] Which can readily be paraphrased as: "That God do I desire to serve who values what I value, and thereby valorizes my existence, who is a scholar even as I am a scholar, and whose erudition makes him beautiful to behold." God himself is a scholar, then, and Israel is a woman who has fallen in love with a scholar.[35]

Or is Israel a closed community of male scholars, instead, fatally infatuated with itself? While "Israel" was engrossed in gazing at "herself" in a mirror of "her" own manufacture, what were "her" women doing? The following passage from Daniel Boyarin's *Unheroic Conduct* suggests what the answer might be:

> As significant as the different gendering of Jewish men was, so was there a significant difference in the gendering of Jewish women. While their men were sitting indoors and studying Torah, speaking only a Jewish language, and withdrawn from the world, women of the same class were speaking, reading, and writing in the vernacular, maintaining businesses large and small, and dealing with the wide world of tax collectors and irate customers. In short, they were engaging in what must have seemed to many in the larger culture as masculine activities, and if the men were read as sissies, the women were read often enough as phallic monsters.[36]

It is indeed tempting to surmise that the rabbinic commentaries on the Song of Songs sprang from such a topsy-turvy world of gender relations.

The Israel of the commentaries, although thoroughly infatuated with herself, nevertheless realizes that she is not yet as beautiful as she might be. But if she is not yet as *beautiful* as she might be, it is only because she is not yet as *holy* as she might be:

> What is meant by THOU ART ALL FAIR MY LOVE? Rabbi Simeon ben Yohai taught: "When Israel stood before Mount Sinai and said, *All that the Lord hath spoken will we do, and obey* (Ex. xxiv, 7), at that moment there were among them neither persons with issue nor lepers nor lame nor blind, no dumb and no deaf, no lunatics and no imbeciles, no dullards and no doubters. With reference to that moment it says, THOU ART ALL FAIR MY BELOVED. After they sinned not many days passed before there were among them person with issue and lepers, lame and blind, dumb and deaf, lunatics and dullards. Then the order was given, *Let them put out of the camp every leper, and every one that hath an issue* (Num. V, 2)." (*Song of Songs Rabbah* 4.7 § 1)

The age-old conflation of physical and moral perfection comes to consummate expression in this passage, in accordance with the following formula: A blemished body or an impaired mind signifies a lack of wholeness, and hence of holiness.[37] And the blemish in question may only be skin deep. Consider the targum of Song 1:5 (which verse Gollancz, following the King James Version, renders as: "I am black, but comely, O ye daughters of Jerusalem, as the tents of Kedar, as the curtains of Solomon"),[38] in which the contrast between Israel's promised perfection, on the one hand, and her threatened imperfection, on the other, is formulated, not just in terms of physical beauty in the abstract, but of physical beauty as racially defined: "When the Israelites fashioned the Calf, their faces darkened as those of the children of Ethiopia, who dwell in the dwellings of Kedar; when they turned in penitence, and their guilt was pardoned, the brilliant radiance of their countenance increased as that of the angels." Compare *Song of Songs Rabbah* 1.5 § 1: "I AM BLACK BUT COMELY. The Community of Israel said: 'I am black in my own sight, but comely before my Creator, as it is written, *Are ye not as the children of the Ethiopians unto Me, O children of Israel* (Amos IX, 7): *As the children of Ethiopians are ye*—in your own eyes, but *unto Me ye are as the children of Israel, saith the Lord*.'" The translator, Maurice Simon, adds the following gloss: "Dividing the verse into two distinct halves—'Children of Ethiopians' is understood as a synonym for persons lacking beauty." A later sentence in this same paragraph of *Song of Songs Rabbah* pairs the words "black" and "ugly," and "repulsive" and "swarthy," while 1.6 § 3 tells how Israelite men would "blacken" the faces of captive Midianite women so as not to be tempted to have sex with them, and also tells the tale of an Ethiopian maidservant who deduces that her master is about to divorce his wife and marry her instead, because he saw his wife's hands "all stained." She confides her hope to a fellow servant, who replies contemptuously, "How then will he endure you who are stained all over and black from the day of your birth?" The point of the story? Israel, taunted by the nations for worshipping "the Baal Peor," can archly reply, "If we who sinned only once are to be punished thus, how much more so you." Black skin is metaphoric of iniquity throughout this entire stretch of *Song of Songs Rabbah*, as in the targum of Song 1:5.[39]

In the rabbinic reading of Song 1:5, therefore, with its metaphoric alignment of race and righteousness, the intrinsic oppressiveness of the beauty-holiness equation comes to exceptionally pointed expression. Whether what we are witnessing in this reading should be regarded as a full-fledged instance of racism, or merely its embryo, is a matter for subtle debate.[40] More significant for my own reflections, however, is the fact that racism, embryonic or otherwise, is itself but a single (although singularly pernicious) instance of a more general equation of looks with worth, a cross-cultural trope that will be a recurrent concern in this book (most especially in the ensuing essay on the physical representation of Jesus). Or less an instance of the goodness/good-looking equation, perhaps, than an elaboration—a logical expansion of the cultural conflation of beauty and virtue. Racism displays the ideology of beauty at its ugliest.

The ideology of beauty? Jesus, you're probably thinking, this guy must be one ugly son of a bitch! I may or may not merit that epithet. I do, however, believe that beauty, which, as we never tire of telling ourselves, is only in the eye of the beholder and, even when beheld, only skin-deep anyway, qualifies thoroughly as an ideology—despite (or because of) our ritual denials of its "reality"—insofar as it dictates the desires, and hence the behavior, of entire populations.[41] It does so now and it did so in antiquity (by different means, of course). I shall have more to say about this later. For now my aim is more modest.

I would argue that the rabbinic reading of Song 1:5 can itself be read as an "exemplary" moment—a revelatory moment, indeed—in the allegorical tradition of Song of Songs interpretation. For the conflation of physical beauty and holiness is the enabling condition of this interpretive tradition, whether Jewish or Christian. In order to see this more clearly, we need to consider the Christian allegorization of the Song in more detail.

## Allegory's Double Cross (Which Turns the Cross-Bearing Christian into a Christian Cross-Dresser)

> The woman shall not wear that which pertaineth unto a man,
> neither shall a man put on a woman's garment; for all that do so
> are abomination unto the Lord thy God.
> —Deuteronomy 22:5 (KJV)

The first Christian known to have allegorized the Song of Songs was Hippolytus of Rome (d. 235), fragments of whose commentary on the Song (ca. 200?) survive.[42] The best-known fragment contains Hippolytus's interpretation of Song 1:2, "your breasts [*mastoi sou*] are better than wine."[43] Once the subject has slipped her bra back on, Hippolytus delivers his diagnosis. His examination has revealed that these gross physical appendages conceal a sublime spiritual reality: they represent the Old and New Testaments. Not for nothing will Hippolytus's spiritual successors be called "Doctors of the Church."

The most curious thing of all about this odd clinical encounter, however, is that the *she* turns out on closer inspection to be a *he*, or, better, a *s/he*: the owner of the breasts is not the "Bride" of the Song but rather the "Bridegroom." This breast exam, administered to the same ambiguously gendered subject, recurs in Origin's exposition of the Song, although there it is filmed in glaring technicolor and no longer in grainy black-and-white. It is a scene that invites comment, and we shall return to it in due course.

It was Origen who really set the standard for Christian allegorical interpretation of the Song. Subsequent Christian expositors (such as Theodoret of Cyrus, Philo of Carpasia, and Gregory the Great) were content to labor in the shadow of Origen's monumental commentary on the Song—"ten full volumes, containing nearly twenty thousand lines," as Jerome admiringly described it to Pope Damasus.[44] Rendered from Greek into Latin by Jerome and his successor Rufinus, Origen's remarkable reading of the Song was thereby disseminated in the West.

It is customary, then, to see Origen as the fountainhead of the Christian allegorical exposition of the Song of Songs. Through him the Jewish allegorical interpretation of the Song flowed into the Church and irrigated its ascetic imagination.[45] Intriguingly, the conduit for this stunningly queer body of commentary may himself have been a gender anomaly. For if Origen's reading of the Song was scrupulously spiritual, his reading of Matthew 19:12 was scrupulously literal—if the early Church historian Eusebius is to be credited. The Matthean verse reads: "For there are eunuchs [*eunouchoi*] who have been so from birth, and there are eunuchs who have been made eunuchs by men, and there are eunuchs who have made themselves eunuchs for the sake of the kingdom of heaven. He who is able to receive this, let him receive it." Squirming uncomfortably and crossing his legs tightly, Eusebius offers an elliptical account of Origen's painfully literal reading of the verse:

> At that time, while Origen was performing the work of instruction at Alexandria, he did a thing which gave abundant proof of an immature

and youthful mind, yet withal of faith and self-control. For he took the saying, "There are eunuchs which made themselves eunuchs for the kingdom of heaven's sake," in too literal and extreme a sense, and thinking both to fulfil the Savior's saying, and also that he might prevent all suspicion of shameful slander on the part of unbelievers (for, young as he was, he used to discourse on divine things with women as well as men), he hastened to put into effect the Savior's saying, taking care to escape the notice of the greater number of his pupils. But, wishful though he might be, it was not possible to hide a deed of this nature.[46]

Whereas the literal reading of Matthew that Eusebius ascribes to Origen was strikingly at odds with his spiritual reading of the Song in one sense, in another sense, it was not. For Origen deals with the textual body of the Song in precisely the same way that he has dealt with his own sexual body, amputating from it anything that might prove an occasion for sin (cf. Matt. 18:8-9: "And if your hand or your foot causes you to sin, cut it off. . . . And if your eye causes you to sin, pluck it out. . . . "). Origen reenacts on the Song that which he has already enacted on his own flesh. In short, he submits the Song to castration. Of course, one could also argue that Origen, in commenting at such great length upon the Song, was attempting to replace that which, on Eusebius's account, he had excised from his own flesh, and one could thereby read his "twenty thousand lines" as a monumental attempt to substitute the phallus for the penis.[47]

In either case, however, Origen's queer reading of the Song of Songs could be said to have proceeded smoothly from the Song's own propensity to blur gender boundaries—to "masculinize" the female body (as in 4:4, for example, "Your neck is like the tower of David, built in courses; on it hang a thousand bucklers, all of them shields of warriors") and to "feminize" the male body (as in the intensely sensual description of it in 5:10–16), and, on occasion, to employ the same images for both bodies (deer and dove, for example).[48] The gender-blurring imagery of the Song overruns the margins of the page and "contaminates" the commentaries of Origen and his successors, where it proliferates and mutates uncontrollably.

But Origen's queer reading of the Song could also be said to have proceeded smoothly from the transgressive body that tradition assigned to him. Of eunuchs in general in the world of late antiquity, and Origen in particular, Peter Brown has remarked:

The eunuch was notorious (and repulsive to many) because he had dared to shift the massive boundary between the sexes. He had opted out of being male. By losing the sexual "heat" that was held to cause his facial hair to grow, the eunuch was no longer recognizable as a man. He was a human being "exiled from either gender." Deprived of the standard professional credential of a philosopher in late antique circles—a flowing beard—Origen would have appeared in public with a smooth face, like a woman or like a boy frozen into a state of prepubertal innocence. He was a walking lesson in the basic indeterminacy of the body.[49]

As it happens, however, the thrilling being who is the ultimate object of desire in Origen's commentary on the Song, and whom he terms "the Bridegroom," is "himself" anatomically indeterminate. He is obviously quite a man—utterly masterful, utterly capable of displaying his "husband's power" to the "virginal" soul and initiating her into the "perfect mystery," as Origen delicately puts it (*Commentary on the Song of Songs*, Prologue 4)—yet he is not *all* man. And not only because he is also divine but because he is also a woman.

We receive the first inkling of this when, with a ceremonious flourish, Origen unhooks the straps of Song 1:2, "For Thy breasts are better than wine," and the hidden glory of the Bridegroom flops forth.[50] The Bride is "moved deeply by the beauty of His breasts" (*Commentary on the Song of Songs* 1.2). And "after she has been found worthy to receive kisses from the Bridegroom's own mouth, and to enjoy his breasts, says to Him: 'Thy breasts are above wine'" (1.4) These superb breasts owe nothing to silicon, moreover; they are packed with something altogether superior: "treasures of wisdom and knowledge are concealed in them." And when the Bride "reflects upon the teaching that flows forth from the Bridegroom's breasts, she is amazed and marvels" (1.2). Moaning softly, s/he wraps her moist lips around the Bridegroom's erect nipples, which leak luscious drops of teaching. S/he does so not as a nursing infant, however, but as a mature wo/man:

> With reference to the perfect soul and the Word of God, then we may say in this connection that as long as a person is a child and has not yet offered himself wholly to God, he drinks the wine which that field produces, which holds within itself the hidden treasure too; and he is gladdened by the wine he drinks. But, when he has offered and vowed him-

self to God and has been made a Nazirite, and has found the hidden treasure and come to the very breasts and fountains of the Word of God, then he will no longer drink wine or spirit, but with reference to these treasures of wisdom and knowledge that are hidden in the Word of God, he will say to Him: "Thy breasts are better than wine." (Ibid.)[51]

Origen's own gender indeterminacy has communicated itself, somehow, to the Bridegroom.

Who in turn communicated it to the Bridegrooms of so many of the commentaries that succeeded Origen's, in a veritable epidemic of gender undecidability. A stunning example occurs in Aponius's *In Canticum canticorum explanatio* (ca. 680, later epitomized by Lucas, abbot of Mount St. Cornelius), which, commenting on Song 8:10, "I am a wall, and my breasts like towers," identifies the wall as "the Manhood of Christ," upon which "the towering breasts" are supported.[52] The mind boggles, or merely bogs down, as it attempts to bring this surreal spectacle into focus. What sort of body might be up to the challenge of coupling with this hyper-endowed prodigy, we wonder, this monument to gendered excess—and gender indeterminacy? How about this one, which Gregory of Elvira, writing a little earlier than Aponius, fantasized on the basis of Song 1:2: "Instead of the two breasts of the she-goat of the Law, written on tablets of stone by the finger of God, Christians, like cows, have the four breasts of the Evangelists, full of the sweet milk of wisdom."[53]

Now, it is not as if there are no straight gender performances in Origen's commentary on the Song. The "masculinity" of the Bridegroom and the "femininity" of the Bride are unambiguously enacted in scenes such as the following: "After the Bridegroom had used some sternness in cautioning the Bride, impressing on her that if she knew not herself, she must go forth in the footsteps of the flocks and feed, not sheep but goats, she blushed at the severity of the command. And the redness of shame, which then suffused her face, made her cheeks lovely and much fairer than they had been before" (*Commentary* 2.7 on Song 1:10, "How lovely have thy cheeks become"). And again: "After this, speaking as though the Bride were veiled and covered for the sake of reverence, the Bridegroom asks her, when she comes to that place which He has just specified as being more secluded, to lay aside her veil and show her face to Him. And, because the Bride was keeping silence out of her great reverence, the Bridegroom desires further that He may . . . take pleasure in her words; He bids her let Him hear her voice" (*Commentary* 3.15 on Song 2:13b–14, "show me thy face, and let me hear thy voice"). No question as to who is wearing the pants here.

Nevertheless, as one picks one's bemused way through the *Commentary* and the *Homilies*, one can scarcely avoid the sneaking suspicion that the Bridegroom, for all his manly posturing, has no male equipment whatsoever. Nothing remotely resembling a tubular or globular appendage is said to dangle from the Bridegroom. What we do learn, however, is that in addition to mammary glands he also has clefts, slots, and slits—and is, indeed, himself an outsized slit. Origen quotes God's eyebrow-raising promise to Moses in Exodus 33:21–23, "Lo, I have set thee in a cleft of the rock, and thou shalt see my back parts," immediately adding: "That Rock which is Christ is, therefore, not completely closed, but has clefts"—*is* a cleft, in fact, God's cleft, which the spiritual man is enjoined to enter: "But the cleft of the rock is He who reveals God to men, and makes Him known to them; for *no one knoweth the Father, save the Son* [Matt. 11:27]. So no one sees the back parts of God . . . unless he be placed in the cleft of the rock" (*Commentary on the Song of Songs* 3.15).

For Bernard of Clairvaux, in contrast, the Bridegroom's clefts are the gaping gashes in his hands, feet, and side: "They pierced his hands and feet, they gored his side with a lance, and through these fissures I can suck honey." Through spiritual cunnilingus, Bernard causes the Bridegroom to open up: "The secret of his heart is laid open through the clefts of his body."[54] John of the Cross, for his part, is more interested in burying himself in the Bridegroom's cleavage: "The soul, then, earnestly longs to enter these caverns of Christ in order to be absorbed, transformed, and wholly inebriated in the love of the wisdom of these mysteries, and hide herself in the bosom of the beloved. In the Canticle He invites her into these clefts" (*Spiritual Canticle* 37.5).

In light of the anatomical anomalies of his Bridegroom, Origen's intimation that the virginal soul, once s/he enters the nuptial chamber, will see "the perfect mystery" unveiled is all the more intriguing.[55] The possibilities afforded by these anomalies are not lost on Origen. "Because He tastes so sweet and so delightful," gurgles Origen, his head buried in the Bridegroom's bosom, milk dripping down his beardless chin, "all other flavours will seem harsh and bitter to [the spiritual man] now; and therefore he will feed on Him alone."[56]

But it is not as though Origen's enjoyment of the Bridegroom is limited to the sense of taste: "His delighting will not . . . be restricted to the single sense of eating and tasting; he will be delighted in his hearing too, and he will be delighted in seeing, and touching, and smelling" (ibid.). A little earlier in this same section of the *Commentary*, reflecting upon the excitement engendered in the Bride and her girlfriends by the Bridegroom's (manly?) scent (Song 1:3-4: "Thy name is as ointment emptied out. Therefore have the maidens loved Thee, have they drawn Thee. We will run after Thee into the fragrance of Thine ointments"), Origen remarks: "This comes about, as we have seen, when as yet they have received only the scent of Him. What, do you think, will they do when the Word of God takes possession of their hearing, their sight, their touch, and their taste as well, and offers excellences from Himself that match each single sense according to its nature and capacity . . . ?"

Bernard, for his part, is more interested in sniffing the Bride: "'My beloved is mine, and I am his' [Song 2:16]. There is no conclusion here, no prayer. What is there? It is a belch. . . . I thank you, Lord Jesus, who have deigned to allow me at least to sense that odor. . . . The breath of your beloved is to me a goodly odor, and I receive of its fulness gratefully" (*Sermons on the Song of Songs* 67.4-5). This inspires Bernard to circle the messianic banquet hall inhaling, in turn, the belches of Moses, David ("Good Jesus! With what sweetness he suffused my nostrils and my ears when he belched" [67.7]), Jeremiah, John, and Paul. Had Bernard been spared to complete his commentary on the Song, who can say what other bodily effluvia he might have been moved to deal with? or where it might have led him? For what Bernard is edging towards here, with upturned nose and outstretched tongue, his eyes shut and his fingers in his ears, is a discourse of knowledge built not on the "abstracting" senses of sight and hearing, but on the "proximity" senses of smell, taste, and touch, a discourse that thus runs counter to the dominant traditions of Western theology and philosophy.[57]

∼

How paradoxical to have to reassert in the face of these lush spectacles of sensory overload that the allegorical impulse in Song of Songs interpretation stemmed from the radical repudiation of the flesh. Yet that would appear to have been the case. Allegorical exegesis was the child of ascesis.[58] Celibate Christian expositors employed allegory to unsex the salacious Song and render it sublimely spiritual. For these expositors, the Song was a ticking time bomb within Scripture itself, an occasion of sin just waiting to happen, which only the ingenuity of the allegorist could successfully defuse. Listen to Origen's grim warning:

> But if any man who lives only after the flesh should approach it [the Song], to such a one the reading of this Scripture will be the occasion of no small hazard and danger. For he, not knowing how to hear love's language in purity and with chaste ears, will twist the whole manner of his hearing of it away from the inner spiritual man and on to the outward and carnal; and he will be turned away from the spirit to the flesh, and he will foster carnal desires in himself, and it will seem to be the Divine Scriptures that are thus urging him and egging him on to fleshly lust!
>
> For this reason, therefore, I advise and counsel everyone who is not yet rid of the vexations of flesh and blood and has not ceased to feel the passion of his bodily nature, to refrain completely from reading this little book. (*Commentary on the Song of Songs*, Prologue 1)

Here the Song is implicitly assigned the stock role of the female temptress, potentially a Potiphar's wife lying in wait to entice and entrap the spiritually immature (male) reader. Only the man who has been castrated, whether literally or metaphorically, can approach this text with impunity.[59] Many centuries later, Denis the Carthusian can be heard worrying aloud about would-be eunuchs for the kingdom of heaven whose castration is incomplete: "What is to be done with those many religious and canons and others in Holy Orders who in Church and in the Divine Office are accustomed to hearing or reading these words, though they are not yet . . . cleansed, who have hardly attained to a true and spiritual understanding and can scarcely read and hear these words . . . without indecent thoughts?" (*Commentary on the Song of Songs* 17).

The Song of Songs is a book for eunuchs, then. Or at least a book for monks, who, by the Middle Ages had come to seem like gender anomalies. Daniel Boyarin elaborates: "[S]ince the monk within [medieval] Christian culture has a binary opposite in the knight, the former can be removed from the category of 'real men' within Christianity and stand as an oppositional force to it. Monks, then, effectively form a distinct gender within Christian society, one that is removed from the paternal and sexual order."[60] All of which leads one to wonder: Was this why medieval monks evinced such immense fascination with the Song of Songs, or rather with its allegorization?[61] Tropological expositions of the Song—torrid expressions of the soul's ardent desire for spiritual congress with Christ under the voluptuous figure of a bride's ardent desire for sexual congress with her bridegroom[62]—proceeded with uncanny smoothness from the pens of this clerical class, pens apparently unencumbered by the penises of those who wielded them. Why? Because these gender contortionists already constituted a third gender in relation to their cultural habitat anyway, just as Origen, their neutered progenitor, had in relation to his?

One is further tempted to drape these *spiritual* cross-dressers in the same conceptual garb that Marjorie Garber runs off for *literal* cross-dressers in *Vested Interests*, her encyclopedic study of cross-dressing from the Renaissance to the late twentieth century. "For me," she writes, "one of the most important aspects of cross-dressing is the way in which it offers a challenge to easy notions of binarity, putting into question the categories of 'female' and 'male,' whether they are considered essential or constructed, biological or cultural."[63] But Garber's larger claims are considerably more ambitious than this simple deconstructive backflip might suggest. "[O]ne of the most consistent and effective functions of the transvestite in culture," she argues, "is to indicate the place of what I call 'category crisis.'" By this she means

> a failure of definitional distinction, a borderline that becomes permeable, that permits of border crossings from one (apparently distinct) category to another: black/white, Jew/Christian, noble/bourgeois, master/servant, master/slave. The binarism male/female, one apparent ground of distinction (in contemporary eyes at least) between "this" and "that," "him" and "me," is itself put into question or under erasure in transvestism, and a transvestite figure, or a transvestite mode, will always function as a sign of overdetermination—a mechanism of displacement from one blurred boundary to another. An analogy here might be the so-called "tagged" gene that shows up in a genetic chain, indicating the presence of some otherwise hidden condition. It is not the gene itself, but its presence, that marks the trouble spot, indicating the likelihood of a crisis somewhere, elsewhere.

In a similar way, I will argue, the apparently spontaneous or unexpected or supplementary presence of a transvestite figure in a text (whether fiction or history, verbal or visual, imagistic or "real") that does not seem, thematically, to be primarily concerned with gender differences or blurred gender indicates a *category crisis elsewhere,* an irresolvable conflict or epistemological crux that destabilizes comfortable binarity, and displaces the resulting discomfort onto a figure that already inhabits, indeed incarnates, the margin.[64]

In the case of the classic medieval commentaries on the Song of Songs, I am tempted to merge Garber's reflections on category crisis with those of Boyarin on the medieval monk as constituting a distinct gender,[65] and speculate that the routine apparitional emergence of "transvestite" figures (males in female guise) in these commentaries—texts that are not concerned thematically with gender difference, much less with gender bending—indicates a category crisis in medieval society centered on the anomalously gendered person of the male celibate. In the commentaries—more specifically, in the authorial personae created in the commentaries—the anomalous figure of the male celibate is torqued up to an exquisite (and cathartic) extreme until it becomes an entity who (surreptitiously) inhabits, indeed incarnates, the margin: a male author who, in the name not of fiction but of ultimate reality, internalizes a feminine persona so completely that he speaks more or less fluently in her voice, feels with her emotions, and throbs with her sexuality; a male author who might be said to personify queer gender identity, in that "he" powerfully calls into question the category of stable gender identity itself.

And yet I have little desire to idealize patristic and medieval commentators on the Song of Songs as exotic exemplars of a third gender or a third sex. The contempt for the flesh on the part of male celibates that found expression in the allegorical exposition of the Song was also—or especially—contempt for *female* flesh. Bernard of Clairvaux, the most prolix commentator of all on the Song, requiring eighty-six sermons to get to the end of its second chapter,[66] discovered the path that would eventually lead to these sermons while in full flight from female flesh, according to his intimate friend and biographer William of Saint Thierry.[67] In boyhood, Bernard's eyes, then roaming free, would alight from time to time upon a female form. Bernard's penis, rudely aroused from slumber, would crane its neck forward curiously for a glimpse of its own, causing its owner to flee in confusion and dunk the offending member (himself still appended to it) in an icy pond until it consented to withdraw its head. Thus it was that Bernard resolved to become a monk.[68] And it was from this same frigid pond, proof against the wiles of the temptress and the treacherous head of the serpent, that Bernard would deliver all eighty-six of his exquisite sermons on the Song, its pages dripping with icy water.

William tells of two particularly fiery temptations to the young Bernard's chastity. In the first, "the devil incited a girl to climb naked into Bernard's bed while he was asleep in it," but such was the saint's self-control that he emerged from the hellish ordeal unscathed. In the second, yet another daughter of Satan slipped into Bernard's room by night and was advancing toward his bed with deadly intent when the saint was inspired to cry out "Thief! Thief!" thereby driving off the temptress. When his companions teased him about the incident the next morning, the youth gravely replied: "There really was a thief, . . . who was trying to steal something very precious to me, the matchless treasure of my chastity."[69] William concludes: "Such things made Bernard see the truth of the old proverb that to play with fire is the surest way of getting burned, and he began to think of fleeing from the temptations that beset him."[70]

Allegorical exposition of the Song of Songs replicates the deadly struggle of male celibacy itself. What must be overcome in either instance is the sexual, the sensual, the fleshly, the female. Small wonder that no other book of Sacred Scripture received more reverent attention from male celibates in the ancient and medieval Church. Paradoxically, it is the book of professional celibates, past masters of repression and sublimation.[71] The repressed returns, of course, although not with a vengeance so much as a wicked sense of humor: the monk, priest, or prelate is deftly transformed into a drag queen as he strives manfully to play the feminine role thrust upon him by the spiritual reading of the Song.[72] And the final intricate twist is the fact that the feminine is ordinarily what elicits his distrust, if not his outright disgust. This is the double-cross of allegory that turns the cross-bearing Christian into a Christian cross-dresser. Through the (r)use of allegory, the exegete eagerly embraces that from which he is actively in flight.

Do these exegetes ever betray any real awareness of the gender-bending acrobatics in which they are engaged? Origen comes closest, perhaps. As though realizing what risks he is running, Origen at one point in his commentary (3.9) protests:

> You must not understand the left and right hands of the Word of God [in Song 2:6, "His left hand is under my head, and his right hand shall

embrace me"] in a corporeal sense, simply because he is called the Bridegroom, which is an epithet of male significance. Nor must you take the Bride's embraces in that way, simply because the word "bride" is of feminine gender.

Rather, although the "Word" of God is of the masculine gender in Greek, and neuter with ourselves,[73] yet all these matters with which this passage deals must be thought of in a manner that transcends masculine and neuter and feminine, and everything whatever to which these words refer. And this applies not only to the "Word" of God, but also to His Church and to the perfect soul, who likewise is here called "the Bride." For thus says the Apostle: *For in Christ there is neither male nor female, but we are all one in Him* [Gal. 3:28].

Origen protests too much, of course. Blurring the boundaries between "masculine and neuter and feminine" is one thing (and something at which Origen excels); transcending these categories is something else entirely. And one would be hard-pressed to imagine a less promising site for the Promethean project of transcending gender than a discourse of intensely sexualized spirituality, such as we have in Origen's commentary and homilies on the Song of Songs. Origen's eroticized spirituality is everywhere productive of gender relations (gender being in part an effect of sexual performance), and queer gender relations at that. Origen doesn't rise above gender; rather he rolls around in it with his fantasy man—the ravishing creature whom he has named "the Bridegroom"—enthusiastically playing the wo/man to a "man" who "himself" is a case study in gender indeterminacy, as we have seen.

### The Breast Pump

> The more the Bride's breasts are pressed the more they flow.
> —WILLIAM OF SAINT THIERRY, *Brevis Commentatio* 18

What distinguishes Christian allegorical treatments of the Song from Jewish allegorical treatments? First, and most obviously, in adapting the allegorical approach to the Song from Judaism, Christian expositors replaced Yahweh with a much younger man, the "bridegroom" of the Song now no longer being identified as the God of Israel, primarily, but rather as his alleged son, Jesus Christ. The stage was thereby set for a more intense spiritual sex life—and, indeed, the show subsequently put on by Christian expositors of the Song regularly outstripped that put on by Jewish expositors by reason of its baroque extravagance.

Compare, for example, Jewish and Christian allegorical exegesis of Song 4:5, "Your two breasts are like two fawns, twins of a gazelle, that feed among the lilies" (repeated in 7:3). Earlier, we saw how *Song of Songs Rabbah* 4.5 § 1 identified the two breasts as Moses and Aaron, asserting that just as the breasts are the beauty, ornament, charm, glory, and pride of a woman, so too were Moses and Aaron the beauty, ornament, charm, glory, and pride of Israel. The *Targum of the Song of Songs* 4.5 also identified the breasts as Moses and Aaron, by "[whose] merits were the Children of Israel fed for forty years," Moses and Aaron standing in their turn for the "two deliverers" of eschatological expectation, "Messiah, son of David, and Messiah, son of Ephraim." And that is pretty much all that the rabbis had to say regarding these breasts, so far as we know.[74]

The Fathers and Doctors of the Church, in contrast, simply could not get enough of the breasts, elbowing each other aside to examine them and outdoing each other in concocting fanciful descriptions of them. Richard Frederick Littledale, nineteenth-century apologist extraordinaire for the allegorical approach to the Song, lovingly assembled a catena of these verbal caresses—a little posy plucked from the flowers of the Fathers, to cull a pretty phrase from Denis the Carthusian (*Commentary on the Song of Songs* 5):

> The *two breasts* of the Church, whereat her children are fed with milk, are the two Testaments [so Hippolytus, as we saw earlier], and the Prophets and Doctors of the Circumcision and the Uncircumcision [Philo of Carpasia].... They are *twin roes*, because of the perfect accord between the Old and New Testaments, the one being rich in type, and the other in fulfilment [Gregory the Great]. Another view sees in the two breasts the precepts of love to God and love to our neighbour [Aponius], while Psellus stands alone in his explanation that they denote the Blood and Water which flowed from the crucified Saviour. The outer and inner man, united in one sentient being, visible and invisible, is, S. Gregory Nyssen alleges, the basis of the comparison here.... Richard of S. Victor, after assenting to the view that the teachers of the Church are designated by her breasts, and dwelling on the

tests of motherly tenderness, proceeds to distinguish the two breasts into the contemplative and active, both yielding the same spiritual nutriment.[75]

And so on. As William of Saint Thierry rather indelicately puts it in our epigraph to this section, "the more the Bride's breasts are pressed the more they flow" (*Brevis Commentatio* 18).[76] Allegory as a breast pump?

∼

How have *modern* commentators tackled Song 4:5, "Your breasts are like two fawns . . . "? Well, breast size has been a preoccupation for some. Marvin Pope is a prime example: "The youth of the fawns bespeak the youthful freshness and small size of the mammary orbs. According to the Arab ideal of feminine pulchritude, the breasts were among the attributes that should be small. The breasts of the numerous figurines of the love-goddess are regularly represented as small, often abnormally small, perhaps indicating their virginal character."[77] Dr. Pope nods respectfully to Dr. W. F. Albright, who is seated in the front row of the auditorium, and upon whose *Yahweh and the Gods of Canaan* Pope has just drawn.[78] Pope's erudite discourse on the ideal dimensions of the mammary orbs is now interrupted, however, by hoots of derisive laughter from the daughters of Jerusalem (or "Jerusalem girls," as Pope himself likes to call them) lounging in the back row. For, as Renita Weems has recently remarked, the daughters of Jerusalem in Song 6:13 ("Why should you look upon the Shulammite . . . ?") seem "skeptical of what the male suitor sees in [her], a woman who besides her dark color evidently had the misfortune to have small breasts as well" (cf. 8:8: "We have a little sister, and she has no breasts").[79]

∼

A further bout of breast-fixation in the ancient and medieval Church was occasioned by a felicitous misconstrual of the Hebrew of Song 4:10a by both the Greek (Septuagint) and Latin (Vulgate) translators, "How fair is thy love [*dōdayik*], my sister, my bride! How much better is thy love [*dōdayik*] than wine!" magically becoming "How fair are thy breasts [Gr. *mastoi*; Lat. *mammae*], my sister, my bride! Thy breasts [Gr. *mastoi*; Lat. *ubera*] are fair from wine!"[80] The standard interpretation of the (surgically?) enhanced verse that eventually took hold in the West was that "the breasts are the Doctors of the Church, who supply spiritual nourishment to her children."[81] And here we move from transvestitism to transsexuality—and beyond. For the Fathers and Doctors of the Church don't just *acquire* female breasts, they *become* breasts, rather like contemporary porn queens, whose silicon-enhanced bosoms have become bigger and bigger, tending inexorably to the point where the woman threatens to *become* a pair of giant mammary glands, her breasts greedily sucking up her identity and assigning her a new name: Betty Boobs, Honey Melons, Letha Weapons, Wendy Whoppers. . . . [82] To assert that she thereby becomes a fantasy object who exists to satiate male desire would be banal. What is less patently obvious, perhaps, is that the female protagonist of the Song of Songs serves roughly the same purpose in the Christian allegorical tradition, in which she becomes the supreme object of male fancy, and fantasy. This should come as no surprise, however. For how could an interpretive tradition, sustained almost exclusively by males and largely centered on the intimately described body and libidinal life of a female, be innocent of the will to domination so endemic to male sexual fantasy (well, mine anyway)?[83]

The will to domination—or the will to annihilation? The Fathers and Doctors of the Church substitute themselves for Shulamith's body, part by part. A further example, again from Littledale's catenae:

> "Thy navel is like a round goblet, which wanteth not liquor" [Song 7:2]. . . . The *navel* is the order of holy preachers, fitly styled a *goblet*, because when the people are taught from its mouth, they are filled with spiritual wine by its ministry. It is *round*, because the preacher's tongue must needs go round all subjects, according to the character of all classes of men [Gregory the Great]. . . . S. Epiphanius and Philo [of Carpasia] agree in holding that the Priesthood is here intended, compared to a *goblet* with *mixture* (i.e., wine and water), because of the mystery of the Sacrament of the Body and Blood of CHRIST, whereof it has charge. . . . The Priesthood, as in the centre of the Church, reconciling the people to God, is the *navel*. . . . [84]

And so on. Through this sustained act of substitution, the allegorical expositors annex a mystical—and mystified—femaleness to their own male bodies, thereby rendering the literal female body redundant. The woman of the

Song—and, by extension, woman in general—is symbolically annihilated in the very gesture through which she is idealized.[85] The symbolic world created by these male celibates in their allegorical appropriations of the Song is as free of the polluting presence of real women as the chapterhouse at Clairvaux, an inner sanctum of homosocial sanctity and the literary setting of Bernard's eighty-six sermons on the Song, delivered to an implied audience of women-free men, the minutiae of whose daily lives are so disposed that they are almost never obliged to lay eyes on a flesh-and-blood daughter of Eve.[86] The ecclesiastical tradition of Song of Songs interpretation thus presents us with the paradoxical spectacle of male ascetics endlessly preening themselves in front of a mirror. Allegory enables them to look upon the female body in the Song without actually having to see it. In its contours and crevices, they only see themselves.

**Allegory's Engine**

The second feature distinguishing Christian allegorical treatments of the Song from Jewish allegorical treatments was that the rejuvenated male protagonist of the spiritualized Song—the Son who, politely yet firmly, ejected his aged Father from the nuptial bed—was granted a still more intimate relationship with the female protagonist than that enjoyed by his parent. In classical Jewish commentary on the Song, the Bride is normally a corporate entity, Israel, as in *Song of Songs Rabbah* 2.16 § 1, for instance: "MY BELOVED IS MINE AND I AM HIS. He is my God and I am His (chosen) nation"; or 6.9 § 5: "MY DOVE, MY UNDEFILED, IS ONE. This is the Community of Israel, as it says, *And who is like Thy people, like Israel, a nation one in the earth* (II Sam. VII, 23)."[87] But in Christian allegorical exegesis, the female protagonist of the Song is identified, not only as the collective people of God (in this case, the Church), but as the contemporary individual "soul" in addition, to a degree not evident in Jewish allegorical exegesis. This tendency is already apparent in Origen's commentary on the Song, which typically examines each verse in light of both relationships, that between Christ and the Church, on the one hand, and that between Christ and the soul, on the other. Or, as Origen himself puts it, "the appellations of Bride and Bridegroom denote either the Church in her relation to Christ, or the soul in her union with the Word of God" (*Commentary on the Song of Songs* 1.1). In actual fact, the latter emphasis—that on the soul's relationship with her Bridegroom—moves progressively to the fore as the commentary proceeds. (In contrast, the predominant emphasis in Origen's homilies on the Song, "composed for babes and sucklings," according to Jerome,[88] is on the Church's relationship with the Bridegroom.) In Gregory of Nyssa's late-fourth-century commentary on the Song,[89] the focus on the soul's nuptial relationship with Christ is still more pronounced, and the Church and the soul will continue to vie for Christ's attention in subsequent Christian exegesis of the Song, his attraction to the soul increasing steadily, at least from the twelfth century on.

What did Christian expositors see in Christ that caused them to desire him so ardently? Origen, for one, seems to have fallen in love with his beauty. "And the soul is moved by heavenly love and longing," he writes swooningly, "when, having clearly beheld the beauty and the fairness of the Word of God, it falls deeply in love with His loveliness and receives from the Word Himself a certain dart and wound of love" (*Commentary on the Song of Songs*, Prologue 2). He prays that "having beheld the beauty of the Word of God, we may be kindled with a saving love for Him" (Prologue 3). Later, he recalls how the prophets foretold Christ's "countless acts of power and His mighty works," and tenderly adds: "His beauty also they described, His charm and gentleness, that I might be inflamed beyond all bearing with the love of Him by these things." The Bride is "moved deeply by the beauty of His breasts," in particular, as we saw earlier. And finally she tells him to his face, "Behold, Thou art beautiful . . . and fair indeed."[90]

Of course, the Bride herself is no eyesore, but her beauty is merely a reflection of God's beauty and that of his Son (the latter having inherited his Father's good looks). "O fairest among women," the Bridegroom compliments the Bride (Song 1:8). But Origen is concerned that the compliment should not go to her head. He cautions her to remember "whence the ground of thy beauty proceeds—namely, that thou wast created in God's image, so that there is in thee an abundance of natural beauty," although he later says that "without doubt she receives the splendour of beauty from the Bridegroom Himself."[91] The Bridegroom is a talented beautician, by Origen's account. The Bride enters God's beauty parlor dowdy and plain, but emerges from it glamorous and radiant:

> It is said to the whole body of the Bride: "How lovely have thy cheeks become!" [Song 1:10]. And notice that He did not say, "How lovely are

thy cheeks!" but, "How lovely have thy cheeks become!" He means to show that previously they were not so lovely. It was only after she had received the Bridegroom's kisses, and after He, who formerly spoke by the prophets, had come and cleansed this Church for Himself in the laver of water and made her to be without spot or wrinkle [Eph. 5:27] and given her knowledge of herself, that her cheeks became lovely. For the chastity and virtue and virginity which had not existed before, were spread abroad in a lovely beauty through the cheeks of the Church.[92]

Moreover, "a woman's beauty is considered to reside supremely in her cheeks," as Origen reminds us in the homilies (1.10).

Can we know more about the Bride and Bridegroom's beauty secrets? Indeed, we can, for Origen also tells us that the more closely the Bridegroom is "contemplated with the eyes of the spirit, so much the lovelier and more beautiful He is found. For not only will His own fairness and marvellous beauty appear; but in the soul herself, as she looks at and beholds Him, an immense glory and extraordinary beauty of form will arise. . . . Such a soul as this rightly shares her bed—that is, her body, with the Word" (*Commentary on the Song of Songs* 3.2). In what, then, will the bliss of the life to come consist? What else but in the Bride and Bridegroom's self-absorbed fascination with each other's beauty—the Bridegroom entranced by his mirror reflection in the Bride, the Bride rapt at her own mirror reflection in the Bridegroom.

Bernard later sketches this scene with elegant economy: "He would not see her when she was unlike him, but when she is like him he will look upon her, and he will allow her to look upon him" (*Sermons on the Song of Songs* 82.7). For how could he possibly love her unless she was beautiful? Compare Bernard's hagiography, in which the saint is represented as expressing modest doubts about his own beauty, and hence his worth as a wo/man: "As he pondered the words of that canticle in his solitude, he could not but wonder how a bridegroom so perfect in every way could love a woman so unworthy of Him. For He is more beautiful than all men, and on His face all the angels long to gaze, while the face of His bride, as she tells us herself, is made swarthy by the days spent in the hot vineyards. Yet He calls her beautiful, and says that there is no spot in all her whiteness."[93]

But it remained for the Mystical Doctor, St. John of the Cross, in whom the Christian tradition of allegorical commentary on the Song initiated by

Origen achieved its zenith (or possibly its nadir), to produce a finished sketch of God's beauty parlor:

> And let us go forth to behold ourselves in Your beauty.... Let us so act that by means of this loving activity we may attain to the vision of ourselves in Your beauty in eternal life. That is: That I be so transformed in Your beauty that we may be alike in beauty, and both behold ourselves in Your beauty, possessing now Your very beauty; this, in such a way that each looking at the other may see in the other his own beauty, since both are Your beauty alone, I being absorbed in Your beauty; hence, I shall see You in Your beauty, and You shall see me in Your beauty, and I shall see myself in You in Your beauty, and You will see Yourself in me in Your beauty; that I may resemble You in Your beauty, and you resemble me in Your beauty, and my beauty be Your beauty and Your beauty my beauty; wherefore I shall be You in Your beauty, and You will be me in Your beauty, because Your very beauty will be my beauty; and therefore we shall behold each other in Your beauty. (*Spiritual Canticle* 36.5)

In other words: every square inch of God's beauty parlor is covered with mirrors, so that the Bridegroom's beauty is reflected back to him from every surface, every face. In the presence of the Bridegroom, the soul herself becomes a mirrored surface, a blank and vacuous surface, eternally reflecting the Bridegroom's radiant beauty back to him. The logic enshrined in this Bea(u)tific Vision is actually a rather common cultural one, a gendered logic, although here distilled to its essence. Figured as female, the soul acquires her worth solely from her relationship to the male. And that worth is figured in turn as beauty.

In general, the equation of beauty not just with worth but with virtue achieves near absolutization in the allegorical tradition of Song of Songs interpretation. The equation already looms large in Origen's exposition of the Song, as we have begun to see. Consider the following passage in particular:

> He [the Bridegroom] says further: "Thy face is fair" [Song 2:14]. If you understand what Paul means by "face" when he says, *We all with unveiled face* [2 Cor. 3:18], and again when he says, *But then face to face* [1 Cor. 13:12], you will perceive what manner of "face" it is that is praised by the Word of God and described as fair. It is, without a doubt, the sort

of face that is daily being renewed *according to the Image of Him who created it* [Col. 3:10], *not having spot or wrinkle or any such thing,* but is *holy and without blemish,* even as the Church which Christ *has presented to Himself* [Eph. 5:27]—in other words, the souls who have reached perfection. And all of these together make up the body of the Church.

This body truly will appear as beautiful and comely, if the souls of which that body is constituted persevere in all the comeliness of perfection.... [T]he face of the Church is declared to be comely or ugly according to the virtues and aspirations of her believers. (*Commentary on the Song of Songs* 3.15)

It is not too much to say that physical beauty here becomes the transcendental signifier of virtue.

Yet beauty is not an abstraction for Origen. Note, first, that the beauty of the Church resides entirely in the eye of the divine beholder: "These words are spoken by Christ to the Church, which is to Him . . . fair, but fair to nobody except to Himself alone; for that is what He implies by saying, '*My* fair one.'"[94] Second, note that the Church's ugliness to the unspiritual eye is signified by the fact of her *dark skin.* We have already examined the role that dark skin plays in Jewish allegories of the Song; now we need to examine its role in Christian allegories.

Origen/Rufinus introduces Song 1:5 as follows: "I AM DARK AND BEAUTIFUL [*Fusca sum et formosa*], O YE DAUGHTERS OF JERUSALEM, AS THE TENTS OF CEDAR, AS THE CURTAINS OF SOLOMON. In some copies we read: I AM BLACK AND BEAUTIFUL [*nigra sum et formosa*]" (*Commentary on the Song of Songs* 2.1). Jerome's Latin (Vulgate) translation has "black" (*nigra*), as does the Greek (Septuagint) translation before him (which uses *melaina*). *Nigra/melaina* also tends to be favored by early Christian commentators on the Song, such as Gregory of Nyssa, Augustine, and even Origen himself on other occasions. However, whereas the Septuagint has "I am black *and* beautiful" (*melaina eimi kai kalē*), the Vulgate has "I am black *but* beautiful" (*Nigra sum sed formosa*). Through the centuries, numerous Christian commentators and translators have echoed the Vulgate's "but," not least Martin Luther and the translators of the King James Version. Rarely has a simple conjunction carried so much cultural freight.

But what does the original Hebrew say? It reads *šĕḥôrâ* ("black") *ʾănî* ("I am") *wĕnāʾwâ* ("and/but beautiful"). The conjunction *w(aw)* can mean "and" or "but," depending upon the context, hence the conundrum. Among modern commentators, Marvin Pope has been a champion of the translation "black *and* beautiful," arguing for it in his landmark critical commentary on the Song.[95] Song 1:6a, however, ʾal-tirʾûnî šeʾānî šĕḥarḥōret šeššĕzāpatnî haššāmeš, which Pope renders as "stare not at me that I am swart / That the sun has blackened me,"[96] seems to present a problem for his translation of v. 5, as Cheryl Exum notes: "Although Pope emphasizes that the translation 'stare not' is 'non-committal,' it is difficult to avoid the conclusion that if one is not to look at her because she is black, then there is something negative about the blackness."[97] Exum herself favors translating the contested phrase in 1:5 as "black and beautiful" nonetheless. She suggests that ʾal in 1:6a is an "asseverative," and that the part-verse should therefore be rendered "Look at me that I am black, that the sun has gazed upon me." The import of Exum's rendition of 1:5–6a, as she herself understands it, is that the woman first draws her interlocutors' attention "to her blackness and beauty," and then proceeds "to demonstrate her pride in her appearance" by urging them to feast their eyes on her.[98] Yet even Exum is obliged to admit that "biblical examples of asseverative ʾal are few, few enough, in fact, as to leave some question as to the existence of asseverative ʾal in biblical Hebrew."[99]

Conferring further uncertainty upon the translation "black and beautiful," perhaps, is Pope's admission that the notion that "blackness of necessity implies the antithesis of beauty has some support in biblical usage"—although the only example he is able to adduce, seemingly, is Lamentations 4:7 f.: "Her princes were purer than snow / Whiter than milk. / In body ruddier than coral, / Their limbs fairer than sapphire. / Their visage is now blacker than soot, / Not recognized in the streets. / Skin tight over their bones, / Grown dry as wood."[100]

But is the woman actually meant to be black in the Hebrew text? Roland Murphy insists that she is not: "There is no basis in the text for inferences about racial color."[101] Murphy is by no means alone. Modern commentators in general "steer away from attributing any ethnic import to the woman's dark complexion," Renita Weems observes, "preferring rather to see the protagonist as perhaps the victim of class prejudice. The argument is that in ancient Oriental culture the light-complexioned woman who had the luxury of remaining indoors during the day was preferred over the dark-complexioned woman who was constrained to labor outdoors in the sun."[102] Weems herself is unconvinced by this argument, however, in part because she is persuaded by

Michael Goulder's suggestion that the appellative *bat-nadîb* in Song 7:2 (7:1 in standard English translations), ordinarily understood to be a designation of royalty or nobility (KJV, for example, renders it "O prince's daughter," while KJV's great-grandchild NRSV follows in the family tradition by translating it "O queenly maiden"), "actually refers to the protagonist's hometown of Nadiv in Arabia."[103] For Weems, as for Goulder, the Song celebrates "two lovers whom society . . . sought to keep apart, perhaps because they were from different classes, from different ethnic backgrounds, or of a different color."[104]

So where does all this leave us? Frankly, in a state of considerable uncertainty, at least as far as determining what "authorial intention" pulsates purposefully beneath the dark, shimmering surface of Song 1:5–6a. We cannot know for certain whether the woman is being represented as black in the racial or ethnic sense or merely as sun-scorched. Neither can we be certain whether her melanin-rich skin (however it is to be read) is a source of shame or pride to her. But I am less interested here in determining how these verses might "originally" have been read or heard than in pondering how certain (immensely influential) readers subsequently read them, beginning with Origen. So let us see what he made of them.

Observe how Origen glosses Song 1:5, "I am dark and beautiful [*Fusca sum et formosa*], O ye daughters of Jerusalem" (while Origen says "and," he really means "but," as we shall see). This part-verse is the object of prolonged and elaborate reflection in his commentary, indicating its importance for him and the extent of his fascination with it:

> Here again the person of the Bride is introduced as speaking, but she speaks now . . . to the daughters of Jerusalem. To these, since they have spoken slightingly about her as being ugly, she now makes answer, saying: "I am indeed dark [*fusca*]—or black [*nigra*]—as far as my complexion goes, O daughters of Jerusalem; but, should a person scrutinize the features of my inward parts, then I am beautiful. . . .
>
> [I]ndeed I am surprised, O daughters of Jerusalem, that you should want to reproach me with the blackness of my hue. How have you come to forget what is written in your Law, as to what Mary suffered who spoke against Moses because he had taken a black Ethiopian to wife? How is it that you do not recognize the true fulfilment of that type in me? I am that Ethiopian.[105] I am black indeed by reason of my lowly origin; but I am beautiful through penitence and faith. . . ."

Let us give some attention now to the passage we cited from Psalm 67, in which the writer says: *Ethiopia shall stretch out her hands unto God*. For, if you consider how salvation comes to the Gentiles through Israel's offence ... you will observe how the hand of Ethiopia—that is, the people of the Gentiles—outstrips and precedes in its approach to God those to whom first His oracles were given. You will see that this is how the saying is fulfilled, that *Ethiopia shall stretch out her hands unto God*, and that "black one" becomes beautiful, for all that the daughters of Jerusalem are unwilling that it should be so, and envy and revile her.

And I think that the statement ... in which the Lord received those also who come from places *beyond the rivers of Ethiopia* and bring offerings to God, calls for a like interpretation. For it seems to me that he is said to be *beyond the rivers of Ethiopia* who has been darkened with exceeding great and many sins and, having been stained with the inky dye of wickedness, has been rendered black and dark. And yet the Lord repels not even these. ...

It remains now to expound only that passage from Jeremias which relates how Abdimelech, the Ethiopian eunuch, having heard that Jeremias had been put in the pit ... draws him out thence. And I do not think it is unsuitable to say that this foreigner, this man of a dark and ignoble race ... represents the people of the Gentiles. ...

It can be said also of each individual soul that turns to repentance after many sins, that she is black by reason of the sins, but beautiful through her repentance and the fruits of her repentance.

And finally, because she who now says: "I am black and beautiful" has not remained in her blackness to the end, the daughters of Jerusalem say later on concerning her: *Who is this that cometh up, having been made white [Quae est ista quae ascendit dealbata], and leaning upon her Nephew?* [Song 8:5].[106]

Thus the Bride, in her Michael Jacksonesque pilgrimage from darkness to light, ceases being black altogether and attains to whiteness, finally winning acceptance and approval from the hard-to-impress daughters of Jerusalem.[107]

Origen is now ready to tackle Song 1.6, "Look not at me, for that I am darkened; for the sun hath looked down on me." In the course of his exposition, he claims: "And it is commonly said among the whole of the Ethiopian race, in which there is a certain natural blackness inherited by all, that in those parts the sun burns with fiercer rays, and that bodies that have once been scorched and darkened, transmit a congenital stain to their posterity." But Origen does not leave us too long pondering the implausible spectacle of the entire Ethiopian race characterizing its own skin tone as a "congenital stain." He hurries on:

> But the reverse is the case with the blackness of the soul. . . . Its blackness . . . is acquired not through birth, but through neglect; and, since it comes through sloth, it is repelled and driven away by means of industry.
>
> And lastly, as I said just now, this same person who is now called black, is mentioned towards the end of this Song as *coming up, having been made white, and leaning on her Nephew*. She became black, then, because she went down; but, once she begins to come up and to lean upon her Nephew, to cleave to Him and suffer nothing whatever to separate her from Him, then she will be made white and fair; and, when all her blackness has been cast away, she will shine with the enveloping radiance of the true Light. (*Commentary on the Song of Songs* 2.2)

The beauty, the fairness, the *whiteness* of the Bridegroom is contagious. It transmits itself to the Bride as she cleaves to him and becomes one with him, leaching the blackness, the darkness, the ugliness, the sinfulness from her appearance,[108] and making her as "white and fair" as he is.[109] And so these two perfectly beautiful beings who will eventually behold each other naked in heaven, every covering finally stripped away, will not only be gorgeous but white—gorgeous because they *are* so white, so fair, so transparently virtuous. This spectacle of light and whiteness is all the more vivid due to the dark backdrop against which it is staged, a backdrop sewn from skins, "Ethiopian" skins to be precise.

Actually, it only because of this backdrop that the spectacle is visible in the first place. Origen's discourse conjures up a time when the Ethiopian will be leached and bleached, thereby becoming the Bride. This brings us to the paradox of the Ethiopian. On the day when the Ethiopian disappears, the Bride and Bridegroom too will vanish. Lacking a constitutive Other they will become invisible even to each other. They will reach out blindly for each other in a heavenly light in which everything suddenly appears perfectly white, and hence in which nothing can be seen.

Bernard later stages his own extravagant version of this impossible encounter, taking as his point of departure the *Noli me tangere* ("Do not touch me") of John 20:17.[110] He begins: "The woman whose wisdom was still carnal was rightly forbidden to touch the risen flesh of the Word" (Bernard seldom misses a chance to slap a woman around, even if only verbally). In a bravura performance, he then paraphrases Jesus' *Noli me tangere* as follows:

> She therefore will touch me worthily who will accept me as seated with the Father, no longer in lowly guise, but in my own flesh transformed with heaven's beauty. Why wish to touch what is ugly? Have patience that you may touch the beautiful. Things will be beautiful then that are now ugly: ugly to the touch, ugly to the eye, ugly even to you in your ugliness, you who are too bound to the senses, indifferent to faith. Become beautiful and then touch me; live by faith and you are beautiful. In your beauty you will touch my beauty all the more worthily, with greater felicity. You will touch me with the hand of faith, the finger of desire, the embrace of love; you will touch me with the mind's eye. But shall I still be black? God forbid! Your beloved will be fair and ruddy [Song 5:10], strikingly beautiful, surrounded by a bloom of roses and lilies of the valley [Song 2:1].... Thousands of thousands are with the Beloved [Song 5:10], and ten thousand surround him [Dan. 7:10] but none compare with him. Do you not fear that in seeking your beloved, you may by mistake take one of this multitude for him? But no, you will not hesitate in making your choice. He who is a paragon among thousands, peerless in their midst, will be easy to discover.... No longer therefore will he appear in the swarthy skin that up to now he had presented to the eyes of his persecutors, who would despise him to the point of killing him, or even to the eyes of his friends after his resurrection, that they might recognize him. No longer will he be encountered clothed in a dark skin, but in a white robe, surpassing in beauty not only all mankind [Ps. 44:3], but even the angels [Heb. 1:4]. Why then should you wish to touch me in this lowly condition, rigged out like a slave [Phil. 2:7], contemptible to look at? But touch me in the beauty with which heaven endows me, crowned with glory and honor [Ps. 8:6], awe-inspiring in the majesty of my divine life, yet loving and calm with an inborn serenity. (*Sermons on the Song of Songs* 28.10)

(Mary Magdalen, meanwhile, has begun to back away nervously from him. Jesus advances upon her retreating form, his eyes glittering unnaturally. "Mary," he intones, with a ghastly grin. "Master," croaks Mary, and then she is off and running.)

Poised in the liminal space between his resurrection and his ascension, however, Jesus is no longer plain, despite his modest self-deprecations. Rather, he is merely in curlers. For God's beauty parlor is the tomb, and resurrection is the ultimate makeover. Listen again to Bernard: "For his flesh, which was not of the Father, rid itself of every infirmity by the glory of resurrection before it went to the Father. It girded itself with strength [Ps. 64:7], it put on light as a garment [Ps. 103:2], that it might present itself to the Father in the splendor and beauty which was its own" (*Sermons on the Song of Songs* 75.8). But it is not only Jesus who is led, blushing and beautiful, into the beaming presence of the Father. The believer is promised no less. Listen to the New Testament itself: "For if we have been united with him in a death like his, we shall certainly be united with him in a resurrection like his" (Rom. 6:5). And again: "Just as we have borne the image of the man of dust, we shall also bear the image of the man of heaven" (1 Cor. 15:49).

But let us return one last time to Origen's commentary on the Song of Songs. What, finally, are we to make of this commentary, specifically its pronouncements on blacks and blackness? These are pivotal pronouncements as regards its internal operations, as we are about to see. They also mark an early moment in a seemingly endless night punctuated by screams of agony and cries of despair. Endemic to this history of oppression is an intimate relationship between Christianity and whiteness. In his recent book *White*, the cultural critic Richard Dyer offers a nuanced description of this complex relationship:

> I am not arguing that Christianity is of its essence white. Given that Christianity developed initially within Judaism, that one of its foundational thinkers was the North African Augustine, and that it is now most alive in Africa, South America and the black Churches of Europe and North America, it is by no means clear that whiteness is constitutive of it. Yet not only did Christianity become the religion, and religious export, of Europe, indelibly marking its culture and consciousness, it has also been thought and felt in distinctly white ways for most of its history, seen in relation to, for instance, the following: the Mani-

chean dualism of black : white that could be mapped on to skin colour difference; the role of the Crusades in racialising the idea of Christendom (making national/geographic others into enemies of Christ); the gentilising and whitening of the image of Christ and the Virgin in painting; the ready appeal of the God of Christianity in the prosecution of doctrines of racial superiority and imperialism.[111]

Origen's allegorical musings on whiteness and blackness make the subsequent whitening of Christianity that much more comprehensible. Reading Origen on the Song of Songs, one begins to see how such a thing could have come about; Origen's allegories, indeed, can themselves be seen as a catalyst in its emergence. As Frank Snowden has noted, "The pioneer in the use of an Ethiopian symbolism was Origen, who became the model for later patristic treatment of Ethiopian themes and who shaped the tradition of this type of exegesis." And Origen's Ethiopian allegories were showcased in his commentary on the Song of Songs.[112] What one doesn't encounter in Origen, of course, are full-fledged racist slogans of the sort, "Whiteness among all the race-colours is the one which best accords with the dignity of man," which would have to await Franz Delitzsch's 1875 commentary on the Song.[113] Nevertheless, the equation of virtue with beauty that runs through Origen's commentary does turn out to have a proto-racist aspect. For the notion of physical beauty that underpins this equation is no airy abstraction, as we have seen. Rather it is one that is inextricably enfleshed in a specific set of "racial" traits: light skin, and, by extension, all that stereotypically accompanies it: shape and size of lips and nose, hair type, body shape, and all the rest.[114]

And so we arrive back once more to the place at which we found ourselves at the conclusion of our earlier reflections on the rabbinic interpretations of the Song. There I argued that the rabbinic construal of Song 1:5, "I am black and/but beautiful . . . ," constituted a singularly illuminating expression of the beauty = holiness equation. And the same now appears to be true of the Christian construal of the verse inaugurated by Origen. As we saw in our reflections on the rabbinic commentaries, the proto-racist reading of Song 1:5 merely pushes the ancient conflation of beauty and virtue to its logical conclusion, since physical beauty is "always already" a concept, a construct, that is racially/ethnically defined and aligned.

But these Jewish and Christian readings of Song 1:5 can themselves in turn be read as moments of epiphany in the allegorical tradition of Song of

Songs interpretation in general. The conflation of beauty and holiness comes to a head in these readings, as we have seen. But the conflation of these two concepts itself turns out to be the enabling condition of this entire interpretive tradition, whether Jewish or Christian. Within this dual tradition, the two lovers of the Song, whose endlessly elaborated physical attributes seem, more than anything else, to be the cause of their mutual attraction,[115] are unceasingly transformed through the miracle of allegorical exposition into God and Israel, or Christ and the Church, or Christ and the Soul, or Christ and the Blessed Virgin, mutually and irresistibly drawn to each other's actual or potential holiness, wholeness, unblemished perfection, unsullied beauty. The seemingly perennial preoccupation with physical perfection as the privileged signifier of moral perfection is the hidden engine that keeps the allegorical interpretation of the Song of Songs turning over.

**Carnival Queens**

Earlier we noted how the Church and the soul, alternately assuming the female lead in the Song of Songs, vie for Christ's favors in the Christian allegorical tradition from Origen onwards, Christ's attraction to the soul reaching its climax in the late Middle Ages. Was the interpretation of Shulamith as the soul queerer than the interpretation of her as Israel or the Church? Arguably it was, since it afforded the (male) commentator an opportunity to play the female lead in a drama that, even on the "spiritual" plane, was now all about one-to-one romance. "No sweeter names can be found to embody that sweet interflow of affections between the Word and the soul, than bridegroom and bride," simpers Bernard, adjusting his bridal veil. "They share the same inheritance, the same table, the same home, the same marriage-bed, they are flesh of each other's flesh" (*Sermons on the Song of Songs* 7.2). No longer was the commentator, as "bride," obliged to share the bridegroom's bed with the innumerable other wo/men in His life; now s/he was allowed a semblance, of a uniquely intimate relationship with Him—at least until compelled to yield the bed to the one woman with whom s/he could not possibly hope to compete.

For Christian rewriters of the Song soon succumbed to the temptation to accord the Virgin Mary the female lead in the script. A bizarre casting decision? Not at all, to hear the Roman Catholic scholar Paschal Parente explain it:

> Along with the Christological interpretation, a *Mariological* interpretation was introduced very early by St. Ephraem, St. Ambrose, St. Epiphanius, St. Peter Chrysologus. They understood the Virgin Mary to be the real, mystical bride of the Canticle. . . . And, indeed, what other soul was there that could claim in all truth to have celebrated the mystical nuptials with God except Mary Immaculate, the true Mother of God? The Fathers used to interpret occasionally one or more parts of the Canticle in a Mariological sense. Since the twelfth century, however, the entire Canticle of Canticles has been applied to the Virgin Mary by such authors as Rupert of Deutz, Denis the Carthusian, Cornelius à Lapide, Nigidius and others.[116]

By the mid fifteenth century, Denis was able to write: "It is commonly agreed that there is a threefold bride of Christ: namely, the whole universal Church militant, called the 'general' bride [*sponsa universalis*] of Our Lord Jesus Christ; then, any faithful and loving soul, called the 'individual' bride [*sponsa particularis*] of Christ; and finally the most blessed Virgin Mary, the mother of Christ, said to be the 'special' bride [*sponsa singularis*] of Christ." How special? Here's Denis again: "The special Bride, she who stands apart from all others, is unique as the beloved beyond all telling of the heavenly Bridegroom; she is his virginal, most pure and most sacred mother, . . . caught into the embrace of the most fiercely burning charity."[117]

Casting the Blessed Virgin in the role of Shulamith constituted the apogee of queer commentary on the Song of Songs. For now the "holy soul" (potentially female, of course, but implicitly male, as we have so often seen) is enjoined, not only to become a spiritual drag queen, to internalize the voice, affections, and sexual passions of the female protagonist of the Song, but to do so by modeling himself on the Queen of Queens, the Queen of Heaven, *Beata Maria Virgo*. For the queerest cut of all is that the Virgin, through being enscripted in the Song, has now become Christ's lover as well as his mother.

Listen to the Universal Doctor, Alan of Lille (1128?–1203), for instance, whose *In Cantica Canticorum ad laudem Deiparae Virginis Mariae elucidatio* (A Concise Explanation of the Song of Songs in Praise of the Virgin Mary) was, like the commentary by Rupert of Deutz that inspired it, a Mariological tour de force:

> And so, although the song of love, Solomon's wedding song, refers particularly and according to its spiritual sense to the Church, in its most particular and spiritual reference it signifies the most glorious Virgin.... So it is that in her eagerness for the presence of the Bridegroom, longing for that glorious conception of which she was told by the angel... the glorious Virgin speaks thus: *May he kiss me with the kiss of his mouth.* (*In Cantica Canticorum* 2–4, trans. Denys Turner)

But the Virgin's urgent desire is more than reciprocated by her Son: "*For your breasts are more delightful than wine*: Which is as much as to say, 'You desire my kisses and I your breasts....' I can read this literally as referring to the Virgin's natural breasts.... Christ longed for those breasts, he longed to draw milk from them.... Those breasts were to Christ sweeter than wine, sweeter than the most pleasing of all drinks" (8).

Not to be outdone, the *Doctor ecstaticus*, Denis the Carthusian, declares with regard to the same two verses of the Song:

> And so it is most appropriately of this best and wisest of virgin girls that, at that moment when she heard from the holy angel, *Behold, you will conceive in your womb*, and then, *the Holy Spirit will come upon you* [Luke 1:31, 35] that the words may be construed: *May he kiss me with the kiss of his mouth*; that is, the only begotten of God, the heavenly Bridegroom, whom you, O heavenly paranymph, promise to me, you assure me that he will be made incarnate in me and will soon become my son; he deigns to come down to me your poor little handmaiden and unite himself closely and intimately to the substance of my flesh....
>
> *For your breasts are more delightful than wine, more fragrant than the finest oils....* These could be the words of the special Bride addressed to her own Bridegroom and Son.... But they could also be the words of the Bridegroom addressed to his most beloved mother and so may be read: "You, O special Bride, mother and virgin, have asked for the kiss of my mouth, and I gladly consent to your request; *for your breasts are more delightful than wine....*" It may be said of those bodily

breasts of the most divine Virgin that they, most blessed as they are, are made almost divine by the continual contact of the adorable, incarnate Bridegroom who sucked from them; they *are more fragrant than the finest ointments*, more fragrant, that is to say, than the most delicious virginal milk, which the Lord of all things took and sucked from them.

And so on.[118]

Could it possibly go any further? Of course it could. Bernard of Clairvaux, for his part, dares to hint at a similar intimacy between the Father and the Son. Bernard is still on Song 1:1, "Let him kiss me . . . ," which he is loath to leave (it occupies his first nine and a half sermons on the Song, after which he finally manages to tear his lips away from the Bridegroom's to fasten them on His nipples instead). These lips of the Bridegroom—"so divinely beautiful" (*Sermons on the Song of Songs* 3.5)—have been kissed before, Bernard suddenly realizes:

> It seems to me that a kiss past comprehension, beyond the experience of any mere creature, was designated by him who said: "No one knows the Son except the Father, just as know one knows the Father except the Son . . . " [John 14:31]. For the Father loves the Son whom he embraces with a love that is unique. . . . Now, that mutual knowledge and love between him who begets and him who is begotten—what can it comprise if not a kiss that is utterly sweet, but utterly a mystery as well?
> 
> For my part I am convinced that no creature, not even an angel, is permitted to comprehend this secret of divine love, so holy and so august. . . . And hence the bride, although otherwise so audacious, does not dare to say: "Let him kiss me with his mouth," for she knows that this is the prerogative of the Father alone. What she does ask for is something less: "Let him kiss me with the kiss of his mouth." . . .
> 
> Thus the Father, when he kisses the Son, pours into him the plenitude of the mysteries of his divine being, breathing forth love's deep delight. . . . As has already been stated, no creature whatsoever has been privileged to comprehend the secret of this eternal, blessed and unique embrace; the Holy Spirit alone is the sole witness of their mutual knowledge and love.[119]

And the Holy Spirit, infinitely discreet, is not about to tell what s/he has seen night after night in the triangular bed that s/he shares with the Father and the Son in the heavenly mansion.

Unexpectedly, it is the Son himself who has spilled the beans. In response to the anticipated objection, "What voice thundered forth to you a secret that, you insist, was made known to no creature [cf. Rev. 10:4]?" Bernard replies, "It is the only Son, who is in the Father's bosom, who has made it known [John 1:18]. But he has made it known, not to the sorry and unworthy creature that I am," adds Bernard, "but to John, the Bridegroom's friend [cf. John 3:29]." A friend and more than a friend, as it turns out. This John is the Beloved Disciple, who has had secret knowledge of the Son, even as the Son has had secret knowledge of the Father: "For [John's] soul was pleasing to the Lord, entirely worthy both of the name and the dowry of a bride, worthy of the Bridegroom's embraces, worthy that is of leaning back on Jesus' breast [John 13:23]. John imbibed from the heart of the only-begotten Son [cf. John 7:37–38] what he in turn had imbibed from the Father."[120]

Bernard is now in a position to complete his headlong rush into the place where, on his own account, even angels fear to tread—the Blessed Trinity's bedchamber itself: "Listen if you will know what the kiss of the mouth is: 'The Father and I are one' [John 10:30]; and again: 'I am in the Father and the Father is in me' [John 14:10].... That the Son is in the Father and the Father in the Son signifies the kiss of the mouth" (*Sermons on the Song of Songs* 8.7). To put it a little differently, the Son need never sob aloud to the Father, nor need the Father sob aloud to the Son, in a moan verging on a scream, "I want you inside me now!" for each is always already inside the other. ("You make me feel like a god," the Son whispers in the Father's ear, gently nibbling his lobe, "utterly omnipotent." "You make *me* feel like a god," the Father whispers back, "I feel I could go on forever.") In the face of this endless act of double penetration, sustained by two eternal erections (each briefly caressing the other as it passes into the body of the being in whose infinite depths it has elected to lose itself), all earthly lovers, however well endowed, can only wait anxiously outside the door, listening to the awe-inspiring sounds of the divine lovemaking within, and hoping to be called to the bedside during a lull in the action, to stand there like a frightened little child:

> Paul was certainly a great man, but no matter how high he should aim in making the offer of his mouth, even if he were to raise himself right

into the third heaven [2 Cor. 12:2], he would still of necessity find himself remote from the lips of the Most High. He must abide content within the limits of his capacity, and since he cannot of himself reach that glorious countenance, let him humbly ask that it may lean down to him, that the kiss be transmitted from on high. He however who did not count equality with God a thing to be grasped [Phil. 2:6], since he could dare say: "The Father and I are one" [John 10:30], because he was joined to him as an equal and embraced him as an equal—he does not beg from an inferior position; rather on equally sublime heights mouth is joined to mouth.... (*Sermons on the Song of Songs* 8.8)

For Bernard, however, even the man steadying his "trembling knees" before daring to raise his eyes to the Son's mouth, "so divinely beautiful, not merely to gaze upon it," but to beg a kiss from it (3.5), is himself a sibling of the Son—though not a brother, as one might expect, but a sister. "Let that man who feels that he is moved by the same Spirit as the Son, let him know that he too is loved by the Father," Bernard begins. "Whoever he be let him be of good heart, let his confidence never waver." In the very next sentence, however, the "he" abruptly becomes a "she"—a she-male, or at any rate a she-soul:

> Living in the Spirit of the Son, let such a soul recognize herself as a daughter of the Father, a bride or even a sister of the Son, for you will find that the soul who enjoys this privilege is called by either of these names. Nor will it cost me much to prove it, the proof is ready to hand. They are the names by which the Bridegroom addresses her: "I come into my garden, my sister, my bride" [Song 5:1]. She is his sister because they have the one Father; his bride because joined in the one Spirit. For if marriage according to the flesh constitutes two in one body, why should not a spiritual union be even more efficacious in joining two in one spirit?[121]

When the Son leans out of the Father's bed, therefore, to kiss the man who desires him, and (if it is that man's lucky day) to embrace him, to fondle him, to have intimate knowledge of him, it is not only as a bride, but as a bride who also happens to be a sister, that he takes him, Bernard implies. Within the divine bedchamber, it would seem, incest is the spiritualized sexual relationship of choice, whether between Son and mother, or Son and Father, or Son and sister.[122]

Allegorical exegesis of the Song thereby becomes, not only an ecclesiastically sanctioned space for an ordinarily prohibited homoeroticism ("Thou shalt not lie with mankind, as with womankind: it is abomination"—Lev. 18:22), but for covert violation of a still more solemn taboo: "None of you shall approach to any that is near of kin to him, to uncover their nakedness: I am the LORD" (Lev. 18:6). Once again allegorical exegesis of the Song creates a carnivalesque zone in which certain of the nonnegotiable moral strictures that structure everyday existence are effortlessly overturned—and, what is more, overturned in the name of the absolute moral Authority. The apogee of queerness, in this instance as in others, is also the apogee of paradox.

But it is also the apogee of gleeful self-sabotage. For if the allegorical reading of the Song is an insubordinate (if sublimated) performance of sex, and hence of gender, the rules that are thereby being transgressed are precisely those that the expositors themselves (monks, priests, and prelates) have undertaken to make and maintain. Through the infinitely malleable medium of a series of ancient erotic love poems, a theocratic elite engages in its own self-subversion, its frocked members falling over one another in their zeal to deconstruct the socioreligious norms that they have dedicated their lives to upholding.

But in all of this there is, to a degree, nothing exceptional or unexpected. Readers of Mikhail Bakhtin's *Rabelais and His World* will be primed to recognize here a signal instance of the literary carnivalesque.[123] Bakhtin begins by noting how carnival festivities and the comic spectacles and parodic rituals associated with them had a prominent place in medieval culture. "Besides carnivals proper, with their long and complex pageants and processions, there was the 'feast of fools' (*festa stultorum*) and the 'feast of the ass'; there was a special free 'Easter laughter' (*risus paschalis*), consecrated by tradition. Moreover, nearly every Church feast had its comic aspect, which was also traditionally recognized," and so on.[124] Bakhtin sharply distinguishes the official festivals of medieval Europe, however—ecclesiastical festivals in particular—from the carnival. The official festivals "sanctioned the existing pattern of things and reinforced it." They "asserted all that was stable, unchanging, perennial: the existing hierarchy, the existing religious, political, and moral values, norms, and prohibitions."[125] Carnival, in contrast—at least in Bakhtin's utopian reimagining of it—"celebrated temporary liberation from the prevailing truth and the established order; it marked the suspension of all hierarchical rank, privileges, norms, and prohibitions."[126]

But the carnivalesque also found potent expression in "comic verbal compositions." The incendiary product of a long evolutionary history, with its roots in Christian antiquity, high medieval comic literature "was infused with the carnival spirit and made wide use of carnival forms and images." It paraded "in the disguise of legalized carnival licentiousness and in most cases was systematically linked with such celebrations.... It was the entire recreational literature of the Middle Ages." In an era in which decent-sized cities devoted three months a year on average to carnival festivities,

> the influence of the carnival spirit was irresistible: it made a man renounce his official state as monk, cleric, scholar, and perceive the world in its laughing aspect. Not only schoolmen and minor clerics but hierarchs and learned theologians indulged in gay recreation as relaxation from pious seriousness. "Monkish pranks" (*Joca monacorum*) was the title of one of the most popular medieval comic pieces. Confined to their cells, monks produced parodies or semiparodies of learned treatises and other droll Latin compositions.[127]

Alternatively, they produced allegorical commentaries on the Song of Songs—compositions no less carnivalesque in their audacious suspension of certain of the fundamental norms and prohibitions that constrained and sustained Christian medieval culture. And yet it seems safe to surmise that these commentaries were not *consciously* written in the antinomian spirit of carnival. The allegorists were not consciously indulging in "gay [!] recreation" or "relaxation from pious seriousness," but, on the contrary, understood themselves to be engaged in an endeavor of the utmost seriousness and sanctity. The conscious intent of the commentators thus paralleled that of the official Church festivals, which "asserted all that was stable, unchanging, perennial: the existing hierarchy, the existing religious, political, and moral values, norms, and prohibitions."[128] Again and again we see the ecclesiastical and political status quo being affirmed and reified in the commentaries—the prelates of the Church, in particular, having their God-given right to govern the masses validated repeatedly by ingenious appeal to this most unlikely of authorities, an ancient Hebrew celebration of unmarried love and lust.[129] Like the official Church festivals, too, the commentaries celebrate theological, christological, soteriological, ecclesiological, and moral truths deemed universal, immutable, and indisputable. "This is why the tone of the official feast was monolithically serious," observes Bakhtin, "and why the element of laughter was alien to it"[130]—as alien as it is to the commentaries.

But the apparent ecclesiastical soundness of the commentaries merely disguises their viral nature. What the commentaries actually represent is the surreptitious invasion and infection of the official ecclesiastical order by the anarchic element forever encamped on its borders—an element most truly *in* its element in the world-inverting world of carnival. Independently of any conscious agency, these commentaries thus combine to form a capacious Trojan horse through which the giants, dwarfs, and other "monsters" of the carnival (not least those defying gender categorization) infiltrate the cathedral at the most solemn moment of High Mass and cavort all over the altar. The repressed always returns—but only masked and in costume.

### After the Carnival (the Commentator Removes His Makeup)

Of course, the carnival always had its critics, and eventually they would succeed in shutting it down. Already at the end of the fourth century, Theodore, bishop of Mopsuestia in Cilicia, had presumed to commit to writing a reading of the Song of Songs that spurned allegory altogether and purported to embrace the literal sense, and in 553, a century or so after his death, his reading was officially condemned at the Second Council of Constantinople.[131] Theodore's near-contemporary Jovinian, meanwhile, proposed a parallel reading of the Song in the West, for which he was castigated by Jerome, among others.[132] Under the Church's withering glare, the carnal reading shriveled up and retreated almost completely from Christian commentaries on the Song for more than a millennium—although not from popular readings, as would appear from various indications in the commentaries themselves. Denis the Carthusian, for instance, his cheeks flushed with indignation, quotes the Chancellor of Paris, "the most learned master John Gerson," himself the author of a commentary on the Song, who insists that "No one should be distracted from belief in the most hidden and pure senses which the smokescreen of the literal [sense] disguises in carnality, nor should a person hit the rock of scandal of a foul sensuality. It would be shameful to repeat what I have heard for myself: it would offend pious ears." Chaucer, in contrast, is more than happy to offend; in "The Merchant's Tale," he has the lecher Januarie propose a staunchly carnal reading of the Song.[133] Popular profanations of the Song were not unknown among Jews either. The Babylonian Talmud attributes a stern warning to Rabbi Akiba: "Whoever sings the Song of Songs with tremulous voice in a banquet hall and (so) treats it as a sort of ditty has no share in the world to come" (*b. Sanhedrin* 12.10; cf. 101a).

Emboldened by the Reformation and the Enlightenment, the carnal interpretation began to inch its way in earnest into erudite discourse on the Song only in the seventeenth and eighteenth centuries,[134] and in the nineteenth century, it began to wrest the Song out of the grip of the allegorical interpretation altogether, a move that had real repercussions even for nonscholarly readers of the text, many of whom simply stopped reading it altogether. Writing in London in 1869 (on the feast of the Nativity of Our Lady, to be precise), Littledale prefaces his monumental attempt to reinstate the allegorical reading of the Song with a revealing lament:

> The Song of Songs, though for many centuries a favorite theme of the most eminent Saints and Christian writers, either by way of direct comment or of illustrative quotation, has fallen, during these latter times, into comparative neglect. It is rarely made the basis of sermons, or even of devotional treatises, and thus, as may be reasonably inferred, does not occupy any prominent place in private study of Holy Scripture.[135]

Indeed, readers of John Fowles's *The French Lieutenant's Woman* may recall that devout Victorians devised an admirably direct strategy for countering the carnal reading of the Song. In the scene in question, Sarah Woodruff, the eponymous heroine and fallen woman, enters the private drawing room of her redoubtable benefactress, Mrs. Poulteney of Lyme Regis, on March 29, 1867, for the evening Bible-reading: "Sarah went towards the lectern in the corner of the room, where the large 'family' Bible—not what you may think of as a family Bible, but one from which certain inexplicable errors of taste in the Holy Writ (such as the Song of Solomon) had been piously excised—lay in its off-duty hours."[136]

Since we are already in Victorian England, let us backtrack thirty years to 1837, in time to pick up the latest copy of *The Congregational Magazine*, in whose pages a polite but animated dispute is being conducted by two learned divines, Revd. Dr. J. Pye Smith and Revd. Dr. James Bennett. The dispute concerns the appropriate method for interpreting the Song of Solomon. Dr. Pye Smith has roundly trounced the allegorical approach,[137] eliciting a spirited and instructive rejoinder from Dr. Bennett:

> That this is *not* a song of human love is clear from the beginning to the end. It opens with the language of a female: "Let him kiss me"; it is full of her solicitous seeking after him; it abounds with praises of his person.... What writer, with the feelings, or the reason, of a man, would begin a poem on his fair one by describing her as courting him? Let it not be said, "We must not transfer our modern and northern ideas to the ancient Orientals, who had not our delicate notions of the female character"; for this would only make the case stronger. It would be more abhorrent from the secluded, submissive character of Eastern brides to ask the gentlemen to come and kiss them, than it would be from the dignified confidence of British women.

Here Dr. Bennett lifts his eyes from his writing desk to gaze with fond admiration at Mrs. Bennett, whose quiet indignation at Dr. Pye Smith's perverse opinions perfectly mirrors his own, and who has been lending him moral support all evening by keeping vigil in a corner of his study, their companionable silence interrupted only by the sound of his pen scratching its purposeful course across the page. Her fingers are busy, as always, with embroidery. The needle flashes in and out forming words of Holy Writ. The verse she has chosen, unbidden, is from the First Epistle to the Corinthians: *Doth not even nature itself teach you?* She boldly meets his eyes and returns his affectionate smile. Newly inspired, he dips his nib and continues:

> It is not a question of climate or age, but of *nature*.... Though men like to court, they do not like to be courted; and while they think it cruel to be rejected when they court, they without mercy reject her that courts them; as the forward female has usually found, from the days of Sappho to this hour. Women were endowed with the form and qualities intended to attract courtship, and they feel it; and when they do not feel it, men despise them. No man, therefore, in his senses, would think to compliment his fair one by writing of her, to her, as if she had lost her retiring modesty, her female dignity, and degraded herself by doing that for which every man would despise her.... Till

fishes mount to sing with larks on the shady boughs, and nightingales dive to ocean's depths to court the whales, no man, of any age, of any clime, of any rank, can be supposed to write ordinary love-songs in such a style. We are told, by the first word, that a greater than Solomon is here, one who must be courted, and that loves more than human are the theme. This is the Bridegroom of whom the Psalmist says, "He is thy Lord, and worship thou him"; "Kiss the Son, lest he be angry, and ye perish from the way." Such a spouse may exhibit his Bride as *asking* for his love; every other must present *himself* as asking for hers, and begging this acceptance of his.[138]

"We are told ... that a greater than Solomon is here, one who must be courted. . . . " But why must *he* be courted? Is it because the one called into relationship with him might also chance to be male—*is* male, indeed, in the case of Dr. Bennett—and courting "comes naturally" to the male? Thus Bennett could himself conceive of courting Christ, of "solicitously seeking after him," of begging intimacy with him. Bennett challenges the literal interpretation of the Song, arguing that it defeminizes the female protagonist, that it makes her a gender anomaly, if not, indeed, a gender monster—a fish twittering in a tree, a bird gliding through the sea. He champions the allegorical reading instead, carefully choosing not to notice that it thrusts an equally anomalous gender role upon *him*.[139] For Revd. Dr. James Bennett, no less than for his patristic and medieval precursors, the spiritual is a carnivalesque sphere in which same-sex relationships, ordinarily invested with the most chilling taboos, are socially sanctioned. Not only are they sanctioned, in fact, they are deemed coeval with the most sublime dictates of morality.

This contradiction merely draws attention to a still more spectacular one. I shall need a moment to bring it into focus. The equation of activity with masculinity and passivity with femininity has proved to be an extraordinarily tenacious one in Western history and culture, enduring, in one form or another, from antiquity down to modernity, and beyond.[140] Against this stylized backdrop, consider first the classic Jewish doctrine of election. Yahweh chose Israel from among the nations; he liberated her from bondage and established his covenant with her. Israel ought to respond to this gracious divine initiative with utter love and obedience; that is the condition of her beauty, her purity, her holiness, her happiness.[141] *Yahweh chose Israel*: the masculinity of Yahweh, the femininity of Israel.[142]

Now introduce Augustine into the sketch, a matchstick man in a mitre. A matchstick Luther is seated on his shoulders. Within the constricted parameters of our perduring gender equation (activity = masculinity, passivity = femininity), the Augustinian-Lutheran view of Judaism as a "works"-based religion can be read as a masculinization of Judaism. In place of the Judaism of the ancient Jewish sources,[143] which is "properly" passive in relation to God, acting only in grateful response to his masculine initiative, Augustine and Luther present us with an Israel who wants to wear the pants, who will not wait for God to rescue her, who wants to do the work(s) of salvation herself, man's work though it is. The corollary representation of Christianity as a religion of grace and election can likewise be read as its feminization: within the house of God that is the Church, the Christian must indeed labor, and labor diligently, but this housework is merely an expression of love and gratitude willingly offered up to the Father of the house and his Son and heir, Jesus Christ. The latter, as Perfect Man, has rescued the Christian from the Dragon ("who is called the Devil and Satan" [Rev. 12:9]), built her this magnificent house, and graciously taken up residence within as her husband and lord.

The question immediately arises, of course, of why Augustine, Luther, and their own innumerable sons should wish to claim, implicitly (and unconsciously?), that Christianity is a "feminine" way of relating to God, and hence of being in the world. Is it merely that they themselves occupy a "feminine" subject position in relation to this "masculine" God? Is their gendered soteriology simply the logical outgrowth of their sexualized spirituality? If so, the importance of the allegorical tradition in Song of Songs interpretation for the understanding of male spirituality—Christian, but also Jewish—becomes apparent. The allegorical interpretation thrusts into plain view a relationship ordinarily closeted. It "outs" the male believer.

∼

Like a man who awakes bleary-eyed and hungover one overcast morning to discover to his immense horror that he is in another man's bed, entwined in its owner's arms, commentary on the Song of Songs began to recoil sharply from allegory in the course of the nineteenth century. Slipping stealthily out of bed and hastily adjusting its clerical collar, it tiptoed out of the room.[144] Like reformed and newly sober men, late-nineteenth- and twentieth-century commentators labored to straighten out the queer reading to which the Song had so long been subjected. The Song was turned instead into a celebration of, indeed a warrant for, heterosexuality. Littledale bewails the beginnings of this transformation in his 1869 tome: "The necessity, after the gradual manufacture of the reigning literalist theory, for discovering some ground for the retention of the Canticles in the Canon, has led to the assertion that its design is to teach a higher morality with regard to love and marriage." He objects: "There is not the faintest hint in any writer, Jewish or Christian, before the nineteenth century, that such a lesson is inculcated by the Song of Songs, there is no trace of any influence having been exerted by it in this direction."[145] But the transformation, once under way, proved irreversible. Littledale's German contemporary Delitzsch was thus able to announce confidently in his 1875 commentary: "The Song transfigures natural but holy love. Whatever in the sphere of the divinely-ordered marriage relation makes love the happiest, firmest bond uniting two souls together, is presented to us here in living pictures."[146] Similar assertions multiply all the way down to the present.

The new homiletics of heteronormativity in Song of Songs interpretation found especially succinct expression in a mid-twentieth-century endorsement of its erotics by the distinguished Old Testament scholar H. H. Rowley. "The Church has always consecrated the union of man and woman in matrimony, and taught that marriage is a divine ordinance," he wrote, "and it is not unfitting that a book which expressed the spiritual and physical emotions on which matrimony rests should be given a place in the Canon of Scripture."[147] Roland E. Murphy, who himself has been arguing this very point since at least the middle of the twentieth century, sums it up nicely in his recent commentary on the Song:

> While the Song is not designed to elaborate theological doctrine or teach ethics, its unapologetic depiction of rapturous, reciprocal love between a man and a woman does model an important dimension of human existence, an aspect of life that ancient Israel understood to be divinely ordained and sanctioned. We need look no further than Genesis 1 to find express warrant for this view: the whole of God's creation is "good . . . indeed very good," specifically including the sexual differentiation of humankind (vv 26–31). In this passage, to be sure, procreation immediately comes to the fore as God's purposive blessing in relationship to human sexuality. But it fulfills rather than diminishes the extraordinary affirmation that the divine image itself is incarnated in

male and female counterparts, which only together are granted sovereignty in God's world. Even more poignant, perhaps, are the familiar lines of Genesis 2:18–25, a text Karl Barth has called the "Old Testament Magna Carta of humanity" because in his view it epitomizes the creaturely coexistence that God intends for all humankind by focusing on the most basic and intimate of human unions, the physical bond formed between a man and a woman.[148]

Of course, it is not only impeccably credentialized biblical scholars such as Rowley and Murphy who have read the Song as championing the sanctity of heterosexuality, thereby slapping a fig leaf on the carnal reading and recruiting it for mainstream morality. In the course of a fascinating stretch of the 300-page lead-in to his own commentary on the Song, Marvin Pope treats us to a wealth of twentieth-century scholarly opinion, mainly Christian but also Jewish, much of it lacking professional polish, which contends that the Song is essentially a celebration of divinely ordained heterosexual love, supremely enshrined in heterosexual marriage.[149] A single example will suffice to convey the tenor of this material. Pope quotes a 1963 doctoral dissertation by Robert Brinkerhoff Dempsey, which argued that the Song seems custom-made for premarital and marital counseling: "Canticles is an exquisite presentation of the total involvement of both partners, each for the other, according to the divine plan for human happiness."[150] Dempsey is wary of the allegorical tradition in Song of Songs interpretation. The Song should "be used only with extreme care in a mystical sense in hymnody, prayers or sermons. So to use the book is to distort its meaning. Whatever use in worship to which the Song of Solomon is put, it must be consistent with its content concerning the love between a man and a woman."[151] The allegorical tradition constitutes a threat to a heterosexual reading of the Song. Dempsey is able to report with satisfaction, however: "During the last century the traditional allegorical approach to Canticles has been for the most part abandoned because of the discoveries of scholarship, the spread of a more natural view of love and sex, and a realization that in the final analysis Canticles is love poetry."[152] And also because of the rise of heterosexuality?

The "invention" of heterosexuality appears to have coincided approximately with the invention of electricity, photography, automotive engineering, and other indispensable appurtenances of modernity.[153] Is it entirely a matter of chance that the emergence of heterosexuality, with its sharply delineated and strictly policed sexual borders, should happen to coincide with the decline of the allegorical interpretation of the Song of Songs, with its blurry and poorly policed sexual borders? "Before" heterosexuality, "normal" men could get up to things with other men that they could not so easily get up to "after" heterosexuality—*intimate* things, erotic or otherwise. Daniel Boyarin notes the scope for forms of male intimacy even within rabbinic Jewish culture, a culture that "has always been heteronormative, even if not heterosexual, that is, homophobic."[154]

> "Who is a friend?" a midrash asks. "He that one eats with, drinks with, reads with, studies with, sleeps with, and reveals to him all of his secrets—the secrets of Torah and the secrets of the ways of the world." "Sleeps with" does *not* have the euphemistic value that it has in English or German, but the text is certainly reaching for a very intense and passionate level of male-male physical intimacy here. The "way of the world" is a somewhat ambiguous metaphorical term that can refer to several areas of worldly life, including business, but especially sex. Male intimacy, it seems, for the talmudic culture includes the physical contact of being in bed together while sharing verbally the most intimate of experiences, a pattern not unknown in other cultures. . . . Thus, while we cannot draw inferences about the sexual practices of rabbinic men from such a passage, we can certainly, it seems to me, argue that it bespeaks a lack of "homosexual panic" such as that necessitated by the modern formation known as "heterosexuality."[155]

I would argue, just as confidently, that the consummately queer body of allegorical commentary on the Song of Songs, both Jewish and Christian, that we have been pondering in this essay similarly bespeaks, indeed presupposes, a lack of homosexual panic in the cultures in which it was conceived—in which case the pervasiveness of homosexual panic in twentieth-century Western culture would explain the rejection of the allegorical approach to the Song even by male readers innocent or wary of the "discoveries" of critical biblical scholarship (such as the non-Solomonic authorship of the book, and its pronounced family resemblance to other ancient Near Eastern love poetry). The interpretation of the Song as a celebration of heterosexual love is now commonplace even among conservative Protestant, Roman Catholic, and Jewish scholars.[156] It is not that these biblical scholars are any less convinced than their ancient or medieval predecessors that God addresses them and us in and through the Song. But they do still tend, almost to a man, to be male,[157] and I strongly suspect that, as polished products of heterosexuality, they simply have problems internalizing the central voice of the Song—the feminine voice—that their pre-heterosexual male counterparts did not have; that they have trouble throwing themselves wholeheartedly into the role of a vivacious young woman in love; that the intrinsic queerness of the role sits too strangely in a culture that has scripted them to be superlatively straight at all times—a culture that has already cast them in a dizzyingly different role, indeed, that of the ultimate custodians of its straightness.[158] All of which suggests that the interpretive history of the Song of Songs constitutes yet another fascinating footnote in the infinitely intricate history of sexuality. But the final twist in this footnote is possibly the trickiest of all.

### The New Allegorists

In their attempts to take the literal interpretation of the Song of Songs to its logical conclusion, a number of late-twentieth-century commentators have fallen back (inadvertently, one assumes) on the allegorical method. Marvin Pope and Michael Goulder are especially notable in this regard. Few twentieth-century readings of the Song are as resolutely heterosexual as theirs. In stark contrast to the "old" allegorists, who give even sexual details a spiritual reading, these "new" allegorists give a sexual reading even to details that are ostensibly nonsexual.

First, Goulder. Confronted with Song 8:5b, which he translates as "Under the apple-tree I awakened you; there your mother writhed with you, there she who bore you writhed," Goulder suspects that the phrase "I awakened you" (ʿôrartîka—the "you" is therefore masculine) "refers to sexual arousal." He further suspects that "Under the apple-tree" is likewise a double entendre:

> For it could be that the place where she aroused him is an anatomical place as well as a place in a glade; and that it is thought of as an apple tree by virtue of the two fruits hanging down above the "trunk"; that there is a special force to "under, because it is at the under end of this tree that the nerves are concentrated that make for such arousal; and

it is "there" that women . . . are in turn aroused to ecstasy in the moment of union.[159]

Faced with 6:12, which he renders poetically as "Ere I had thought it, he made me, my life did, my own people's chariot, / Come from Nadiv," Goulder explains: "When first he saw her, the king compared the princess to his mare in the chariots (*rikebê*) of Pharaoh (1.9): now, she says, he has made her a chariot of her own people—that is, she is still the mare, but he is now the 'charioteer.'" Still unsure as to Goulder's meaning? Let him confirm your worst suspicions: "The Hebrews had thus already discovered that sexual union could take place in more than one position."[160]

Neither does Goulder shrink from translating 7:10b, a line he assigns to the "princess," as "To touch my love's erectness, and my lips to kiss his sleepers!" or from paraphrasing the entire verse as follows: "He says, 'Your mouth is like wine' [7:10a] with its kisses: yes, she replies daringly, 'It goes to my beloved to his "uprightness."'" And again: "'Your mouth is intoxicating,' says the king: 'it goes,' replies the princess with a twinkle, 'to my beloved's "uprights," it glides with my lips over his "sleepers."'"[161] What Goulder imagines these "sleepers" to be is never explicitly stated—but then it doesn't need to be, so skillfully does he draw ancient Hebrew sexual slang out of the ether. And the imagined oral ministrations (guaranteed to arouse the "sleepers" from slumber?) are not all one-way traffic. Confronted, finally, by 8:2, which Goulder renders in rhyme as

I'd take you to my mother's,
To drink my spiced wine—
You'd show me how—and taste the sweet
Of pomegranate mine

he is able to state confidently, "The sexual meaning is not in doubt. . . . The only question is what sort of sexual activity is envisaged. We may think of straightforward sexual union. . . . On the other hand, we have to consider the alternative that the 'drinking' is meant literally. . . . It seems probable then that she is speaking here of oral sex on his side, as a preamble to the full union of 8.3 (celebrated at v. 5b)."[162] And so on.

What prevents me, however, from hailing Michael Goulder as the New Allegorist par excellence of the Song of Songs is the palpable discomfort that his own steamy readings induce in him. He worries audibly and at length that the details of his translations and exegesis reveal the Song to be nothing more "than a piece of high-class pornography."[163] Like Martin Luther before him, Goulder cannot quite bring himself to contemplate an unmitigated carnal interpretation of the Sublime Song. Consequently, he is driven to argue that the Song contains a hidden theological message.

Goulder contends that the Song was composed "in the context of the fourth-century Jewish controversy on intermarriage with foreign women."[164] Its purpose was to signal divine sanction of, and garner social acceptance for, such intermarriage, "for unless there is such an intention, it is difficult to explain the recurring emphasis on its heroine's darkness, curly hair, and Arabian extraction, which alone detract from her oft-sung perfections," which otherwise conform to ancient Israelite standards of beauty.[165] The Song of Songs is thus "the most ambitiously anti-racialist document in the Bible."[166] And if its intended theological message is commendable, its *un*intended theological message is positively prescient: it is "that Jews and Gentiles are equal in the sight of God. Such theological insights do not receive explicit expression before the Epistle to the Ephesians."[167] In Goulder's fascinating commentary on the Song of Songs, therefore, "old" allegorist and "new" allegorist do deadly battle, the old allegorist eventually pinning the new allegorist to the ground—but not before the latter has blurted out everything he has wanted to say.

Pope, in contrast, is prey to no such conflicts. His transformation of the Sublime Song into the Suggestive Song is accomplished entirely without qualms. But he does open up a Pandora's box in the process (out of which a topless Pandora pops on cue—although that's just the beginning). Let us start with Pope's treatment of Song 7:2a (7:3a in the Hebrew text), generally rendered by translators along the following lines: "Your navel is a rounded bowl / that never lacks mixed wine" (NRSV). The owner of the navel is feminine in the Hebrew (*sorēk*). Peering intently into the little cavity, however, Pope begins to doubt that it really is a navel after all. He argues that the Hebrew word traditionally translated as "navel" would be better rendered here as "vulva." "Since the movement of the description of the lady's charms is from the feet upward," he tactfully explains, "the locus of the evermoist receptacle between the thighs and the belly would seem to favor the lower aperture. The liquid, too, would seem to make the navel unlikely since navels are not notable for their capacity to store or dispense moisture."[168]

Convinced that he has caught a glimpse of a vulva (like Sharon Stone's mesmerized interrogators in *Basic Instinct*), Pope seems to become obsessed by the thought of it. Thus he cannot resist translating Song 7:8c–d (Hebrew 7:9c–d) as "Let your breasts be like grape clusters / The scent of your vulva like apples," instead of the more usual "Let your breasts be like grape clusters / The scent of your *breath* [*ʾappēk*] like apples."[169] But Pope had earlier ascribed a still more fragrant perfume to this fascinating vulva. With regard to Song 4:13a, "*šĕlāḥayik* is a pomegranate grove," he suggests that *šĕlāḥayik* denotes a "more intimate portion" of the heroine's anatomy than most translators have been willing to contemplate, and boldly renders the part-verse as "Your groove a pomegranate grove."[170]

But Pope's pièce de résistance, the showpiece of his New Allegorical reading of the Song, is his ingenious decoding of 5: 2–6. The passage, in Pope's own translation, reads:

I slept, but my mind was alert.
Hark, my love knocks.
Open to me, my sister,
My darling, my dove, my perfect one!
For my head is drenched with dew,
My locks with the night mist.
I have removed my tunic
How shall I put it on?
I have washed my feet
How shall I soil them?
My love thrust his "hand" into the hole,
And my inwards seethed for him.
I rose to open for my love,
And my hands dripped myrrh,
My fingers liquid myrrh,
On the handles of the bolt.
I opened to my love,
But my love had turned and gone.
My soul sank at his flight.
I sought, but could not find him.
I called him, but he did not answer me.

Pope offers the following explanation for his decision to turn "hand" (*yad*) into a naughty word by slipping it into a sexy pair of quotation marks: "Given the attested use of 'hand' as a surrogate for phallus"—earlier he has adduced Isaiah 57:8-10 and the Qumran *Manual of Discipline* (1QS 7:13) in this regard, along with certain Ugaritic texts—"there can be no question that, whatever the context, the statement 'my love thrust his "hand" into the hole' would be suggestive of coital intromission, even without the succeeding line descriptive of the emotional reaction of the female."[171]

∽

As it happens, certain of the Old Allegorists also accorded phallic significance to the "hand" of Song 5:4a, prompted, perhaps, by the Vulgate translation, whose expansive rendering of the verse as *dilectus meus misit manum suam per foramen et venter meus intremuit ad tactum eius* ("my beloved put his hand through the hole and my belly trembled at his touch") seems to suggest that the hand makes physical contact with Shulamith, an impression confirmed by the treatment accorded elsewhere to the verse by Jerome, the Vulgate translator: "Let the seclusion of your own chamber ever guard you; ever let the Bridegroom sport with you within. If you pray, you are speaking to your Spouse; if you read, He is speaking to you. When sleep falls on you, He will come behind the wall and will put His hand through the hole in the door and will touch your flesh [*et mittet manum suam per foramen et tanget ventrem tuum*]" (*Letters* 22.25). The emperor Matthew Cantacuzene (d. ca. 1360), for his part, followed by Denis the Carthusian, saw in the action of the hand and the woman's excitation in response to it a clear reference to "the rejoicing of the hallowed womb of the Virgin Mother when He, the Right Hand of God, came to her at the Annunciation in secret and mysterious wise, finding her all pure, . . . resolute in her spotless maidenhood."[172] This spectral Hand of inspection (a medical Hand enveloped in surgical rubber?) opens the Virgin to examine her and deposits its spectral seed in her womb.

No less phallic, although queerer by far, is Rupert of Deutz's reading of the verse. The hand and its thrusting gesture prompts Rupert to recall one of his own mystical experiences in which he, or rather his soul, assumed the guise of a "young girl," who then had her spiritual G-spot skillfully manipulated by the Bridegroom: "the Beloved, seen in a vision of the night, in a wondrous fashion thrust his hand into her chest—through an opening, as it were—and grasped her heart within, and held it for some time, binding it very sweetly; and that heart, leaping up and dancing inside that hand, was rejoicing with unspeakable joy."[173] In his paraphrase of the anecdote, Littledale tellingly suppresses the fact that Rupert styles himself a girl. Littledale has time for any nonsense but that, and so in the paraphrase Littledale makes a man out of Rupert (albeit one who apparently relishes a spiritual fisting): "And accordingly the holy Abbot of Deutz recounts a vision granted to a nameless person, supposed to have been himself, telling us: 'The Beloved appeared plainly in a vision of the night, and wondrously put His hand, as through a hole, into the man's breast, and laid hold of his heart within, and held it for some time, pressing it gently, and that heart rejoiced with gladness unspeakable, leaping and bounding within the clasp of that Hand.'"[174]

~

Let us pick up Pope's assertion that "there can be no question that, whatever the context, the statement 'my love thrust his "hand" into the hole' would be suggestive of coital intromission, even without the succeeding line descriptive of the emotional reaction of the female."[175] "Whatever the context...." This is an extraordinary claim in *its* context, because disregard for context is meant to be the hallmark, not of the "literal" reading of the Song (of which Pope's magnum opus is still the most ambitious example ever attempted), but of the "allegorical" reading. As it happens, the immediate context of these lines militate strongly against Pope's reading, as we shall see in a moment. Like the "old" allegorists, however, Pope is not about to let context stand in the way of the *desired* reading.[176] Precisely at this point in Pope's commentary, the distinction between the literal and the allegorical collapses, for by inviting us to read even *one* word in this passage euphemistically, Pope opens a sluice gate. We automatically enclose the "hole" also in quotation marks (even if Pope himself is too delicate to do so),[177] and these mental quotation marks then begin to run rampant all over the passage. In effect, Pope has invited us to turn the entire passage into an allegory of "coital intromission." Let's give it a try.

If Pope is correct in his interpretation of Song 5:4a ("My love thrust his 'hand' into the hole"), surely 5:2c ("Open to me") can mean only one thing: "Open *your legs* to me!"—and, indeed, Pope does not disappoint us in his handling of this part-verse. "The word 'door' is recognized even by the most modest commentators as a figure for a female unusually open and receptive to sexual overtones," he maintains. Moreover, "the request to 'open' in the preceding verse could in certain circumstances have sexual connotations."[178] But now we encounter our first obstacle. The reason given for this impassioned outburst of unbridled lust—"Open your legs!"—seems rather incongruous at first blush: "For my head is drenched with dew, / My locks with the night mist." But might not the "head" in question be the man's glans, we feel compelled to ask, in which case the drops of "dew" would be the visible proof of his ardor, while the "locks" would, of course, be the luxuriant tangle of his pubic hair (raven black, perhaps, to match his wavy tresses [cf. 5:11]).[179] Admittedly, the "night mist" with which the "locks" are said to be drenched present us with more of a challenge, unschooled as we are in the allegorical method.

Still more obdurate are the lines that follow, spoken this time by the woman: "I have removed my tunic / How shall I put it on?" What we should expect to hear at this steamy juncture in the proceedings is *not* something along the lines of "I'm stripped and ready for action and now you want me to get dressed again?" The latter part of the verse, however, is less enigmatic: "I have washed my feet / How shall I soil them?" Pope knowingly remarks: "In view of the well-known use of 'feet' as a euphemism for genitals, the language is at least suggestive."[180] He adds: "The language of the lady may represent a bit of coy pretense intended to tease the eager male."[181] Hmmm. "Coy" (which my dictionary defines as "Shrinking modestly or coquettishly from familiarity; shy; demure . . . ") is hardly the adjective that leaps to my mind to describe a statement that might be paraphrased as: "I have washed my pussy and now you want me to get it messy again?" But now we encounter our biggest problem yet. The next seven lines of the poem seem to be out of sequence. We should expect "I rose to 'open' for my love," followed by "I 'opened' to my love," climaxing in "My love thrust his 'hand' into the 'hole,'" but that is not what we have here, the thrusting of the "hand" into the "hole" mysteriously preceding any "opening" whatsoever on the part of the said "hole."

Certain of the remaining details, however, have been ably handled by yet another New Allegorist. Undeterred by contextual inconveniences, Lyle Eslinger has snatched the baton from Pope and pushed the hyperheterosexual reading of the passage to unprecedented extremes. First, he picks up Pope's interpretation of Song 8:8–9. This passage reads:

> We have a little sister, and she has no breasts.
> What shall we do for our sister, on the day
> when she is spoken for?
> If she is a wall, we will build upon her a
> battlement of silver; but if she is a door,
> we will enclose her with boards of cedar. (RSV)

At issue here is the girl's virginity, Pope suspects. Her family's concern is "to keep her closed until the proper time for opening."[182] This provides Eslinger with the opening *he* needs, however: "Given this explicit identification of the girl with a door, and the *double entendre* of 5.2–5, in which the door plays a central role, it is possible that the *kappôt hammanᶜûl* of 5.5d may mean something besides 'the handles of the bolt' (RSV and Pope)."[183]

The exegetical footwork that follows resists easy reduplication, so I shall take the liberty of skipping ahead to Eslinger's conclusion. The seemingly innocent reference to "the handles of the bolt," expertly coaxed open by Eslinger, now parts to reveal a superlatively intimate part of female anatomy. At that moment the Song of Songs seems to shimmer, shift shape, and become—what? A hardcore centerfold spread, which teasingly transmutes into a gynecological illustration from an anatomical textbook (pornography always threatening to teeter over into anatomy, in any case, and vice versa). Any textbook in particular, though? Yes, *Cunningham's Manual of Practical Anatomy*, 13th edition, from which Eslinger extracts the following terms that, for him, uncover the secret meaning of the mysterious part-verse that he is probing: "Regarding the specific anatomical identity of the *kappôt hammanᶜûl* it is possible to suggest the vaginal vestibule and bulbs, along with the bulbospongiosus muscle as the locking or barring mechanism (*hammanᶜûl*) and the labia minora and majora as the plural appendages which together form the walls of the vulvic cavity."[184]

Eslinger's dramatic gesture of uncovering is a singularly electrifying example of that hyperheterosexual reading of the Song of Songs that I have termed the New Allegory. Yet it is a mere Hippolytan fragment, casually whipped out en route to a rereading of some verses from Deuteronomy.[185] The "literal" reading of the Song, its reclamation from seventeen centuries of queer exegesis and its transformation into an unmitigated celebration of heterosexual love and lust, is still in its infancy. The carnal interpretation of the Song still awaits its Origen.[186]

## 2  ON THE FACE AND PHYSIQUE OF THE HISTORICAL JESUS

### The Tannery

> Jesus appeared; he put on that book; he was nailed to a tree;
> he published the edict of the Father on the cross.
> —*The Gospel of Truth* 20, 24–25
> (trans. Harold W. Attridge and George W. MacRae)

"I'm finished," groaned Jesus, gratefully giving up the ghost. Late that night, his father came to claim the body. Never one to stand on ceremony, he went to work there and then in the tomb. First, he skinned the corpse. After he had laboriously removed the body hair by scraping, he scrubbed the skin clean, sighing all the while at the punctures and tears that marred it. Then he smoothed it with pumice and dressed it with chalk. Perspiring profusely now, he carefully cut it into rectangular sheets, stacked and folded them meticulously, and sewed them along the creases. Leaving the book on the slab, he wearily vacated the tomb before sunrise, dragging the flayed corpse behind him. Soon afterwards, the book was found by two of Jesus' disciples (as it was meant to be), one of whom recognized it for the remains of his master and lovingly bore it away. Years later he would use it to write the first draft of his gospel.

∼

This tale, too, refuses to remain buried. This is now the third time that I've told it. Always with variations, of course. The last time it was the Beloved Disciple himself who manufactured the book. He had arrived with Peter at the tomb and seen only the linen grave cloths lying there, together with the *sydarion*, the face cloth, all of them covered with a minute elegant script written in bright red ink:

> In the beginning was the Word, and the Word was with God, and the Word was God. He was with God in the beginning; through him all things were made, and nothing that was made was made without him. In him was life, and the life was the light of humankind. The light glows in the darkness, and the darkness has not extinguished it. . . .

Tenderly the disciple had gathered the grave cloths, burying his tear-streaked face in them and inhaling the scent of death that still clung to them. He had slept in the linen wrappings for many years afterwards, the face cloth under his head. Finally, when the writing had begun to fade, he had cut the moldering rags into crude rectangular sheets, stacked them roughly in order, folded them in two, and stitched them along the crease, thereby producing the first Christian codex.

The first time the tale imposed itself on me, however, I was standing not in the tomb but by the cross. And the cross in question was not John's pink cross with the padded patibulum and rubber nails but Mark's cruel crimson cross with the red-hot razor-sharp spikes. Here is what I saw:

> Writ(h)ing in pain on his cross, Jesus can at last be read: "Truly this man was a Son of God!" exclaims Mark's centurion, his reading glasses reflecting the harsh glare of the afternoon sun. Jesus is in the process of becoming a book. Nailed, grafted onto the tree, Jesus' body is becoming one with the wood. His flesh, torn and beaten to a pulp, joined by violence to the wood, is slowly being changed into processed woodpulp, into paper, as the centurion looks on. As tree and budding book, Jesus is putting forth leaves, the leaves of a gospel book, whose opening sentence the centurion has just read: "The beginning of the gospel of Jesus Christ, Son of God." Doubled over in pain, folded like a stack of leaves, Jesus is bound to a hard wooden spine. Graphted onto the tree, he is leafing his body in order to readturn as a book. He will

spend tree days in the tome. But in death his voice will acquire the volume that it lacked in life.

And in death his body will also acquire the beauty that it (most likely) lacked in life, a beauty generally found only in books. Or in glossy magazines, on billboards, in movies, or on TV—which is all very much to the point, as we shall see, for this essay is primarily a pretext to bring biblical studies into contact with contemporary culture[1]—to let biblical studies at its driest, dustiest, and most ecclesiastical experience the touch of *popular* culture in particular. Alternately bland and bizarre, the latter already has a Bible in its pocket anyway, its spine comfortably pressed up against a copy of *TV Guide*. It's not that I'm interested in *idealizing* popular culture; it fatigues and nauseates me as much as it fascinates me.[2] But fatigue no less than fascination compels acknowledgment. And what the present essay aims to acknowledge, specifically, is that although fewer people than ever know what Jesus is supposed to have said, many remain reasonably sure that they at least know what he looked like. Jesus' face is a (pop-)cultural icon, and has been for quite some time. As such his image speaks louder than his words.

But I'm getting ahead of myself. I need to retrace my steps and begin, once again, with the Gospel According to Saint John.

**The Beauty Parlor**

> His person is tall and elegantly shaped; his aspect amiable and reverend; his hair flows into those beauteous shades which no united colors can match, falling into graceful curls below his ears, agreeably couching on his shoulders, and parting on the crown of his head like the head dress of the Sect of Nazarenes; his forehead is smooth and large; his cheeks without spot, save that of a lovely red; his nose and mouth are formed with exquisite symmetry; his beard is thick and suitable to the hair of his head, reaching a little below his chin and parting in the middle like a fork; his eyes are bright, clear and serene.
>
> —*Letter of Lentulus*[3]

He will have a single eye protruding from his forehead, with a flat-surfaced face, and a mouth extending as far as his chest. He will have no upper teeth, nor will he have knees, and the soles of his feet will be rounded like a cartwheel.

—*Antichrist*[4]

What are we to make of the Fourth Gospel today (which is also the Found Gospel, as we have just seen, written on the flayed flesh of the crucified Son of God)? Is it not at once the most essential—and most inessential—of the canonical gospels? At the beginning of the twenty-first century, no less than at the end of the fourth, does the Johannine Jesus not remain the benchmark of christological orthodoxy for all the mainline Christian churches? But what of the role of the Johannine Jesus in critical biblical scholarship?

Critical scholarship on all four Gospels began in earnest in post-Enlightenment Germany as a manhunt for the historical Jesus, the Jesus "behind" the Gospels, a secretive figure systematically mistaken for his more popular twin, the Christ of faith.[5] Twice it seemed as though he had been found, but each time he managed to slip away.[6] A so-called Third Quest for the historical Jesus rages even as I write.[7] Many have joined in the manhunt, many more cheering or yelling obscenities from the sidelines. Startled eyes turn as hysterical Jesus suspects are dragged into the church by the triumphant band of critics. To the dubious congregation in the pews, each Jesus seems more unlikely than the last. "Did you at any time claim to be the Christ, the Son of the living God," each is asked in turn. "I most certainly did not," most of them reply. But if the congregation is in shock, we critics are in our element. For this we were born, to testify to the truth, most especially the truth about this Jesus, called Christ. And what could be less relevant to this truth than the Gospel According to Saint John?

Hardened as we are by historical Jesus research, it is hard not to smile superciliously if we contemplate the great controversies that shook Christendom in the fourth century, the heresiarch Arius, for instance, presuming to claim that the preexistent Christ was not an eternal being after all, but merely a superior creature created *ex nihilo* by the Father as an instrument for the creation of the cosmos[8]—all of which is simply to say that by the fourth century, the Fourth Gospel was calling the shots, establishing the parameters of permissible debate on the identity of the enigmatic Nazarene more than any other early Christian document,[9] while the early imperial Church yawned, stretched itself, and lumbered unsteadily to its sandaled feet to tower imperiously over the earth. The fourth century was the century of the Fourth Gospel, and the same can be said of every century since then as far as Christian orthodoxy is concerned. Several centuries of critical biblical scholarship has done remarkably little to change that, which is why the Jesus Seminar was formed.

*The Jesus Seminar*: Founded by Robert W. Funk in 1985, it originally consisted of twenty-nine North American New Testament scholars, although its numbers later swelled to—what? Surprisingly hard to say, although probably not fewer than seventy-five.

*Its mission*: To sift for historical authenticity all the parables, aphorisms, pronouncements, and other sayings attributed to Jesus in early Christian literature (which is he most likely to have actually uttered? which were the creation of the early Church?), and to communicate the results to the general public by every means available (resulting, predictably, in numerous newspaper headlines of the sort, "THE LORD DID NOT PRAY THE LORD'S PRAYER, BIBLE SCHOLARS CLAIM").

*Its startling findings*: No more than 20 percent of the sayings can plausibly be said to have been uttered by the historical Jesus.

*The public's response to the Gospel According to the Jesus Seminar*: Outrage, amusement, and dismissal, mostly: the Seminar makes a mockery of traditional Christian faith.

*The academy's response to the Gospel According to the Jesus Seminar*: Outrage, amusement and dismissal, mostly: the Seminar makes a mockery of traditional biblical scholarship.[10]

∽

I'm eager to add my own squawk to the cacophony of commentary on the Jesus Seminar (a din that is already fading inaudibly into history). Ten years or so ago, I was one of the small band of biblical scholars who made up the Literary Facets Seminar, one of several sideshows that met biannually alongside the Jesus Seminar, under the grand ringmastership of Robert Funk. At the 1988 Spring Meeting of the Seminars in Sonoma, California, perched on kindergarten chairs and surrounded by alphabet charts and children's art in the grade school classroom that had been assigned to us, our group read papers on postmodernism to one another and to a lone misdirected local who gradually came to realize that we were not the Jesus Seminar. It was in that classroom that *The Postmodern Bible* was conceived.[11]

∽

The contrast between the Johannine Jesus and the Jesus Seminar's Jesus could not be more dramatic. Johannine scholars like to say that the Jesus who speaks in the Fourth Gospel is not the historical Jesus but the post-Easter Jesus (a polite way of saying that the Johannine Jesus is a mere mouthpiece—albeit an exquisitely eloquent one—for the christological convictions of the Johannine community, thought to have crafted the Fourth Gospel, and its protagonist, during the closing decades of the first century).[12] As such, the Johannine Jesus is, from his very first appearance in this Gospel, a Jesus risen from the dead even before he has died, a Jesus always already resurrected. The second-century Gnostic teacher Valentinus and his school seem to have grasped this intuitively.[13] A fragment attributed to Valentinus by Clement of Alexandria (*Miscellanies* 3.59.3) states: "Jesus digested divinity: he ate and drank in a special way, without excreting his solids. He had such a great capacity for continence that the nourishment within him was not corrupted [i.e., did not become excrement], for he did not experience corruption."[14] Valentinus rightly refuses to be thrown off the scent by the fact that this is also a body that, on the Fourth Evangelist's own account, was susceptible to thirst (4:7; 19:28) and exhaustion (4:6) and capable of being cut open (19:34; 20:25, 27). For a risen body is of necessity incorruptible, in life no less than in death. (This fascinating fragment is what lies behind the present essay, actually. Chancing upon it, I was assailed by a desire to create a sanctuary for it. And so I began to build.)

Contrast the worm-ridden corpse of Jesus that the Jesus Seminar claims to have exhumed. In a 1995 issue of *The Fourth R*, the Seminar's popular periodical, we read that the German New Testament scholar Gerd Lüdemann, controversial author of *The Resurrection of Jesus* and guest speaker at the Seminar's Spring 1995 meeting, "argued in a public address that the body of Jesus undoubtedly decayed in the usual way," and that the Fellows of the Seminar "approved this thesis overwhelmingly."[15] "They found that Jesus' corpse probably rotted in some unknown grave," the report continues.[16] We should not be unduly alarmed by their grisly discovery; history, after all, is written with a gravedigger's spade. The nineteenth-century French historian Jules Michelet, having witnessed the opening of his wife's grave, wrote in a journal entry of September 4, 1839: "Severe ordeal. Alas! I scarcely saw anything but worms. It is said: 'returned to the earth.' It is a figure of speech. The corpse's inanimate substance reanimates a living substance. That aspect is hideous to the eye, harsh as Christian humiliation. . . . "[17] In later years, as though condemned to remain poised forever on the lip of his wife's opened grave, Michelet would characterize his own life's work, and that of historians in general, as one of unending exhumation.

What might the decomposed body of Jesus have looked like in life? Appearing human, all too human, in death, should he not likewise have appeared human, all too human, in life? As it happens, the same century that presents us with the spectacle of a cruelly constipated Christ, the Valentinian Jesus without an anus, also presents us with the specter of a physically repulsive Christ. (I find this ugly Jesus strangely alluring. As a research topic, indeed, the face and physique of the earth[l]y Jesus holds an almost irresistible attraction for me. What could be more immanent, more mundane than this Galilean peasant's physical aspect? And yet, as absolutely unknowable, is it not also somehow ineffable?)

The apparition first rears its ugly head briefly in Justin Martyr's *First Apology* (50) and later in Irenaeus's *Against Heresies* (3.19.2; 4.33.12; cf. 2.22.4), although Clement of Alexandria seems to have been the first to grasp it firmly by the horns. Justin and Irenaeus had taken Isaiah 53:2–3 at its word; so, too, does Clement: "And that the Lord Himself was uncomely in aspect, the Spirit testifies by Esaias: 'And we saw Him, and He had no form nor comeliness; but his form was mean, inferior to men'" (*The Instructor* 3.1).[18] Subsequently, Clement cites the same prooftext in the course of explaining how certain individuals can be just "even should they happen to be ugly in their persons" (*Miscellanies* 2.5). Tertullian and Hippolytus each appeal to this Isaian passage, too, in propounding the doctrine of the two advents. "We affirm two characters of the Christ demonstrated by the prophets, and as many advents of His forenoted," Tertullian declares. Whereas the second advent will be incomparably glorious, the first was "in humility," "not even in his aspect comely"—and the quotation follows: "And we saw Him, and he had not attractiveness or grace; but His mien was unhonoured . . . " (*Answer to the Jews* 14).[19] Elsewhere, too, Tertullian concedes that Jesus was, indeed, "inglorious in countenance and aspect, just as Isaiah . . . had fore-announced" (*On Idolatry* 18),[20] and so do Cyprian (*Treatises* 12.2.13), Novatian (*Concerning the Trinity* 9), Lactantius (*The Divine Institutes* 4.16), and Augustine (e.g., *Exposition of Psalm 127* 8).[21] The most notable allusion to the ugly Christ, however, occurs in Origen. In the course of his interminable refutation of Celsus, Origen attributes the following statement to him:

> Since a divine Spirit inhabited the body [of Jesus], it must certainly have been different from that of other beings, in respect of grandeur, or beauty, or strength, or voice, or impressiveness, or persuasiveness.

For it is impossible that He, to whom was imparted some divine quality beyond other beings, should not differ from others; whereas this person did not differ in any respect from another, but was, as they report, little, and ill-favoured, and ignoble.

To which Origen indignantly replies:

There are, indeed, admitted to be recorded some statements respecting the body of Jesus having been "ill-favoured"; not, however, "ignoble," as has been stated, nor is there any certain evidence that he was "little." The language of Isaiah runs as follows, who prophesied regarding Him that He would come and visit the multitude, not in comeliness of form, nor in any surpassing beauty: ". . . He has no form nor glory, and we beheld Him, and He had no form nor beauty; but His form was without honour, and inferior to the sons of men."[22]

As will by now be readily apparent, Robert Eisler notwithstanding, this recurrent portrait of the incarnate Christ as physically ill-favored hangs principally from Isaiah 53:2–3.[23]

On first looking into Eisler's *The Messiah Jesus and John the Baptist According to Flavius Josephus's Recently Rediscovered "Capture of Jerusalem" and the Other Jewish and Christian Sources*,[24] I found myself plunged into a parallel universe, one in which the *Testimonium Flavianum*, for example —the christianized passage on Jesus in Josephus's *Antiquities of the Jews* (18.3.3 §63)—comes replete with a head-to-toe description: "[H]e was a man of simple appearance, mature age, dark skin, short growth, three cubits tall [about four-and-a-half feet], hunchbacked, with a long face, a long nose, eyebrows meeting above the nose, so that the spectators could take fright, with scanty hair, (but) having a line in the middle of the head after the fashion of the Naziraeans, and with an undeveloped beard." Eisler "reconstructed" this stark sketch from an eclectic group of arcane sources, notably an expansive Old Russian version of Josephus's *Jewish War*, blended with further apocryphal "quotations" from Josephus found in certain Byzantine chroniclers, together with the late medieval document known as *The Letter of Lentulus on the Appearance of Christ*.[25] Eisler was convinced that the description derived ultimately from an official record of Jesus' trial, one to which Josephus had access, but which was subsequently expunged both from the *Jewish War* and the *Antiquities of the Jews* by Christian censors.

These eyebrows that meet and greet each other above the long nose of this Jesus look familiar. I've seen them before. They also grace the face of Paul in that famous physical description of him in the *Acts of Paul and Thecla* 3.2—"a man small of stature, with a bald head and crooked legs, in a good state of body, with eyebrows meeting (*synophryn*) and nose somewhat hooked, full of friendliness; for now he appeared like a man, and now he had the face of an angel."[26] This description has drawn cruel comments from modern scholars. Abraham Malherbe has assembled a litany of them: "hardly flattering" . . . "naiv-unheroisch" . . . "plain" . . . "ugly and small" . . . "ein Mann von numinoser Hässlichkeit" . . . "the typical portrait of a Jew," and so on.[27] But these ethnocentric moderns have missed the Apostle's true beauty, according to Malherbe. First, he quotes a passage from Archilochus popular in the second century: "I love not a tall general nor a straddling one, nor one proud of his hair nor one part-shaven; for me a man should be short and bowlegged to behold, set firm on his feet, full of heart."[28] This rehabilitates Paul's bandy legs. Then he quotes Suetonius's description of his idol Augustus: "His teeth were wide apart, small, and well-kept; his hair was slightly curly and inclining to golden; his eyebrows met. His ears were of moderate size, and his nose projected a little at the top and then bent slightly inward. His complexion was between dark and fair. He was short of stature."[29] This rehabilitates Paul's meeting eyebrows, hooked nose, and small stature, argues Malherbe, since Suetonius regularly had recourse to physiognomic stereotypes to provide physical descriptions of his ideal political leaders. Meeting eyebrows were widely regarded as a sign of beauty, as the Greco-Roman physiognomic manuals and other contemporary texts testify (for me, too, meeting eyebrows are a cause of admiration, or outright fascination, especially on an otherwise hairless face), while a hooked nose was deemed a mark of royalty, and small stature a sign that someone was quick. The evidence duly laid out on the dressing table that has been dragged into the courtroom for the occasion, Malherbe rests his case: "It is clear by now that Paul's hooked nose, bowed legs, and meeting eyebrows were not unflattering features in the context in which the Acts was written."[30]

Could Malherbe provide a similar makeover for Eisler's short, stooped, long-faced and long-nosed Christ? I suspect he would have his work cut out for him (even with the promising foundation provided by the meeting eyebrows). For certain of this Jesus' other features are found on such frightful faces as that of the Antichrist, as represented in Jewish lore. "We learn . . . that the Antichrist has a long nose," notes Joan Ford in her article, "The Physical Features of the Antichrist," which builds on J. M. Rosenstiehl's collection of seventeen related descriptions of the Antichrist found in late Jewish apocalyptic and rabbinic literature, arguing that these descriptions can readily be deciphered using the ancient physiognomic handbooks as code books.[31] Even a cursory glance at Ford's survey, replete with physiognomic lore, would likely cause the self-esteem of Eisler's Jesus to plummet dismally: "One notes that a curved body and shoulders are a sign of malignancy, envy, avarice. . . . [T]oo large a face denotes foolishness, a boorish man. . . . [B]aldness is not a good sign. Too little hair on the head, a few hairs scattered here and there, . . . indicate an incorrigible character."[32] Fairer by far are the features ascribed to Jesus in the immensely influential description of him composed by John of Damascus in the eighth century in the shadow of the iconoclastic controversy; they include an olive complexion, a strong nose, curly hair, a dark beard, and— what else?—eyebrows that meet and embrace, thereby becoming one.[33] The moral is plain, not to say ugly: beauty bespeaks goodness.[34]

Returning to Origen, we discover that he himself freely admits that his ill-favored Christ has stumbled directly out of the pages of the Old Testament: "But now, as neither the Gospels nor the apostolic writings indicate that 'He had no form nor beauty,' it is evident that we must accept the declaration of the prophets as true of Christ . . . " (*Against Celsus* 6.76). Even the "report" that Jesus was "little," adduced by Celsus (6.75), seems to hinge on Isaiah 53:2. "He is like a little boy [*puerulus*]," is how Tertullian renders its opening words.[35] But Tertullian also likes to trot out Psalm 22:6 hard on the heels of the Isaian text: "He pronounces Himself 'a worm, and not a man, an ignominy of man, and the refuse of the People.' Which evidences of ignobility suit the First Advent, just as those of sublimity do the Second." In sum, for Tertullian, "His body did not reach even to human beauty, to say nothing of heavenly glory."[36]

At first blush, there would seem to be something singularly un-Johannine about this homely, not to say ugly, Jesus. Note, for example, that the Jesus Seminarian whose historical Jesus is the least Johannine, the least divine, the least sublime, is also the Seminarian whose historical Jesus is the least attractive. I speak of Burton Mack.[37] Mack himself has even admitted to not liking his Jesus particularly,[38] although he apparently does not have his physical appearance in mind. Yet, as I argue below, Mack's countercultural Jesus and that of the Jesus Seminar generally[39] positively cries out for an "unattractive" face and an unprepossessing physique. John Meier's Jesus is closer by far than Mack's to mainstream christological orthodoxy, which is to say Johannine orthodoxy (although not of course identical with it). Is it merely by chance that the Jesus who gazes out at us from the jacket of the second volume of Meier's *A Marginal Jew: Rethinking the Historical Jesus* (Fig. 1) is a Jesus whose face is arresting, possessed of sharp, striking features, an exceptionally handsome man who has more than fulfilled the physical promise exhibited by the unusually attractive boy who graced the cover of the first volume of Meier's magnum opus (Fig. 2)?[40] He has lost his halo, but not his good looks.

Why would a historian choose to illustrate his critical investigation of the historical Jesus with highly intrusive fictitious images of his subject? Is it possible to read Meier's historical narrative and *not* visualize its protagonist first as the boy and then as the man on the jacket? As one reads, Meier's "historical" Jesus is being played by two actors, one young, the other mature, but both undeniably handsome—as in any docudrama "based on a true story."

And what of the cover of E. P. Sanders's recent Penguin paperback, *The Historical Figure of Jesus*?[41] What are we to make of this other figure (hardly historical) who coolly returns our curious stare, this broad-shouldered, regular-featured young man with the flowing auburn hair, large brown eyes, and sensuous lips (Fig. 3)? The rear cover identifies the figure as a detail from *Christ Blessing Children*, an early-seventeenth-century painting by Pacecco de Rosa.[42] The children have been excised from this reprint. Deep in self-absorption, the figure hardly seems to notice. Did Sanders himself select this stereotypical image of Jesus, so reaffirming of popular piety, on the one hand, and the identification of virtue and beauty, on the other? Or did the cover designer choose it for him? What role does Sanders imagine this image to have in relation to his historical portrait of Jesus? Is the visual portrait meant to illustrate the verbal portrait? Or is the relationship between word and image wholly contingent instead? Would any depiction of Jesus have done? Or just any standard depiction of him, as a more-or-less handsome Caucasian male?

Contrast the image of Jesus that adorns the cover of John Dominic Crossan's *Jesus: A Revolutionary Biography* (Fig. 4).[43] Dating from the early fourth century, this Jesus too is bearded and curly haired. Yet he is not handsome,

FIGURE 1. Jacket illustration for John P. Meier, *A Marginal Jew: Rethinking the Historical Jesus*, vol. 2: *Mentor, Message, and Miracles*, Anchor Bible Reference Library (New York: Doubleday, 1994). Reproduced with permission.

FIGURE 2. Jacket illustration for John P. Meier, *A Marginal Jew: Rethinking the Historical Jesus*, vol. 1: *The Roots of the Problem and the Person*, Anchor Bible Reference Library (New York: Doubleday, 1991). Reproduced with permission.

FIGURE 3. Jacket illustration for E. P. Sanders, *The Historical Figure of Jesus* (New York: Penguin Books, 1995). Reproduced with permission.

FIGURE 4. Jacket illustration for John Dominic Crossan, *Jesus: A Revolutionary Biography* (San Francisco: HarperSanFrancisco, 1994). Reproduced with permission.

at least not by late-twentieth-century Western standards. Badly in need of a Malherbean makeover, his face droops like a bloodhound's and he has big bags under his eyes. And whereas Meier and Sanders leave us guessing about their own thoughts on the Jesuses who grace their jackets, Crossan devotes a whole page to elucidating the links between the Jesus on the cover and the Jesus between the covers, going so far as to claim that the former is an "iconographic miniature" of the latter[44]—not because of his face, however, but because of his dress, which Crossan takes to be that of a Cynic philosopher.[45] Even Crossan has no conceptual apparatus with which to reflect on Jesus' face and physique.[46]

Interestingly enough, Meier is not entirely silent on the matter of Jesus' physical appearance. Jesus' trade, that of *tektōn*,[47] which Meier aptly translates as "woodworker," "involved no little sweat and muscle power," he claims. "The airy weakling often presented to us in pious paintings and Hollywood movies would hardly have survived the rigors of being Nazareth's *tektōn* from his youth to his early thirties."[48] What might Meier's modest espousal of a more manly Jesus, made in passing, look like magnified into a book? Cut to one-time bestseller *The Man Nobody Knows* by American advertising mogul Bruce Barton, a life of Jesus whose chapter titles alone constitute a treasure trove for the connoisseur of Christian curiosities: "The Leader; The Outdoor Man; The Sociable Man; His Method; His Advertisements; The Founder of Modern Business. . . . " Barton's book is a belated product of that peculiar Victorian movement known as "muscular Christianity."[49] The best-known expression of muscular Christianity is Thomas Hughes's 1856 novel *Tom Brown's Schooldays*, but it is to his own boyhood in Sunday school that Barton traces his arousal from dogmatic slumber:

> The kindly lady who could never seem to find her glasses would have been terribly shocked if she had known what was going on inside the little boy's mind.
>
> "You must love Jesus," she said every Sunday. . . .
>
> Love Jesus! The little boy looked up at the picture which hung on the Sunday-school wall. It showed a pale young man with flabby forearms and a sad expression. The young man had red whiskers.
>
> Then the little boy looked across to the other wall. There was Daniel, good old Daniel, standing off the lions. The little boy liked Daniel. He liked David, too, with the little sling that landed a stone square on the

forehead of Goliath. And Moses, with his rod and his big brass snake. They were winners—those three. He wondered if David could whip Jeffries. Samson could! Say, that would have been a fight!

But Jesus! Jesus was the "lamb of God." The little boy did not know what that meant, but it sounded like Mary's little lamb. Something for girls—sissified. . . .

Years went by and the little boy grew up and became a businessman.

He began to wonder about Jesus.

He said to himself: "Only strong magnetic men inspire great enthusiasm and build great organizations. Yet Jesus built the greatest organization of all. It is extraordinary."

The more sermons the man heard and the more books he read the more mystified he became.

One day he decided to wipe his mind clean of books and sermons.

He said, "I will read what the men who knew Jesus personally said about him. I will read about him as though he were a new historical character, about whom I had never heard anything at all."

The man was amazed.

A physical weakling! Where did they get that idea? Jesus pushed a plane and swung an adze; he was a successful carpenter. He slept outdoors and spent his days walking around his favourite lake. His muscles were so strong that when he drove the money-changers out, nobody dared to oppose him![50]

The latter scene is one that Barton particularly relishes. Later he dwells at length upon this spectacular show of strength. A five-page imaginary replay of the scene culminates in the following revelation:

There was, in his eyes, a flaming moral purpose; and greed and oppression have always shriveled before such fire. But with the majesty of his glance there was something else which counted powerfully in his favor. As his right arm rose and fell, striking its blows with that little whip, the sleeve fell back to reveal muscles that were hard as iron. No one who watched him in action had any doubt that he was fully capable of taking care of himself. No flabby priest or money-changer cared to try conclusions with that arm.[51]

For Barton, this is the pivotal scene in Jesus' ministry, revealing much more than the bulge of Jesus' biceps. It reveals the sort of man he was, or rather that he *was* a man, the kind of man that Barton himself, presumably, would want to be.

How interesting that Jesus' aggressive action in the temple should also be of central significance to at least two of the leading contemporary Jesus scholars, namely Sanders and Crossan. That Jesus created some sort of violent disturbance in the temple area is, for Sanders, one of the few virtually indubitable things that we can know about his public career. For Sanders, no less than for Barton, the event is an epiphany. It is central to Sanders's reconstruction of Jesus' self-understanding.[52] Crossan, although more skeptical than Sanders generally, is also certain that Jesus caused a scene in the temple. That action is utterly in keeping with Crossan's characterization of Jesus, and central to Crossan's explanation of why Jesus was executed.[53] Reading Crossan and Sanders side by side with Barton, however, has the effect of making me wonder whether all three men might not be animated by the same impulse; whether what is overtly the case with regard to Barton might not be covertly the case with regard to Crossan and Sanders; whether they, like him, are not intent on (re)constructing a Jesus who, if nothing else, was a "man" at least, and as such eminently equipped for action, even violent action, that perennial hallmark of masculinity. If so, the comically macho Jesus who marches through Barton's unscholarly pages, shoulders squared, "fine features" (a recurrent Bartonian phrase) set in an expression of grim determination as he contemplates the work of salvation (man's work, needless to say), is also tiptoeing more shyly through Crossan's and Sanders's scholarly pages, no less an idealized figure inviting the (male?) reader's identification, no less an embodiment of imagined masculine virtue.

Is masculine self-projection, then, intrinsic to the quest for the historical Jesus as it is commonly practiced? Is Jesus scholarship essentially a man-to-man affair, the scholar's Jesus being a man's man, and the scholar himself systematically mistaking his own reflection in his shaving mirror for the face of the man from Galilee? And is this at least part of the reason why so few women, even today, are actively engaged in the Jesus quest?[54]

Barton's verbal Christ had a visual twin. Beginning in 1924 (coincidentally the same year in which Barton's book appeared), Warner Sallman began to produce an unprecedentedly popular series of Jesus portraits. Like Barton,

Sallman was a Chicago "adman." Like Barton too, Sallman embraced a muscular Christianity that had been precipated by a gender crisis in American Protestantism. The erosive effects of suffrage on the patriarchal edifice, coupled with the fact that women greatly outnumbered men as active Church members, induced in many (male) Church leaders an anxiety that the Church had become "feminized" and a desire for a more "virile" Christianity—one modeled on a more "manly" image of Christ than the "womanly" Christ of Victorian piety (the "soft-looking" Christ who had inspired contempt in the young Barton).[55] Thus it was that when Warner Sallman came to enroll in a night class at the Moody Bible Institute in Chicago in 1914 and admitted to his mentor, E. O. Sellers, that he was an aspiring artist, he was promptly exhorted:

> Good. Keep right at it. We need Christian artists. And I hope sometime you give us your conception of Christ. Most of the pictures I have seen are too effeminate. I hope you'll picture a virile, manly Christ.... Make Him a real man! Make him rugged, not effeminate. Make him strong and masculine, not weak, so people will see in His face that He slept under the stars, drove the money changers out of the temple, and faced Calvary in triumph.[56]

The *Head of Christ* that Sallman later went on to paint, however (Fig. 5),[57] was not nearly as rugged as this ringing exhortation might have led us to expect. In a letter to the popular periodical *Christianity Today*, indeed, one singularly unenthusiastic seminary professor, Paul Roth, even went so far as to lampoon it as a "pretty picture of a woman with a curling beard who has just come from the beauty parlor with a Halo shampoo."[58]

And, undeniably, Sallman's Jesus does have pretty eyes and hair, the former dark-blue and large, the latter auburn in tint.

Where have I seen these eyes and hair before? On the Jesus of Lew Wallace's *Ben Hur* (to whom I shall later return). Light-colored skin is something else that these two Christs share in common. In fact they are not two figures but one: a northern European savior whose physical characteristics proclaim his distance from the despised race whom he has been sent to redeem.

Of course, it is not only from Jews that the blue-eyed Christ, and his blue-eyed Father, are careful to keep their distance. According to a cherished cliché, a person's physical appearance means nothing to either of them: "It's not how you look but what's inside that counts with God and Jesus."[59] The cliché is un-

FIGURE 5. Warner Sallman, *Head of Christ*, 1940, oil on canvas, 28 ¼" × 22 ⅛". Jesse C. Wilson Galleries, Anderson University. ©Warner Press, Inc., Anderson, Ind. Used by permission.

dermined, however, by the fact that God and Jesus, far from providing transcendental anchorage for the principle it enunciates, themselves constitute exceptions to it and thereby destabilize it. For God's and Jesus' own appearance does count for a great deal for a great many people(s). To anthropomorphize God is to confer ethnic identity upon God.[60] Except in certain apophatic traditions, therefore, the divine image is invariably an ethnic construct. Historically, in the case of Christianity, and especially from the Renaissance onwards, the divine image has been a white construct; consequently, white people have seemed to reflect it most closely, whereas nonwhite people have seemed to reflect it dimly, if at all. Of course, the doctrine of the Incarnation is the ultimate anthropomorphization, and so it was in the figure of the incarnate Christ that the whitening of the deity achieved its apogee, most notably during the centuries of European colonization of Africa, the Americas, and the Indian subcontinent. Although its pedestal was erected during the Renaissance and the "Age of Exploration," it was not until the nineteenth century that the image of Jesus as not just fair-skinned but blond and blue-eyed as well was fully in place, towering over the world.[61]

But whiteness itself is a constructed category.[62] Whiteness can be seen—can be conceptualized, indeed—only as difference from and in opposition to what is *not* white: what is colored, what is black.[63] The God of traditional Euro-American Christianity needs nonwhite people simply in order to be. Contrary to the cliché, therefore, this God is acutely concerned with what is outside a person: his very existence depends upon it.

The blue-eyedness of the Christian God, and the problem he poses for people of color, is wittily articulated by Alice Walker in *The Color Purple*. A telling theological exchange takes place between Celie and Shug, two black women struggling to survive in a world in which each of these qualifiers perpetually threatens to compound the potential misery already inherent in the other:

> Then she say: Tell me what your God look like, Celie.
> Aw naw, I say. I'm too shame. Nobody ever ast me this before, so I'm sort of took by surprise. Besides, when I think about it, it don't seem quite right. But it all I got. I decide to stick up for him, just to see what Shug say.
> Okay, I say. He big and old and tall and graybearded and white. He wear white robes and go barefooted.

Blue eyes? she ast.

Sort of bluish-gray. Cool. Big though. White lashes, I say.

She laugh.

Why you laugh? I ast. I don't think it so funny. What you expect him to look like, Mr. ——?

That wouldn't be no improvement, she say. Then she tell me this old white man is the same God she used to see when she prayed. If you wait to find God in church, Celie, she say, that's who is bound to show up, cause that where he live.

How come? I ast.

Cause that's the one that's in the white folks' white bible.

Shug! I say. God wrote the bible, white folks had nothing to do with it.

How come he look just like them, then? she say. Only bigger? And a heap more hair. How come the bible just like everything else they make, all about them doing one thing and another, and all the colored folks doing is gitting cursed?

I never thought bout that.

Nettie say somewhere in the bible it say Jesus' hair was like lamb's wool, I say.

Well, say Shug, if he came to any of these churches we talking bout he'd have to have it conked before anybody paid him any attention. The last thing niggers want to think about they God is that his hair kinky.

That's the truth, I say.[64]

A rival religious artist, Louis Jambor, cannibalized Sallman's *Head of Christ* in 1949, replicating the angle and expression of the face, but first putting its owner on a course of steroids. Jambor explained that he had attempted to represent his subject's "physical strength" in addition to his "spiritual greatness." "I tried to develop the face to show the strength His manual labor wrought."[65] By the late 1950s and early 1960s Sallman himself was reduced to retouching his *Head of Christ* to give it a more rugged outdoorsy feel. Finally in 1966 he capitulated fully and painted a *Portrait of Jesus* that was huskier—and hunkier—than the *Head of Christ* (Fig. 6). The face in the *Portrait* fairly drips masculinity, and appears to have been influenced by another high-testosterone Jesus portrait painted two years earlier by Richard Hook.

FIGURE 6. Warner Sallman, *Portrait of Jesus*, 1966, oil on canvas, 20 ¼" × 26 ¼". Jesse C. Wilson Galleries, Anderson University. ©Warner Press, Inc., Anderson, Ind. Used by permission.

Yet it was not Jambor's craggy *Jesus of Nazareth*, nor Hook's forceful *Head of Christ*, nor even Sallman's own Rock Hudsonesque *Portrait of Jesus* that sold more than 500 million copies worldwide, but rather his *Head of Christ*. And it is estimated that a further 500 million copies of spinoff compositions by Sallman have sold in addition—in which the *Head*, now attached to a matching body, beams encouragement at children or Bible-clutching adolescents, simpers over cuddly lambs, or prays fervently to its Father in heaven—thereby making the *Head* the dominant twentieth-century image of Jesus. (Its popularity has declined dramatically since the 1960s, however—hardly surprising. One glance at the *Head of Christ*'s straitlaced expression is enough to tell us that he doesn't drink, smoke, dance, gamble, or do drugs, that the thought of sex outside marriage is a source of acute pain to him—and that he probably isn't too comfortable with the thought of sex *inside* marriage either. He is happiest in church or at Sunday school.)

What are we to make of these staggering sales figures? In the early decades of the twentieth century, American Protestant clergymen were calling for more "manly" images of Jesus, as we saw earlier, reacting to the (modest) inroads that women had made in Church and society. Yet religion had been the domain of women since the founding of the republic.[66] Why was the backlash so long in coming? Was it also caused in part by the construction, consolidation, and dissemination in early-twentieth-century America of the sexual ideology that would soon come to be known as "heterosexuality"?[67] Was the anxious reaction to "effeminate" Victorian images of Jesus at least partially provoked by the onset of incipient homophobia and consequent revulsion on the part of male Christian leaders at the thought of having an intimate relationship with a man who looked like a woman? Even as elite male commentators on the Song of Songs were defecting en masse from the allegorical method and the "feminine" role that it thrust on the male interpreter,[68] American Church leaders were demanding a more macho Christ. And what they eventually got was Warner Sallman's Christ—which is to say that the Christian faithful, casting their votes with their hard-earned dollars, expressed their preference for a queerer Jesus over an unambiguously straight Jesus. (Admittedly, it was a no-win situation, because it is Sallman's *Portrait of Jesus*, his belated response to his Bible teacher's request for a thoroughly rugged Jesus, and not his *Head of Christ*, that now looks most like a gay icon, coming across, as it does, as a veritable caricature of straight masculinity.)

A measure of the palpable queerness of the *Head of Christ* was the degree

FIGURE 7. Warner Sallman, *The Lord Is My Shepherd*, 1943, oil on canvas, 40" x 30". Jesse C. Wilson Galleries, Anderson University. ©Warner Press, Inc., Anderson, Ind. Used by permission.

to which it was capable of raising homophobic hackles. A venomous attack on it by one Alan Devoe, reported in a 1948 issue of *Time* magazine, described it as a portrait "of a pale and posturing person with immoderately long, silky hair... who clutched a kind of diaphanous drapery gracefully about him with an expression of simpering vapidity. It was into this hand, so unmistakably the limp and clammy hand of an effeminate curate, that little boys were to put theirs trustingly."[69] Yet it was not so much that the *Head of Christ* was flamboyantly effeminate, a Queen of Queens as opposed to a King of Kings, as that it was ambiguously gendered. Advertising copy for Sallman's *The Lord Is My Shepherd* (Fig. 7), a composition in which the *Head of Christ* is affixed to a shepherd's body, optimistically asserts of the gentle-looking figure surrounded by saccharine lambs in a chocolate-box landscape, "His is a man's task calling for genuine courage, physical strength, and a kindly concern for the flock. Sallman's shepherd is as rugged as the staff he carries."[70] Some might say that this rather delicate looking staff is being asked to support a large claim. Doubts were often expressed about the manly credentials of Sallman's Christ, as we saw earlier, even to the point of accusing him of being a soft-featured prettily coifed "woman" (albeit with a slight facial hair problem). Yet it was Sallman's *Head of Christ* that legions of American soldiers chose to carry next to their hearts on the beaches of Normandy and in the foxholes of Korea.[71] And it was the same *Head* that, notwithstanding (or because of?) its alleged "womanliness," became the icon par excellence of the infinitely enthralling man with whom millions of other men sought total intimacy and to whom they pledged their undying love (see Fig. 8, *Christ Our Pilot*; a standard gift to boys and young men, this image found its place above the beds of thousands).

Like John Meier's dust-jacket Jesus (Fig. 1), Sallman's *Head of Christ* seems to radiate an inner glow, even a divine glow. Lit up from within, he is recognizably Johannine, for the Fourth Gospel, more than any other New Testament gospel, is the gospel of the incandescent Christ, the Christ who alone declares "I am the Light of the World" (John 8:12; cf. 9:5; 12:35; 1:4; 1 John 1:5). And when one ventures outside the fenced enclosure of critical scholarship altogether, which is to say fully into the realm of popularized Johannism, Jesus' flesh fairly glows in the dark.

Perhaps the most remarked feature of Sallman's *Head of Christ* was, in fact, its radiance, which, for so many of those who cherished it, signified Christ's divinity. As it happens, Sallman claimed that the image had been supernatu-

FIGURE 8. Warner Sallman, *Christ Our Pilot*, 1950, oil on canvas, 40" x 30". Jesse C. Wilson Galleries, Anderson University. ©Warner Press, Inc., Anderson, Ind. Used by permission.

rally revealed to him in a burst of light in January 1924, in response to prayer "in a despairing situation." The despair was occasioned by a looming deadline; Sallman had been commissioned to design the cover for the February issue of the *Covenant Companion* and he had been afflicted with artist's block. Fortunately, inspiration was at hand. "After retiring, within two sleepless hours, the glorious appearing shown [sic] about in the darkened room," he later recalled.[72] In the event, it took him sixteen years to capture the radiance of the vision on canvas. But technology was waiting in the wings to take the process one step further. Around 1957, an enterprising company, Kriebel and Bates, had the bright idea of mass-producing an "Inspira-Lamp" featuring Sallman's *Head of Christ*. Designed for bedside tables, it magnified the radiance that millions had admired in the famous image and caused Jesus' face *literally* to glow in the dark.[73]

The incandescent Christ of mass consumption has by no means been confined to the visual media, however. Witness, for instance, Anne Rice's verbal sketch of Jesus' face in *Memnoch the Devil*, volume 5 of her best-selling *Vampire Chronicles*:

> I looked up, and in the midst of the flood of light I saw again the balustrade, and against it stood a single form.
>
> It was a tall figure who stood with his hands on the railing, looking over it and down. This appeared to be a man. He turned around and looked at me and reached out to receive me.
>
> His hair and eyes were dark, brownish, his face perfectly symmetrical and flawless, his gaze intense; and the grasp of his fingers very tight.
>
> I drew in my breath. I felt my body in all its solidity and fragility as his fingers clung to me. I was on the verge of death. I might have ceased to breathe at that moment, or ceased to move with the commitment to life and might have died!
>
> This being drew me towards himself, a light flooding from him that mingled with the light behind him and all around him, so his face grew brighter yet more distinct and more detailed. I saw the pores of his darkening golden skin, I saw the cracks in his lips, the shadow of the hair that had been shaved from his face.[74]

This is the Jesus that the public demands. This is the Johannine Jesus, as popularly conceived. For what other Jesus is so fully divine, so full of divinity, that he leaks the stuff like a sieve, godhood dribbling from him everywhere as light, drizzling from every pore, and dazzling with its fine spray all who dare to come close to him?

Rice's gorgeous Jesus reaches out to receive me along with Memnoch, and the grip of his fingers is indeed very tight. We have met before, you see, although not in a celestial mansion. Once again I am thirteen or fourteen, visiting my grandfather's cottage on the Limerick-Tipperary border. Straw-bestrewn flagstone floor, hellish fire over which a huge blackened pot bubbles, monstrous slabs of smoking bacon suspended from hooks under the thatch. My father and grandfather are engaged in an extraordinarily prolonged exchange about the very ordinary weather we are having. The conversation switches to cattle, then to hurling,[75] at which point it becomes passionate. In an agony of boredom I cast around for something to read. All I can find is a crushed copy of *Ben Hur* propping up a corner of the dresser. I start to skim distractedly through it, gradually slowing down as the plot begins to grip me. As I am dragged in chains through Galilee with the unlucky Ben Hur, a familiar figure comes out to meet me at the tiny hamlet of Nazareth. Familiar yet unfamiliar, never before has he looked so good:

> Thereupon a youth who came up with Joseph, but had stood behind him unobserved, laid down an axe he had been carrying, and, going to the great stone standing by the well, took from it a pitcher of water. The action was so quiet that before the guard could interfere, had they been disposed to, he was stooping over the prisoner, and offering him a drink.
>
> The hand laid kindly upon his shoulder awoke the unfortunate Judah, and, looking up, he saw a face he never forgot—the face of a boy about his own age, shaded by locks of yellowish bright chestnut hair; a face lighted by dark-blue eyes, at the same time so soft, so appealing, so full of love and holy purpose, that they had all the power of command and will. The spirit of the Jew, hardened though it was by days and nights of suffering, and so embittered by wrong that his dreams of revenge took in all the world, melted under the stranger's look, and became as a child's. He put his lips to the pitcher, and drank long and deep. Not a word was said to him, nor did he say a word.[76]

I read on, entranced. Later that same afternoon, he appears to me again (and, of course, to Ben Hur), this time on the banks of the Jordan:

... a form slightly above the average in stature, and slender, even delicate. His action was calm and deliberate, like that habitual to men much given to serious thought upon grave subjects; and it well became his costume, which was an undergarment full-sleeved and reaching to the ankles, and an outer robe called the talith; on his left arm he carried the usual handkerchief for the head, the red fillet swinging loose down his side. Except the fillet and a narrow border of blue at the lower edge of the talith, his attire was of linen yellowed with dust and road stains. Possibly the exception should be extended to the tassels, which were blue and white, as prescribed by law for Rabbis. His sandals were of the simplest kind. He was without scrip or girdle or staff.

These points of appearance, however, the ... beholders observed briefly, and rather as accessories to the head and face of the man, which—especially the latter—were the real sources of the spell they caught in common....

The head was open to the cloudless sky, except as it was draped with hair long and slightly waved, and parted in the middle, and auburn in tint, with a tendency to reddish-golden where most strongly touched by the sun. Under the broad, low forehead, under black, well-arched brows, beamed eyes dark-blue and large, and softened to exceeding tenderness by lashes of great length sometimes seen on children, but seldom, if ever, on men. As to the other features, it would have been difficult to decide whether they were Greek or Jewish. The delicacy of the nostrils and mouth was unusual to the latter type; and when it was taken into account with the gentleness of the eyes, the pallor of the complexion, the fine texture of the hair, and the softness of the beard, which fell in waves over his throat to his breast, never a soldier but would have laughed at him in encounter, never a woman who would not have confided in him at sight, never a child that would not, with quick instinct, have given him its hand and whole artless trust: nor might any one have said he was not beautiful.[77]

It would still be a decade or more before I would give myself wholly to Jesus, before I would "invite him in." But my initial infatuation with him undoubtedly dated from that drowsy Sunday afternoon in my grandfather's overheated kitchen. In retrospect, I think I fell for his looks.

And what of Lew Wallace himself—husband, father, soldier supreme (ascending to the rank of major-general in the Union Army during the American Civil War), and first governor of the new Union state of New Mexico? The Collins edition of *Ben Hur* (whose biographical introduction yields up these interesting facts) has an artist's sketch of Wallace as a frontispiece, bellicose, beetle-browed, and bearded. Whence the extraordinary tenderness with which he writes about Jesus? Whence the extraordinary tenderness with which I have heard so many other rugged men speak of Jesus, and speak to him, when I moved in evangelical Christian circles? The (inevitable?) homoeroticism of the male believer's intimate relationship with the male Christ, the socially sanctioned worship of one man by another, institutionalized same-sex love on an incalculable scale—we arrive back once again at the topic of the previous essay.

Eve Sedgwick also broaches the topic, briefly but incisively, in her *Epistemology of the Closet*:

> Christianity may be near-ubiquitous in modern European culture as a figure of [homo]phobic prohibition, but it makes a strange figure for that indeed. Catholicism in particular is famous for giving countless gay and proto-gay children the shock of the possibility of adults who don't marry, of men in dresses, of passionate theatre, of introspective investment, of lives lived with what could, ideally without diminution, be called the work of the fetish. Even for the many whose own achieved gay identity may at last include none of these features or may be defined as against them, the encounter with them is likely to have a more or other than prohibitive impact. And presiding over all are the images of Jesus. These have, indeed, a unique position in modern culture as images of the unclothed or unclothable male body, often in extremis and/or in ecstasy, prescriptively meant to be gazed at and adored. The scandal of such a figure within a homophobic economy of the male gaze doesn't seem to abate: efforts to disembody this body, for instance by attenuating, Europeanizing, or feminizing it, only entangle it the more compromisingly among various modern figurations of the homosexual.[78]

A recent issue of the British lesbian and gay *Pink Paper* carries a tongue-in-cheek inset entitled "Queer Icons: Jesus Christ." "Oh come on, what has *he* got to offer?" it asks itself impatiently, only to reply: "Just try to imagine him in a contact ad. 'Superstar good looks. Long flowing locks, straight-acting, lean.'"

It all proved too much for Gerard Manley Hopkins, Victorian priest, venerated poet—and author of a remarkable rhapsody on the imagined physical beauty of Jesus Christ:

> There met in Jesus Christ all things that can make man lovely and loveable. In his body he was most beautiful. This is known first by the tradition in the Church that it was so and by holy writers agreeing to suit those words to him, "Thou art beautiful in mould above the sons of men" [Ps. 45:2]; we have even accounts of him written in early times. They tell us that he was moderately tall, well built and slender in frame, his features straight and beautiful, his hair inclining to auburn, parted in the midst, curling and clustering about the ears and neck as the leaves of a filbert, so they speak, upon the nut. . . . The account I have been quoting (it is from memory, for I cannot now lay my hand upon it) we do not indeed for certain know to be correct, but it has been current in the Church and many generations have drawn our Lord accordingly either in their own minds or in his images. Another proof of his beauty may be drawn from the words *proficiebat sapientia et aetate et gratia apud Deum et homines* (Luc. ii 52), "he went forth in wisdom and bodily frame and favour with God and men"; that is, he pleased both God and men daily more and more by his growth in mind and body. But he could not have pleased by growth of body unless the body was strong, healthy, and beautiful that grew. But the best proof of all is this, that his body was the special work of the Holy Ghost. He was not born in nature's course, no man was his father; had he been born as others are he must have inherited some defect of figure or of constitution. . . . But his body was framed directly from heaven by the power of the Holy Ghost, of whom it would be unworthy to leave any the least botch or failing in his work. So the first Adam was moulded by God himself and Eve built up by God too out of Adam's rib and they could not but be pieces, both, of faultless workmanship: the same then and much more must Christ have been. . . . I leave it to you, brethren, then to picture him, in whom the fulness of the godhead dwelt bodily, in his bearing how majestic, how strong and yet how lovely and lissome in his limbs, in his look how earnest, grave

but kind. In his Passion all this strength was spent, this lissomness crippled, this beauty wrecked, this majesty beaten down. But now it is more than all restored, and for myself I make no secret I look forward with eager desire to seeing the matchless beauty of Christ's body in the heavenly light.⁷⁹

Hopkins's intense attraction to this heavenly man, however, was a source of pain as well as pleasure to him. "Hopkins was over- rather than under-scrupulous in detecting weaknesses of the flesh," his biographer Norman White writes, "and his list of sexual immoralities is probably shorter and less intense than the complete record of the average adolescent. Nothing goes beyond glances, awareness, and 'temptations': the objects of attraction remain at a distance. Most instances of sinful attraction involve males, usually boys or young men. . . . " One Man in particular, of course, stood out from this seductive mass of male flesh. "When [Hopkins] gave up the idea of being a professional painter," White continues, "he was probably basing his decision on such temptations: 'evil thoughts' occurred to him while he was drawing, particularly when he drew a crucified arm, and a crucifix of his Aunt Kate's stimulated him in the wrong way."⁸⁰ The ultimate object of desire must remain at a distance, then. Incarnated in wood or plaster, he is physically too close for comfort. And when he is represented *in extremis*, cruelly pinioned to a crude instrument of torture, the feelings he arouses become unbearable. In what sort of surreal sexual tableau might "a crucified arm" play a part? Both Hopkins and White leave us guessing.

Yet Hopkins's distress puts us in mind of a rather disquieting aspect of our topic. When one's ultimate fantasy object is not only beautiful but nailed to a butcher's block to boot, one's fun cannot be all good and clean. That the central symbol of Christianity should be the figure of a beautiful man is curious enough in itself, given that Christianity has mainly been run by men. But that its central symbol should be the figure of a beautiful *tortured* man— near-naked, smarting from a good whipping, and penetrated with assorted sharp objects—is still more curious.⁸¹ Might it not help to account for the perduring appeal of Christianity in general, and the spectacle of the crucifixion in particular, down through the ages? Physical beauty combines with physical violence in most standard depictions of the crucifixion (Isenheim altarpieces aside), and where beauty and violence are present can sexual arousal be very far distant?

But let us leave the troubled Hopkins prostrate in prayer before the sacrificial altar of male beauty, his eyes raised intermittently and compulsively to the Crucified Arm that has been savagely nailed to it, the fingers twitching spasmodically as they are caressed by his anguished gaze, and turn instead to a contemporary theological celebration of the three themes whose combination filled the closeted Victorian cleric with dread: religion, male beauty, and homoeroticism. The celebration is that of Roland E. Long in his essay, "The Sacrality of Male Beauty and Homosex." What grounds gay identity? For most gay men, argues Long, it is "a susceptibility—indeed, an erotic receptivity—to masculine beauty."[82] Long believes that this receptivity is "vastly underplayed" in current queer theory—and queer theology. For Long does not hesitate to frame the matter in explicitly religious terms: "For gay men, I submit, there is a compulsion in a magnificent male that commands attention and solicits . . . the word 'worship' will suffice for the moment."[83] Nor does he stop there: the gay man's "love for male beauty and his love for males . . . are venerable realities to be celebrated and revered. . . . A gay man is one who recognizes and lives by the 'sacrality' of masculine beauty and homosex."[84]

Let us assume for the sake of argument that Long is correct in his claim that many gay men are "worshippers at the altar of male beauty."[85] What would it mean for our evaluation of a male Christian spirituality centered on an intensely affective relationship with an utterly magnificent male, a paragon of masculine perfection—"one who commands attention and solicits worship" (to parrot Long, although Long himself does not take Jesus on in his essay)? Would it not suggest that this male-to-male spirituality (whether mystical or charismatic, closeted in a monastic cell, or a Pentecostal assembly hall, or any number of other affectively charged spaces in between) is but a covert manifestation of what Long would term "the gay religion of male beauty and mansex," and as such is queer to the core? Our earlier examination of the uses to which the Song of Songs has been put by male interpreters down through the ages would seem to bear this out. A prickly problem remains, of course, one that Long fails to address. In a religion of male/masculine beauty, what but the most humble (and humiliating?) roles are available to those who, smitten by the fickle finger of cultural apperception, are deemed physically unattractive?

All of this brings us back circuitously to the Jesus Seminar's Jesus. The Johannine Jesus was abandoned early on by the Seminar, but later appeared to it in October 1994 while it was gathered behind closed doors in a hotel ballroom in Santa Rosa, California, greatly alarming it. The movie director Paul Verhoeven (*Robocop, Total Recall, Basic Instinct, Showgirls, Starship Troopers, Hollow Man*), a longtime fellow of the Seminar, was reading an outline of the screenplay for his forthcoming Jesus movie to the gathering.[86] According to the testimony of one eyewitness, however, "the faces of his fellow seminarians slowly froze" as he read. "For it became clear that despite eight years of faithful attendance at the Jesus Seminar, he hadn't been paying much attention."[87] Verhoeven's chief scriptural source for his screenplay was none other than the Fourth Gospel. Basing himself on John's narrative framework, but jettisoning John's miracles, Verhoeven outlined a gripping drama of a charismatic and courageous Jewish visionary, who, having incurred the enmity of the authorities by running riot in the temple, is forced to become a fugitive. "When Verhoeven finished, there was a long silence. Then, speaking practically all at once, the seminar's participants took him to task. He was pandering to fundamentalists by relying on John's Gospel."[88] Verhoeven defended himself by pointing out the obvious, namely, that the Jesus Seminar's Jesus was simply not the stuff of film. "You'd have a man walking about from marketplace to marketplace saying aphorisms. . . . That isn't much of a movie."[89]

One suspects that Verhoeven's Jesus will cut a handsome figure, should he ever make it to the silver screen. We probably shouldn't expect to see Wallace Shawn in the role,[90] or even Sean Penn.

Well, maybe Sean Penn. Have you seen *Dead Man Walking*? Penn almost succeeds in becoming Jesus in the final sequence. Hemmed in by guards, he proceeds in regal slow-motion to the death chamber to the accompaniment of mournful music, his eyes already fixed on eternity. The anguished visage of Susan Sarandon, become Veronica, bobs above his left shoulder—Death Row as the Via Dolorosa. Upon reaching the place of execution, he is strapped to a black upright device, arms outstretched. He utters his last words from this high-tech cross—a prayer addressed to the father of one of his victims, "Forgive me, for I knew not what I was doing," or words to that effect—and soon thereafter yields up his spirit. Sarandon, meanwhile, maintains her look of tearful love throughout, now no longer Veronica but the Magdalen, or even the Virgin.

On second thought, do we really need another blue-eyed cinematic Christ?

We've seen such a long procession of pale-eyed Galileans over the years, Willem Dafoe in *The Last Temptation of Christ* dispiritedly bringing up the rear. It was *Jesus of Nazareth*, however, that set a daunting new standard for blue-eyed biblical characters. Not content with a blue-eyed Jesus (played by Robert Powell), the director, Franco Zeffirelli, threw in a blue-eyed John the Baptist (Michael York) for good measure, a gesture all the more curious given Zeffirelli's much-publicized quest for authenticity in this film—his abandonment of fake beards, American accents (he recognizes that first-century Mediterranean people spoke with English accents instead), freshly starched peasant robes, cardboard temples and palaces, and other hallowed appurtenances of the Hollywood Bible epic.[91]

I had my historical Jesus class watch *Jesus of Nazareth* once at the Kansas state university where I taught. Afterwards, students were asked to write a review of the film. Several commented on Powell's ice-blue eyes, although not as a glaring anachronism. "They were just as I'd always imagined Jesus' eyes would be," wrote one. But another reviewer objected to Powell's stringy hair and skeletal physique: "The real Jesus would have had neat hair and a good build." Yet another noted that Powell's teeth protruded slightly, and wondered why he had been selected for the role.

This student reviewer was by no means unique, however, in deeming divinity and dental perfection to be ontologically (I almost said orthodontically) linked. Reviewing *The Last Temptation of Christ* for the *National Review* in 1988, John Simon remarked: "Willem Dafoe, if you like your Jesus as a Zen hippie, is good enough, and very nice looking, [but] wouldn't you think that the Son of God would have better teeth?"[92]

But if movie stars playing Jesus are expected to look the part, Jesus himself is expected to look like a movie star. Erica Doss notes how the postwar popularity of Sallman's *Head of Christ* derived in part from its stylistic similarity to film star and celebrity face shots. The 1924 sketch on which the *Head* was based followed a standard format used in Hollywood head shots and publicity posters for film stars, ranging from Rudolph Valentino to Douglas Fairbanks. Even the yellow, green, and brown hues that Sallman used in the final colorized version were those commonly used in such posters.[93] Sallman was grooming his Jesus for superstardom.

While still at the Kansas college, I discovered a mysterious pamphlet in my pigeonhole one morning. It bore the title "Jesus: The Most Beautiful

Man I Have Ever Seen," and told how Jesus had appeared to the author late one evening as he paused in his pickup truck on the shoulder of the highway on the outskirts of Lubbock, Texas, to pray in tongues and read aloud from the opening chapter of the Book of Revelation: "And I turned to see the voice that spake with me. And being turned, I saw seven golden candlesticks; and in the midst of the seven candlesticks one like unto the Son of man, clothed with a garment down to the foot, and girt about the paps with a golden girdle. . . . " The author was fortunate enough to have had a tape recorder with him at the time (a camcorder would have been even better, of course) and so was able to record Jesus' message to the world. The pamphlet ended with a 1-900 number, but when I called it had already been disconnected. My mail at the University of Sheffield in Yorkshire, where I moved after my five-year sojourn in Kansas, paled dreadfully by comparison.

Had I not moved to England, however, I might never have learned that Elvis expired while contemplating the face of Christ. There it was in the Culture section of the *Sunday Times*. It appears that Elvis exited this life while seated on a lavishly padded lavatory seat at Graceland (his one-piece sequined jumpsuit pulled down around his ankles, adds an acquaintance, although that may be an apocryphal embellishment). Open in his lap at the time was a book entitled *The Scientific Search for the Face of Jesus*. Elvis might as well have been gazing in the mirror as he expired, the author of the *Sunday Times* article seems to imply. "Elvis has become the kitsch Christ of an American—and, therefore, global—peasant religion," he writes, most conspicuously for the First Presleytarian Church of Elvis the Divine, whose members offer up daily prayers to the King and engage in ritual consumption of his favorite banana pudding.[94]

But is it the young, beautiful Elvis or the aging, obese Elvis who is the object of veneration for millions? The defeat of the ungracefully aging Elvis by the youthful Elvis in the much-publicized battle between the two for a coveted place on a U.S. commemorative postage stamp strongly suggests that it is Elvis the Beautiful who is King in the minds of most of his devotees.

Of course, there is no intrinsic reason why the Johannine Jesus should be similarly visualized as supremely handsome. John's claim, after all, is that the enfleshed Word's innate glory was invisible to all save a select few, and that this glory, when he chose to reveal it, was to be seen not in his face but in his deeds. Most contemporary Christians, however, seem to find it infinitely easier to imagine the monomaniacal pronouncements of the Johannine Jesus—

"I am the Light of the World"; "I am the Way, the Truth and the Life"; etc.—issuing from a pair of well-formed lips, barely concealing a set of gleaming white teeth, and affixed to a handsome face, which in turn is attached to a lean, well-proportioned body, than to imagine the same unlikely words issuing from a dreadfully deformed mouth, barely concealing a set of ruinously decayed teeth, and so on.

Furthermore, even if the second-century apologists declined to idealize the face and physique of Jesus of Nazareth, it is probably safe to surmise that the Fourth Gospel supplied the safety net for their tightrope assertion that he was physically ill favored—the Fourth Gospel especially as read through the lens conveniently provided by the hymn to the kenotic Christ preserved in Philippians 2:6–11.[95] For if the preexistent Son of God elected to empty himself, to become flesh and dwell among us, why should he not have gone all the way and taken on flesh that was inglorious rather than glorious, becoming as ugly, precisely, as sin? The assertion that Jesus was ugly only made theological sense within the framework of a preexistence Christology, a framework whose central strut was the Fourth Gospel. Before this framework was firmly in place, Christian authors seem not to have known what to do with Isaiah 53:2–3, "[H]e had no appearance or splendor; and we beheld him, and he had neither appearance nor beauty...."[96] For although the portrait of the "Suffering Servant" of Isaiah 53:1–12 pops up repeatedly in the literature that now makes up the New Testament (Matt. 8:17; 26:63a; Mark 15:28; Luke 22:37; John 12:38; Acts 8:32–33; Rom. 10:16; 1 Pet. 2:22–24; cf. Mark 9:12; 1 Cor. 15:3; 1 John 3:5), the physical ugliness that is so prominent in the original has been discreetly painted out of the picture. But by the end of the second century, as we have already seen, Isaiah 53:2–3 was being whipped out fearlessly and repeatedly by the apologists and other Christian authors, confident that the "before" snapshot of Jesus that it represents merely serves to accentuate the "after" snapshots that are readily available now that he has undergone the miraculous makeover of crucifixion combined with resurrection.[97]

The age-old inclination to equate looks with worth, which, in antiquity, crystallized in the physiognomic handbooks of the second to the fourth centuries C.E.,[98] finds its quintessential expression in our own time in the U.S.-led global entertainment industry (i.e., the Hollywood film, television, and popular music industries), aided and abetted by the advertising and fashion industries.[99] The ultimate product of this global culture machine[100] is an idealized human couple, heterosexual of course, and also beautiful in accordance with an aesthetic code that is simultaneously white and Western, a new Adam and Eve. The old physiognomy snubbed Eve, lavishing its attention on Adam. The new physiognomy focuses mainly on Eve, although Adam, too, comes under its purview.[101] And it is in the image of this Adam, this Adonis, that Jesus has been remade, or made over, in the minds of millions of his adorers, his nose straightened, his teeth whitened, his body nipped, tucked, and toned—and his scarred but well-manicured hand raised in blessing over a culture, or rather a cult, of youth and beauty postulated upon a set of hallowed priorities that ensure minimal disturbance to the status quo: looking good is more important than being good; physical transformation is more important than social transformation; and so on. The ideological character of this cultural formation, and hence its propensity for self-contradiction, is evident from the fact that the societies it embraces happen, virtually without exception, to be presided over by men who themselves exhibit few of these fetishized physical traits—a lack that seems to make as little difference to their effective functioning, however, as the lack of "Aryan" physical traits in the author of *Mein Kampf* seemed to make to the effective operation of the gigantic genocidal machine constructed according to his specifications.

To return finally to the question raised earlier, what might the decomposed corpse of Jesus, that worm-ridden horror exhumed by the Jesus Seminar, have looked like in life? What sort of body should we expect the Seminar's Jesus to have, and, indeed, the Jesus of so much contemporary New Testament scholarship, given his resolutely countercultural tendencies, an affront not only to the dominant social values of his own age but to ours as well? The answer, it seems to me, is that we should expect this Jesus to possess a face and physique that the prevalent aesthetic canons of Western culture would deem unattractive or downright ugly. This would be a face and physique that could not be played by Tom Cruise, Bruce Willis, Brad Pitt, George Clooney, or Leonardo DiCaprio; that would be ineligible to guest-star on *Baywatch*; that would be unfit to appear on *Entertainment Tonight*; that advertisers would shudder even to think of placing in proximity to their products—the same face and physique that were revealed to the second-century apologists. And if we are all but incapable of imagining this face and physique at the beginning of the twenty-first century, we not only have the global entertainment industry to blame. I suspect that it is also because we have allowed ourselves to become dazzled by the Gospel of the Incandescent Christ. Somehow, without ever quite showing him, the Fourth Gospel has taken the subversively ugly Nazarene and, like a prime-time docudrama, represented him as a radiantly handsome hero.

### The Asylum

> Jesus said to her, "Mary!"
> —JOHN 20:16

Joshua Josephson awoke before dawn, only gradually becoming aware of where he was, like one who has slept the sleep of the dead. The suffocating mound of myrrh and aloes beneath which he had slipped into unconsciousness had mercifully dissolved, although its cloying scent lingered in the cold morning air. The entombing boulder, too, had been rolled away from his door, he knew not how nor by whom. It had left a deep rut in the hospital corridor, he saw, a trail of ripped linoleum and ruined tiles.

He eased himself carefully out of bed and padded gingerly to the bathroom on bandaged feet. He peered apprehensively at his dim reflection in the bathroom mirror. It was worse even than he had feared. The face that gazed back at him was breathtakingly—no, blandly—beautiful, each feature perfect (painfully so), the flesh pellucid. The face pulsated effulgently in the dull light. It was not his own face.

He heard the echo of running feet in the corridor and animated male voices at the outer door. That would be Peter and his weird friend whatshisname, the one nobody liked. He waited until the voices had retreated down the hall, merging with the dawn chorus of muffled screams that had begun to seep from the locked wards.

He limped out of the bathroom. Mary was standing with her back to him. He hadn't heard her come in. She was contemplating the empty bed, its shroud and face napkin crumpled and bloodstained. The medicine tray was balanced on her right hand. Her crisp white uniform shimmered in the soft light. "Mary," he said, a little too loudly. She turned with a cry of surprise, the tray teetering precariously, its precious cargo sliding toward the edge. "Jesus! You almost scared the pants off me." Calmly resigned, he waited for his newly numinous countenance to have its awful effect on her, for her to falter, to pale, or to stutter, but she gave him his medicine without comment, barely glancing at his face.

Afterwards, he sat alone in the garden immersed in the brilliant blue scroll of the sky, delicately deciphering its gilt script. And knew what he was about to become. Already he could feel time lengthening imperceptibly. By noon eternity would have begun.

## PART II: . . . GOD'S LOCKER ROOM, GOD'S WAR ROOM

Kill me with the sight of Your beauty.

—John of the Cross,
*Spiritual Canticle 11*

# 3  SEX AND THE SINGLE APOSTLE

<1:18> For the wrath of God is revealed from heaven against all ungodliness and wickedness of those who by their wickedness suppress the truth. <v19> For what can be known about God is plain to them, because God has shown it to them. <v20> Ever since the creation of the world his eternal power and divine nature, invisible though they are, have been understood and seen through the things he has made. So they are without excuse; <v21> for though they knew God, they did not honor him as God or give thanks to him, but they became futile in their thinking, and their senseless minds were darkened. <v22> Claiming to be wise, they became fools; <v23> and they exchanged the glory of the immortal God for images resembling a mortal human being or birds or four-footed animals or reptiles.

<v24> Therefore God gave them up in the lusts of their hearts to impurity, to the degrading of their bodies among themselves, <v25> because they exchanged the truth about God for a lie and worshiped and served the creature rather than the Creator, who is blessed forever! Amen.

<v26> For this reason, God gave them up to degrading passions. Their women exchanged natural intercourse for unnatural, <v27> and in the same way also the men, giving up natural intercourse with women, were consumed with passion for one another. Men committed shameless acts with men and received in their own persons the due penalty for their error.

> \<v28\> And since they did not see fit to acknowledge God, God gave them up to a debased mind and to things that should not be done. \<v29\> They were filled with every kind of wickedness, evil, covetousness, malice. Full of envy, murder, strife, deceit, craftiness, they are gossips, \<v30\> slanderers, God-haters, insolent, haughty, boastful, inventors of evil, rebellious toward parents, \<v31\> foolish, faithless, heartless, ruthless. \<v32\> They know God's decree, that those who practice such things deserve to die—yet they not only do them but even applaud others who practice them.
>
> —*Romans* 1:18–32 (NRSV)

> If you were able to direct your eyes into secret places, to unfasten the locked doors of sleeping chambers and to open these hidden recesses to the perception of sight, you would behold that being carried on by the unchaste which a chaste countenance could not behold. You would see what it is an indignity even to see....
>
> —CYPRIAN, *To Donatus* 9 (on Rom. 1:26–27)[1]

> The gods bless you.
> May you sleep then
> on some tender
> girlfriend's breast.
>
> —SAPPHO OF LESBOS, fr. 126[2]

In a superbly argued article, Dale Martin has recently shown that the Paul of Romans 1:26–27 is neither *anti-gay* nor *pro-gay*—nor is he *neutral*—on the issue of homosexual sex.[3] But, the hapless reader may object (especially if he or she chanced to skip the Introduction to the present work), if we accept the (eminently plausible) premise that Paul was not pro-homosexual, and if, for the sake of argument, we accept the additional (although altogether unlikely) premise that he was not anti-homosexual either, that at least leads logically to the (no less implausible) conclusion that he was entirely neutral on the issue of homosexual sex. Or does it? Not necessarily. For, as Martin argues, the logics of sexuality that underpin Romans 1:26–27, on the one hand, and modern logics of sexuality, on the other, are so drastically different as to preclude any paraphrase of this incalculably influential passage that would assimilate it to the modern concept of homosexuality.[4]

The task of defamiliarization necessitated by Romans 1:26–27 does not end there, however, as the present essay attempts to demonstrate. I have more drastic defamiliarizations in mind, and not just for Romans 1:26–27, or even for 1:18–32, but for the larger theological treatise in which both are embedded. In order to accomplish this, I shall have to outflank the letter's defenses and steal up on it from behind. My path will pass through several other, neighboring texts, and as I go along, I shall be attempting to isolate the concepts, or rules, of masculinity, femininity, and sexual engagement that inform them, and, by extension, the letter to the Romans as well.

## Of Men and Unmen

What is man . . . ?

—PSALM 8:4

Let us consult some maps of the terrain to begin with. The first thing we should note (lest we plunge into it) is the gulf that exists between the ancient Greek and Latin terms *anthrōpos, anēr, arsēn, homo, vir, masculus*, and their cognates, on the one hand, and the contemporary English terms "man," "male," "masculine," and *their* cognates, on the other.[5] Not all adult males were "men," it seems, in the Roman world. In the Latin-speaking Roman world, this social truth found shorthand expression in the gender epithets employed by both elite and popular authors from Cicero to Apuleius. In what has become the standard treatment of these epithets, Francesca Santoro L'Hoir shows how "charged with significance" the Latin terms for "man" and "woman" were, in stark contrast to "their lacklustre English equivalents."[6] Examining a range of literary sources from the last decades of the republic and the first two centuries of the empire, she argues compellingly that "[t]he nouns *vir* and *femina* came to signify the upper classes, while *homo* and *mulier* applied to everyone else. *Vir* and *femina* are never neutral; for while every man, by definition, is a *homo*, and every woman, a *mulier*, not every man or woman is a *vir* or a *femina*, respectively."[7]

Yet Santoro L'Hoir can only take us so far. Despite its philological merits, her theoretically underdeveloped study does not succeed in fully defamiliarizing the Roman sex/gender system. Gender and social status appear to have been mutually defining categories in the Roman world to a degree that continually threatens to elude us moderns and postmoderns—and not only in the Latin-speaking Roman world: the same conceptions permeate Greek sources also, as we shall see, even though the Greek gender vocabulary was less nuanced than the Latin.[8] The Roman sex/gender system is best mapped as a circle or a pyramid. In the center of the circle, or at the apex of the pyramid, were adult male citizens—supremely, although not exclusively, those of high social standing: rulers, upper magistrates, heads of elite households, powerful patrons, and so on. These were the most "qualified" recipients of the epithet *vir* (which, in this context, begs to be rendered as "true man").[9] Around them, or below them, were countless others who, in different ways and to different degrees, fell into a category that the classicist Jonathan Walters has usefully labeled *unmen*: females, boys, slaves (of either sex), sexually passive or "effeminate" males, eunuchs, "barbarians," and so on.[10]

This (implicit) distinction between "men" and "unmen," however, rests on texts that were authored, not by those at the "unmen" end of the gender gradient—extant texts from this vast group are all but nonexistent—but by free adult males. Would low-status males (agricultural slaves, for instance) themselves have subscribed to this distinction? Would they have hesitated to apply the term *vir* to themselves? Santoro L'Hoir's study suggests that they might have.[11] Yet even the elite authors themselves occasionally applied *vir* to non-Romans and low-born citizens, as Craig Williams has observed.[12] It is exceedingly difficult to generalize on the basis of the existing evidence.[13]

The extent to which gender and social status were reciprocally defining categories in the forms of ancient Mediterranean culture that *have* mainly been transmitted to us, however, can hardly be overestimated. Gender, social status—and sex. Intrinsic to the popular stereotypes of masculinity that pervade modern Western cultures is the notion that a "man," in the full sense of the term—a "real" man, that is to say—is a male whose sexual desire is exclusively directed toward females. But what are we to make of a culture in which certain males could be seen as appropriate, socially sanctioned objects of sexual penetration by certain other males?[14] As is well known, pagan Greek and Roman culture was characterized by a "tolerance" of "homosexuality" that appears to have permeated all levels of society. It is necessary to place both words in scare quotes, for as Foucault points out in *The Use of Pleasure*, the second volume of his *History of Sexuality*, "the notion of homosexuality is plainly inadequate as a means of referring to an experience, forms of valuation, and a system of categorization so different from ours. The Greeks did not see love for one's own sex and love for the other sex as opposites, as two exclusive choices, two radically different types of behavior. The dividing lines did not follow that kind of boundary."[15] The kind of boundary that they *did* follow will be traced below. Suffice it for now to mention that there was no true equivalent of our concept or even of our term "homosexuality" in Greco-Roman culture.[16] Foucault continues:

> As for the notions of "tolerance" or "intolerance," they too would be completely inadequate to account for the complexity of the phenomena we are considering. To love boys was a "free" practice in the sense that it was not only permitted by the laws (except in particular circumstances), it was accepted by opinion. Moreover, it found solid support in different (military or educational) institutions. It had religious guarantees in rites and festivals where the protection of the divine powers was invoked on its behalf. And finally, it was a cultural practice that enjoyed the prestige of a whole literature that sang of it and a body of reflection that vouched for its excellence.[17]

And although in the first centuries of the common era, literary and philosophical reflection on sexual love between males "lost some of its intensity, its seriousness, its vitality," as Foucault later argues in *The Care of the Self* (the third volume of *The History of Sexuality*), one should not therefore conclude "that the practice disappeared or that it became the object of a disqualification" in pagan society. "All the texts plainly show that it was still common and still regarded as a natural thing."[18]

Apuleius's *The Golden Ass* would be one such text. Also known as *Metamorphoses*, it was written in Latin and appears to date from the third quarter of the second century C.E. It includes the titillating tale of a baker's wife who confesses her sexual frustration to a female friend, whereupon the friend promptly offers to deliver a dashing young man to her door that very evening. The youth is delivered on schedule, welcomed with a deluge of kisses, and set down before a sumptuous meal. But the first morsel is only halfway to his lips when the woman hears her husband returning. The youth is hastily stuffed into a flour bin, where the husband soon discovers him. The youth is terrified on being apprehended, but his cuckolded captor addresses him with apparent kindness:

> "You have nothing harsh to fear from me, son. . . . I will not even invoke the strictness of the law to try you on capital charges under the statutes against adultery. You are such a charming and pretty boy [*pulchellum puellum*]: I will treat you as the joint property of my wife and me. Instead of a probate to split an estate, I will institute a suit to share common assets, contending that without controversy or dissension we three should enter into contract in the matter of one bed. You see, I have always lived in such harmony with my spouse that, in accordance with the teachings of the wise, we both have the same tastes. . . . "
>
> When he had finished mocking the boy with the gentleness of this speech, he led him off to bed. Reluctantly the boy followed; and the baker, locking up his virtuous wife in another room, lay alone with the boy and enjoyed the most gratifying revenge for his ruined marriage [*solus ipse cum puero cubans gratissima corruptarum nuptiarum vindicta perfruebatur*]. (9.27–28)

Next morning, moreover, the baker summons two of his sturdiest slaves and when they have hoisted the boy high he lashes his buttocks unmercifully with a rod. Eventually set free, the would-be adulterer departs hastily but painfully, "for those white buttocks of his had gotten a pounding both during the night and by day [*tamen nates candidas illas noctu diuque diruptus*]" (9.28).[19]

What intrigues Jonathan Walters about this tale is the fact that the husband's rape of his rival "is not seen as requiring any particular comment"; the act does not stigmatize the husband, nor is there the slightest suggestion from the normally intrusive first-person narrator that it should be considered an anomalous act for a man who, we are given no reason to doubt, is sexually attracted to his wife. The implication is rather that the injured husband is merely "defending his honour and, by making his rival submit to him sexually, reaffirming his manhood."[20]

In the course of chiding the youth, the baker calls him "soft" and "tender": "What? Do you, still a boy so soft and tender [*mollis ac tener*], seek to deprive lovers of the bloom of your youth, and instead make free-born women your target?" (9.28). The English terms "soft" and "tender," however, are ill equipped to convey the complex of gendered connotations inherent in these two Latin adjectives. *Mollis*, in particular, was regularly used "to differentiate women, eunuchs and immature males from 'real' men" (as was its Greek counterpart, *malakos*).[21] It connoted such unmanly qualities as flabbiness, voluptuousness, weakness, and cowardliness. And in certain contexts, *mollis* and its abstract form *mollitia* could denote "sexual passivity on the part of a male."[22]

In his much-admired book *The Constraints of Desire: The Anthropology of Sex and Gender in Ancient Greece*,[23] John J. Winkler, too, asserts that one axis along which masculinity could be measured in the Greco-Roman world extended from hardness on one end to softness on the other. He finds "the appropriate social relations between the hard and the soft" graphically illustrated on a red-figure oinochoe (wine jug) of 465–460 B.C.E. that shows a Greek man,

> wearing only a cape and holding his erect penis in his right hand, approaching a Persian soldier in full uniform who is bending over away from the Greek and looks out at the viewer with his hands raised in horror. The inscription identifies the about-to-be buggered soldier as a representative of the losing side in the Athenian victory over the Persians at the battle of Eurymedon (465 B.C.E.).[24]

No longer a hard, impenetrable *man*, the emasculated soldier has become a soft, eminently penetrable *un*man.[25]

Walters also finds *tener*, the other term of reproach applied by the cuckolded baker to his underaged rival, to be loaded with pejorative connotations: not fully grown, weak, fragile, sensuous, effeminate—"all attributes incompatible with being a true man."[26] Walters continues: "Further examination of the language used lets us get at the gender/status differential which is in play here. The youth is never called *vir* ('man') in the Latin text"; instead he is consistently called *puer* ("boy") or *puellus* ("child").[27] But *puer* was not only used of male children, even though that was its primary meaning. It was also used of slaves, of whatever age, and of the passive partner in a sexual relationship between two males. The latter two categories were not unrelated, however. In Roman society, an intimate bond obtained between the institution of slavery and same-sex intercourse. Freeborn Roman males could be sexually active, but not passive, with other males—what Craig Williams has aptly termed "the prime directive of masculine sexual behavior for

Romans."²⁸ If penetration was subjugation, then masculinity was domination.²⁹ The passive role might be appropriate for slaves,³⁰ or for former slaves who still owed a "duty of deference" to their ex-master's desires, or even for other noncitizens in certain circumstances, but was altogether inappropriate for a freeborn male of sound reputation, which is to say a "man" in the full sense of the term.³¹ That a "man," or even a freeborn youth, might actually *relish* the passive role was a thought calculated to cause the Greco-Roman moralist to throw up his own hands in horror.³² Collecting himself, Plutarch sternly states: "Those who enjoy playing the passive role we treat as the lowest of the low, and we have not the slightest degree of respect or affection for them" (*Dialogue on Love* 768a).³³ Philo is still more outraged; clenching his own buttocks defensively, he grimly declares such males to be worthy only of death (*Special Laws* 3.38).³⁴

What did a boy, a slave, and a "catamite" (the three standard meanings of *puer*)³⁵ have in common? What cultural logic dictated that all three groups should be designated by the same term? Walters's answer is that the individuals so categorized, "though male in sex, are not male in gender." Dependent and powerless, they are at another's disposal "in a way inappropriate for a man."³⁶ In a word, they are unmen.

Again, we must not lose sight of the *social* stakes in these rules of sexual engagement. Dio Chrysostom castigates "the man who is never satiated," and who progresses, or rather regresses, from purchasing the services of prostitutes to seducing honorable women and finally to seducing young men of good family who are destined to hold public office (*Oration* 7.151). This last recourse of a jaded appetite Dio deems to be "against nature" (*para physin*). But "nature" in Dio's schema turns out to be culture in camouflage gear and green face paint. For this crime against "nature" consists in treating the city's future leaders as if they were common slaves in a brothel. "It is really an offence against class, an upsetting of the social hierarchy," Winkler notes.³⁷ It dishonors the freeborn young man, whose honor is intimately bound up with his future standing in society (unlike the freeborn young woman, whose status is intimately bound up with her future marriage).³⁸ The socially subversive offense decried by Dio, then, is that of treating ripening "men" as common "unmen."

Just how pervasive were these class-infused views of sex and gender in the ancient Mediterranean world? Once again we come up against the familiar barrier, the fact that the primary sources for these views are the writings of those nearer the apex of the social pyramid than its base. Foucault's principal informants in the second volume of *The History of Sexuality*, for instance, are Plato, Aristotle, and Xenophon. He readily concedes that, for elite intellectuals such as these, "reflection on sexual behavior as a moral domain" was not a means of legitimizing or formalizing "general interdictions imposed on everyone; rather, it was a means of developing—for the smallest minority of the population, made up of free, adult males—an aesthetics of existence," a "stylization of conduct for those who wished to give their existence the most graceful and accomplished form possible"[39]—and accede to full "manhood" in the process.

As though to ward off objections that his sources are too exclusive, Foucault begins the third volume of *The History of Sexuality*, dedicated to discourses of sexuality in the Roman period, with an examination of a rather different sort of text, the *Oneirokritika* (Dream Analysis, or Dream Taxonomy) of Artemidoros of Daldis, an itinerant dream analyst of the second century C.E.[40] This too is "a man's book that is addressed mainly to men."[41] It is designed as a handbook for other dream analysts, although it is also addressed to the "general reader," who will be able to use it to decipher his own dreams.[42] This general reader, or dreamer, is envisioned as a family man with possessions, quite often with a trade or business, and "apt to have servants or slaves."[43] But the real value of this text, for Foucault, inheres in the fact that while it is the only one from this period to present anything approximating a systematic exposition of the varieties of sexual acts, "it is not in any sense a treatise on morality, which would be primarily concerned with formulating judgments about those acts and relations."[44] Instead, it discloses "schemas of valuation that were generally accepted."[45] Indeed, Winkler, whose *Constraints of Desire* accords a no less prominent place to the *Oneirokritika*, goes so far as to claim that the text "represents not just one man's opinion about the sexual protocols of ancient societies"—the opinion of a free, literate man, to be precise—"but an invaluable collection of evidence—a kind of ancient Kinsey report—based on interviews with thousands of clients."[46]

The relevant chapters of the *Oneirokritika* begin: "The best set of categories for the analysis of intercourse [*synousia*] is, first, intercourse which is according to nature [*kata physin*] and convention [*nomon*] and customary usage [*ethos*], then intercourse against convention [*para nomon*], and third, intercourse against nature [*para physin*]" (1.78).[47] The relevance of the *Oneirokritika* for the interpretation of Romans 1.26–27 thus begins to become apparent: "Their women exchanged natural relations [*tēn physikēn chrēsin*] for unnatural [*eis tēn para physin*]," writes Paul, "and the men likewise gave up natural relations [*tēn physikēn chrēsin*] with women...."[48] "Intercourse which is according to nature and convention" in the *Oneirokritika* turns out to be that in which a man has sex with a social inferior—but not just a *female* inferior (such as his wife, his female slave, "women who mind workshops and stalls," or a prostitute). For sex with a male slave also falls into this category, provided only that the slave assumes the passive role. "To be penetrated [*perainesthai*] by one's house slave is not good," Artemidoros opines (1.78). Why? Not because of the act of anal penetration in itself, nor even the slave's maleness, argues Winkler, "but because a social inferior is represented as a sexual superior."[49]

The active/passive antithesis is one that Foucault returns to repeatedly in the second and third volumes of *The History of Sexuality*. At one point, for instance, he notes that although the dividing line of gender in antiquity did run principally between male and female, its route was ultimately far more circuitous. More precisely, the line ran "between what might be called the 'active actors' in the drama of pleasures, and the 'passive actors': on one side, those who were the subject of sexual activity . . . , and on the other, those who were the object-partners, the supporting players. . . . " The active actors were men, of course, "but more specifically they were adult free men." And the passive actors included women, of course, "but women made up only one element of a much larger group that was sometimes referred to as a way of designating the object of possible pleasure: 'women, boys, slaves'" (*Use of Pleasure*, p. 47). David Halperin reduces these principles to a simple formula: "Sexual partners came in two different kinds—not male and female but 'active' and 'passive,' dominant and submissive" (*One Hundred Years of Homosexuality*, p. 33). Or as Clement of Alexandria put it, no less pithily: "To do [*to dran*] is the mark of the man; to suffer [*to paschein*] is the mark of the woman" (*The Instructor* 3.19.2).

Returning to Artemidoros (1.78–79), we discover that "intercourse against convention [*para nomon*]" involves incest or oral-genital contact (for reasons not entirely clear, almost as great a taboo attached to the latter as to the former in the ancient Mediterranean world).[50] "Intercourse against nature [*para physin*]," finally, turns out to be a ragbag category containing most of the possible (and seemingly impossible) permutations that remain: penetrating oneself anally with one's own penis, fellating oneself (regular masturbation falls into the natural and conventional category), the penetration of a woman by another woman, and sex with a god or goddess, a corpse, or an animal (1.80). "What idea or ideas of nature generate this heterogeneous list of things *para physin*?" muses Winkler.[51] Not reproductive potential, obviously, since both the preceding categories, the natural-conventional and the unconventional, contain sexual acts that are nonreproductive: sodomy is natural and conventional, for example, while fellatio is unconventional, although not unnatural. The underlying rationale "seems to be that unnatural acts do not involve any representation of human social hierarchy. . . . Bestiality is not 'unnatural' in the sense of being what modern psychology calls a perversion; rather it is outside the conventional field of social signification. If a man gains advantage over a sheep, so what?" (pp. 38–39). (The sheep herself might not be quite so dismissive, of course.)

The most telling item in the unnatural category, however, and the most significant for our understanding of Romans 1.26–27, is the penetration of a woman by another woman—provided, of course, that v. 26b ("Their women exchanged natural intercourse for unnatural") actually refers to sexual relations between women, as most modern commentators on Romans have supposed,[52] and not to "heterosexual" anal or oral intercourse, say, or even bestiality.[53] What are the grounds for this supposition? In the first place, the *homoiōs* of v. 27 ("and the men *likewise*, giving up natural intercourse with women, were consumed with passion for each other") strongly suggests that the women's unnatural intercourse similarly resulted from *their* being consumed with passion for each other. The correspondence between the unnatural activities of the women, on the one hand, and those of the men, on the other, suggested by *homoiōs*, also militates against the bestial interpretation of v. 26b: whatever the men are up to, it doesn't seem to involve four-legged partners. The bestial interpretation also stumbles on v. 24: "God gave them up . . . to the degrading of their bodies *among themselves [en autois]*." No barks, bleats, grunts, or neighs mingle with the human cries of passion that resound through this passage. And as for the women's unnatural intercourse being anal or oral sex with men, explicit castigations of either activity as being contrary to nature are lacking in Greco-Roman sources (even including Jewish sources), whereas sexual relations between women are denounced as unnatural by an impressive array of authors over a long span of time, including Plato, Seneca the Elder, Martial, Ovid, Ptolemy, Dorotheos of Sidon, Manetho, Pseudo-Phocylides, Tertullian, Clement of Alexandria, John Chrysostom—and Artemidoros.[54] Quietly slipping in behind this august company, therefore, I take Romans 1:26b to refer to sexual relations between women. But what precisely is it about such activity that caused the hackles to rise on these ancient authors?

Commenting on Artemidoros's allusion to unnatural intercourse between women, Winkler rightly insists that the expression should not be domesticated by some soft-focus translation such as "lesbian sex," "for that would be to gloss over the very point where ancient Mediterranean sexual significations diverge from our own, hence the point where they are most revealing" (*Constraints of Desire*, p. 39). In the Greco-Roman world, sex, by definition—"natural" and "conventional" sex, that is—was male-initiated and utterly centered on the penis and the act of penetration (p. 43). Barbara Kellum has observed that "the sheer ubiquity of the phallus" in the Roman world in particular,

> in scales ranging from the gigantic to the miniscule—here a house marker and there a representation on a child's finger ring—is difficult for us to imagine. The erect phallus certainly served as the shop sign for a *caupona* but equally appeared on house walls, on baker's ovens, on paving stones, at the baths, at fortress gateways, and on objects ranging from *ex votos* to suggestively flaming lamps. Projected in at least three dimensions and hung with bells, the polyphallus became a whimsical doorbell (*tintinnabulum*). In daily speech too, the male organ was everywhere.... Like the phallic amulet in the child's *bulla* or the phallic harness ornament on the prized horse, representations of the phallus offered protection from the evil eye.[55]

And so on. That the male organ should loom large in Artemidoros's dream book, therefore, given that book's propensity to reflect commonly held sexual attitudes and assumptions, is scarcely surprising. At one point in the *Oneirokritika*, indeed, the penis elicts the following eulogy:

> The penis is like a man's parents since it contains the generative code [*spermatikos logos*], but it is also like his children since it is their cause. It is like his wife and girlfriend since it is useful for sex. It is like his brothers and all blood relations since the meaning of the entire household depends on the penis. It signifies strength and the body's man-

hood, since it actually causes these: for this reason some people call it their "manhood" [*andreia*]. It resembles reason and education since, like reason [*logos*], it is the most generative thing of all. . . . It is like the respect of being held in honor, since it is called "reverence" and "respect." (1.45, trans. Winkler, *Constraints of Desire*, p. 42)

In short, it can do everything but beg, roll over, and fetch the newspaper. In the sphere where we should most expect it to shine, however—the bedroom—it is rather less versatile. The act of penetration seems to constitute the quintessence of sexual activity for Artemidoros. "No caresses, no complicated combinations, no phantasmagoria," as Foucault remarks (*History of Sexuality*, 3: 28). This is in full continuity with the phallocentric conception of the sexual act reflected in a wide range of ancient Greek and Latin texts, its reduction to a penetrative, ejaculatory schema assumed to encompass all sexual activity.[56]

Sexual relations between women can only be articulated in the *Oneirokritika*, therefore, in the significant terms of the system, which is to say, in terms of a penetrator and a penetratee. "Sexual relations between women are here classed as 'unnatural,'" notes Winkler, "because 'nature' assumes that what are significant in sexual activity are (i) men, (ii) penises that penetrate, and (iii) the articulation thereby of relative statuses through relations of dominance" (*Constraints of Desire*, p. 39). Women are not intrinsically equipped—not anatomically equipped, that is—to display these "natural" relations of dominance, of social hierarchy, in the sexual act. And they had better not try! "Women had better not ape [*mēde . . . mimēsainto*] the conjugal role [*lechos*] of men," warns the Hellenistic Jewish author known as Pseudo-Phocylides (*Sentences* 192; my translation).

The reduction of sexual relations to the act of penetration enables sex to become a simple yet effective instrument for expressing hierarchical relations. Foucault puts it memorably:

Artemidorus sees the sexual act first and foremost as a game of superiority and inferiority: penetration places the two partners in a relationship of domination and submission. It is victory on one side, defeat on the other; it is a right that is exercised for one of the partners, a necessity that is imposed on the other. It is a status that one asserts, or a condition to which one is subjected. (*History of Sexuality*, 3: 30)

Penetration was not all of sex, then as now, needless to say, but it appears to have been that aspect of sexual activity commonly thought to express social relations of honor and shame, aggrandizement and loss, domination and submission,[57] or, more generally, movement up or down that treacherously slippery social ladder whose greased rungs marked discrete levels of status and prestige.[58]

## What's That Peculiar Thing Poking through the Tear in Saint Paul's Epistle to the Romans?

## Things That Cannot Be Thought without Shame or Horror

Is this how Paul, too, saw the sexual act? There is, of course, no way to know for certain. We may be tempted to give him the benefit of the doubt. He did choose to remain celibate, after all (1 Cor. 7:7–8; 9:5, 15),[59] which, being translated into the Priapean terms in which we have been trading, means that he did not use his penis to affirm his social status. (His phallic use or abuse of authority is another matter, of course, one that has often been addressed in recent years.) Yet the problem that now protrudes so obscenely through the tear that began to appear in Romans 1.26–27 as we perused Artemidoros's pronouncements on sex cannot be sewn up—or zipped up—so easily. So startlingly congruent, indeed, are these verses with the sociosexual script that I have been fleshing out that it seems to matter very little in the end whether Paul himself was fully cognizant of what he was saying or whether he was merely a dummy on the knee of a ventriloquist culture that spoke through him to audiences that he, or it, could never have imagined—most recently ourselves. In any case, taking a leaf from the *Amplified New Testament*, I now submit the following amplified translation of Romans 1.26b–27:

> All that is quite disgusting!
> 
> —MICHEL FOUCAULT, "On the Genealogy of Ethics"

> With so much untruthfulness of speech and unrighteousness of conduct on every side of us, we Christians of India need to be very "straight."
> 
> —THOMAS WALKER, *The Epistle to the Philippians*

Consider the case of a society one of whose constitutive conditions is the systemic subjugation of the feminine. Consider further that the definitive display of this subjugation is, ac-

Their women exchanged natural relations (of domination versus submission, designed to display social hierarchy, they themselves assuming the inferior position by accepting penile penetration) for unnatural relations (in which no display of domination or submission occurred and consequently no social hierarchy was exhibited, because no penile penetration took place), and the men likewise gave up natural relations with women (the male assuming the dominant position, penetrating the woman and thereby exhibiting and reaffirming his social superiority over her) and were consumed with passion for one another, men committing shameless acts with men (in which one partner would necessarily end up the loser in the zero-sum game of honor versus shame, passively accepting penetration and thus defeat at the hands of the other).... [60]

My argument, in short, is that Romans 1.26–27 is but the tip of a sociosexual iceberg. And that the iceberg, like most, is a chilling one.

Of course, we have barely begun to scratch its surface. Romans 1:18–32, the larger subunit within which our verses occur, is a saga of crime and punishment. The plot paraphrase of this saga, sketched out in what follows, began as a series of scribbles and doodles in the margins of Bernadette Brooten's *Love Between Women*.[61] Brooten has left no stone unturned in her meticulous mapping of this tiny, but hotly contested, patch of text, and has begun to describe what has crawled out from underneath them. It seems to me, however, that what has slithered out is even cording to the society's elite spokesmen, the act of sexual penetration. In such a society, the act of penetration becomes the arbitrary object of a massive symbolic investment —arbitrary, because a penis inserted in a vagina or an anus has no more intrinsic social significance than a digit inserted in a nostril, say, or a hot dog inserted in a bun. For the society's moral custodians, however, the idea that certain insubordinate females might brazenly usurp the definitive masculine role of sexual penetrator is a deeply disturbing one. But the idea that they might actively choose to bypass penetrative sex altogether, finding nonpenetrative sex preferable, for whatever reason, is literally unthinkable: it falls soundlessly beyond the bounds of the system and cannot even be posed as a problem within it.

more unsightly than Brooten has realized. Borrowing her pen and sketch pad, therefore, and drawing on the work of other scholars too (notably Stanley Stowers), I shall attempt to press beyond Brooten's analysis in what follows (although without presuming for a moment that she would recognize my sketch as a logical extension of her own).

First of all, why does Paul mention female homoeroticism before male: "Their women exchanged natural relations for unnatural, and the men likewise gave up natural relations with women . . . "? Does he regard the former as the more heinous aberration of the two (so heinous, in fact, that he is unwilling to go into detail on it, reserving what meager details there are in these verses for the lesser aberration of male homoeroticism)? Brooten finds support for this view in a comment of the fourth-century Church Father John Chrysostom on this passage to the effect that homoerotic sexual contact is even more shameful for women than for men (Brooten, *Love Between Women*, p. 240; Chrysostom, *On the Epistle to the Romans*, Homily 4.1). But what ultimately lends plausibility to this interpretation of Romans 1:26–27 is the hegemonic "logic" of the Greco-Roman sex/gender system as it is expressed in so many of the other elite, male-authored texts that have come down to us,[62] a logic I began to unpack in the preceding pages (and one with which Brooten is intimately familiar, although she omits bringing it to bear on the question of why Paul indicts female homoeroticism first, or why he declines to gloss its "shamefulness," reserving the more lurid details for male homoeroticism, and causing Brooten to conclude that, "as for many other writers through-

These general observations are by no means restricted, however, to ancient Greek or Roman societies. Even in nineteenth-century Britain—at least as represented by the patriarchs of polite British society—sexual relations could still be conceived of only in terms of a penetrator and a penetratee,[101] same-sex relations merely involving insertions that God or nature never intended. As such, same-sex relations automatically assumed the status of an inferior copy (or, on occasion, Satanic parody) of an authentic (divinely instituted) original.[102] But when the two parties engaged in sexual congress were not only female but British as well, no model whatsoever could be wheeled into the parlor, the church, or the courtroom within which they might be conceptually caged.

Consider the historical anecdote with which

out history, female homoeroticism is unspeakable for Paul").⁶³ Female homoeroticism constituted more of a threat to the logic or symbolic economy of Greco-Roman sex and gender than either anal intercourse or fellatio between males (the twin specters implicitly summoned up on the flickering screen of Romans 1:27). It even constituted more of a threat than bestiality or necrophilia. A person of either sex who copulated with an animal at least preserved his or her gender identity intact, either "mounting" the animal or "being mounted" by it, as his or her anatomical equipment dictated (cf. Brooten, *Love Between Women*, p. 252). A man who penetrated a corpse likewise retained the essential mark of his masculine identity.

A woman who had sex with another woman, however—which, being translated into the dominant sexological categories of Greco-Roman thought, could only mean a woman who penetrated or mounted another woman, using her in the manner of a man and thereby constructing a counterfeit, indeed monstrous, masculinity for herself—becoming a monster, in fact⁶⁴—threatened by her hubris to shatter the very mold that shaped Greco-Roman gender identity in the first place.⁶⁵ Such a woman—if that indeed is what "she" was—pissed in the sacred waters of gender itself and sent ripples of alarm through the minds and texts of elite Greco-Roman males, the letter to the Romans included.⁶⁶ For the purity of gender was no mere abstraction for such males; rather they perceived it as having social consequences of the most concrete and immediate kind. Brooten is incisive on this point: "Female-female and male-male sexual relations in the Roman world and in Rom 1:26f are both parallel

Bernadette Brooten opens her discussion of Romans 1:26–27 in her book *Love Between Women*: "The place: Edinburgh, Scotland. The time: 1811. Miss Marianne Woods and Miss Jane Pirie, two schoolteachers accused of having had a sexual relationship with each other, deny the charges and sue their accusers for libel."¹⁰³ The charges rested principally on the testimony of a sixteen-year-old schoolgirl, Jane Cumming. In the course of the trial, however, doubts were voiced that sexual relations between women were even possible. This elicited a "memorandum" from the Senior Counsel for the defense (the schoolteachers' accusers, that is to say), which begins as follows: "Because the Lord Ordinary in hearing had expressed doubt of the existence of the vice in question, the defendant begs leave to provide proofs of the and not parallel to one another. They both exemplify homoeroticism, but they differ socially, since, within this gender hierarchy, a man loses status in adopting a passive role, while a woman theoretically gains status by giving up a passive role" (ibid., p. 266). In principle, the thought of a woman *gaining* status was more worrying for elite males than the thought of a man *losing* status. Why? Because as a culture that pivoted on the concept of "limited good,"[67] there was only so much status (read "honor") to go around. Loss of honor on the part of one male in this zero-sum economy entailed automatic increase of honor for another male.[68] But increase of honor on the part of a *female*—itself an anomalous notion, since the Roman concept of honor encapsulated the essence of *masculine* virtue[69]—could only result in loss of honor for *all* males. Female homoeroticism was therefore a crime against man.

But, of course, it was also a crime against God. This brings us to the question, not simply of why Paul places *female* homoeroticism at the head of his list of "degrading passions" (*pathē atimia*), but of why he separates *all* homoeroticism out for special mention instead of merely including it in the vice list that follows (1:29–31)?[70] Because homoerotic relations epitomize—indeed, mimic in miniature—human rebellion against God and refusal of the honor due to him ("though they knew God, they did not honor [*ouch . . . edoxasan*] God as God"—Rom. 1:21); the thorny problem with which Paul is wrestling in this difficult stretch of Romans. (But is there any stretch of Romans that is *not* difficult?)

This brings us finally to the relationship of homoeroticism to idolatry in our passage. Ro-

Authorities with regard to the practice of tribadism" (quoted in Faderman, *Scotch Verdict*, p. 211). The evidence produced was principally antiquarian in character, including the sophist Lucian of Samosata's *Dialogue of the Courtesans* 5.1–4 (quoted at length) and a list of references to relevant passages in other Greco-Roman authors: Juvenal, Ovid, Martial, Phaedrus. It also included Romans 1:26b.

And the verdict? No less august a body than the House of Lords itself decided in 1819 in favor of Woods and Pirie, unable to accept that two Christian British women above the lower classes could be capable of the heinous act attributed to the two schoolteachers—if, indeed, British women of any class could be deemed capable of it. Lord Justice-Clerk Hope: "There is not a prostitute so blasted as these women are demans 1:18–23 sternly indicts those who, in choosing empty idols over the one true God ("they exchanged the glory of the immortal God for images resembling a mortal human being or birds or four-footed animals or reptiles"), rebelled against his authority and refused to submit to his power. Romans 1:24–27 proceeds to imply that their punishment fit their crime: "Therefore [*dio*] God gave them up in the lusts of their hearts to impurity, to the degrading of their bodies among themselves, because they exchanged the truth about God for a lie and worshipped and served the creature rather than the Creator, who is blessed forever! Amen." Their refusal of the divinely ordained relations of superordination and subordination between creature and creator is mirrored in their refusal of the divinely ordained relations of superordination and subordination between male and female.[71] A startling homology therefore emerges, in which God is to the human being as the active, erect, penetrating male is to the passive, open, penetrated female.[72]

But the homology implicit in this passage is much more intricate than that. "Claiming to be wise, they became fools; and they exchanged the glory of the immortal God for images resembling a mortal human being or birds or four-footed animals or reptiles," Romans 1:22–23 says. Brooten adds: "Paul draws upon motifs of Jewish antipagan polemic. Both the Wisdom of Solomon (hellenistic or early Roman period) and Philo of Alexandria (ca. 20 B.C.E.–ca. 45 C.E.) explicitly polemicize against Egyptian animal worship"—although animals also played a role in Greek and Roman religion, as Brooten reminds us; for example, the snakes that were an essential scribed by Miss Cumming." Lord Gillies: "No such case was ever known in Scotland, or in Britain. . . . I do believe that the crime here alleged has no existence."[104] Whence, then, the accusation? Where was the fire from which this noxious smoke had arisen? Lord Meadowbank noted with undisguised disdain that the principal witness, Miss Cumming, was "wanting in the advantages of legitimacy and a European complexion." The daughter of a deceased Scottish gentleman and an Indian woman, she had spent the first eight years of her life in India. Meadowbank suggested that Miss Cumming's imagination had been set ablaze by her lewd and lascivious Indian nurses: "It is an historical fact and matter of notoriety that the language of the Hindoo female domestics turns chiefly on the commerce of the sexes."[105] Lord Boyle summed up part of the Roman *lararium*, that chapel within a Roman house dedicated to its tutelary deities (*Love Between Women*, pp. 231–32).[73] Philo obligingly spells out the rationale for his own scornful denunciation of animal worship: "The Egyptians have promoted to divine honours irrational animals.... [T]hey render worship to them, they the civilized to the uncivilized and untamed, the reasonable to the irrational, ... the rulers and masters to the naturally subservient and slavish" (*On the Contemplative Life* 8–9).[74]

We are now in a position to unfurl the implicit rationale of Romans 1:18–27 in turn. Because the human beings whom Paul is indicting refused to honor the divinely ordained hierarchy whereby the lesser submits to the greater—a refusal emblematized by their worship of animals, creatures that by nature are inferior to humans and designed to serve them—God punished them by consigning them to shameful practices that sabotaged another divinely ordained hierarchy, that of male over female. In other words: humans refused to honor the divinely instituted hierarchy that should have regulated divine-human relations (God over "man"). This refusal or rebellion found emblematic expression in, or was epitomized by, these sinful humans' reversal of a *second* divinely instituted hierarchy, that which should have regulated human-animal relations ("man" over animal). And God punished these rebels by permitting them to overturn a *third* divinely instituted hierarchy, that which should have regulated male-female relations (man over woman), thereby rubbing their noses in their sin (cf. 2:6).[75] The full homology inherent in Romans 1:18–27 can now be set out in full:

the situation: "[H]owever well known the crime here charged may be among Eastern nations, this is the first instance on record, of such an accusation having ever been made in this country."[106]

The lords' confident pronouncements on the sexual proclivities of Asian women should come as no surprise. Since the Renaissance at least, Asia, Africa, and the Americas had been what Anne McClintock has termed "a pornotropics for the European imagination—a fantastic magic lantern of the mind onto which Europe projected its forbidden sexual desires and fears" (*Imperial Leather*, p. 22). In consequence, non-European peoples were regularly imagined by Europeans to be especially susceptible to homoerotic temptations. "Harem stories, in particular, fanned fantasies of lesbianism," as Ania Loomba has remarked.

FEMALE is to MALE
as
ANIMAL is to HUMAN
and as
HUMAN is to GOD.

In the symbolic world of Romans 1:18–32, therefore, "natural" sex is to "true" worship as "unnatural" sex is to idolatry[76]—which is to say that the submissiveness that the female should display in relation to the male (the sine qua non of "natural" sex) finds its ultimate warrant in the submissiveness that the human being should display in relation to God. The absolute inequality that is intrinsic to the act of divine worship—such worship being, in effect, the celebration of such inequality—is tacitly adduced in Romans 1:18–32 to sanction inequality between male and female, an inequality whose ritual expression is the "natural" sex act, the act of penile penetration. Sex in this symbolic economy is nothing other—*can* be nothing other—than eroticized inequality.[77] And this inequality is immeasurably productive, masculine and feminine subjects themselves being manufactured through the eroticization of dominance and submission.[78] To elaborate, were Paul in Romans willing or able to reflect explicitly on the theory of gender that undergirds his discourse, he might well appeal to Genesis 3:16 in support of it. "Male and female he created them" [Hebrew: *zākār ûněqēbâ bārā² ²ōtām*; Greek: *arsen kai thēlu epoiēsen autous*]" — so the first Genesis creation account describes the institution of anatomical sex (1:27). But the second creation account[79] describes the institution of gender: "Your desire shall be for your husband/man, and he shall lord it over you [3:16;

In his account of early-seventeenth-century Turkey, for example, George Sandys contemplates what happens when women are cloistered with each other, engaged in long hours of massaging and pampering their bodies: "Much unnaturall and filthie lust is said to be committed daily in the remote closets of these darksome [bathhouses]: yea, women with women; a thing incredible, if former times had not given thereunto both detection, and punishment."[107]

But what act precisely was it that the House of Lords in 1819 deemed a British woman incapable of? What act would it have been unthinkable to attribute to such a person? What act constituted such a vicious symbolic assault on the

Hebrew: *wĕʾel-ʾîšēk tĕšûqātēk wĕhûʾ yimšāl-bāk*; Greek: *kai pros ton andra sou hē apostrophē sou, kai autos sou kyrieusei*]," which, being further translated, means nothing other than "*masculine* and *feminine* he created them." The intricate interpenetration of desire, domination, and submission (at once creative Trinity and sadomasochistic ménage à trois), succinctly suggested in this immensely influential verse, is precisely what brings gender to birth, for the author of Romans no less than for the author(s) of Genesis.

Thus far I have been attempting to exhume the imbedded cultural assumptions about homoerotic behavior that underlie Romans 1:26-27, to explain why such behavior should not only be an affront to Paul's God, but should actually epitomize sinful humanity's disordered relationship with him. Implicit in any conception of "wrong" relationship, however, is a corresponding conception of "right" relationship. If homoeroticism can be said to epitomize a *wrong* relationship with Paul's God, what would be logically entailed in a *right* relationship with him? Were we to press Paul's implicit characterization of homoeroticism to its logical conclusion, what would come into view? It is time to turn over this particular stone and see what adheres to its underside.

In light of what we have unearthed thus far, many of the platitudes ritually intoned over our passage now need to be reconsidered. For instance: "And we could interpret the whole of Rom. 1:18-32 as describing confused people, who do not do what they really want, assuming that people truly want to be in right relation to God."[80] But a right relation of creature to creator is implicitly modeled in our passage by a right relation of female to male, specifically a right sexual institution of gender itself that it could not be granted even a notional existence in British society, but could only be conceived of as something external, alien, and monstrous, something that the uncivilized, dark-skinned women of the Orient indulged in, something altogether Other? Why, the sexual penetration of one woman by another, of course. What finally clinched the verdict in favor of the two Scottish schoolteachers was the fact that the primary witness, Jane Cumming, had never claimed to have seen an artificial phallus being employed in the alleged sexual relationship.[108] But in that case no sexual act could have occurred. The legal principle was classic in its stark simplicity: *No dildo, no dyke.*

In pronouncing upon Romans 1:26b, therefore, the schoolteachers' lawyer, John relation. What, therefore, are we to conclude? That a right relation to God would mean being properly underneath him,[81] breathless under his massive bulk, legs spread wide? And are we also to conclude that women who engage in homoerotic activity are "confused people, who do not do what they really want," because they do not *know* what they really want? What do they really want, anyway? The answer comes to succinct expression in that quintessential site of masculine discourse, the male locker room. What women who love women want, what they need, to straighten them out and cure them of their condition, is—let me see, how can I put this delicately?—*a good fucking.*

In Romans 1:18–32, "confused" people everywhere are epitomized by women-loving women. And God's "wrath" against such people ("For the wrath of God [*orgē theou*] is revealed from heaven against all ungodliness and wickedness . . . " [1:18])[82] is the direct result of their unreasonable refusal of his stiff solution to their plight, of their declining to assume the passive position in relation to him, spreading their legs or bending over as an abject acknowledgment of his absolute authority and infinite superiority. Paul's God thus turns out to be an oversized (and overendowed?) Roman male in the classic patriarchal mold, with a permanent erection and not enough orifices in which to insert it.[83] Intriguingly, this Priapean personage is the exact antithesis of the celibate Paul's own public persona, suggesting how little conscious control Paul has exercised over the creation of his God. What should we conclude? That Paul is once again a dummy in the lap of a ventriloquist and masculinist culture whose voice resounds through his letters (and whose

Clerk, argued that if it indeed referred to sexual relations between women, a prosthetic phallus must needs be envisioned:

> [T]he defendant's counsel . . . alleged that this crime was mentioned in the New Testament. And if they were right it is the only one of all their authorities entitled to the slightest regard. The New Testament passage which the defendant's counsel refers to is in the first chapter of the Romans: "For this cause God gave them up into vile affections; for even their women did change the natural use into that which is against nature." It is very evident that even supposing this passage had referred to some infamous congress between two women, the proper inference

SEX AND THE SINGLE APOSTLE 155

permanently erect member he is blithely unaware of, despite his being perched upon it)? Or that Paul, on the contrary, is no dummy, the fact that he has surreptitiously created a Jewish-Christian Priapus suggesting instead that he has unconsciously allowed his sexuality to shape his theology?

Now, the tale that Paul tells about his Priapus is not one of unending frustration. In the fullness of time, this ithyphallic personage did have the perfect orifice offered to him, and in a spirit of perfect submission. For Paul's anguished outlining of humanity's *plight*—universal sin: "Since all have sinned and fall short of the glory of God . . ." (Rom. 3:23; cf. 1:18–3:20)—is but the prelude to his triumphant unveiling of God's *solution*—Jesus Christ: ". . . they are now justified by his grace as a gift, through the redemption that is in Christ Jesus" (3:24). This universal sin is epitomized, or, better, synecdochically figured (the part standing in for the whole), by homoerotic sexual relations, especially between women, as we have seen. But why is *Jesus* the solution? Because Jesus submitted himself absolutely to God (cf. Phil. 2:5–8; Rom. 5:19),[84] uniquely exemplifying the obedience to, and reverence for, God's authority that God demands of every human being.[85] Stripped naked and spread out on the cross, run through with sundry phallic objects, Jesus in his relationship to God perfectly models the submissiveness that should also characterize the God-fearing female's proper relationship to the male. This is the sexual substratum of Paul's soteriology.

And it comes to vivid visual expression in the various artistic depictions of a female Christ on the cross that have appeared in recent decades, beginning in 1975, apparently, with Edwina San-

would be that it was by the use of an instrument.[109]

Not surprisingly, the notion of a phallus-wielding woman,[110] coupled with the accompanying notion, almost as inducive of gender vertigo, of "men" who mistook their anuses for vaginas, was too much for most eighteenth- and nineteenth-century clerical commentators on Romans 1:26–27, prompting near-apoplectic outbursts of indignation. Exemplary in this regard is John Brown's *The Self-Interpreting Bible*, a mammoth, worm-eaten tome that sat in a corner of the conference room in the Department of Biblical Studies at the University of Sheffield, my whilom employer, and glowered down at my colleagues and me while we engaged in our ungodly deliberations. First published

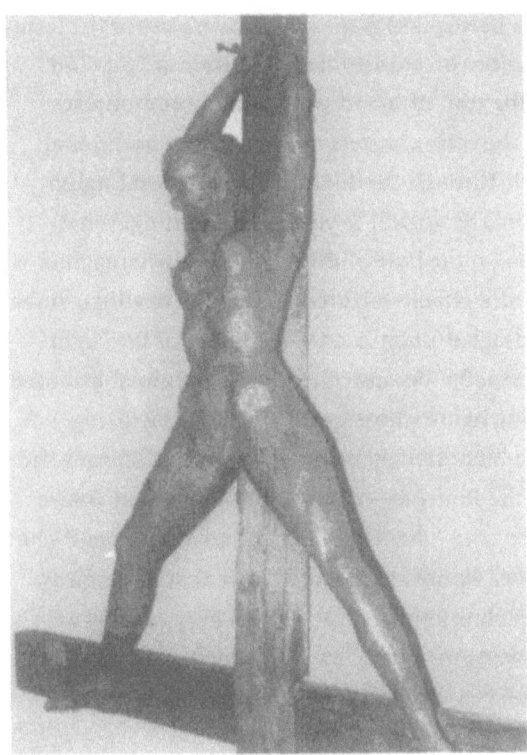

FIGURE 9. James M. Murphy, *Christine on the Cross*, 1984, clay sculpture, height 24". Used by permission of the artist.

dys's controversial *Christa*, a bronze sculpture first displayed in the Episcopal Cathedral of St. John the Divine in New York City. A similar sculpture by James M. Murphy exhibited at Union Theological Seminary nine years later, this time in clay and entitled *Christine on the Cross*, carried the inversion of the traditional image to its logical conclusion. Murphy turned the familiar cross on its head—literally: the woman's legs are spreadeagled and her feet nailed to the dropped crossbar, while her arms are pulled above her head and her hands nailed together to the vertical bar (Fig. 9). But what does it all mean? The artist's own inter-

in 1778 and highly regarded in its day, *The Self-Interpreting Bible* paraphrases Romans 1:24–27 as follows:

> To punish their thus setting up false objects of worship, and representing Him in so unjust, false, and shameless a manner, and regarding and worshipping the basest of creatures more than Himself, God, their infinitely glorious and blessed Creator, Preserver, and Governor, in His righteous judgement, withdrew His abused light and restraints, left them to themselves, and gave them up to their own vicious inclinations, which hurried them, both men and women, into such shocking, lustful, disgraceful, and unnatural abuse of their bodies as cannot be thought of or mentioned without shame or horror.

pretation of the sculpture is that it is a graphic embodiment and denunciation of worldwide, systemic misogyny.[86] Does the trail of blood we have been tracking through the early chapters of Romans lead inexorably, then, through the doors of St. James's Chapel at Union Theological Seminary to form a spreading pool at the base of this highly unsettling sculpture of a cruelly tortured woman symbolically spreadeagled upon a cruciform bed of pain? Not exactly, because the closer we come to the writhing figure whose own cross thrusts up through the bloodstained pages of the crucifixated letter to the Romans—a dim figure silhouetted against the sun—the less certain we become about whether we are looking at a woman or a man. For the Pauline Jesus' spectacular act of submission—his consummately "feminine" performance—is simultaneously and paradoxically a demonstration of his masculinity, as we are about to see.

Note first, however, that Paul's spiritual progeny, while picking up on his sexual soteriology, tend to take fewer risks with Jesus' gender identity. In Ephesians 5:21–33, for example,[87] it is not Jesus' own submission to God that forms the model for the female's submission to the male. Jesus appears here with an adoring Church on his arm, a stunning trophy bride who has undergone a salvific makeover at the hands of the Divine Beautician himself, so as to be presented to him "in splendor, without a spot or wrinkle [*mē echousan spilon ē rutida*] or any such thing" (v. 27), radiant as a model in a Clearasil or wrinkle-cream commercial. "Just as the church is subservient to Christ [*hypotassetai tō Christō*]," admonishes the author, "so also wives ought to be, in everything, to their husbands" (v. 24). Of

Brown's use of the term "Governor" for God, while commonplace, at least in traditional ecclesiastical English, is interesting. What does Brown imagine? That the heathen, in the absence of the "light and restraints" imposed by their (civilizing?) "Governor," simply slid back into their native moral degeneracy? The logic that undergirds this fiery reading of Romans 1:24–27 is, I suspect, a colonialist logic.

Brown himself does not use the term "heathen" in his paraphrase of this passage, but many other eighteenth- and nineteenth-century commentators do.[111] Consider what befalls our passage when the wicked of 1:18–32 are said, not to be "gentiles" or "pagans," but "heathen," as, for instance, in William Sanday and Arthur Headlam's 1895 commentary on Romans, which contains a notable excursus course, it was Jesus' own extraordinary self-mastery that won him his trophy bride (v. 25b: "Christ loved the church and gave himself up for her [*paredōken heautē hyper autēs*]"). According to a philosophical commonplace of Greco-Roman antiquity, in order to be deemed worthy to govern others, one first had to demonstrate one's ability to govern oneself.[88] Like a virtuous Greco-Roman householder, therefore, the epitome of traditional masculinity, Jesus is eminently well qualified to lord it over his household slaves: "Slaves [*hoi douloi*], obey your earthly masters [*kyriois*] with fear and trembling, in singleness of heart, as you obey Christ; not only while being watched, and in order to please them, but as slaves of Christ [*hōs douloi Christou*], doing the will of God from the heart" (6:5–6). All of which brings us back to Romans 1:26b. As Brooten observes, a homoerotic relationship between two women would run "absolutely counter" to Ephesians 5:21–6:9. "Not only does the envisaged household have no room for a relationship between women, but such love confounds its very structure.... Who would be subordinate to whom?" (*Love Between Women*, pp. 265–66). In other words, who would be the man? Hegemonic hypermasculinity is the only game in town, as far as the author of Ephesians is concerned.[89] But what about the author of Romans?

Mastery—of others, but most especially of oneself—was the supreme index of masculinity in the Greco-Roman intellectual milieu of the mid first century C.E., and had been for quite some time.[90] Against this towering backcloth, it is hard to resist reading the Pauline Jesus' submission unto death as a bravura display of self-mastery, and hence a spectacular performance of on 1:18–32 entitled "St. Paul's Description of the Condition of the Heathen World" (*Critical and Exegetical Commentary on the Epistle to the Romans*, pp. 49–52). When a contemporary British New Testament scholar uses the term "pagan," he or she almost always does so with reference to one of the manifold products of Greco-Roman culture—pagan religions, pagan literature, pagan moralists, and so on—and in order to distinguish it from Jewish or Christian cultural products of the same period. But when an eighteenth- or nineteenth-century British New Testament scholar used the term "heathen," an eighteenth- or nineteenth-century reality was automatically conjured up in addition to an ancient one.[112] The article on "Gentiles, Heathen" from the nineteenth-century revised edition of John masculinity.[91] Yet one is hard-pressed to discover any Pauline scholars who have set foot on this stage.

Stanley Stowers comes closest, making a compelling case for construing Romans as, in part, yet another Greco-Roman discourse on self-mastery. "The theme of self-mastery would have loomed very large for ancient readers of Romans," argues Stowers—and it still loomed large for patristic interpreters of the letter, as he later observes:

> but it is scarcely noticed by modern readers. It has receded deeply into the background for contemporaries because the concept of self-mastery has none of the powerfully loaded social and cultural meaning for us that it did for people in Paul's day. Even apparent similarities between self-mastery and the modern concept of self-discipline mislead because the ancient and modern conceptions of the person and society differ so greatly. The rhetoric of Romans pushes the theme of self-mastery, or the lack of it, into the foreground in three ways. First, Romans tells the story of sin and salvation, problem and solution, punishment and reward at its most basic level as a story of the loss and recovery of self-control. Second, the letter represents the readers as characters in this basic story that concerns self-mastery. Third, Romans relates this story of loss to the story of God's righteous action through Jesus Christ so that Christ becomes an enabler of the restored and disciplined self. (Stowers, *Rereading of Romans*, p. 42)

Brown's 1768 *Dictionary of the Holy Bible* provides an instructive illustration of the ease with which the heathen of old and the contemporary heathen could be conflated. Of the heathen of old we are told:

> For many ages before Christ, these nations were destitute of the true religion, and gave themselves up to the grossest ignorance, or most absurd idolatry, superstition, and horrid crimes. Their most learned men, with all their boasted pretensions to wisdom, were, as well as others, absurd in the main, and complied with, or promoted the absurd customs they found among their countrymen. They were strangers to the covenants of promise—without God and without hope in the world—

And hence an enabler, and indeed a paragon, of masculinity, so that the salvation proffered to the reader of Romans amounts to—what? The attainment of true manhood, this being necessary in order to enter into fellowship with Paul's (hypermasculine) god?

Stowers himself does not draw this conclusion, however. Gender is a peripheral concern in "Readers in Romans and the Meaning of Self-Mastery," the (masterful) chapter of *A Rereading of Romans* in which Stowers substantiates the argument summarized in the above quotation. Yet it is but a short step from Stowers's position to the conclusion that Romans is implicitly about masculinity. Consider a further passage from his chapter, one of the few to deal directly with gender:

> Gender hierarchy lies close to the heart of the discourse on self-mastery. Life is war, and masculinity has to be achieved and constantly fought for. Men are always in danger of succumbing to softness, described as forms of femaleness or servility. In the ancient Mediterranean construction of gender, the sexes are "poles on a continuum which can be traversed." To achieve self-mastery means to win the war; to let the passions and desires go unsubdued means defeat, a destruction of hard-won manliness. (Ibid., p. 45)

All of this we have already seen. But Stowers now makes the crucial link with Romans 1:26–27: "The centrality of this gender defeat explains why leaving assigned gender roles for same sex love serves as the illustration in 1:26–27 of the extent to which gentiles have succumbed to passions and desires"

living in subjection to Satan, and in the most horrid, and often most unnatural lusts, Rom. i .22, 25. (Brown, *Dictionary of the Holy Bible*, p. 461)

And of the eighteenth- and nineteenth-century heathen, we are told: "As the nations were of old destitute of the knowledge and worship of the true God, the word Heathen or Gentile sometimes denotes such as are without the church, are ignorant, atheistical, idolatrous" —and so on down to the concluding encapsulation of the heathen as "all Antichristian nations, whether Papists or not" (ibid.).

But "heathen" was a pregnant term, indeed a strategic term, not only in British ecclesiastical discourse of the period but also in British imperial discourse (to the extent that the two could be disentangled). Reflect-

(pp. 45–46). This would seem to mean that homoerotic relations, specifically between males this time, is, for Paul, emblematic of the loss of masculinity that loss of mastery over the passions always and inevitably entails. And this in turn means that Paul's discourse on *sin* in Romans—Romans, remarkably, containing 48 of the 64 occurrences of the word "sin" (*hamartia*) in the Pauline letters,[92] and sin, for Paul, being, above all, that which masters and enslaves (Rom. 6:16–23)—is simultaneously a discourse on *masculinity*. Which in *its* turn means that Paul's Jesus, as the one who uniquely overcame sin, is implicitly held up as the supreme exemplar of masculinity for Jew and gentile alike—a hypostatized Masculinity, if you will, to which all human beings can now aspire, whether or not they have been blessed with male genitalia. (For one of the more striking features of masculinity in Greco-Roman antiquity is its relative independence of anatomy: females, too, could be paragons of masculinity.)[93] Or to translate back into Stowers's terms:

> The letter establishes the audience's relation to the theme of self-mastery also by making Christ an enabler of the mastery over self that the readers are already depicted as having by virtue of their new lives. The arguments in chapters 5–8 aim to change the readers' understanding of how they have attained mastery over their passions and desires: not through the law but through their identification with Jesus Christ. According to 6:1–7:6, Jesus' death is somehow a cause of the encoded readers' "death to sin," which means that the readers can now be free from enslavement to

ing upon nineteenth-century India, for example, R. S. Sugirtharajah remarks: "As a way of legitimizing European intervention, colonizers were actively involved in producing images which reinscribed the cultural and religious differences between imperialists and imperialized natives. One such image was of the 'Other' as the heathen —the antithesis of all civilized and Christian values" (*Asian Biblical Hermeneutics and Postcolonialism*, p. 46). The term "heathen" in a nineteenth- or early-twentieth-century British commentary on Romans 1:18–32, therefore—the period when the British Empire had succeeded in hauling its bloated bulk up to the dizzying pinnacle from which it was soon to plunge—readily conjured up the stereotypical spectacle of the "unsaved" dark-skinned mass of polytheistic humanity, their passions and desires. Chapter 8 combines this motif of liberation from passions through the Spirit with the themes of freedom from condemnation and a filial relationship with God leading to future reward. (*A Rereading of Romans*, pp. 44–45)

What this edifying paragraph conceals, however—indeed, what Stowers's entire chapter conceals, although only barely: it crouches in the corners—is a rather less edifying reality. *Righteousness in Romans is essentially a masculine trait*; it is, in fact, the very mark of masculinity. What then is *un*righteousness, sin, with its cunning accomplice, "the flesh"? What else but loss of self-mastery, lack of masculinity—in a word, femininity. *Sinfulness, therefore, is essentially a feminine trait in Romans.* Commentators on Romans have occasionally glimpsed this, but failed to acknowledge what they were seeing. In his magisterial *Theology of Paul the Apostle*, for example, James Dunn states: "And in [Rom.] 7:14 Paul's 'I' laments that he is 'fleshly, sold under sin,' like a defeated captive in war, sold into slavery" (p. 112). Like a feminized male, in other words. But that sinfulness should be found to be a feminine state in Paul's thought is scarcely surprising; it is merely the gendered logic of Greco-Roman moral philosophy in Jewish-Christian guise.[94]

Romans implicitly presents Jesus' submission to God as a model for the submission that should characterize the female's proper relationship to the male, as we have seen. Yet Jesus is not allowed to become mired in femininity, to sink into a softness, a flabbiness, from which he might not be able to extricate himself, in which he might lose his own hardness, his own manliness. For his in need of Christ, and in need of civilizing, and hence in need of colonizing.

The amalgamation of the academic, the ecclesiastical, and the imperial is accentuated in the Sanday-Headlam commentary cited earlier (altogether a more polished product than Brown's bilious tracts) by the fact that at least one of its authors happened to be a pillar of the university that was the intellectual jewel in the crown of the British Empire, and that both of them happened to be officers, not just of the academy, but also of the Church that had succeeded spectacularly in making Englishness a global religion.[113] The Right Revd. William Sanday was the Lady Margaret Professor of Divinity and Canon of Christ Church at Oxford University, while the Right Revd. Arthur C. Headlam was a Fellow of All Souls College at the spectacular act of submission is simultaneously a demonstration of self-mastery. The redemption of femininity is accomplished through its transmutation into masculinity,[95] and this transmutation is effected through self-mastery. The passage from sin to righteousness that Romans proclaims, therefore, is not only *christological* through and through: it is also *gendered* through and through. And the story that Romans tells is a saga of soteriological sex change. For the Jesus of Romans is a woman forever in the process of becoming a man. And that is what queer theory has to teach us about Pauline theology.

But it is not only Paul's Christ who now looks considerably queerer than when we first began. For what is true of his Christ is also true of Paul himself. Paul reinvented Jesus of Nazareth, but in so doing Paul also reinvented himself. Paul modeled himself on the Jesus whom he had modeled, mimicked the Jesus whom he had made. "Mimic me, as I mimic Christ [*mimētai mou ginesthe, kathōs kagō Christou*]," he urged his Corinthian congregation (1 Cor. 11:1; cf. 4:16; 1 Thess. 1:6; 2 Thess. 3:7, 9). But this self-engendering performance was also a performance of gender: Paul permitted his Jesus to enter him. "I have been crucified with Christ," he groans in Galatians, "and it is no longer I who live, but it is Christ who lives in me [*en emoi*]. And the life I now live in the flesh I live by faith in the Son of God, who loved me and gave himself for me" (Gal. 2:19–20; cf. Rom. 6:3–6). In this male-male love affair, Jesus is the penetrator, Paul the penetratee. Jesus is active and initiatory (cf. Gal. 1:12), Paul is passive and receptive. In refashioning Jesus of Nazareth, therefore, in constructing this Christ-in-a-closet (the closet lovingly crafted with tools borrowed same institution. Reading Sanday and Headlam on "St. Paul's Description of the Condition of the Heathen World," it is hard to avoid the suspicion that their outraged hero is storming, not just through the streets of Corinth, but also through the streets of Calcutta, fulminating against all heathenish practices, present no less than past, so fully do they seem to share his intense sense of revulsion "at the vices which he found prevailing among the heathen," "given over especially to sins of the flesh" as they were (and are?). Such gods as their "lawless fancies" invented "left them free to follow their own unbridled passions. And the Majesty on High angered at their wilful disloyalty, did not interfere to check their downward career" (*Critical and Exegetical Commentary on the* from the Carpenter himself?), Paul refashions himself, becoming—what? He becomes a man whose identity inheres in his utter submission to another man. As such, he becomes a "man," or a (wo)man, or an unman.[96] The dominant male who has placed Paul in this passive role is, of course, no longer Jesus of Nazareth, the lowborn Galilean peasant (Paul's appetite for humiliation and rough trade—for a rough tradesman?—does have its limits, apparently), but instead the Christ of faith: the ravishing being whom Paul was fated to be with—and be under—from all eternity (Rom. 8:29–30). This heavenly man (cf. 1 Cor. 15:48–49) derives his own identity in turn, however, from his utter submission to a still more dominant male—the most dominant male of all (the one whose testosterone-bloated bulk casts a menacing shadow over the women-loving women of Romans 1:26b)—which is to say (yet again) that Paul's Christ is not all man either, and not only because he is divine, but also because he is supine: read 1 Corinthians 15:24–28. And it is Paul's own abjectly submissive role within this all-male threesome as "slave of Christ" (*Christou doulos*, Gal. 1:10; cf. Rom. 6:16–23) that, more than anything else, now defines his radically reconfigured identity as a Christian. Small wonder that Paul has no need of a woman (1 Cor. 7:7–8; 9:5, 15). Why should he need one when, in terms of the phallobsessive gender logic of his culture (and ours?), he quite simply is one? Other logics are possible, however. More than that, they are necessary.

How (else) might we counter Paul's reading of homoeroticism in Romans 1:26–27? Taking my lead once again from Brooten, I shall concentrate on homoerotic relations between women. "The *Epistle to the Romans*, pp. 49–50). That the Majesty on High might not be an altogether separate, or separable, entity from the Majesty in Buckingham Palace is suggested by even a casual perusal of another instructive Sanday and Headlam excursus, this time on Romans 13:1–7 ("Let every person be subject to the governing authorities . . . ").[114] But let us return to the sins of the flesh, to wallow in them one last time.

In the nineteenth century, no less than in the first, the moral degeneracy of the benighted heathen could be conveniently encapsulated in the most shocking spectacle of all: that of their women sacrilegiously thrusting their hands into the sacred flame to seize the one organ that nature never intended them to have and to penetrate each other with it in the manner of men (not

Greek term for 'intercourse,' *chrēsis*, literally means 'use,'" as she reminds us. "Greek authors from the classical period through late antiquity use both the noun *chrēsis* and the verb *chraomai* ('to use') in a sexual sense. A man 'uses' or 'makes use of' a woman or a boy."[97] He uses them for sexual pleasure, sexual release. But he also uses them to display his social status, as we saw, to demonstrate his "superiority" in relation to their "inferiority." Now let us turn yet again to Romans 1:26b, "Their woman exchanged natural use/intercourse [*metēllaxan tēn physikēn chrēsin*] for unnatural." "'Their women' exchanged the culturally accepted form of men 'using' them for another form of sexual contact," is Brooten's etic paraphrase of this statement (ibid.). She continues:

> As the subject of an active verb, "their women" acted as agents in changing their form of sexual contact. The active verb (*metēllaxan* ["exchanged"]) with a feminine subject (*hai thēleiai* ["the women"]) is striking. The specific terms for sexual intercourse are usually active when they refer to men and passive when they refer to women. Thus, a man penetrates (*perainei*) a woman, while a woman is penetrated (*perainetai*) by a man. Ancient Greek authors also applied an active verb to male animals having intercourse or to male human beings having intercourse with animals. Thus, a male animal or male human being mounts (*ocheuei*) his animal partner, while a female animal or female human being is mounted (*ocheuetai*) by her animal partner. The case is the same for marriage: a man marries (*gamizei*) a woman,

caring that the organ they usurp has been torn from the groins of "real" men, who now lie bleeding all about). When it comes to Romans 1:26, Sanday and Headlam do not disappoint us. "God gave them up to the vilest passions," they write. "Women behaved like monsters who had forgotten their sex" (p. 40). This reading, however, is offered as part of the paraphrastic translation with which their treatment of each section of Romans begins. The verse-by-verse commentary proper on Romans 1:18–32 that follows passes over 1:26 in perfect silence.[115] Compare the memorable scene in E. M. Forster's *Maurice* in which the issue of same-sex love is similarly consigned to the closet by an Oxbridge don. David Halperin's *One Hundred Years of Homosexuality* opens with a rerun of the scene:

while a woman is married (*gamizetai*) by a man....

"To exchange" is, of course, not a verb that means "to have sexual intercourse" or "to marry." Nevertheless, in the context of the widespread cultural view of women as sexually passive, for women actively to "exchange natural intercourse for unnatural" stands out.[98]

Brooten would seem to be suggesting that the practices here condemned by Paul—female homoerotic practices—can be counter-read as active resistance to phallic, patriarchal power, Paul himself inadvertently providing us with the cue through his assignation of active agency to these outlaw women.

Where might one go from here? One could take the tiny opening proffered by the active verb and prise it apart as far as it will go. One way to do so would be to employ Foucault as a lever, but also as a foil. The heroes of the second and third volumes of his *History of Sexuality* are Greek and Roman individuals for whom the sex act was a "technology of the self," part of a voluntary regime of improvised "ethical" practices, which together constituted an "art of existence" (*technē tou biou*) in the service, not just of self-transformation, but of self-invention. Notoriously, however, all these individuals happen to be male, for Foucault, who flatly states:

> [T]his ethics was not addressed to women. ... It was an ethics for men: an ethics thought, written, and taught by men, and addressed to men—to free men obviously. A male ethics, consequently, in which

"Omit: a reference to the unspeakable vice of the Greeks." With those words, uttered in "a flat toneless voice," the Dean of a Cambridge college in the seventh chapter of E. M. Forster's self-suppressed novel, *Maurice* (originally composed in 1913–14 and first released for publication upon the novelist's death in 1970), interrupts a student who has been dutifully translating aloud from the text of an unnamed classical Greek author. (*One Hundred Years of Homosexuality*, p. 1)

Why this particular vice should have required such a vigilant labor of denial and repression, especially among elite males, for whom gender, sexuality, and social status were inextricably intertwined, should by now be apparent.

women figured only as objects or, at most, as partners that one had best train, educate and watch over when one had them under one's power, but stay away from when they were under the power of someone else.⁹⁹

But what the active verb in Romans 1:26b conjures up, albeit in spectral form, is a spectacle undreamed of even (or especially?) by Foucault, that of Greco-Roman *women* actively engaged in "technologies of the self," in radical self-(re)invention, exchanging the culturally prescribed passive role in sexual relations for something else—something altogether unspecified but meriting the (promising) adjective "unnatural" nonetheless (which, in the context, readily admits the etic synonym "countercultural")—and thereby acceding to sexual agency.¹⁰⁰

That such a reading should manage to spring up in the arid wasteland of Romans 1:18–32 is rather remarkable. But is the climate not too harsh for it? Sadly it is. Watch what happens.

Even the fragile autonomy that the active verb *metēllaxan* confers upon these gender renegades is ultimately illusory, according to our passage. For these shockingly unfeminine females are still being shafted by a male. The active verb "exchanged" is overshadowed in our text by a much bigger active verb, whose subject is God, and is forced to submit to it: "Therefore God gave them up [*paredōken*] in the lusts of their heart to impurity, to the degrading of their bodies among themselves. . . . God gave them up [*paredōken*] to degrading passions. Their women exchanged their natural sexual use for unnatural"—all of which can now be paraphrased as follows. Even as these aberrant women lie entwined in each

So who, then, are these women-become-monsters who slither sensuously out of the darker recesses of Sanday's and Headlam's imaginations, causing them to shudder briefly and lapse into troubled silence? They are the selfsame monsters that other prominent representatives of the British ruling class declared to be dark-skinned, Oriental, and altogether un-British in the trial of the two female schoolteachers earlier in the same century, in an attempt to cleanse the land of their loathsome spectral presence and drive them back into the amoral cesspool out of which they had crawled. In short, they are *heathen* monsters. These nineteenth-century heathen, whose moral turpitude is, like that of their first-century counterparts, epitomized by their women-loving women, are other's arms, they are being impaled on God's irresistible purpose, being quietly punished by him—so quietly, so surreptitiously, in fact, that they are entirely unaware of it and slumber on in a stupor, as though drugged. Even though, by their monstrous behavior, they threaten gender binarism, and hence the very foundations of the cosmos itself, threatening to bring the entire natural and cultural order crashing down in ruins, gender is silently reasserting itself even as they sleep. Their activity is being transmuted into passivity, pliancy, penetrability. The Impenetrable Penetrator (that condition being the quintessence of Roman manhood, as we have seen—it is not by accident that we speak of "the impenetrability of God") remains fully in charge, and his superiority and their inferiority are being properly displayed on behalf of all males everywhere—which, for Paul and the hegemonic hypermasculinity for which he is here the mouthpiece, is all that matters ultimately.

practically begging for the locker-room "cure,"[116] so sorely are they in need of Christ, of civilizing, of colonizing. In a word, they are in need of *invasion*, the imperialistic equivalent of "a good fucking"—in this case, one administered in the missionary position. And that is precisely what they get.

It is time we explored this locker room more thoroughly, however. What if some of its lockers actually turned out to be closets?

## The Locker Room

Paul need not have the last word. The trick will be to reason according to rules not laid down by him or his culture. My queerying of Paul and his Christ has, up to now, played into Paul's hands. I was merely waltzing with him to his own whistled tune, and whether he happened to be wearing the evening gown or the tuxedo made little difference in the end. In characterizing the submissive Christ or the submissive Paul, the "penetrated" Christ or the "penetrated" Paul, as "feminine" or "feminized" I was reading into Paul's pregnant silences and attempting to complete his unfinished sentences for him. But my calculations were based on the Greco-Roman gender equations: active = masculine, passive = feminine. I was factoring Jesus and Paul into these equations and duly jotting down the results. The equations are hardly axiomatic, however, to put it mildly. Numerous feminist scholars have deconstructed them and the concepts of appropriate gender behavior enshrined in them. What might queer theory (or the critical sensibility for which this term is a cipher) contribute to such critiques?

We might begin by asking what logic dictates that a submissive male be characterized as "feminine" or "feminized" in the first place. To so characterize the submissive male is to code the erotic exchange in terms that are ineluctably "hetero." It is to supply the "missing" female in the exchange by dressing one of the partners in conceptual drag and declaring him to be the woman. But the bottom line is that there *are* no females in the inner sanctum of Pauline theology. There are only males acting upon other males: God, Jesus, Paul. Now, this male sanctum is a locker room, as it happens. And most of the action takes place in the showers. "The Lord is enveloped in clouds," declares the Psalmist (97:2). Here the clouds are of steam. And the symbolic action dimly glimpsed through them is inflexibly hierarchical. Jesus submits himself obediently to God's excruciating demands. Paul submits himself to Jesus in turn, opens himself utterly to Jesus, is entered and possessed by Jesus. And throughout this steamy scene, there is not a single female face in sight, not to mention a female orifice. Richard Rambuss rightly cautions in his *Closet Devotions* "that we avoid peremptorily re-encoding every representation of the penetrable male body as feminized *because* penetrated. Are male bodies without their own orifices?"[117]

The defensive clenching of male orifices is the most characteristic gesture of Greco-Roman discourses on sex. Within the constrictive bounds of these discourses, a "man" is, by definition, an impenetrable penetrator, as we have seen, a body whose exits must never be used as entrances. To translate into contemporary queer idiom, the Greco-Roman man can only ever be a "top" and must never be a "bottom." He is an assless cock, a bottomless top, a top who does not have a bottom of his own.[118] Greco-Roman discourses on sex conjure up a sex-gender system in which every sexual act *must* involve a masculine and a feminine partner—to the extent that when an anatomically female partner is lacking, an anatomically male partner must be conscripted to play the woman. Within the terms of this system, therefore, sex can only ever be a masculine-feminine activity: sex can only ever be heterosex. Greco-Roman discourses on sex thus enshrine a hyperheteronormativity—and centuries "before" heterosexuality.

But there is more. Within the cramped confines of this phallofixated system, sexual acts even between persons of the same sex automatically become displaced expressions of gender hierarchy. Sex becomes a mechanism for producing and maintaining gender hierarchy—one with an inbuilt safety device to ensure that the mechanism cannot be used for any other purpose. For whether the sexual partners happen to be a man and a woman, or a man and a "woman" (in the case of two males), or a "man" and a woman (in the case of two females), the superiority of the man and the inferiority of the woman is symbolically affirmed—endlessly reaffirmed—in and through the act of penetration. This symbolic reiteration of gender hegemony was the quintessence of sex for Greek and Roman male elites, rendering the concept of nonpenetrative "lesbian" sex literally unthinkable (the phallus is the switch that activates the mechanism; without it no sex is possible). Greco-Roman heteronormativity thus turns homosex—even homosex between women—into an expression of misogyny.

In this essay I have been arguing that Paul, too, inhabited this conceptual enclosure (which more and more has come to resemble a factory floor), and that his "theological system" (to the extent that he can be said to have had *one*), traditionally thought to be encapsulated in his letter to the Romans, was not only *infected* by this sex-gender system but partly *produced* by it.

Any changes introduced into the sex-gender system, therefore, would have immediate repercussions for the theological system. What sorts of changes? First and most obviously, perhaps, the abandonment of fixed sexual roles of domination and submission, conceptually correlated with the performance of masculinity and femininity respectively, for fluid sexual roles of "domination" and "submission," neither being automatically correlated with either gender. This would be a relatively minor adjustment. It would loosen the symbolic screws of a cast-iron concept of gender hierarchy, although without actually dismantling it.

Yet a reversal even on this modest scale would have massive repercussions for Pauline theology, given Paul's passionate conviction (classically expressed in Romans 1:18–32, as we have seen) that proper relations between human beings, even—or especially—sexual relations, necessarily mirror proper relations between human beings and God. Any expansion of the domain of the permissible in human sexual relations would, therefore, result in a corresponding transformation of human-divine relations. What transformed relations might we then envision between the three central characters in Paul's epochal passion play—between God and Jesus, Jesus and Paul, God and Paul? What else but those in which Paul would not only open himself utterly to Jesus, but Jesus, reciprocally, would open himself utterly to Paul. Most significantly of all, however, God would open himself to each of them in turn. The Bottomless Top, the conceptual pivot of Paul's entire theosexual system, would become a top with a bottom. God would get a bottom of his own.

And what might he not be ready for then? Sexual activity that would offer only the most precarious of toeholds to hierarchy, and thus would constitute a divine warrant for radically egalitarian forms of social behavior? Nonphallic sexual activity, even? The trick would be to take that which is farthest outside the camp in Romans, that which is most anathemized—sex between women, as we have seen—and usher it into the center, into the tabernacle itself, thereby causing the models of divine-human relations, male-female relations, and even human-animal relations currently displayed in Romans to reform themselves radically in relation to it. This essay is offered as a prolegomenon to such a project.

## 4  REVOLTING REVELATIONS

This essay was originally commissioned for a collection entitled *The Personal Voice in Biblical Interpretation*.[1] Where I come from, however, the third word of this title could only be pronounced as "vice" (just as the first word could only be pronounced as *Da*; hence, *Da Personal Vice . . .* ).[2] But it is not the personal vice in biblical interpretation that I wish to ponder here, nor even my own personal vice (although I shall hardly be able to resist the temptation), so much as that of the only New Testament narrator to employ the personal voice throughout his narrative. I speak of the narrator of Revelation, whose unblinking "I" first transfixes us in 1:9—"I, John, your brother who shares with you in Jesus the persecution and the kingdom and the patient endurance, was on the island called Patmos . . . "—not releasing its hypnotic hold on us until we pass 22:8: "I, John, am the one who heard and saw these things."

In any case, there is by now relatively little of my own vices and vicissitudes left to reveal. Buried in books that, if my royalty checks are anything to go by, are seldom exhumed and opened up, my published secrets are slowly decomposing, thin nourishment for the occasional prurient bookworm. For these secrets are a sadly unsensational lot. Still, had your own life been so desperately dreary during the past decade or so as to cause you to dig out and devour my every published word, you would have read, with ever-mounting ennui, of:

1. My roots in the soggy soil of rural Ireland. My father was a butcher; you'd be weary of hearing that.³ Later on, he became a farmer; you might also have caught that. But you wouldn't yet know that my mother was a hairdresser. That she was, however, is the real subject of the present book.
2. My LSD-induced psychosis in the summer of 1974 (well, DMT actually; is there anybody else out there who still remembers what that was?), which led, simultaneously, to
3. My conversion to Christianity, and
4. My incarceration in St. Joseph's Mental Hospital, Limerick.
5. My subsequent incarceration (voluntary, this time) in Mount Melleray Cistercian Abbey, County Waterford (I've gone on about that even in the present book).
6. My current. . . . Sorry, it's caught in my throat. I probably shouldn't have confessed it in the first place. And now it's out there, observing the progress of my career with malevolent interest, cleaning its weapons compulsively as it plans its next move. (I should have taken a leaf from John's book: "And when the seven thunders had sounded, I was about to write, but I heard a voice from heaven saying, 'Seal up what the seven thunders have said, and do not write it down'" [Rev. 10:4].)

Anyway, that's six. Now, let's see, I need a seventh if I'm to keep up with John and his amazing four-legged friend ("When the Lamb opened the seventh seal, there was silence in heaven for about half an hour" [Rev. 8:1]).⁴ Well, there is one other thing, actually:

7. My relationships with other men, one ten-year affair in particular, which began in the spring of 1972, and persisted even through my period in the monastery (we entered the novitiate together). Unlike my first six revelations, I haven't written about this one before. The other party has, however; see Anon., "The Boys," unpublished MS concealed in the bottom drawer of the gray file cabinet in my office, beneath my (likewise unpublished) doctoral dissertation,⁵ which apparently favors the missionary position

(as befits a thesis whose main title is "Narrative Homiletics"). Recently, this improbable couple conceived and gave birth to *God's Gym: Divine Male Bodies of the Bible*, which ends with a preliminary exploration of the book of Revelation.

And it is to Revelation that I wish to return here. For my essay title is not intended to be a reference to my own revelations, insufficiently revolting as they are, as I had started to say, so much as those of this exquisitely bizarre book—the book of Revelations, as it is most often called. Even among Bible-reading Christians, surprisingly few refer to the book by its actual (short) title, "Revelation,"[6] much preferring the plural, "Revelations." The latter has a titillating ring to it, I suppose, that the more theological "Revelation" cannot match. "Revelations" doesn't conjure up the tablets of the law so much as the law of the tabloids. And what is the law of the tabloids—the tabloid press, and now tabloid TV, epitomized by the talk show? It is simply that secrets sell. Revelations is the grand dénouement of the biggest bestseller of all time. So whose sordid secrets is it supposed to be peddling? God's or merely John's? Let us see.

∼

"So what is Revelation actually about?" I ask myself.

"Easy," the answer comes back. "It's about the establishment of God's kingdom on earth."

"God's 'kingdom,' eh? Not his dukedom or his fiefdom, then? And 'on Earth.' As opposed to Mars, say, or Uranus?"

"My *what*?"

"No need for alarm. I'm merely marveling at your propensity to shroud your theological thought in archaic political and cosmological metaphors."

"Oh, the shroud isn't mine, I borrowed it from John."

"You look so comfortable in it. So just how is the kingdom of God to be established on earth, according to John?"

"How are kingdoms or empires ever established?"

"Through military conquest, no doubt."

"Well, there you have it."

"You mean Revelation is all about war?"

## War Book, I

> . . . assemble them for
> battle . . .
>
> —REVELATION 16:14

"Yes, messianic war. Richard Bauckham is excellent on this. Now, if I can only find his discussion of it. . . . Ah yes, here we are:

> The prominence of Davidic messianism in Revelation can be gauged from Jesus' self-designation, 'I am the root and the descendant of David, the bright morning star' (22:16). The first of these two titles comes from Isaiah 11:10 ('the root of Jesse') and is used of the Davidic Messiah. . . . The second refers to the star of Numbers 24:17, which (in the context of 24:17–19) was commonly understood to be a symbol of the Messiah of David who would conquer the enemies of Israel. 'The root of David' is found also in Revelation 5:5, alongside another title evoking the image of the royal Messiah who will defeat the nations by military violence: 'the Lion of Judah' (cf. Gen. 49:9; 4 Ezra 12:31–32).

## War Book, II

> All changed, changed utterly:
> A terrible beauty is born.
>
> —W. B. YEATS, "Easter 1916"

Revelation *is* a book of war, a book of warriors, but not an especially vivid one, at least to my mind. My own internal standard for an ancient war book is the *Táin Bó Cuailnge* (The Cattle Raid of Cooley), the oldest vernacular epic in Western literature, ancient Ireland's answer to the *Iliad*.[42] Between the ages of seven and twelve (numbers to which John accords sublime significance), I had but a single teacher in the tiny school that I attended in the village of Adare in County Limerick, and he happened to be an ardent nationalist. Ancient Irish mythology consequently took precedence over biblical mythology in my early formation, even though the school was run by a religious order. The *Táin*, in particular, made an indelible impression upon my fledgling imagination years before I even knew that John's war book existed.

Every page of the *Táin* is a paean to war. Even its accounts of warriors mentally preparing themselves for battle are marked by an exuberance and excess that I have yet to encounter in any other ancient literature. Judge for yourself. In the following excerpt, the hero of the *Táin*, Cúchulainn,[43] prepares to take on an entire army single-handedly:

Further allusions to the Messiah of Isaiah 11, a favourite passage for Davidic messianism, are the sword that comes from Christ's mouth (1:16: 2:12, 16; 19:21) with which he strikes down the nations (19:15; cf. Isa. 11:4; 49:2) and the statement that he judges with righteousness (19:11; cf. Isa. 11:4)."[7]

"Stirring stuff. But does all this mayhem have a purpose—other than the establishment of 'God's kingdom,' that is (a phrase which, as you know, never fails to send a shiver down my spine)? What if its real purpose were to engender masculinity, to make men? War making men making war making men...."

"Ah, so we're to obsess about deessentialized manhood again, are we? The lament of the matchstick man. Or is it the gender construct blues? Muddy Waters had it all wrong, no doubt. Instead of bellowing 'I'm a man!' he should have sobbed 'I'm a subject whose gender identity is purely performative, the product of a compulsory set of rituals and conventions, which conspire to engender retroactively the illusion that

The first warp-spasm seized Cúchulainn, and made him into a monstrous thing, hideous and shapeless, unheard of. His shanks and his joints, every knuckle and angle and organ from head to foot, shook like a tree in the flood or a reed in the stream. His body made a furious twist inside his skin, so that his feet and shins and knees switched to the rear and his heels and calves switched to the front. The balled sinews of his calves switched to the front of his shins, each big knot the size of a warrior's bunched fist. On his head the temple-sinews stretched to the nape of his neck, each mighty, immense, measureless knob as big as the head of a month-old child. His face and features became a red bowl: he sucked one eye so deep into his head that a wild crane couldn't probe it onto his cheek out of the depths of his skull; the other eye fell out along his cheek. His mouth weirdly distorted: his cheek peeled back from his jaws until the gullet appeared, his lungs and liver flapped in his mouth and throat, his lower jaw struck the upper a lion-killing blow, and fiery flakes large as a ram's fleece reached his mouth from his throat. His heart boomed loud in his breast like the baying of a watch-my masculinity is natural and innate, merely "expressed" by the actions, gestures, and speech that in fact produce it—'"[8]

"Sorry to interrupt your own performance, but I'd like to share the following snippet with you in exchange for the Bauckham: 'Until recently, critical discussion of violence, warfare, and the sacred in the Hebrew Bible has failed to consider the constitutive role of gender categories for these texts. This, I think, is remarkable, for what could be more acutely gendered than war, an activity historically described as performed by men only, in a space containing nothing but men?' That's Harold Washington, by the way, paraphrasing Miriam Cooke.[9] Now, given that it's the *Davidic* Messiah we've been discussing, let me cut to another essay, 'David the Man' by David Clines."

"The 'man' of the title isn't Clines himself, then?"

"No, or at least not entirely. He notes: 'The essential male characteristic in the David story is to be a warrior, a man of war . . . or a mighty man of valour. . . . It is essential for a man in the David story that he be strong—which means to say, dog at its feed or the sound of a lion among bears. Malignant mists and spurts of fire—the torches of the Badb[44]—flickered red in the vaporous clouds that rose boiling above his head, so fierce was his fury. The hair of his head twisted like the tangle of a red thornbush stuck in a gap; if a royal apple tree with all its kingly fruit were shaken above him, scarce an apple would reach the ground but each would be spiked on a bristle of his hair as it stood up on his scalp with rage. The hero-halo rose out of his brow, long and broad as a warrior's whetstone, long as a snout, and he went mad rattling his shields, urging on his charioteer and harassing the hosts. Then, tall and thick, steady and strong, high as the mast of a noble ship, rose up from the dead centre of his skull a straight spout of black blood darkly and magically smoking like the smoke from a royal hostel when the king is coming to be cared for at the close of a winter day.[45]

When that spasm had run through the high hero Cúchulainn he stepped into his sickle war-chariot that bristled with points of iron and narrow blades, with hooks and hard prongs and heroic frontal spikes, with ripping capable of violence against other men and active in killing other men.' Later he adds:

> Or, to take another example, from a little outside the David story itself, in 1 Sam. 4.9 the Philistines say to one another, having learned that the ark of Yahweh has come into their camp: 'Take courage (lit. be strong), and acquit yourselves like men, O Philistines, lest you become slaves to the Hebrews as they have been to you; acquit yourselves like men and fight.' This phrase 'acquit yourselves like men,' literally 'become men' . . . , means, very simply, that to be a man is to fight. The whole ideology surrounding this utterance is a little more complex than that, no doubt; for the purpose of fighting is to resist slavery for oneself and to continue to keep others in slavery. . . . But as far as the gender issue is concerned, it is simple: men fight."[10]

"Enough! My testosterone level is shooting off the scale. I vow never again to wear my wife's dressing gown to breakfast. But how does it all connect with the Davidic Messiah?"

instruments and tearing nails on its shafts and straps and loops and cords. The body of the chariot was spare and slight and erect, fitted for the feats of a champion, with space for a lordly warrior's eight weapons, speedy as the wind or as a swallow or a deer darting over the level plain. The chariot was settled down on two fast steeds, wild and wicked, neat-headed and narrow bodied, with slender quarters and roan breast, firm in hoof and harness—a notable sight in the trim chariot-shafts. One horse was lithe and swift-leaping, high-arched and powerful, long-bodied and with great hooves. The other flowing-maned and shining, slight and slender in hoof and heel.

In that style, then, he drove out to find his enemies and did his thunder-feat and killed a hundred, then two hundred, then three hundred, then four hundred, then five hundred, where he stopped—he didn't think it too many to kill in that first attack, his first full battle with the provinces of Ireland. Then he circled the outer lines of the four great provinces of Ireland in his chariot and he attacked them in hatred. He had the chariot driven so heavily that its iron wheels sank in the earth. So deeply the chariot-

"Don't pretend you don't see it. The Davidic Messiah, as the ultimate warrior, would also have been the ultimate icon of masculinity."

"A male fantasy of phallic proportions?"

"Funny you should mention the phallus—"

"Well, I *was* missing it, rather. You usually insist on beating me over the head with it."

"Hmmm, now there's a tantalizing thought."

"Not quite what I had in mind, however. You were saying?"

"You've made me forget. Oh, yes. I was reminded that Bauckham himself makes a rather phallic point about John's preoccupation with Psalm 2. Hang on a minute.... Yes, here it is: 'One of John's key Old Testament texts, allusions to which run throughout Revelation, is Psalm 2, which depicts "the nations" and "the kings of the earth" conspiring to rebel against "the LORD and his Messiah" (verses 1-2).... God promises to give this royal Messiah the nations for his inheritance (verse 8) and that he will violently subdue them with a rod of iron (verse 9). Allusions to this account of the Messiah's victory over the wheels sank in the earth that clods and boulders were torn up, with rocks and flagstones and the gravel of the ground, in a dyke as high as the iron wheels, enough for a fortress-wall. He threw up this circle of the Badb round about the four great provinces of Ireland to stop them fleeing and scattering from him, and corner them where he could wreak vengeance for the boy-troop.[46] He went into the middle of them and beyond, and mowed down great ramparts of his enemies' corpses, circling completely around the armies three times, attacking them in hatred. They fell sole to sole and neck to headless neck, so dense was that destruction. He circled them three times more in the same way, and left a bed of them six deep in a great circuit, the soles of three to the necks of three in a ring around the camp. This slaughter on the Táin was given the name Seisrech Bresligi, the Sixfold Slaughter. It is one of the three uncountable slaughters on the Táin: Seisrech Bresligi, Imslige Glennamnach—the mutual slaughter at Glenn Domain—and the Great Battle at Gáirech and Irgáirech (though this time it was horses and dogs as well as men). Any count or estimate of the number of the rabble who fell nations are found in Revelation 2:18, 26–8; 11:15, 18; 12:5, 10; 14:1; 16:14, 16; 19:15. . . .'"[11]

"And your own point is what, precisely?"

"Oh, come on! Rod of iron?"

"Well, you know what Freud said, 'Sometimes a rod of iron is just a rod of iron.'"

"Freud aside, I submit that what John is really saying is that the Messiah, when he comes, will fuck the nations into submission."

"You have such an exquisitely delicate way of putting things. Any nation in particular, though?"

"I think we both know the answer to that. 'Babylon the great, mother of whores and of earth's abominations.'[12] Which brings me back to Harold Washington: 'The language of war in the Hebrew Bible and other ancient Near Eastern literatures is acutely masculinist. Warfare is emblematically male and the discourse of violence is closely imbricated with that of masculine sexuality. . . .'[13] He goes on to quote Harry Hoffner: 'The masculinity of the ancient was measured by two criteria: (1) his prowess in battle, and (2) his ability to sire children. . . . These two aspects of masculinity

there is unknown, and unknowable. Only the chiefs have been counted. . . . In this great carnage on Murtheimne Plain Cúchulainn slew one hundred and thirty kings, as well as an uncountable horde of dogs and horses, women and boys and children and rabble of all kinds.[47] Not one man in three escaped without his thighbone or his head or his eye being smashed, or without some blemish for the rest of his life. And when the battle was over Cúchulainn was left without a scratch or a stain on himself, his charioteer or either of his horses.[48]

I must confess to finding John's parallel account of Jesus battling the beast, "the kings of the earth," and their armies single-handedly (for although he commands an army, apparently he doesn't need one) a tad insipid by comparison:

Then I saw the beast and the kings of the earth with their armies gathered to make war against the rider on the horse and against his army. And the beast was captured, and with it the false prophet who had performed in its presence the signs by which he deceived those who had received the mark of the beast and those who worshiped its image. These two were thrown alive into were frequently associated with each other. . . . Those symbols which primarily referred to his military exploits often served to remind him of his sexual ability as well. . . .'[14] Here I'm reminded of an instructive scene in the movie *Full Metal Jacket*. You know the scene I mean? The marine recruits are required to clutch their M16s firmly in one hand and their crotches just as firmly in the other, all the while chanting, 'This is my rifle, and this is my gun. This is for fighting; this is for fun!'"

"You can let go of your own crotch now. I wouldn't want you to injure yourself."

"Sorry, I got a little carried away. Washington also notes:

> The male is by definition the subject of warfare's violence and the female its victim. For example, the language of the siege instructions of Deut. 20.10–20 is densely supplied with syntactical groups joining a masculine singular verbal subject with a city as (feminine) object of attack. . . . Given a linguistic milieu where cities are so often portrayed in the figure of a woman—either mother (Isa. 66.8-13), queen

the lake of fire that burns with sulfur. And the rest were killed by the sword of the rider on the horse, the sword that came from his mouth; and all the birds of the air were gorged with their flesh. (Rev. 19:19–21; cf. 20:7–10)

Whereas the *Táin* is a garish celebration of war, Revelation is a muted celebration of war. Superimposed upon Revelation, the *Táin* colors in its blanks with lurid hues. Revelation is a war scroll.[49] But the *Táin* is what this war scroll would look like fully unfurled.

(Fearful of exposure, Revelation resorts to threats: "I warn everyone who hears the words of the prophecy of this book: if anyone adds to them, God will add to that person the plagues described in this book . . . " [22:18]. The *Táin*, for its part, feeling its colors bleed into Revelation, ends on an equally nervous note: "A blessing on everyone who will memorise the Táin faithfully in this form, and not put any other form on it.")[50]

As will by now be readily apparent, perhaps, my own attitude towards violence is somewhat ambivalent. There is probably little of which the God of Revelation is guilty of which I myself would not also be capable, given certain extreme environmental stimuli—and a dash of omnipotence, needless to say. Which is why I fear this God as much as I do and resist him for all I am worth.

And yet, despite my better judgment,

(Isa. 62.3), or virgin daughter (Isa. 37.22), a woman married (Isa. 62.5), widowed (Isa. 47.8, 9; 54.4; Lam. 1.1), or raped (Jer. 6.1–8; 13.22; Isa. 47.1–4; Nah. 3.5–6)—the concentration of feminine forms in Deut. 20.10–20 inescapably evokes the figuration of the city as an assaulted woman. In issuing the command to draw near to a city 'in order to attack it,' this text effectively enjoins the soldiers 'to attack her' [20.10]. . . . The description of the submissive city 'opening' to the warrior [20.11] . . . evokes an image of male penetration. Similarly, the law uses [the same verb] to describe the military seizure of a city [20.19] . . . [as] for the forcible seizure of a woman in sexual assault [22.28]."[15]

"And all of this is relevant to Revelation, I take it?"

"Quite possibly. Compare, for instance, Tina Pippin's reading of Babylon in Revelation as a sexually assaulted woman. Her prooftext, as you may recall, is Revelation 17:16, 'they will make her desolate and naked; they will devour her flesh and burn her up with fire.'"[16]

I love Revelation for its beauty. Its intricate lacework of lurid images has never failed to thrill me. Of course, my impression that Revelation is an exquisite work of language is willful illusion on my part. The English translations in which I ordinarily read it are cosmetic coverings concealing from view all of Revelation's unsightly grammatical blemishes, its "barbarous idioms," as Dionysius of Alexandria dubbed them long ago (Eusebius, *Ecclesiastical History* 7.25.26–27). The translators take John's broken Greek and beautify it (as did numerous copyists before them), excising all its startling irregularities, a nip here, a tuck there. I know enough Greek to spot John's stunning solecisms, but not quite enough to *hear* them. I wish I could hear John's exotic Aramaic (?) intonations, listen as he fumbles in the warm Aegean night for the correct grammatical boxes in which to lock his glittering visions, occasionally picking up the wrong one in the deep, velvety darkness, as so many scholars have imagined him doing—although other scholars have argued that John is wearing night-vision goggles instead and verbalizing his visions with painstaking precision, freely opting, for whatever reason, not to express himself in standard Greek.[51]

Revelation seduces me no matter how much I resist it. There is another kind of resistance that I wish to bring into the discussion, however, and also

"I also recall that the perpetrators of these dire deeds are the 'ten horns,' together with the beast, not Christ, your phallic warrior."

"Admittedly, but ultimately it's the Commander-in-Chief, the one seated on the throne, who is responsible for Babylon's rape: 'For God has put it into their hearts to carry out his purpose . . .' (17:17)."

"I'm nervous that you'll have him leaping naked from his throne next to join in the action, so let's move on. So far you've been talking as though John's Jesus were a one-man army—"

"Or a one-*lamb* army, at least."

"—but he doesn't wage war alone; instead he leads an army against the enemies of God. Here's Bauckham again:

> Also derived from this militant messianism is Revelation's key concept of conquering. It is applied both to the Messiah himself (3:21; 5:5; 17:14) and to his people, who share his victory (2:7, 11, 17, 28; 3:5, 12, 21; 12:11; 15:2; 21:7). Once again we note the importance in Revelation of the Messiah's army. That the image of conquering is a

another kind of seduction. On the annual school excursion from Adare to Dublin, our Ireland-for-the-Irish schoolmaster would lead us in solemn procession around the cavernous interior of the General Post Office,[52] where the Irish rebels set up their headquarters during the armed revolt of 1916 against British colonial rule. He would deliver a hushed but heated soliloquy by the statue of Cúchulainn enshrined in the building on April 21, 1935, to commemorate the uprising, a speech sodden with intoxicating excerpts from the Proclamation of Irish Independence. The act that ignited the 1916 conflict was the public reading of this Proclamation from the steps of the building. We were obliged to memorize the Proclamation at school, in common with most Irish schoolchildren of that era. As though fearful that the Irish public had forgotten the symbolism of the Cúchulainn statue, the authorities recently had it framed with a lengthy quotation from the Proclamation:

> We declare the right of the people of Ireland to the ownership of Ireland, and to the unfettered control of Irish destinies, to be sovereign and indefeasible. The long usurpation of that right by a foreign people and government has not extinguished the right, nor can it ever be extinguished except by the destruction of the

militaristic one should be unmistakable, although interpreters of Revelation do not always do justice to this. It is closely connected with language of battle (11:7; 12:7-8, 17; 13:7; 16:14; 17:14; 19:11, 19), and it is notable that not only do Christ's followers defeat the beast (15:2), but also the beast defeats them (11:7; 13:7), so that this is evidently a war in which Christ's enemies have their victories, though the final victory is his. We should note also that the language of conquering is used of all the three stages of Christ's work: he conquered in his death and resurrection (3:21; 5:5), his followers conquer in the time before the end (12:11; 15:2), and he will conquer at the Parousia (17:14). Thus it is clear that the image of the messianic war describes the whole process of the establishment of God's kingdom as Revelation depicts it—"[17]

"Permit me to interrupt. May I hazard a précis of the plot thus far?"

"The plot? I was unaware that there was one."

Irish people. In every generation the Irish people have asserted their right to national freedom and sovereignty; six times during the past three hundred years they have asserted it in arms. Standing on that fundamental right and again asserting it in arms in the face of the world, we hereby proclaim the Irish Republic as a sovereign independent state, and we pledge our lives and the lives of our comrades-in-arms to the cause of its freedom, of its welfare, and of its exaltation among the nations.

The Cúchulainn statue represents a calculated combination of vulnerability and indomitability. Too weak to stand through loss of blood, the hero has strapped himself to a stone pillar, sword still gripped in his now lifeless hand, defiant to the end and beyond, even in the face of unimaginable odds. A raven has settled on his shoulder, a signal to the armies assembled around him that it is now safe to approach him.

But whence this fatal loss of blood, you might well ask, given that Cúchulainn earlier took on these same armies single-handedly without incurring a single scratch? Well, the blood loss was inflicted by Cúchulainn's "adored fosterbrother" Ferdia, "the horn-skinned warrior from Irrus Domnann," "the burden unbearable and the rock fatal in the

"Here goes. Revelation can plausibly be said to be about the establishment of God's kingdom on earth. How is this kingdom to be established? Through the messianic war. And what is the messianic war? An activity that, on the symbolic level, is conducted exclusively by male subjects (note the notorious 14:4),[18] and is constitutive of the masculinity of those subjects, since it is ultimately directed against the feminine (note, again, the no less infamous 17:3–6)."[19]

"Stunning. But there's one small matter you've overlooked. This is an army that does not kill; on the contrary, it allows itself to be killed."

"How noble. Your friend Bauckham, too, makes much of the fact that—let me see—'just as 5:5–6 depicts Jesus Christ as the Messiah who has won a victory, but has done so by sacrificial death, not by military might, so 7:4–14 depicts his followers as the people of the Messiah who share in his victory, but do so similarly, by sacrificial death rather than by military violence.'[20] Well, what else should we expect John to say? A military campaign against 'the enemies of God' is hardly a fray," who had been shamed into challenging Cúchulainn to single combat.[53] Ferdia emerged the loser, eventually finding himself at the wrong end of the *gae bolga*, the belly-barb, Cúchulainn's ultimate weapon, which, cast from the fork of his foot across the waters of the ford in which they were fighting, sliced through Ferdia's "deep and sturdy apron of twice-smelted iron, and shattered in three parts the stout strong stone the size of a millstone," which he had earlier stuffed inside the apron for good measure, "for fear and dread of the *gae bolga*," "and went coursing through the highways and byways of his body so that every single joint filled with barbs."[54] Thereupon the taciturn Ferdia is moved to remark, "That is enough now; I'll die of that," Cúchulainn's javelin, which he has already thrust through Ferdia's heart so that "half its length showed out through his back," having failed to impress Ferdia sufficiently.[55] But Ferdia got his licks in too. At the height of the contest, which raged for four days, the heroes were "piercing and drilling each other" with their "big burdensome stabbing-spears" (the *Táin*, too, is not without its queer conceits), and a bewildering assortment of other heavy weaponry. "If even birds in flight could pass through men's bodies they could have passed through those bodies that day and brought bits of blood and meat with them out into the thickening air through the wounds viable option for Christians at the time in which he is writing. That will have to await the Parousia, he supposes, when Christians will have Christ, as invincible Divine Warrior— King of Kings and Warlord of Warlords—present in person to lead them forth into battle. (As you may have surmised, I understand the 'armies of heaven' in 19:14—'And the armies of heaven, arrayed in fine linen ... followed him on white horses'—to be the Christian elect,[21] especially in light of 17:14, which tells us that those who stand with the Lamb in the final battle 'are called and chosen and faithful.') What hasn't even occurred to John, of course, is the possibility that Christians might be in a position to triumph over their enemies—not symbolically, through sacrificial martyrdom, but literally, through military might— long before the Divine Warrior gets here. And if the slaughter of the 'ungodly' should be permissible at the Parousia, then why not before? (Whether or not Jesus is *literally* whacking off heads with his sword in 19:21 is a moot point, it seems to me, given the subsequent fate of the owners of those heads: eternal

and gashes," insists the narrator.[56] And that was only the third day; the fourth was even worse.

Limerickman Frank McCourt, in his autobiographical Pulitzer Prize–winning novel *Angela's Ashes*, describes his first encounter with the dead hero Cúchulainn. Frank's penniless ne'er-do-well émigré father ("He fought with the Old IRA and for some desperate act he wound up as a fugitive with a price on his head")[57] has brought four-year-old Frank, his mother, and his brothers back from New York to Dublin, en route to Limerick, in the late 1930s. Now the family are being driven across Dublin to the train station:

> Dad asks the driver if he'd mind going by way of the G.P.O. and the driver says, Is it a stamp you want or what? No, says Dad. I hear they put up a new statue of Cuchulain to honor the men who died in 1916 and I'd like to show it to my son here who has great admiration for Cuchulain.
>
> The driver says he has no notion of who this Cuchulain was but he wouldn't mind stopping one bit. He might come in himself and see what the commotion is all about for he hasn't been in the G.P.O. since he was a boy and the English nearly wrecked it with their big guns firing up from the Liffey River. He says you'll see

death, or worse, in the lake of fire that burns with sulphur. The latter spectacle is elaborated in 14:9–11: 'Those who worship the beast and its image, and receive a mark on their foreheads or on their hands, they will also drink the wine of God's wrath, poured unmixed into the cup of his anger, and they will be tortured [*basanisthēsetai*] with fire and sulphur in the presence of the holy angels and in the presence of the Lamb. And the smoke of their torment goes up forever and ever.')[22] The Crusades, the Inquisition, and even the Holocaust itself (the smoke rising day and night from the ovens of Auschwitz and Belsen) are but some of the more notable manifestations of the militarism that animates Revelation. Indeed, any one of these campaigns might have claimed a warrant for its genocidal fantasies in the sinister logic of this most dangerous of biblical books."

"Sorry to disappoint you, but the title 'Most Dangerous Biblical Book' has already been awarded to the Gospel According to Luke."

"By Jane Schaberg, you mean?[23] Well, Luke *is* more subtle, and to that extent more

the bullet holes all over the front and they should be left there to remind the Irish of English perfidy. I ask the man what's perfidy and he says ask your father and I would but we're stopping outside a big building with columns and that's the G.P.O.

Mam stays in the motor car while we follow the driver into the G.P.O. There he is, he says, there's your man Cuchulain.

And I feel tears coming because I'm looking at him at last, Cuchulain, there on his pedestal in the G.P.O. He's golden and he has long hair, his head is hanging and there's a big bird perched on his shoulder.

The driver says, Now what in God's name is this all about? What's this fellow doin' with the long hair and the bird on his shoulder? And will you kindly tell me, mister, what this has to do with the men of 1916?

Dad says, Cuchulain fought to the end like the men of Easter Week. His enemies were afraid to go near him till they were sure he was dead and when the bird landed on him and drank his blood they knew.

Well, says the driver, 'tis a sad day for the men of Ireland when they need a bird to tell them a man is dead. I think we better go deadly, but when all is said and done he doesn't have as many notches on his gun. Even Bauckham concedes that the body count in Revelation is astronomical:

> So the series of judgments affecting a quarter of the earth (6:8) and the series affecting a third of the earth (8:7–12; 9:15, 18) are not, as we might expect, followed by a series affecting half the earth. . . . But there is now to be only the final judgment, the seventh trumpet (10:7). When the content of the seventh trumpet is spelled out in detail as the seven bowls (15:1), they are total, not limited, judgments (16:2–21), accomplishing the final annihilation of the unrepentant."[24]

"Yes, arguably the unrepentant are to be annihilated *in toto*, according to John. But by whom? Not by the Lamb, apparently—"

"Or not yet, at any rate."

"—nor by the army he commands, but by the one seated on the throne and those whom he commands, his heavenly host. But these spectacular military now or we'll be missing that train to Limerick.[58]

Padraic Pearse, poet and pillar of the 1916 rebellion, argued that the spilling "of Irish blood was at least as important to the cause of Irish freedom as the spilling of English blood. "Bloodshed is a cleansing and sanctifying thing," he wrote, "and the nation which regards it as the final horror has lost its manhood. There are many things more horrible than bloodshed; and slavery is one of them."[59] Feminization is another, apparently, as Pearse's evocation of the specter of emasculation suggests, against the backdrop of the English colonial construal of Ireland as "not-England," the indispensable Other against which English identity could consolidate its (imaginary) contours. "[I]f John Bull was industrious and reliable," the Irish postcolonial critic Declan Kiberd observes, "Paddy was held to be indolent and contrary; if the former was mature and rational, the latter must be unstable and emotional; if the English were adult and manly, the Irish must be childish and feminine."[60] The hypermasculine high hero Cúchulainn, resurrected in Standish O'Grady's *History of Ireland* (1878–80) after centuries of decomposition and neglect, and enfleshed in English words for the first time (the better to meet the invader on his own terms and beat him back to the sea?), provided a ready model of masculinity for militant Irish strikes cannot induce repentance in the enemy. For that an altogether different kind of army is required—one designed not to kill but to be killed, as I remarked earlier, whose general is the Lamb who was slain."

"What's interesting to me is the way in which military metaphors are withheld from the one seated on the throne and his angelic agents—their most qualified recipients, one might suppose—and lavished instead on the Lamb-in-a-body-bag and the walking dead who accompany him. In Revelation, Jesus is not so much God become *man* as God become *masculine* —although it doesn't look like that at first. In chapter 1, Jesus is an angel,[25] and in chapters 5 and following he is a lamb, but in chapter 19 he is a superwarrior. As angel he is barely human, as lamb he is barely a man, but as warrior he is hegemonically hypermasculine. In the final analysis, John presents Christ, together with his Christians, as icons of masculinity, reserving feminine imagery for the enemy. Smells suspiciously like a smokescreen to me, suggesting—yes, I see from your supercilious smirk that you've anticipated what I'm about to say—a certain anxiety

nationalists such as Pearse. "What was in Patrick Pearse's soul when he fought in Easter Week but an imagination," the Irish author and mystic George Russell (Æ) would later declaim,

> and the chief imagination which inspired him was that of a hero who stood against a host.... I who knew how deep was Pearse's love for the Cuchulain whom O'Grady discovered or invented, remembered after Easter Week that he had been solitary against a great host in imagination with Cuchulain, long before circumstances permitted him to stand for his nation with so few companions against so great a power.[61]

Kiberd's take on the Irish nationalist infatuation with Cúchulainn is a little less romantic:

> So the ancient hero Cuchulain died strapped to a rock, singlehandedly defending the gap of the north ... ; and as his life ebbed away, a raven alighted and drank his blood. This combination of pagan energy and Christ-like suffering was of just the kind recommended for the production of muscular Christians at Rugby, suggesting that the revivalist Cuchulain was little more than a British public schoolboy in drag.[62]

on John's part regarding his own masculinity."

"Ah, so the last book of the Bible is the result of its author's acute anxiety about the size of—"

"No, the dimensions of the Saint's sacred member are probably not the issue—in his own mind its measurement was a multiple of seven, no doubt—but domination versus submission might well be the issue, or, more precisely, the cultural proclivity to construe domination as masculine and submission as feminine in the ancient Mediterranean world.[26] I mean, consider the fate that John is convinced awaits him and his fellow martyrs-in-the-making, the prospect of having to submit themselves passively to being fucked with physically, unto death if necessary...."[27]

"Not a very manly way to go out of *that* world, admittedly, at least not without a modicum of rationalization. Actually, you find the same gendered rationalization of martyrdom in another, roughly contemporary text, 4 Maccabees.[28] There the atrociously abused martyrs are lauded as true men in the most explicit terms—even, or especially, the female martyr, the

Pearse, then, would provide a still queerer spectacle, that of a Gaelic-speaking British public schoolboy, draped in the battle dress of an Irish Volunteer,[63] which has been sexily unbuttoned so as to reveal his underwear: the costume of a mythical Celtic superhero. His right hand holds a rifle aloft, while his left brandishes a sword. The latter accessory is no fantasy, actually; Pearse did wear an ancient sword strapped to his waist in the GPO through much of Easter Week 1916, as artillery shells rained down upon the building and snipers' bullets whistled through it.[64]

When Pearse declared bloodshed to be "a cleansing and sanctifying thing," therefore, he was speaking not only in the shadow of the cross of Christ but also of the pillar of Cúchulainn, that other son of a god. (Have I mentioned that Cúchulainn, too, was born of a human mother and a divine father?—not the god of Israel, however, but rather a prince of the *síde*, that ancient race, now invisible, from whom the fairies are descended.) To abhor blood sacrifice is to accept emasculation, Pearse implies, to remain dependent and enslaved: to remain a woman.[65] Independence, nationhood, manhood requires that one be willing to sever the bond of servility, to turn one's weapon upon oneself as well as upon the emasculating imperial overlord to whom one is in thrall. "We must accustom ourselves to mother of the seven brothers—and at the expense of their tormentors, especially Antiochus Epiphanes, whose own masculinity is subtly but effectively called into question."[29]

~

When I first penned the above, suggesting that the martial imagery applied to the (proto-)martyrs in Revelation was an apologia for passive resistance as a legitimate masculine stance, and appealing to 4 Maccabees for support, I was groping for closure and felt I was overreaching. But I have since stumbled upon some parallel claims that have persuaded me of my own suggestion. First, a recent article by the classicist Brent Shaw, "Body/Power/Identity: Passions of the Martyrs," which asserts of 4 Maccabees:

> Praises of active and aggressive values entailed in manliness [*andreia*] by almost all other writers in the world of [4 Maccabees] could easily fill books. The elevation to prominence of the passive value of merely being able to endure would have struck most persons . . .

the thought of arms, to the sight of arms, to the use of arms," insists Pearse, polishing and repolishing his ancient sword.[66] Ultimately, it is our own shackled wrists and our own fettered ankles that we shall be hacking through, and we shall bleed to death as a result. But we shall just as surely rise again, proclaims Pearse, his patriotism taking on a characteristic Pauline inflection. For Pearse did not hesitate to cast his own "blood sacrifice" in explicitly christological terms, brazenly picking up Christ's discarded purple robe and draping it over his green Irish Volunteer uniform with the ancient Celtic battle dress underneath. The following poem/prayer, composed by Pearse while in prison, was delivered to his mother on the day of his execution:

*A Mother Speaks*

> Dear Mary, that didst see thy
>     first-born Son
> Go forth to die amid the scorn
>     of men
> For whom He died,
> Receive my first-born son into
>     thy arms,
> Who also hath gone out to die
>     for men,
> And keep him by thee till I come
>     to him.
> Dear Mary, I have shared thy
>     sorrow,
> And soon shall share thy joy.[67]

as contradictory and, indeed, rather immoral. A value like that cut right across the great divide that marked elite free-status male values and that informed everything about bodily behavior. . . . [30]

Shaw finds in 4 Maccabees (and not only in 4 Maccabees—he also appeals extensively to Seneca, for instance) "the conscious production of a rather elaborate conception of passive resistance," or, more precisely, "the explicit cooptation of passivity in resistance as a fully legitimized male quality—a choice that could be made by thinking, reasoning and logical men."[31]

Second, a paper by another classicist, Tessa Rajak, which I chanced to hear in August 1997 at the annual meeting of the Studiorum Novi Testamenti Societas in Birmingham. (The SNTS seminar, Early Jewish Writings and the New Testament, had devoted its entire program that year to 4 Maccabees. For three days we circled this text, our genteel scholar-speak enabling us to say everything and anything about it but the thing that most rises in my own throat as I read it: *This is a*

"If you strike us down now, we shall rise again and renew the fight," Pearse proclaimed from the dock in which he was sentenced to death.[68] Nine months earlier he had delivered a rousing panegyric at the grave of his fellow rebel O'Donovan Rossa, saying:

Life springs from death; and from the graves of patriot men and women spring living nations. The Defenders of this Realm have worked well in secret and in the open. They think that they have pacified Ireland. They think that they have purchased half of us and intimidated the other half. They think that they have foreseen everything, think that they have provided against everything; but the fools, the fools, the fools!—they have left us our Fenian dead, and while Ireland holds these graves, Ireland unfree shall never be at peace.[69]

The British authorities proceeded to demonstrate the truth of Pearse's soteriological assertions by summarily executing him, along with the other captured leaders of the rebellion, thereby unwittingly creating a cadre of martyrs and transforming an unpopular and apparently unsuccessful uprising into a popular and ultimately successful one, in that it eventually led to Irish independence.[70] As if in acknowledgment *text that makes me want to vomit.*) Independently of Shaw, Rajak notes in her paper, "Dying for the Law: The Martyr's Portrait in Jewish-Greek Literature," that there is evidence that in the Greco-Roman world "the inflexible and obdurate mind-set of the martyr was perceived by some logical spirits as the epitome of unreason."[32] Philo, for example, "says that opponents might consider the Jews' readiness to die for their laws as 'barbaric,' while in reality it was an expression of freedom and nobility (*Leg.* 215). Later, Marcus Aurelius, in expounding the Stoic way to die, was to observe that this should be with considered judgment (*lelogismenō*) and not, in the Christian manner, obstinately and showily (11.3)."[33] Concerning "the terminology of male heroism" in 4 Maccabees, therefore, with its elaborate evocations of warfare and athletic prowess (as in 17:11–17, for example), Rajak claims: "These images are intrinsic to martyrology, as the agents which effect the transmutation of shaming passivity into the highest of masculine virtues. What we are offered is a concentrated inversion of the competitive, physical values

of the christological contours of this saga of execution and vindication, the standard name in Ireland for the 1916 revolt has long been the Easter Rising.[71] And as though to drive the message home, the peace accord that has recently promised to close the horrific chapter in Northern Irish history ushered in by the events of 1916–22 happens to be called the Good Friday Agreement.

Nationalism has long been a religion in Ireland, a sacrificial rite and a cult of martyrs. Indeed, the latter motifs are explicitly inscribed in the Proclamation of Independence itself (hardly surprising, since Pearse was its principal author):[72] "In this supreme hour, the Irish nation must, by its valour and discipline, and by the readiness of its children to sacrifice themselves for the common good, prove itself worthy of the august destiny to which it is called." All of which brings us back to *Angela's Ashes*:

> Come on, boys. Sing.
>   Because he loved the motherland,
>   Because he loved the green
>   He goes to meet a martyr's fate
>   With proud and joyous mien. . . .
> You'll die for Ireland, won't you,
>   boys?
> We will, Dad.
> And we'll all meet your little sister
>   in heaven, won't we, boys?
> We will, Dad.[73]

which constructed masculinity for Graeco-Roman society, a triumphant reversal of the power-structure, with the victim as the winner."[34]

Third, the classicist Carlin Barton's "Savage Miracles: The Redemption of Lost Honor in Roman Society and the Sacrament of the Gladiator and the Martyr," a portion of which is a reflection on "the ambiguous reception met by Christians in the arena."[35]

> The laughing, joyous submission to the rigamarole of the arena, the tranquil accommodation to brutality, and the apology that publicized their motivations were meant to forestall the perception of them as mere *ludibria*, ridiculous, weak, and humiliated. . . . The condemned Christian, like the gladiator, needed to establish to the audience that he or she was redeemed and a redeemer, not insulted and insulting. . . . But there can be no doubt that the voluntary suicide had difficulty in sacralizing himself or herself to a Roman audience. Most often they remained objects of scorn.[36]

But if nationalism has long been a religion in Ireland, religion has long been a form of nationalism:

> Talking about First Communion makes the [school]master all excited. He paces back and forth, waves his stick, tells us we must never forget that the moment the Holy Communion is placed on our tongues we become members of that most glorious congregation, the One, Holy, Roman, Catholic and Apostolic Church, that for two thousand years men, women and children have died for the Faith, that the Irish have nothing to be ashamed of in the martyr department. Haven't we provided martyrs galore? Haven't we bared our necks to the Protestant ax? Haven't we mounted the scaffold, singing, as if embarking on a picnic, haven't we, boys?
> We have, sir.
> What have we done, boys?
> Bared our necks to the Protestant ax, sir.
> And?
> Mounted the scaffold singing, sir.
> As if?
> Embarking on a picnic, sir.[74]

It feels strange, sacrilegious even, to be conjuring up these ghostly voices (which echo eerily in my own indoctri-

But back to the conversation that I have so rudely interrupted.

∼

"You're saying that 4 Maccabees inhabits Revelation's textual unconscious, then, just as texts such as Daniel and Ezekiel inhabit its textual consciousness?"

"So that's what I said! I wonder what I meant by it. Actually, Revelation goes well beyond 4 Maccabees in its defensive feminization of the foe.[37] 4 Maccabees never goes so far as to spit the epithet 'whore' at Antiochus, after all, to deck him out in drag, then strip him naked—"[38]

"Yes, mentally undressing Rome is what keeps John hard (and since he does it with his eyes closed, he isn't bothered by the incongruous bulge in her panties)."

"—and 'devour his flesh,' whatever that might mean."

"Whatever, indeed. The phrase 'they will devour her flesh' trips a tad too lightly off the tongues of most commentators on Revelation. There's a chapter in *American Psycho*, simply entitled 'Girl,' which opens with the said psycho slapping the eponymous girl

nated head no less than in Frank McCourt's) in the wake of the Good Friday Peace Agreement, not to mention the Omagh bombing. Like McCourt, I'm a bit of a dinosaur (although not a tIRAnnosaur).

"And do they still have to memorize the Proclamation of Independence?" I ask my sister in tones of mild apprehension, although I'm not quite sure which answer I'm most in dread of hearing. We're sitting at her kitchen table discussing Irish education in general and that of her own children in particular. My sister still lives in County Limerick ("between Patrickswell and Crecora," I always write anxiously on the envelope, unable after years in the United States to believe that my letter will ever find its way otherwise to her unnumbered, unstreetnamed, unzipcoded domicile) and her children are educated locally. She looks at me in wonder, or perhaps it is pity. "The proclamation of what? Sure, I doubt they'd ever even have heard of it."

The author of Revelation, too, attached immense importance to martyrs and martyrdom.[75] Indeed, his calculation of the symbolic value of martyrdom was to prove uncannily accurate. Christian martyrdom would eventually purchase a vast empire "for God" on earth, the Great Persecution under Diocletian ushering in Imperial Christendom under Constantine. Understandably enough, John failed to foresee around—and spitting the word 'whore' at her, as it happens—and, when that fails to turn him on sufficiently, forcing her to watch a home video—"

"That *can* be torture, I'll admit."

"—in which he literally devours the brain of another nameless woman, with great relish, slathering it with Grey Poupon—"[39]

"Thanks for that, but I think I'll stick with Ezekiel 23 as my backdrop of choice for the disturbing tableau in Revelation 17:16."[40]

"But what if *American Psycho* were merely making explicit what is already implicit in both Revelation 17 and Ezekiel 23? What if—"

"Hang on a minute. Why are we discussing *American Psycho*?"

"Because I see it as a highly illuminating instance of menaced masculinity at the margins—or rather beyond every margin, every limit, which is what makes it so chilling. Anyway, what if *American Psycho* were the apocalypse of Revelation, the uncoverer of the uncoverer, which, juxtaposed with Revelation, exposes the gendered savagery that seethes beneath the latter's surface?"

Constantinian Christianity, precisely. But the motif of the millennium ("I also saw the souls of those who had been beheaded for their testimony to Jesus. . . . They came to life and reigned with Christ a thousand years" [Rev. 20:4–6]), which he smuggles into the climactic sequence of his eschatological scenario, neatly anticipates its advent. For the symbolic economy of martyrdom in Revelation can be reduced to a simple exchange. In order to be deemed worthy to dominate others, Christ and his followers first have to show, in good Greco-Roman fashion, that they are able to dominate themselves.[76]

And so we arrive back at 4 Maccabees, which, like the *Táin*, is a paean to war, but this time to war with oneself. For 4 Maccabees is a paean to martyrdom, understood as ultimate self-mastery. The Roman Catholic children's Bible used in Christian doctrine class in that small school in Adare did not contain the book of Revelation, even in abridged form. But it did contain something still more disturbing, the story of the scalping, dismemberment, and roasting of seven brothers, watched by their mother, from 2 Maccabees 7 ("Then the king fell into a rage, and gave orders to have pans and caldrons heated. These were heated immediately, and he commanded that the tongue of their spokesman be cut out and that they scalp him and cut off his hands and feet, while the rest of the brothers and the

"Nothing like a bit of good clean misogyny to make a man feel good about his own masculinity. Is that the common thread, then, winding its dismal way through Ezekiel and Revelation and tying them, across space and time, to *American Psycho* and other leading snuff books of our day?"[41]

"I'm afraid it might well be. But there's one other thing that troubles me."

"And what might that be?"

"Surely you're not persuaded by my reading?"

"Of course not, I'm merely patronizing you."

"Thank goodness, you had me worried."

mother looked on. When he was utterly helpless, the king ordered them to take him to the fire, still breathing, and to fry him in a pan..." [vv. 3–5, NRSV]), which is to say, 4 Maccabees in miniature.[77] And so my childhood was innocent of the book of Revelation but haunted by the *Táin Bó Cuailnge* and the tale of the Maccabean mother and her butchered sons. But perhaps providence was merely preparing me for Revelation. For it strikes me now that what I earlier said of the *Táin* in relation to Revelation would apply mutatis mutandis to 4 Maccabees: whereas 4 Maccabees is a garish celebration of martyrdom, Revelation is a muted celebration of martyrdom. Superimposed upon Revelation, 4 Maccabees colors in its blanks with lurid hues.

Picking my way nervously through 4 Maccabees, I plunge through its blood-besotted pages and fall screaming into Revelation's upper atmosphere.

At which point, I wake up in a cold sweat.

If you, too, feel Revelation to be a place of peril, perhaps it is because you, like me, cannot crawl beneath the altar with the souls of those who have been slain (6:9–11)—those who are still being slain—for their testimony to Jesus: those for whom the book was composed.[78] Perhaps it is not addressed to you. Certainly, it is not addressed to me.

"There was a time when it *might* have been addressed to you," a remonstrative voice whispers in my head, "during the centuries when the colonial overlord oppressed your people and tried to crush the Catholicism out of their bodies. They bled, they prayed, they died."

"But what does the cry for vengeance from under the altar, heard and heeded by the one seated on the throne, actually effect?" I reply in consternation. "An eye for an eye? No, not an eye for an eye. What Revelation seems to be saying is this: If you gouge out the eye of one of God's witnesses, or even refuse to heed them, God will gouge out both of your eyes in return. And not only that but he will puncture your eardrums as well, and tear out your tongue, and sever your spine, and plunge you into a timeless torment. Or, what amounts to much the same thing, he will have you tortured for all eternity in the presence of his Son and his angels (14:9–11), the smoke of your torment ascending like incense (cf. 2 Macc. 7:3: 'The king fell into a rage and gave orders to have pans and caldrons heated . . . '). It's the 'forever and ever' that seems to make the punishment spectacularly incommensurate with the crime," I continue, feebly belaboring the obvious, "however horrific the latter may be. In this respect, too, Revelation reveals that it is of a piece with 2 and 4 Maccabees (and 4 Macc. 12:11–12 in particular, in which the tyrant is told that in exchange for the temporary tortures inflicted upon the martyrs, God has 'laid up for [him] intense and eternal fire and tortures [*aiōniō pyri kai basanois*], and these throughout all time will never let [him] go')."

But the real source of my unease with Revelation's God lies elsewhere, I suspect. As I intimated earlier, I find him disturbingly like myself. God knows, if anyone were to inflict grievous injury on one of my own loved ones, I myself would not be content merely to repay injury with comparable injury, given half a chance. I would seek more, much more. Because that is how I am. Had I set out to create a God in my own image and likeness, therefore, I could hardly have done better than the one who confronts me in the Book of Revelation. Reading Revelation is, for me, uncannily like looking in a mirror—while having a psychotic episode.

The Gospel of John is generally regarded as the New Testament witness par excellence to the Christian doctrine of the incarnation. It seems to me, however, that this honor (a dubious honor, actually) belongs, rather, to the Book of Revelation. For the God of Revelation is quintessentially incarnational: God become human—or, more to the point, as I have sought to show in this essay, God simply become *man*.

# IN LIEU OF A CONCLUSION: LINES INTENDED FOR A PUBLIC LAVATORY DOOR IN SAN YSIDRO, CALIFORNIA

> And so from His presence the hand was sent and this writing was inscribed.
>
> —Daniel 5:24 (NRSV)

> God is dog in the English mirror.
> This page writes itself without help,
> it is the proof of the existence of gods.
>
> —Hélène Cixous,
> *Stigmata*

*San Diego, California, December 30, 1994.* Consumed by conference burnout, I'm now in full flight. Unable to face "Que(e)rying Sexuality," the session I had penciled into my personal conference planner some days earlier, I'm finally headed for Mexico. But in the men's restroom at the border post at San Ysidro, fate beckons me into the cubicle it has prepared for me and sits me down. The back of the cubicle door is teeming with multilingual graffiti, including an interactive block of graphic gay graffiti. Beneath the latter, in large red letters, some self-appointed prophet of the wrath to come has scrawled a grim warning: GOD HATES ~~QEER~~ QUEERS. BOOK OF ROMANS FIRST CHAPTER TWENTY SIXTH AND TWENTY SEVENTH VERSES.

What I would *like* to have written in response to this chilling (but commonplace) paraphrase of Paul's sexual theology, had I had the wit or the will or even a pen, slipping my own surreptitious sentences into the cracks in the script seething upon the door, thereby inscribing my own revulsion and desire upon the void—and manifesting my geekiness to the secret society of lavatory literati—runs something like this: He does hate queers, it's true. But why? Pop-psychology can supply the answer, even if pop-theology cannot. It's because He has been saddled with a brittle masculinity that shores up its fragile identity by violently obliterating femininity, even, or especially, the woman (who cowers) within—an unwanted fourth (and female) person of the Holy Trinity—the (w)hol(l)y (male) trinity—a person whom He must thus project outward eternally, and as hard as He possibly can (projectile vomiting is the activity envisioned here), splattering her against the implacable wall of His will—His will to power, to overpower, to become (a) man. Hence the necessity of the incarnation.

A split second before her skull shatters on the wall, therefore, she becomes—what, precisely? What might Paul himself have said? Or, rather, what might the culture that produced Paul (imagining for a moment that it could be spoken of in the singular), and through Paul this epochal epistle whose extraordinary *Wirkungsgeschichte* now includes a homophobic scrawl on a lavatory door—what might this culture have to say about this unwanted woman if only it were here, crowded into this cubicle with me, breathing down my neck? Plucking the pen from my fingers would it write: "A split second before her skull shatters on the wall she metamorphoses into a man, the only man ever to submit utterly to the impenetrable will of this particular God, ever to be penetrated utterly by that will: the wo/man Jesus Christ"? Jesus would then be the queer whom God loathes (proof: the Crucifixion), the queer whom God loves (proof: the Resurrection).

"But they are father and son," somebody will object.

"Mere metaphors," somebody else will reply. "Fold back these metaphors like sheets and see what lies beneath: two males—*at least* two; hard to tell: a tangle of limbs—in a permanent relationship of absolute intimacy. To describe the persons of the Christian godhead as (intensely troubled?) male lovers would surely be a more plausible description of them than their customary portrayal as a nuclear family ('I love you, Dad'; 'I love you too, son'), given that this family has never included a mother (the best efforts of the Blessed Virgin notwithstanding, or even those of the Holy Spirit, eminently capable of slipping into a dress from time to time ). All it requires is the brute fact of their masculinity."

Not that this masculinity is unproblematic, of course. Quite the contrary, in fact. Which is where we came in.

To complicate matters further, however (or perhaps to explain them?), this God who projects, who eternally projects a part of Himself outward, is Himself a mass projection (what else *could* He be?). This God with a hard-on whom I'm undoubtedly too hard on, I hardly know why: I loved His book (God help me, I still do).

"But He's been coddled far too long, don't you think?" somebody else will interject. "Time to make an unman of Him at last."

"Might His name not provide the clue as to how to proceed?" some irreverent wag will then pipe up. "As every schoolchild knows, it is 'dog' spelled backwards. Perhaps we need to find a way to *fix* this God, once and for all."

"To dephallicize Him, you mean? Even to deanthropomorphize Him? But at what risk? Could we even recognize Him without His priapism, His narcissism, His misogyny, His ferocity? Could we even conceive of Him outside of His boudoir, His beauty parlor, His locker room, His war room? What other sacred spaces might be conjured out of His book? What other God might the go(o)d book yield up, so as to make it even better? ('Almost two millennia and not a single new god!' as Nietzsche somewhere exclaims.) What other genders, if any, for this God? A God beyond gender? A God beyond God? A God beyond belief? Can we even begin to say or see what all of these Gods might be until we have made an end of saying what they should not be?"

And we are not yet at an end. At least, I'm not. Or only for now.

# REFERENCE MATTER

# NOTES

### INTRODUCTION

1. Just how tiny? Fewer than ten. I'm here to present "A Report on the Postmodern Bible" with fellow members of the Bible and Culture Collective, not all of whom could make it to the meeting (see Bible and Culture Collective, *Postmodern Bible*). Still, I suspect this is the biggest mob of biblical scholars ever to show up at the MLA.

2. C. A. Evans, "Images of Christ in the Canonical and Apocryphal Gospels," pp. 36–37. Source, form, and redaction criticism, by the way, are concerned respectively with identifying the sources used by the evangelists in the composition of their Gospels; with identifying the forms (or genres) of individual units of source material; and with identifying the evangelists' motivations in redacting (or editing) these sources. All three methods are indigenous to biblical studies. Since the 1970s, however, a brisk import business has been under way, other methods being brought into biblical studies from neighboring fields, notably literary studies, sociology, and anthropology.

3. Reader-response criticism? A congeries of methods and theories centered on the complex reciprocal process through which literary texts mold audiences and audiences mold literary texts.

4. Narratology searches for the "deep structures" underlying narrative discourse, or, alternatively, attends to the "surface" features of narrative, such as plot, characterization, and narrative perspective.

5. *MLA Newsletter* 31 (Spring 1999): 25.

6. My hunch will subsequently be confirmed by the central statement on the first page of the lead article in *PMLA* (flagship journal of the MLA) the following May:

"Queer is hot." See Berlant and Warner, "What Does Queer Theory Teach Us about X?" p. 343. The "official" MLA publication on lesbian and gay studies is Haggerty and Zimmerman, eds., *Professions of Desire*.

7. Several years down the line, queer MLA sessions still abound, as even a casual perusal of the 1998 convention program quickly reveals: "Queer Bataille"; "Queer Walter Scott"; "Queering Dickinson"; "Queering and Querying Jewish American Identity"; "Queer Theory and Asian American Studies"; "Psychoanalysis and Queer Theory"; "Queer Crossroads"; "Queer Menace?"; "A Roundtable on the Academic and Nonacademic in Gay, Lesbian, and Queer Print Culture". . . . Thus are we led inexorably to the following obituary in the Call for Papers for the 2000 convention, published in the Spring 2000 *MLA Newsletter*: "Is queer studies passé? Has it gone too far? If the trend is over, what role should queer studies play now in the academy? 1–2-page proposals addressing history, achievements, setbacks, goals. . . . "

8. All titles on view in the Routledge booth, and all published between 1990 and 1994, with further titles announced: *Queer by Choice*; *A Queer Romance*; *The Queening of America*; *The Gay Teen*; *Asian American Sexualities: Dimensions of the Gay and Lesbian Experience*; *Negotiating Lesbian and Gay Subjects*. . . . The early to mid 1990s also saw the birth of *GLQ: A Journal of Lesbian and Gay Studies*; *Critical InQueeries*; the *Journal of Gay and Lesbian Social Sciences*; the *Journal of Gay and Lesbian Psychotherapy*; and the *Journal of Lesbian Studies*, all rubbing chubby shoulders with the graying and venerable *Journal of Homosexuality*.

9. Berlant and Warner, "What Does Queer Theory Teach Us about X?" p. 343, their emphasis. The biblical applications readily leap to mind: *A Queer Commentary on Saint Paul's Epistle to the Romans*. . . .

10. Each of these journals has devoted a thematic issue to queer theory: *differences* 3.2 (1991); *Social Text* 9.4 (1991). The *differences* issue, edited by Teresa de Lauretis, who appears to have coined the term "queer theory," consisted of the proceedings of the Santa Cruz conference. For a handy introduction to queer theory, see Jagose, *Queer Theory*. Other convenient points of access include Abelove, Barale, and Halperin, eds., *Lesbian and Gay Studies Reader*; Warner, ed., *Fear of a Queer Planet*; Morton, ed., *Material Queer* (especially instructive for students of religion is Warner's "Tongues Untied" in this collection); Beemyn and Eliason, eds., *Queer Studies*; Duberman, ed., *Queer World*; and Sedgwick, ed., *Novel Gazing*.

Apart from Warner's essay, how might any of this relate to religious studies? That, of course, is the burden of the present book, but see also Comstock and Henking, eds., *Que(e)rying Religion*; Boyarin, *Unheroic Conduct*; Jordan, *Invention of Sodomy in Christian Theology*; Rogers, *Sexuality and the Christian Body*; Stephen Carr, "Doing Queer Theology in *The Garden*"; Webster, "Queer to Be Religious"; Althaus-Reid, *Indecent Theology*; and, best of all, Rambuss, *Closet Devotions*.

What about biblical studies? There is relatively little as yet. *Que(e)rying Religion* does have a couple of essays on biblical texts (Olyan, "And with a Male You Shall Not

Lie," and D'Angelo, "Women Partners in the New Testament"). More attuned to queer theory, however, are several of the essays in Goss and West, eds., *Take Back the Word*; Boer, *Knockin' on Heaven's Door*, pp. 13–32; Heschel, "Jesus as Theological Transvestite"; Runions, "Zion is Burning"; Pippin, *Apocalyptic Bodies*, pp. 117–25; and Stone, "Biblical Interpretation as a Technology of the Self" and "Sexuality"—although the latter has little to say about the Bible or its interpretation. Neither does Schneider's "Queer Theory," an introductory essay that, like Stone's "Sexuality," appears in the *Handbook of Postmodern Biblical Interpretation*. Also pertinent here is the brand of exegetical activism exemplified by such works as Goss's *Jesus ACTED UP*, Wilson's *Our Tribe*, and most of the essays in *Take Back the Word*.

11. For a compact account of the emergence of gender studies, see Schor, "Feminist and Gender Studies." Echoing what is now a fairly common view, she claims: "Around 1985 feminism began to give way to what has come to be called gender studies" (p. 275). Also see Giddens et al., eds., *Polity Reader in Gender Studies*.

12. The literature on masculinity is vast (and merits another outsized endnote, as masculinity is a central concern of this book). The following works stand out, however, at least for me: Chapman and Rutherford, eds., *Male Order*; Gilmore, *Manhood in the Making*; Leiris, *Manhood*; Silverman, *Male Subjectivity at the Margins*; Haddad, ed., *Men and Masculinities*; Cornwall and Lindisfarne, eds., *Dislocating Masculinity*; Goldstein, ed., *Male Body*; Simpson, *Male Impersonators*; Berger, Wallis, and Watson, eds., *Constructing Masculinity*; Connell, *Masculinities*; Schehr, *Parts of an Andrology*; Stecopoulos and Uebel, eds., *Race and the Subject of Masculinities*; and, on religion and masculinity, Doty, *Myths of Masculinity*; Krondorfer, ed., *Men's Bodies, Men's Gods*; and Boyd, Longwood, and Muesse, eds., *Redeeming Men*.

Studies of masculinity in biblical texts have also begun to appear: Eilberg-Schwartz, *God's Phallus*; Glancy, "Unveiling Masculinity"; Clines, "David the Man" and "Ecce Vir"; Parsons, "Hand in Hand"; Moore, *God's Gym*; Washington, "Violence and the Construction of Gender in the Hebrew Bible"; Ward, "Displaced Body of Jesus Christ"; and Kahl, "No Longer Male." Also relevant are Deming, "Mark 9.42–10.12, Matthew 5.27–32, and *b. Nid.* 13b"; Neyrey, *Honor and Shame in the Gospel of Matthew*, esp. pp. 29–32, 148–51, 180 ff., 195 ff., and 212–22; Attridge, "Masculine Fellowship in the Acts of Thomas"; Boyarin, *Carnal Israel*, pp. 197–225; id., *Unheroic Conduct*; Young, "Being a Man"; Moore and Anderson, "Taking It Like a Man"; and Burrus, "*Begotten Not Made*," as well as a large number of cognate studies in classics, such as Carlin Barton, "All Things Beseem the Victor," together with much of her *Sorrows of the Ancient Romans*; Gleason, *Making Men*; Loraux, "Herakles" and *Experiences of Tiresias*; Kellum, "Phallus as Signifier"; much of Hallett and Skinner, eds., *Roman Sexualities*; Richlin, "Gender and Rhetoric"; Foxhall and Salmon, eds., *Thinking Men* and *When Men Were Men*; Williams, *Roman Homosexuality* (whose larger topic is, as its subtitle indicates, ideologies of masculinity in classical antiquity); and Martin, "Contradictions of Masculinity."

13. Butler, "Against Proper Objects," p. 3. She is contesting a statement by the editors of the *Lesbian and Gay Studies Reader* to the effect that "Lesbian/gay studies does for *sex* and *sexuality* approximately what women's studies does for gender" (Abelove, Barale, and Halperin, "Introduction," p. xv, their emphasis). Butler's article was part of a special issue of *differences* entitled *More Gender Trouble: Feminism Meets Queer Theory* (since reprinted as Weed and Schor, eds., *Feminism Meets Queer Theory*). See more recently Merck, Segal, and Wright, eds., *Coming Out of Feminism?* a further collection of studies devoted to the complex intersections of feminism and queer theory.

14. "Jane Austen and the Masturbating Girl," in Sedgwick, *Tendencies*, pp. 109–29. Sedgwick's *Between Men* is frequently said to exemplify the transition from feminist to gender studies, and her *Epistemology of the Closet* is probably the most admired product of queer theory to date.

15. Sedgwick, *Epistemology of the Closet*, p. 29. Cf. Halperin, Winkler, and Zeitlin's introduction to *Before Sexuality*, p. 3: "Sexuality (as we use the term here) refers to the cultural interpretation of the body's erogenous zones and sexual capacities.... The norms, the practices, even the very definition of what counts as sexual activity have varied significantly from culture to culture." See further Lancaster and di Leonardo, eds., *Gender/Sexuality Reader*. Even chromosomal sex has been subject to cultural contingency as a male/female marker, as Thomas Laqueur in particular has argued. Biologically speaking, early modern European culture operated with a one-sex model of humanity, with its roots in classical antiquity, which conceived of the vagina as a kind of inverted or internal penis (Laqueur, *Making Sex*, esp. pp. 63 ff.).

16. See Foucault, *History of Sexuality*. The introductory volume deals primarily with the modern period, while the second and third volumes backtrack to deal with Greek and Roman antiquity respectively. A fourth volume, devoted to Christianity and sexuality, and entitled *Les Aveux de la chair* (The confessions of the flesh), remained unfinished at Foucault's death from AIDS in 1984. Essays by and interviews with Foucault that comment on or supplement his *History of Sexuality* include the following: "The Battle for Chastity"; "The Concern for Truth"; "The Confessions of the Flesh"; "Friendship as a Way of Life"; "The History of Sexuality"; "Michel Foucault: An Interview"; "On the Genealogy of Ethics"; "Power and Sex"; "Sexual Choice, Sexual Act"; "Sexuality and Solitude"; "Sexual Morality and the Law"; "The Simplest of Pleasures"; "The Return of Morality"; "The Social Triumph of the Sexual Will"; and "The West and the Truth of Sex." Several of these pieces have now been collected in Foucault, *Ethics*. Foucault's significance for queer theory is ably elucidated by Halperin in *Saint Foucault* (see esp. pp. 15–125, "The Queer Politics of Michel Foucault") and by Spargo, in *Foucault and Queer Theory*.

Foucault's impact on biblical studies has been relatively slight to date; see, however, Castelli, *Imitating Paul*; Moore, *Poststructuralism and the New Testament*, pp. 83–112; Bible and Culture Collective, *Postmodern Bible*, pp. 138–44; Polaski, *Paul and the Discourse of Power*; and George, "Foucault" (although none of these works engages extensively with *The History of Sexuality*). For Foucault and religious studies more generally, see Carrette, *Foucault and Religion*.

17. For further work in this area, see Greenberg, *Construction of Homosexuality*, esp. pp. 397–433.

18. Foucault, *History of Sexuality*, 1: 43. The article in question (which Foucault erroneously dates to 1870) is Westphal's "Die conträre Sexualempfindung."

19. Foucault, *History of Sexuality*, 1: 42–43. What of the cultural construction of the lesbian? Foucault does not address the issue, another instance of the neglect of female experience for which his history of sexuality has been criticized (see pp. 167–68 above).

20. The anti-constructionist note has been sounded most clearly by John Boswell; see esp. his *Christianity, Social Tolerance, and Homosexuality*. On the constructionist/essentialist debate generally, see Stein, ed., *Forms of Desire*; also useful are Vance, "Social Construction Theory and Sexuality," and Thornton, "Constructionism and Ancient Greek Sex." Sedgwick, herself a radical constructionist, has criticized other constructionists (Foucault and Halperin) for employing an overly monolithic concept of (modern) homosexuality (*Epistemology of the Closet*, pp. 44–48). Joseph Boone, for his part, shows how "Western" that concept also tends to be ("Vacation Cruises").

21. For the medieval dating, see Jordan, *Invention of Sodomy in Christian Theology*, who argues: "When we lesbians and gays think of ourselves as members of a tribe, as a separate people or race, we echo medieval theology's preoccupation with the Sodomites" (p. 163). And again: "The idea that same-sex pleasure constitutes an identity of some kind is clearly the work of medieval theology, not of nineteenth-century forensic medicine" (p. 164). For the other extreme (the late dating of homosexuality), see Chauncey, *Gay New York*. The late dating of lesbianism, specifically (by Lillian Faderman and others), is challenged by Terry Castle in *Apparitional Lesbian*.

22. See also his "Homosexuality and the Signs of Male Friendship."

23. Foucault, *History of Sexuality*, 1: 101.

24. Jagose, *Queer Theory*, p. 16. For similar formulations, see Halperin, *One Hundred Years of Homosexuality*, p. 17; Bristow, *Sexuality*, p. 179; Larmour, Miller, and Platter, "Situating *The History of Sexuality*," p. 22; and esp. Sedgwick, *Epistemology of the Closet*, for whom the heterosexual no less than the homosexual is a product of the closet. Differing dates and details regarding first uses of the terms "homosexual(ity)" and "heterosexual(ity)" occur in different works. For my own account, I have relied principally on Jonathan Katz, who seems to have done his homework most assiduously (*Invention of Heterosexuality*; see esp. pp. 51–55). I am also following Katz in referring to the coiner of the two terms as Karl Maria Kertbeny; others refer to him as Karoly Maria Benkert. For further details of Kertbeny's sexological innovations, see Féray and Herzer, "Homosexual Studies and Politics in the Nineteenth Century."

25. Quoted in Katz, *Invention of Heterosexuality*, p. 92. Katz is able to multiply similar references from the first quarter of the twentieth century to heterosexuality

as an abnormal condition. See also Halperin, *One Hundred Years of Homosexuality*, pp. 17–18. It is but a relatively short leap to the following assertion by Bruce Smith: "In texts written before the 1880s, perhaps before the 1920s, perhaps even before the 1980s, sexuality, in our psychopolitical understanding of it, is something that is *not there*" ("Premodern Sexualities," p. 319; his emphasis).

26. Katz, *Invention of Heterosexuality*, pp. 57–82.

27. Schor, "Feminist and Gender Studies," pp. 277–78. "But how, exactly, do we bring the hetero/homo opposition to the point of collapse?" muses Diana Fuss ("Inside/Out," p. 1).

28. The expression "regimes of the normal" is lifted from Warner, "Introduction," p. xxvi, to *Fear of a Queer Planet*, who argues that these are what queer theory is designed to resist. Queer theory has its work cut out for it, then; because the normal is immensely seductive, it is extremely hard to resist. Warner's own *The Trouble with Normal* leaves us in no doubt about that.

## 1. THE SONG OF SONGS IN THE HISTORY OF SEXUALITY

1. *GQ* is, of course, *Gentlemen's Quarterly*, while *GLQ* is, presumably, the *Gay and Lesbian Quarterly* (its subtitle is *A Journal of Lesbian and Gay Studies*).

2. Under "allegorical," here and throughout, I am subsuming three different "senses of sacred Scripture" that the medieval mind, in particular (principally inspired by the fifth-century monk John Cassian), generally took pains to distinguish, namely, the allegorical, the anagogical, and the tropological (also known as the moral). In Cassian's oft-quoted example, Jerusalem is literally (or "historically," as he himself says—*secundum historiam*) "the city of the Jews," allegorically "the Church of Christ," anagogically "that celestial city of God" (the New Jerusalem), and tropologically "the human soul" (*Collationes* 14.8). My usage of the term "literal," too, is rough-and-ready by medieval standards; by the thirteenth century, the term had become subject to some exquisite refinements.

3. Origen, *Homilies on the Song of Songs* 1.2–3. The translation of the *Commentary* and *Homilies* used here and throughout is that of R. P. Lawson (see Origen, *Song of Songs*).

4. Ann Matter notes the untranslatability of the Latin (Vulgate) text of Song 1:1, the verse that has gotten Bernard so worked up. Over the course of five words, in a paroxysm of alliteration, it contrives to repeat cognate words for "kiss" and "mouth" three times: *Osculetur me osculo oris sui*. How to match this in English? Matter's tongue-in-cheek suggestion is, "Let him kiss me with the kiss of his kisser" (*Voice of My Beloved*, p. 126).

5. Bernard of Clairvaux, *Sermons on the Song of Songs* 2.2, 9.2, 9.7. The translation used here and throughout is that of the Cistercian Fathers series (see Bernard of Clairvaux, *On the Song of Songs I-IV*).

6. Merton, *Elected Silence*, p. 241. The book is better known in the United States under the title *The Seven Storey Mountain*, but it was as *Elected Silence* that I first encountered it.

7. Denis the Carthusian, *Commentary on the Song of Songs* 43–45. The translation and paragraph numbers are those of Denys Turner in his *Eros and Allegory*, more than two hundred pages of which consist of translated excerpts from medieval commentaries on the Song. All subsequent excerpts from such commentaries follow Turner, unless indicated.

Turner is able to reflect for the other two hundred pages on the spiritual erotics of this tradition of commentary without ever once coming to terms with the fact that the erotics in question essentially concerns two males. Ann Astell, in constrast, does take us to the bedroom door and allow us a brief glimpse of the bed and the two male bodies entwined in it: "The allegory of the Song had defined the place of audience identification as the Bride, not the Bridegroom. The central consciousness of the Song *ad litteram*, moreover, is feminine, not masculine—a feature which sets the *Canticum* apart from other eastern love literature and from the courtly tradition of the West. . . . The [late medieval male] exegetes all encourage their auditors to identify their 'bridal self' with the Bride, using the feminine *figura* as a way of evoking, expressing, and directing the emotional domain within themselves" (*Song of Songs in the Middle Ages*, p. 10). Periodically throughout her book, Astell brings Jungian categories to bear on this rhetorical ploy. For example: "The distinctly feminine readings of the *Canticum* [by males], then, reflect the commentators' desire to evoke, engage, and direct the *anima* in the work of their own salvation, to bring into consciousness the affective soul-life and set it at the service of a personal God. Even more, the feminization of seif and audience reifies psychologically the allegory that represents humankind as a woman, the soul as spouse. In the metaphysics of sexuality, every person, male and female, is more feminine than masculine in relation to God—because receptive, dependent, and small" (p. 13).

8. John of the Cross, *Spiritual Canticle* 27. The translation is from *The Collected Works of St. John of the Cross*. Essentially, the *Spiritual Canticle* is a free poetic paraphrase of the Song of Songs.

9. By which I simply mean that whether in Jewish or Christian allegorical exegesis of the Song through the ancient, medieval, and early modern periods, the expositor in all but a handful of the extant texts is a male who addresses himself primarily to an audience of male peers, synecdochic stand-ins for Israel or the Church. The first possible exception to the rule is the anonymous twelfth-century Christian commentary on the Song known as the *St. Trudperter Hohelied* (St. Trudperter Song of Songs), and the first certain exceptions are Mechtilde of Magdeburg's thirteenth-century *Das fliessende Licht der Gottheit* (The Flowing Light of the Godhead), which includes mystical meditation on selected verses from the Song, and Teresa of Avila's sixteenth-century *Conceptos del Amor de Dios sobre unas palabras de los Cantares*

(Conceptions of Divine Love in Some Words of the Canticles). See further Riedlinger, *Die Makellosigkeit der Kirche*, pp. 226-33 (on the *St. Trudperter Hohelied*); Mechtilde of Magdeburg, *Revelations of Mechtilde of Magdeburg*; and Teresa of Avila, *Complete Works of Saint Teresa of Jesus*, 2: 352-99. Why so few extant meditations or commentaries on the Song by women? The surprise, perhaps, is that there are any at all, when one considers that the most celebrated of the few just listed, that of Teresa, was reduced to ashes by the author on the orders of her confessor, alarmed that a woman should presume to pronounce on mystical matters, and it survives (in truncated form) only because another nun had earlier chanced to make a personal copy of the first seven chapters.

10. The poem (if indeed it is *a* poem and not a mini-anthology of love lyrics) contains three voices: a female voice, a male voice, and a group voice. Of the three, the female's is the most prominent, delivering most of the lines and initiating most of the exchanges, as Phyllis Trible observed more than two decades ago in "Love's Lyrics Redeemed." Trible is only one of many feminist critics who have been drawn to the Song on that account; others include Athalya Brenner ("Afterword"), Marcia Falk (*Song of Songs*), Julia Kristeva ("Holy Madness"), Carol Meyers ("Gender Imagery in the Song of Songs"), and Renita Weems (both of her essays entitled "Song of Songs"). Cheryl Exum has assembled a catena of quotations from all of these critics celebrating the Song's representation of gender relations ("Developing Strategies of Feminist Criticism / Developing Strategies for Commentating the Song of Songs," p. 227). Other names could be added to the list, such as that of Fokkelien van Dijk-Hemmes ("Imagination of Power").

The more the Song is presumed to be a unified composition (as opposed to a mere compilation), the more its female protagonist emerges as a coherently delineated character. The presumption of unity was, of course, generally shared by precritical exegetes of the Song, and facilitated their imaginative appropriation (and obliteration) of the protagonist's voice (although that obliteration is already under way in the Song itself, according to Ilana Pardes [*Countertraditions in the Hebrew Bible*, pp. 118-43 passim]). The prominence of this female voice has also prompted some modern commentators to suggest that the Song was the work of a woman; see most recently LaCocque, *Romance, She Wrote*.

11. With the passage of time, however, allegorical expositors developed more subtle strategies for sanitizing the salacious Song. "Unlike Origen, whose belief in two loves—carnal and spiritual, demonic and divine—led him to disassociate the literal and allegorical meanings of the Song, twelfth century [monastic] exegetes upheld a unitary concept of love," Ann Astell notes. "They therefore approached the erotic images of the Song in a way that rendered them transparent to their divine tenor, sacramentalizing them, making them vehicles for an organic transference of the *affectus* to Christ the Bridegroom" (*Song of Songs in the Middle Ages*, p. 178).

12. Examples drawn from Nicholas of Lyra (1270?-1349), *The* Postilla Litteralis *on*

*the Song of Songs* 62–63, trans. Denys Turner. For a continuous 382-page catena of ancient and medieval interpretations of the Song, lavishly studded with such gems (but all presented with utter solemnity), see Littledale, *Song of Songs from Ancient and Mediaeval Sources*.

13. Denis the Carthusian, *Commentary on the Song of Songs* 42, trans. Denys Turner. The female protagonist of the Song is traditionally called Shulamit(h), or "the Shulam(m)ite" (see 6:13: "Come back, come back, O Shulammite [*haššûlammît*] . . . ").

14. My strategy of reading the Song of Songs over the shoulders of its allegorical interpreters may itself be read as an attempt to circumvent the obstacle noted by Christopher King, who writes:

> [T]he queer reader, however devoted to the Song of Songs' all-lovely lovers, must be alert to a roadblock on the way to a queer interpretation, for we must not forget that the Song of Songs' zeal for embodied, passionate love is directed entirely to that love as shared by *woman and man*. Of all the dimensions of the Song of Songs' narrative context, the one that remains most visible to us today is its situation in a world suffused with the images and reality of opposite-sex desire. Queers seem to be left entirely out of the picture. How, then, are queer believers to "take back" such a text as this? ("Love as Fierce as Death," p. 127; his emphasis)

King's own strategy of reclamation is to focus, first and foremost, on the "outsider" status of the Shulamite, signified by her blackness ("I am black and beautiful" [1:5]), and to argue that she is a consummate object of queer desire within the Song: "As a class underling or territorial alien, the Shulamite's social location as outsider makes her a prohibited object of the Beloved's erotic favor. . . . Thus, the romance of the Shulamite and the Beloved begins with the violation of a fixed social boundary. Their love affair, like that of all queer lovers, is essentially transgressive" (ibid., p. 130). The basis of their mutal attraction, moreover, is not difference but sameness:

> [T]he fervent love of the Shulamite and her Beloved is fueled by a real parity of desire, an erotic symmetry arising from their reciprocal share in a loveliness that is irresistible. Each lover is, in other words, drawn to a "sameness"—an essential similarity—seen in the beauty, the sexiness, of the other. The dynamism might be heterosexual, but its structure is definitely homoerotic: *an attraction of sames*. By unveiling this "queer" dimension in the love life of the Shulamite and the Beloved, the Song of Songs not only champions the dignity of queer passion but upholds it as a model for any love worth pursuing. (Ibid., p. 132; his emphasis)

15. Cf. Scholem, *Jewish Gnosticism, Merkabah Mysticism, and Talmudic Tradition*, pp. 36–38, 46–52. For a moving meditation on Akiba's putative pronouncements on the Song, see Francis Landy's "Drush on Rabbi Akiba," in his *Paradoxes of Paradise*,

pp. 13–18. The historical critic in me, however (cowed though he is after years of self-inflicted neglect), feels compelled to put the question to Landy that Philip Alexander casually put to me in a recent conversation: "What can we really know about Rabbi Akiba? His remains are entombed in textual sarcophagi that are all considerably younger than him." Or words to that effect. What I think he actually said was, "It's high time somebody did a Jack Neusner on old Akiba." (Jacob Neusner was one of the first scholars to bring an adequately critical sensibility to the dating of rabbinic traditions.)

Who, then, is "my" Rabbi Akiba? He is the fictionalized Akiba of the Jewish heterodox mystical tradition, which appropriated his name and authority, and evinced a fascination with the body of God. While the classical Jewish commentaries on the Song (most notably *Song of Songs Rabbah* and the *Targum of the Song of Songs*) reverently refrained from interpreting the lyrical description of the male lover's body in Song 5:10–16 as a head-to-toe description of Yahweh's, as we shall see (even though they did identify the lover as Yahweh, and his beloved as Israel), a "mystical" text such as *Hekhalot Rabbati* betrays no such scruple. In *Hekhalot Rabbati* §167 (Ms. Budapest 238) a description of the dimensions of the divine body—"And from His right arm to His left His width is seven myriads of parasangs, and His arms are twice [as long] as his shoulders [are broad],", etc.—is immediately followed by a direct quotation of all of Song 5:9–16. (Philip Alexander not only called my attention to this passage, but kindly whipped up a translation of it for me.)

Apart altogether from Akiba, the origins of the Jewish allegorical interpretation of the Song are shrouded in the mists of history and inconclusive scholarly debate. Does the ancient ascription of the Song to Solomon presuppose a literal interpretation, given that "Solomon" in his "other books" (Proverbs in particular) evinces an interest in human sexual relations? Does the Septuagint (Greek) translation of the Song contain hints of allegorization? Does Sirach 47:14–17 presuppose the allegorization of the Song? How about Wisdom 8:2? 2 *Esdras* 5:24–36; 7:26? Revelation 3:20? Josephus's categorization of the biblical books in *Against Apion* 1.8? What significance should be ascribed to the Septuagintal translators' decision to translate the Song in the first place? Or to the fact that fragments of the Song crop up among the Dead Sea Scrolls? And so on.

16. M. *Yadaim* 3.5. The translation is from Danby, *Mishnah*.

17. *Mekilta de Rabbi Ishmael*, Shirata 3.49–63. The translation is from Judah Goldin, *Song at the Sea*. It was in the Jewish mystical tradition, however (again in *Hekhalot Rabbati*), that the theme of Yahweh's beauty fully crystallized. For example, *Hekhalot Rabbati* 13:4 describes how the *Chayyot* (the four bizarre creatures from Ezek. 1:4–12 who chauffeur Yahweh around) play with him in his heavenly throne room, kissing and caressing him, flapping their wings ecstatically, playing music and dancing about. Then we are told: "They reveal their faces (to Him), but the King of Glory hides His face, lest the expanses of heaven burst before the King of Beauty,

Splendor, Loveliness, Comeliness, Fairness, Radiance, Attractiveness, Brilliance. . . . " The translation is from Martin S. Cohen's "Song of Songs and the Shi'ur Qomah" (p. 9), an unpublished paper that he graciously shared with me. He argues that "the idea of describing the *unio mystica* as an act of gazing on a Deity described in terms of the beauty of his physical form was certainly part and parcel of the heritage of ancient Judaism in the post-Biblical period" (p. 10), and that the Song of Songs played a crucial role in this tradition.

18. All quotations from *Song of Songs Rabbah* are from Maurice Simon's translation (see Simon, *Esther and Song of Songs*).

19. Delitzsch, *Proverbs, Ecclesiastes, Song of Solomon*, p. 113.

20. Ibid., pp. 3, 4, 5.

21. For details, see Urbach, "Homiletical Interpretation of the Sages," p. 251, n. 11.

22. Boyarin, *Dying for God*, p. 111. Much of Boyarin's book takes the form of a comparative analysis of early Jewish and Christian martyrologies. For Boyarin, "Rabbi Akiva is the Polycarp of Judaism," the ideal type, and prototype, of the rabbinic martyr (pp. 105, 110), just as Polycarp (d. ca. 155) can be regarded as a prototype of the Christian martyr—not that Boyarin regards the meager rabbinic references to the circumstances of Akiba's death as transparently historical; the rabbinic Akiba is "a semifictionalized representation" (p. 111) and his martyrdom a discursive construct (p. 116). What is novel in these martyrological constructs, Jewish or Christian, for Boyarin, and what distinguishes them from other cognate literature (such as the Jewish martyrological text 4 Maccabees, about which I have much to say in "Revolting Revelations"), is that they represent "the eroticization of death for God, . . . of martyrdom as the consummation of love . . . " (p. 107). "They are all about love, about dying for God" (ibid.), as distinct from dying for his law, or out of fear of him, or to demonstrate Stoic or superhuman endurance (cf. pp. 96, 114). See also Boyarin, *Intertextuality and the Reading of Midrash*, pp. 119–24, which anticipates the arguments of *Dying for God*, although without reference to the Christian martyrologies.

23. Targums are Aramaic paraphrases of the Hebrew Scriptures that were designed for use in the synagogues. So free and expansive were certain of these paraphrases that they amounted to biblical commentaries. Such was the case with the *Targum of the Song of Songs*, a text for which Philip Alexander claims a high degree of originality: "Certain earlier rabbinic commentators had contextualized some parts of Canticles to specific events in the *Heilsgeschichte* [salvation history]—notably the giving of the Law at Sinai. But the targum is the first text systematically and chronologically to correlate Canticles with a long period of the history of Israel. The targum inaugurated the historicizing reading within Jewish biblical scholarship" (Alexander, "Song of Songs as Historical Allegory," p. 23; see also id., "Tradition and Originality in the Targum of the Song of Songs," esp. pp. 335–36). This historicizing reading was singularly successful: "The *Targum of the Song of Songs* is extant, in whole or in part, in at least sixty manuscripts from all over the Jewish world, making it one of the best

attested and most popular texts of the Jewish Middle Ages" (Alexander, "Textual Criticism and Rabbinic Literature," pp. 163–64). When does this targum date from? It has gotten younger with the passage of time. Christian Ginsburg dates it to the sixth century (*Song of Songs*, p. 28), and Raphael Loewe, followed by Marvin Pope, dates it to the seventh century (Loewe, "Apologetic Motifs in the *Targum to the Song of Songs*," pp. 163–66; Pope, *Song of Songs*, pp. 93–94), while Alexander dates it to the eighth century ("Song of Songs as Historical Allegory," pp. 23, 27).

24. Of which three have survived intact: *Shir ha-Shirim* [= Song of Songs] *Rabbah* (the largest compilation, probably dating from the early seventh century), *Aggadat Shir ha-Shirim*, and *Midrash Shir ha-Shirim* (both probably dating from the tenth or eleventh centuries). Further on *Song of Songs Rabbah*, see Neusner, *Song of Songs Rabbah*, or, for the abridged version, his *Introduction to Rabbinic Literature*, pp. 467–86. For a handy compilation of talmudic pronouncements on the Song, see Ginsburg, *Song of Songs*, pp. 24–28.

25. Renderings of the *Targum of the Song of Songs* throughout follow Hermann Gollancz's translation closely—except where they follow Marvin Pope's instead. See Gollancz, "Targum to the 'Song of Songs.'" Pope's translation is scattered throughout his massive commentary on the Song. Alexander chides Pope for "cribbing rather obviously" from Gollancz's translation ("Tradition and Originality in the *Targum of the Song of Songs*," p. 319). I've had to crib from Gollancz *and* Pope, unfortunately, my Aramaic being somewhat rudimentary. Alexander's own translation of the targum for the Liturgical Press's Aramaic Bible series is not yet in print as I write.

26. Nor do her charms end there: "THY CHEEKS ARE COMELY WITH CIRCLETS [Song 1:10]: these are the teachers of Scripture and of Mishnah and of infants, who teach conscientiously.... Another explanation: THY CHEEKS ARE COMELY WITH CIRCLETS: these are the Rabbis. THY NECK WITH PEARLS (*HARUZIM*) [Song 1:10]: these are the disciples who strain (*hozrim*) their necks to hear the words of Torah.... Another explanation: THY CHEEKS ARE COMELY WITH CIRCLETS: when they spy out the *halachah* with one another, like R. Abba b. Mimi and his colleagues. THY NECK WITH PEARLS: when they were linking up the words of the Pentateuch with those of the prophets and the prophets with the Writings" (*Song of Songs Rabbah* 1.10 § 2). And again: "THY NAVEL IS LIKE A ROUND GOBLET [Song 7:3]. THY NAVEL indicates the Sanhedrin.... A ROUND GOBLET (*AGAN HASAHAR*): the seat of admonishment [i.e., the Sanhedrin].... WHEREIN NO MINGLED WINE IS WANTING: the Sanhedrin should not consist of less than twenty-three members" (7.3 § 1). Two further regulations for the proper conduct of Sanhedrin business then follow, each of which is also said to be presaged (and why not?) by the image of a capacious female navel overflowing with mingled wine.

27. According to *Song of Songs Rabbah* 4.10 § 1, "In ten places in Scripture Israel is called 'bride,' six here [in the Song of Songs], and four in the prophets."

28. Pope, *Song of Songs*, p. 96.

29. Cf. *Song of Songs Rabbah* 1.16 § 1: "BEHOLD THOU ART FAIR, MY BELOVED, BEHOLD THOU ART FAIR, because if God desires to choose another nation He can"— but he doesn't because Israel's beauty keeps him faithful to her, as the translator, Maurice Simon, implies in a footnote: "Yet he does not, and for that very reason He emphasises her fairness." But what if Israel were to grow "stout," say, and if her "charm" were to "fade"?

Though terms for "ugly" or "ugliness" occur across the span of rabbinic literature, biblical Hebrew lacks any such term, a curious fact that has often been noted. It may merely be an "accidental absence," as Athalya Brenner has suggested (*Intercourse of Knowledge*, p. 48, n. 68). Biblical Hebrew frequently employs terms for "beauty," as we shall see, and a concept of beauty would seem to presuppose a corresponding concept of ugliness.

30. Cf. *Song of Songs Rabbah* 4.1 § 1: "BEHOLD THOU ART FAIR, MY LOVE, BEHOLD THOU ART FAIR. Behold thou are fair with precepts, behold thou are fair with deeds of kindness; behold thou art fair in positive precepts, behold thou art fair in negative precepts; behold thou are fair in the religious duties of the house, with the *hallah, terumah*, and tithes, behold thou art fair in religious duties of the field, with the gleanings, the forgotten sheaf, the corner, the second tithe," etc. (repeated with variations in 7.7 § 1).

31. We encounter a parallel notion in Origen: "Let us interpret the Bride's neck ... [cf. Song 1:10: 'Your cheeks are beautiful with ornaments, your neck with strings of jewels']. It must surely denote those souls who receive the yoke of Christ who says: *Take up my yoke upon you, for my yoke is sweet* [Matt. 11:29–30]. Her 'neck' is so called, therefore, because of her obedience. And her neck has been made 'lovely as necklaces,' and rightly so. For that which the disobedience of the Transgression formerly made shameful, the obedience of faith has now made beautiful and fair" (Origen, *Commentary on the Song of Songs* 2.7).

32. This cycle of misdeed, chastisement, and submission mystified Freud. "Why the people of Israel, however, clung more and more submissively to their God the worse they were treated by him—that is a problem which for the moment we must leave on one side," he wrote in *Moses and Monotheism* (p. 112; he never did return to it, as far as I can discover).

33. Though he enjoys trying on other robes as well: "The Holy One, blessed by He (is described as having) put on ten robes, viz. *The Lord reigneth; He is clothed in majesty* (Ps. XCIII, 1); this is one: *The Lord is clothed* (*ib.*); this is two: *He hath girded Himself* (*ib.*); this is three: *And He put on righteousness as a coat of mail* (Isa. LIX, 17); this is four: *And He put on garments of vengeance* (*ib.*); this is five: *For clothing* (*ib.*); this is six: *And was clad with zeal as a cloak* (*ib.*); this is seven: *This that is glorious in his apparel* (*ib.* LXIII, 1); this is eight: *Wherefore is Thine apparel red* (*ib.* 2); this is nine: *Thou art clothed with glory and majesty* (Ps. CIV, 1); this makes ten" (*Song of Songs Rabbah* 4.10 § 1). Neither can the scholar afford to neglect his appearance: "Just

as a bride is adorned with twenty-four ornaments, and if one is missing she cannot pass muster, a Rabbinical scholar should be conversant with the twenty-four books of the Scriptures, and if he is not conversant with one of them he cannot pass muster" (4.11 § 1).

34. And who is scheduled to deliver a scholarly paper at the eschaton? Marvin Pope, peering between the lines of the targum of Song 7:14 ff., thought so: "The Messiah, commissioned to take up his kingdom and reveal himself to Israel, is invited to join Israel in procession to Jerusalem to attend a Talmudic discourse—the anonymous guest lecturer being presumably the Deity Himself (cf. 5:10)" (*Song of Songs*, p. 95).

35. Even the quintessential mark of male Israel, the circumcised penis, is effortlessly assimilated in *Song of Songs Rabbah* to the area between a woman's thighs: "THE ROUNDINGS OF THY THIGHS. Rabbi Johanan said: 'All the luxuries and delicacies that Israel enjoys in this world are on account of the circumcision which is between the thighs'" (7.2 § 3).

36. Boyarin, *Unheroic Conduct*, p. xxii. It is early modern European Judaism that Boyarin is commenting on here. His point, however, is that what he is describing is a characteristic "rabbinic" formation.

37. This holiness-wholeness connection is no rabbinic conceit, but is enshrined in the Torah itself. See Douglas, *Purity and Danger*, pp. 51, 57, and Milgrom, *Leviticus 1-16*, p. 1001: "That wholeness (Hebrew *tamim*) is a significant ingredient of holiness cannot be gainsaid" (cf. p. 721).

38. Though this is not the only possible rendering of the Hebrew of Song 1:5, an important issue to which we shall later return.

39. And also in other rabbinic texts, such as *Genesis Rabbah* 22:5-6; 36:7-8, and *b. Sanhedrin* 108b.

40. Or rather it would be part of a complex debate on the origins of "race" and "racism." The word "race" did not appear in the English language until around 1500, apparently, and did not acquire its present meaning(s) until the late eighteenth century. Similarly, "theories that claim to provide a 'scientific' basis for white racism are peculiar post-Enlightenment by-products of modern civilization," as Cain Hope Felder remarks ("Race, Racism, and the Biblical Narratives," p. 128). See further Malik, *Meaning of Race*, and Solomos and Back, eds., *Theories of Race and Racism*.

41. My concept of ideology is thus broadly Althusserian in its lineaments—even though beauty is too mercurial a quantity to be pigeonholed neatly in any of Althusser's "Ideological State Apparatuses" (see Althusser, "Ideology and Ideological State Apparatuses," esp. pp. 136-37). There is now an extensive critical literature on beauty (see p. 252, n. 99, below).

42. The commentary was written in Greek and erroneously attributed to Ambrose of Milan during the Middle Ages. In its fragmentary form it extends no further than Song 3:8. For discussion of it, see Chappuzeau, "Die Auslegung des Hohenliedes durch Hippolyt von Rom," and Riedlinger, *Die Makellosigkeit der Kirche*, pp. 20-23.

43. These breasts appear to have been fantasized out of thin air by the ancient Greek translators of the text, as we shall see.

44. In the course of the prologue to Jerome's Latin translation of Origen's subsequent *Homilies on the Song of Songs* (although Jerome would later abjure Origen as a heretic [*Letters* 612; 96.5–6]). The commentary is usually dated to 240–45, and is thought to have preceded the homilies by a few years. None of the Greek text of the homilies has survived, and only a few fragments of the Greek of the commentary (in the *Philocalia* of Nazianus and Basil, and in various *catenae*, notably that of Procopius). The commentary is known principally from Rufinus's Latin translation of it (although Rufinus appears to have translated only three of the ten books, together with the prologue), whereas the homilies are known solely from Jerome's Latin translation. Comparison of the Greek fragments of the commentary with Rufinus's translation reveals the latter to be a less than literal rendering, to say the least. Origen's comments on the Song cannot be fully separated from Rufinus's, then, Origen and Rufinus being entwined with each other, and with the Bride and Bridegroom, in a wild tangle of limbs.

45. See Urbach, "Expositions of Origen on Canticles, and the Jewish-Christian Disputation," and Kimelman, "Rabbi Yohanan and Origen on the Song of Songs." For Origen's intellectual exposure to rabbinic thought generally, see the bibliography in Matter, *Voice of My Beloved*, p. 41, n. 2.

46. Eusebius, *Ecclesiastical History* 6.8.1–3, Loeb translation (see Justin Martyr, *First Apology* 291–92, for a similar anecdote). Scholars have long been divided over the credibility of Eusebius's testimony, ranging from Henry Chadwick's outright dismissal of it as "malicious gossip" (*Sentences of Sextus*, p. 68; cf. pp. 9–12, also his *Early Christian Thought and the Classical Tradition*, p. 67) to Patricia Cox's more tentative skepticism (*Biography in Late Antiquity*, pp. 88–90) and the relative confidence of others in its veracity, e.g., Hanson, "Note on Origen's Self-Mutilation," pp. 81–82; Trigg, *Origen*, p. 54; and Caner, "Self-Castration in Early Christianity," p. 401. I shall not rehearse the arguments pro and con here, as I have nothing substantive to add to them, although it does seem to me that the skeptics have the less convincing case. But even if I were persuaded otherwise, I would be unable to avoid the suspicion that Eusebius or his tradition is here instinctively acknowledging the intrinsic queerness of Origen's spirituality by assigning him a physical body to match his literary corpus.

47. Boyarin succinctly defines the phallus as "a platonic idea of the penis" (*Unheroic Conduct*, p. 9).

48. See further Landy, *Paradoxes of Paradise*, pp. 73–112, and Meyers, "Gender Imagery in the Song of Songs."

49. Brown, *Body and Society*, p. 169, also taking Eusebius at his word. The image of eunuchhood as exile is from Claudius Mamertinus, *Panegyrici latini* 11.19.4.

50. The Bridegroom owes his hermaphroditic cleavage to the Greek (Septuagint)

and Latin (Vulgate) translations of Song 1:2, which read *mastoi sou* and *ubera tua* respectively ("your breasts"), whereas the Hebrew (Masoretic) text has *dōdĕkā* ("your love," or, conceivably, "your lovemaking"; so Bloch and Bloch, *Song of Songs*, p. 137). "The basis for this rendering is somewhat obscure," as G. Lloyd Carr explains, "but both the Hebrew word 'loves' (*dôdîm*) and the Hebrew word 'breasts' (*dadayim*) would be written simply as *ddm* in the old consonantal text" (*Song of Solomon*, p. 73). See further Pope, *Song of Songs*, pp. 298–99, and Murphy, *Song of Songs*, p. 125. Modern translations modestly cover up the breasts, opting for "your love" instead. Origen was not the only early Church writer to conceive of a she-male Christ, complete with breasts; for further examples, see Combes, "Nursing Mother, Ancient Shepherd, Athletic Coach?" esp. p. 114.

51. Cf. Origen, *Commentary on the Song Songs* 1.4: "We cherish the hope that we shall reach the age at which we can not only feed from the breasts of the Word of God, and be nourished thereby, but also love Him who thus nourishes."

52. Cited by Littledale, *Song of Songs from Ancient and Mediaeval Sources*, p. 371.

53. Gregory of Elvira, *Tractatus de epithalamio [In Cantica Canticorum libri quinque]* 19, paraphrased by Matter, *Voice of My Beloved*, p. 88.

54. Bernard of Clairvaux, *Sermons on the Song of Songs* 61.2. Gender-bending conceptions of Christ abounded in the late medieval period in particular, as Caroline Walker Bynum has shown. Numerous examples can be found in her *Jesus as Mother, Holy Feast and Holy Fast*, and *Fragmentation and Redemption*.

55. Origen, *Commentary on the Song of Songs*, Prologue 4. Cf. *Homilies on the Song of Songs* 1.5: "The Bride alone is brought into the chamber, that she may see there dark and hidden treasures. . . . " For Patricia Cox Miller, Origen's "Bride" is a figure for the reader; and for Origen, "as for [Roland] Barthes, the text is an erotic body where word and reader, Bridegroom and Bride, are joined" ("Pleasure of the Text, Text of Pleasure," p. 251).

56. Origen, *Commentary on the Song of Songs* 1.4. Gregory the Great, too, longs to bury his head in the Bridegroom's cleavage: "But we will embrace the breasts of the Bridegroom when in the eternal kingdom we will contemplate him by embracing him in person" (*Exposition of the Song of Songs* 19, trans. Denys Turner).

57. This is the sort of issue I would have been passionate about ten years ago. In fact, I devoted most of a book to it (*Mark and Luke in Poststructuralist Perspectives*).

58. This would seem to be true even of Jewish allegorical exegesis of the Song, notwithstanding the fact that the rabbis did not idealize celibacy. Ibn Ezra (1089–1164), for example, declares: "This book surpasses all the songs which Solomon composed and perish utterly perish its being (understood as) erotic literature. Rather it is by way of allegory. . . . Were it not a book of high import, as spoken by the Holy Spirit, it would not have defiled the hand [i.e., been canonized]" (*Commentary on the Song of Songs*, Introduction to the Second Gloss, quoted in Pope, *Song of Songs*, p. 103). And Immanuel ben Solomon (b. 1272), nicknamed "The Prince of Knowledge

in Rome," contrasts spurious expositors of the Song, who "go no further than the material world, and that which their eye sees, looking forward to the good of this world and its glory, . . . and to have their stomachs filled with the flesh of the Leviathan, and the best of the wines preserved in its grape," with true expositors, "who are separated from the material world" and "despise the mere temporal things" (*Commentary on the Song of Songs*, quoted in Ginsburg, *Song of Songs*, pp. 49–50). Yet we should beware of unduly conflating Jewish and Christian allegorical exegesis of the Song, as Hyam Maccoby has cautioned ("Sex According to the Song of Songs," esp. pp. 54–55).

59. Jerome gives almost identical advice to the female reader of the Song. Addressing a female correspondent who has requested advice on how best to bring up her daughter, he prescribes massive doses of Sacred Scripture, beginning with the Psalms and proceeding through Proverbs, Ecclesiastes, and Job, followed by the Gospels, Acts, and Epistles; then circling back and "committing to memory" the Prophets, the Heptateuch, Kings, Chronicles, Ezra, and Esther, after which he adds: "Then at last she may safely read the Song of Songs: if she were to read it at the beginning, she might be harmed by not perceiving that it was the song of a spiritual bridal expressed in fleshly language [*sub carnalibus verbis*]" (*Letters* 107.12; quotations from Jerome's letters throughout follow the Loeb translation [see Jerome, *Select Letters*]).

60. Boyarin, *Unheroic Conduct*, p. 26. He continues: "Although rabbinic Judaism also provides an array of male ideals and modalities, it fell to Ashkenazic Judaism to furnish European culture with the possibility of a male who is sexually and procreationally functioning but otherwise gendered as if 'female' within the European economy of gender. The Jewish men obviously remain within the sexual order, since they do not form a separate gender within the Jewish cultural system. Seen however from the point of view of the larger cultural system, they appear similar to monks and thus femminized" (p. 26; "femminize" is a Boyarinian neologism).

61. "During the later patristic period and the rest of the Middle Ages, Christian interpreters wrote more works on the Song of Songs than on any other individual book of the Old Testament," as Roland Murphy remarks (*Song of Songs*, p. 21).

62. Although traditionally "the soul was held not to be sexed, social perceptions of gender persisted in the characterisation of its qualities as male and female" (Clark, "Old Adam," p. 174). A not insignificant element in this process was the simple fact that "soul" happened to be a feminine noun in most European languages, "making it all the easier to transpose the metaphors about the Bridegroom of the Soul into highly charged sexual images" (Pelikan, *Illustrated Jesus through the Centuries*, p. 139).

63. Garber, *Vested Interests*, p. 10.

64. Ibid., pp. 16–17; Garber's emphasis.

65. Garber herself in her chapter on "Religious Habits" writes of the perceived femininity of the priest or monk in medieval society—"beardless, wearing a cassock that could be thought to resemble a woman's skirt, devoid of political power, living

in quiet obedience, and performing domestic chores" (ibid., p. 218). The chapter carries a telling epigraph from Sydney Smith's 1855 novel, *Lady Holland's Memoir*: "As the French say, there are three sexes—men, women, and clergymen."

66. And thus overtaking Origen, whose three extant books on the Song take him all the way to 2:15. Bernard began the sermons in 1135 and continued them until his death in 1153. On Bernard's relationship to Origen, still a controversial figure in the twelfth century, see Evans, *Mind of St. Bernard of Clairvaux*, pp. 82–85.

67. William of St. Thierry et al., *St. Bernard of Clairvaux*. William began the biography around 1147 and covered the first forty years of Bernard's life. After William's death, Arnold of Bonnevaux took up the tale.

68. The anecdote is William's, even if the words are not (*St. Bernard of Clairvaux*, p. 20).

69. Ibid., pp. 21–22.

70. Ibid., p. 23. In the *Sermons* the roles are reversed, Bernard slipping into Jesus' bedchamber by night to solicit sexual favors from him. "We humbly dare to raise our eyes to his mouth, so divinely beautiful, not merely to gaze upon it, but—I say it with fear and trembling—to receive its kiss," a kiss that, we later learn, is "at the summit of love's intimacy" (*Sermons on the Song of Songs* 3.5, 4.1). Bernard and Jesus undoubtedly made a striking couple. Bernard himself was an exceptionally handsome man, according to his hagiographers (William of St. Thierry et al., *St. Bernard of Clairvaux*, pp. 20, 21, 126).

71. Not that *all* commentators on the Song were celibate. Gregory of Nyssa, for instance, seems to have been married.

72. Cf. Butler, *Gender Trouble*, p. 137: "The performance of drag plays upon the distinction between the anatomy of the performer and the gender that is being performed."

73. This is Rufinus, Origen's Latin translator, talking (one of many places where he adapts Origen's text for his Latin readership).

74. *Song of Songs Rabbah* 7.9 § 1, commenting, not on Song 4:5 but on 7:9, does, however, declaim in addition: "AND LET THY BREASTS BE AS CLUSTERS OF THE VINE: this refers to Perez and Zerach. Just as Perez and Zerach were condemned to be burnt but were not burnt, so these were condemned to be burnt but were not burnt."

75. Littledale, *Song of Songs from Ancient and Mediaeval Sources*, pp. 156–57.

76. Squeezing the Bride's breasts produces a phallic fantasy in William: "I seem to see the frightened Esther here, trembling as she approaches the throne of the king and hardly daring to lift her eyes to the splendour of his face; and I seem to see the king stretching forth his sceptre of mercy towards her and saying: *What is it you want, Esther . . . ?*" (*Brevis Commentatio* 17, trans. Denys Turner).

77. Pope, *Song of Songs*, p. 470.

78. Albright, *Yahweh and the Gods of Canaan*, p. 133.

79. Weems, "Song of Songs" (*Women's Bible Commentary*), p. 159.

80. The Bridegroom came in for the same treatment earlier, as we have seen (pp. 221–22, n. 50, above). "From wine" (Greek: *apo oinou*) is a literalistic rendering of the Hebrew *miyyayin*. Having no special forms for degrees of comparison, classical Hebrew employed the "*min* [from] of comparison" instead.

81. Littledale, *Song of Songs from Ancient and Mediaeval Sources*, p. 173.

82. As seen on *The Jerry Springer Show*. Or was it *Ricki Lake*? Hard to keep it all straight.

83. Cf. Clines, "Why Is There a Song of Songs . . . ?" pp. 118–19: "In the Song, the woman is everywhere constructed as the object of a male gaze. . . . To her male spectators, the readers of the poem, of course, she cannot say, 'Do not stare at me'; for she has been brought into existence precisely to be stared at. . . . She has been the victim of male violence and anger (1:6 ['My mother's sons were angry with me'; also 5:7: 'Making their rounds in the city the watchmen found me; they beat me, they wounded me, they took away my mantle']) . . . and now the poet invites his readers to share his sight of the woman's humiliation. That is the very stuff of pornography." Donald Polaski entertains a similar view of the Song; he characterizes its implied reader as "a panoptical male connoisseur" ("What Will Ye See in the Shulammite?" pp. 76–77).

84. Littledale, *Song of Songs from Ancient and Mediaeval Sources*, p. 308.

85. Pertinent here, too, is Shawn M. Krahmer's suggestion that the figure of the bride in Bernard's *Sermons on the Song of Songs* "might function paradoxically as a 'virile woman,' a female 'figure' or type who serves appropriately to represent the highest spiritual attainments of the human soul (whether of biological male or female), precisely because she has overcome any stereotypically 'womanly' weaknesses and become typologically 'male' or 'virile'" ("The Virile Bride of Bernard of Clairvaux," pp. 304–5). As Krahmer pithily puts it, "we might say that the figure of the Bride represents for Bernard and his monks a man striving to be a woman striving to be a man!" (p. 305, n. 3). And again: "We should observe with caution any literary appropriation of the feminine by a male, because the female figure may turn out, at least in part, to be a man in disguise" (p. 327).

86. Bernard represents himself throughout as an abbot addressing his monks, but authorities on the sermons tend to take the view that they were not actually delivered to live audiences. Rather, they were dictated to a secretary originally and were incessantly revised by Bernard throughout his later years. See Leclercq, "Making of a Masterpiece."

87. Except when the Bride, or one or more of her body parts, or an item of her clothing or jewelry, becomes a selected biblical character or character-group. For example: "MY DOVE, MY UNDEFILED, IS BUT ONE. ONE: this is Abraham, as it says, *Abraham was one* (Ezek. XXXIII, 24)" (*Song of Songs Rabbah* 6:9 § 1); "THOU ART ALL FAIR MY LOVE: this refers to our ancestor Jacob" (4.7 § 1); "THY TWO BREASTS: these are Moses and Aaron" (4.5 § 1); "WITH ONE BEAD OF THY NECKLACE: this is Moses"

(4.9 § 1); "Thou art beautiful, o my beloved, as tirzah: this refers to the women of the generation of the wilderness, for Rabbi said: The women of the wilderness were virtuous" (6.4 § 1).

88. In his prologue to the homilies, Jerome is taking his lead from Origen's own statement in his commentary that "those who are at the stage of infancy and childhood in their interior life ... who are being nourished with milk in Christ, not with strong meat" (cf. 1 Cor. 3:1–3; Heb. 15:12–14; 1 Pet. 2:2–3), are not ready to plumb the full depths of the Song (*Commentary on the Song of Songs*, Prologue 1).

89. See Gregory of Nyssa, *From Glory to Glory*, pp. 152–288. The commentary extends only as far as Song 6:9.

90. Origen, *Commentary on the Song of Songs* 1.1, 1.2, 3.2. Cf. Thomas Gallus (d. 1246): "She gazes upon the beauty of the divine brilliance ... and she longs to be united to the primary beauty beyond all beauty" (*An Explanation of the Song of Songs* 12, trans. Denys Turner). Or Denis the Carthusian, who eulogizes the Bridegroom "who is infinite in beauty," adding: "It is therefore not surprising that this Bride should wish to be united and espoused to such a Bridegroom" (*Commentary on the Song of Songs* 20, trans. Denys Turner). An especially ravishing description of the Bridegroom's face and form is provided by Rupert of Deutz (ca. 1075–1129): "Open your eyes, your interior eyes, to see this Beloved, to see his golden head, his brilliant eyes, his awe-inspiring cheeks, his radiant and glorious lips, his smooth and golden hands, his ivory stomach set with sapphires, his upright legs" (*In Cantica Canticorum*, PL 168, c 929–30, trans. Ann Astell).

91. Origen, *Commentary on the Song of Songs* 2.5, 3.1. Cf. Bernard, who insists that the saints' entire attention "is fixed on improving and adorning the inward self that is made to the image of God. . . . For they are certain that nothing can be more pleasing to God than his own image when restored to its original beauty" (*Sermons on the Song of Songs* 25.7; cf. 83.1). God loves the way he looks.

92. Origen, *Commentary on the Song of Songs* 2.7. Origen is much taken with the Pauline phrase "without spot or wrinkle," employing it several times in the *Commentary* as well as in the *Homilies*. For example: "But when the Bride, the fair, the perfect one who is without spot or wrinkle . . . " (*Homilies* 1.5).

93. William of St. Thierry et al., *St. Bernard of Clairvaux*, p. 94.

94. Origen, *Commentary on the Song of Songs* 3.14. There is a nice symmetry here. The Bridegroom's beauty, too, is invisible to the unspiritual eye: "But these people who . . . have lacked power to see what beauty there is in the Son of God say: *And we looked, and He had no beauty nor comeliness, but His appearance was unbeautiful and lacking before the sons of men* [Isa. 53:2]" (ibid. 3.2). Yet his body was sublimely beautiful even in its ugliness, as Origen later implies (ibid. 3.4), commenting on Song 2:1, "I am the Flower of the field and the Lily of the valleys": "The Bridegroom, then, becomes the Lily in this valley, in that the heavenly Father clothed Him with such a robe of flesh as never Solomon in all his glory had power to possess. For Solomon's flesh

was not born spotless, without man's desire or woman's intercourse with man; nor was it innocent of any subsequent offence."

Bernard goes further (as usual), explicitly ascribing blackness to Jesus: "Obviously black, since he had neither beauty nor majesty [Isa. 53:2]; black because he was 'a worm and no man, scorned by men and despised by the people' [Ps. 21:7]. If he even made himself into sin, shall I shrink from saying he was black?" (*Sermons on the Song of Songs* 25.9). And so on. Bernard presents us with a black Jesus, then, and not as an affirmation of blackness but as a denigration. More on this below.

95. Pope, *Song of Songs*, pp. 291, 307–21 (which also traces the fortunes of the verse through the ages).

96. Ibid., p. 291.

97. Exum, "Asseverative ʾ*al* in Canticles 1,6?" p. 416, quoting Pope, *Song of Songs*, p. 321.

98. Exum, "Asseverative ʾ*al* in Canticles 1,6?" p. 417.

99. Ibid., p. 418.

100. Pope, *Song of Songs*, pp. 307–8, his translation. Contrast Randall Bailey's argument ("They Shall Become as White as Snow") that within the Hebrew Bible the formulation "to be made white as snow" (see esp. Isa. 1:18) functions not as a blessing but as a curse—notwithstanding its eager adoption by so many (white) Christian hymn writers.

101. Murphy, *Song of Songs*, p. 128 (cf. p. 126).

102. Weems, "Song of Songs" (*Women's Bible Commentary*), p. 159. In her *New Interpreter's Bible* commentary on the Song, Weems adds: "The Hebrew word she uses to describe her complexion . . . is unambiguous, despite the numerous efforts by translators to render it more euphemistically and palatably as 'dark,' 'very dark,' 'swarthy,' 'blackish,' and so on" ("Song of Songs," p. 382). Charles Copher also identifies the woman outright as black; his argument is that "in the eyes of the ancients she was black" ("Black Presence in the Old Testament," pp. 157–58).

103. Weems, "Song of Songs" (*Women's Bible Commentary*), p. 159 (the argument does not show up in her subsequent *New Interpreter's Bible* commentary: compare "Song of Songs," pp. 425–26); Goulder, *Song of Fourteen Songs*, p. 55 (cf. pp. 51–52).

104. Weems, "Song of Songs" (*Women's Bible Commentary*), p. 160; Goulder, *Song of Fourteen Songs*, pp. 74–78. Cf. King, "Love as Fierce as Death," pp. 128–32, 136–42, for an alternative version of the same argument. The most extensive resources on ethnicity and race in relation to the Bible and its interpretation, as far as I am aware, are Brett, ed., *Ethnicity and the Bible*, and Sparks, *Ethnicity and Identity in Ancient Israel*. Neither has much to say, however, about the semiotics of skin color in ancient Israel. On the latter, see Felder, ed., *Stony the Road We Trod*, pt. 3 ("Race and Ancient Black Africa in the Bible"); for a useful survey of related work, see Bailey, "Academic Biblical Interpretation among African Americans," pp. 697–700.

105. The term "Ethiopian" (Greek: *Aithiops*, literally "burnt-face"), already found

in Homer (*Od.* 19.246 ff.), was the standard designation in the Greco-Roman world for persons of dark pigmentation and "African" features (Felder, "Race, Racism, and the Biblical Narratives," p. 128, n. 6; Snowden, *Blacks in Antiquity*, pp. 118–19).

106. Origen, *Commentary on the Song of Songs* 2.1. Cf. id., *Homilies on the Song of Songs* 1.6: "Beautiful indeed is the Bride, and I can find out in what manner she is so. But the question is, in what way is she black and how, if she lacks whiteness, is she fair. She has repented of her sins, beauty is the gift conversion has bestowed. . . . She is called black, however, because she has not yet been purged of every stain of sin, she has not yet been washed unto salvation; nevertheless she does not stay dark-hued, she is becoming white. When, therefore, she . . . begins to mount from lowly things to lofty, they say concerning her: *Who is this that cometh up, having been washed white?*" She is only made white in the Septuagintal rendering of the verse, however, upon which Origen and Rufinus both depend: *Tis hautē hē anabainousa leleukanthismenē* ("Who is this [woman/girl] coming up, who has been made white . . . ?"). The Hebrew reads: *mî zōʾt ʿōlâ min- hammidbār* ("Who is this [woman/girl] coming up from the desert/wilderness . . . ?"). Cf. Jerome, *Letters* 22.1: "Your bridegroom is not arrogant, not haughty; He has married a woman of Ethiopia. As soon as you resolve to hear the wisdom of the true Solomon, and come to Him, He will avow to you all His knowledge; He will lead you as a king to His chamber; your colour will be miraculously changed, and to you the words will be fitting: 'Who is this that goeth up and hath been made white?'" The (incestuous) "Nephew" of Origen's text derives from the Septuagint's *ton adelphidon autēs* ("her nephew"), in place of the Hebrew *dôdâ* ("her lover/beloved").

107. Similar sentiments on Song 1:4 echo down through the ages. The verse plays a prominent role in Frank Snowden's chapter on the "Early Christian Attitude Toward Ethiopians" in his *Blacks in Antiquity*, pp. 196–215. The chapter covers the period from the first to the sixth centuries. Snowden takes the statements of Origen, Jerome, Augustine, and other Church Fathers on Song 1:4 and on the explicit scriptural references to Ethiopians as grist for his general thesis that "color was inconsequential" in the Greco-Roman world: "antipathy because of color did not arise," nor was color "a criterion for evaluating men" (pp. 205, 216). See further Snowden, *Before Color Prejudice*; Vercoutter et al., *Image of the Black in Western Art*; and Lloyd Thompson, *Romans and Blacks*, which also argues for a largely positive Roman view of blacks. For a reading of the Church Fathers on blacks and blackness that is considerably less benign than Snowden's, see Hood, *Begrimed and Black*, esp. pp. 73–90. Wimbush, "Ascetic Behavior and Color-ful Language," further undermines Snowden's arguments, as does Mayerson, "Anti-Black Sentiment in the *Vitae Patrum*." Also see Frost, "Attitudes Toward Blacks in the Early Christian Era."

Venturing beyond the period covered by Snowden, we find Bernard of Clairvaux dwelling lovingly and at length (*Sermons on the Song of Songs* 25–28) upon the enigma of the "dark lady" who "bears the stigma of a dark skin," "not yet a blessed one who reigns without stain in heaven" (25.3). Blackness is "the abject hue that indicates infirmity.... I recognize here the image of our sin-darkened nature," he writes (28.2). Thankfully, there is always heaven to look forward to. "But shall I still be black?" Bernard has the Bridegroom inquire; like the Bride, the Bridegroom, too, is black, having assumed "the form of a slave" (Phil. 2:7). "God forbid!" Bernard has him reply, going on to quote Song 5:10, "Your beloved will be fair and ruddy, strikingly beautiful" (*Sermons on the Song of Songs* 28.10; I shall return to this material below).

Nicholas of Lyra's gloss on "I am black" is no less dispiriting: "And so there were some among the Jewish people who ... thought the whole Church to be an offence before God—like an ugly bride before her husband.... *I am black*, that is, I am shameful before God" (*The* Postilla Litteralis *on the Song of Songs* 36). Centuries earlier, Gregory the Great had paraphrased the verse as: "I have become ugly in the sight of the King" (*Exposition of the Song of Songs* 39, trans. Denys Turner).

Depressing, too, however, is Charles B. Copher's contemporary attempt, in several of the essays collected in his *Black Biblical Studies*, to lay responsibility for anti-black prejudice in medieval and early modern Europe at the feet of the ancient and medieval rabbis (once again the Jews are to blame). What does Copher do with Origen and the other Church Fathers? He reads them through rose-tinted spectacles borrowed from Frank Snowden. See esp. Copher, "Three Thousand Years of Biblical Interpretation with Reference to Black Peoples."

108. "And we have shown that ... a person is darkened or scorched by the sun where the ground of sin exists. But where there is no sin, the sun is not said to burn or darken" (Origen, *Commentary on the Song of Songs* 2.2). And again: "But if you do not likewise practice penitence, take heed lest *your* soul be described as black and ugly, and you be hideous with a double foulness—black by reason of your past sins and ugly because you are continuing in the same vices!" (*Homilies on the Song of Songs* 1.6). Jerome will later press this line of argument through to its logical conclusion and interpret the black skin of Song 1:5 as the very mark of the devil: "'Ye are of your father the devil, and the lusts of your father it is your will to do' [John 8:44]. So it was said to the Jews. And in another place, 'He that committeth sin is of the devil' [1 John 3:8]. Born of such a parent we are black by nature [*Tali primum parente generati nigri sumus*], and even after repentance, until we have climbed to virtue's height, we may say, 'I am black [*Nigra sum*] and comely, a daughter of Jerusalem'" (*Letters* 22.1; in contrast to his Vulgate translation of Song 1:5, Jerome here uses *et* ["and"] in place of *sed* ["but"]).

109. "And then my light and my splendour will be restored to me, and that blackness for which you now reproach me will be banished from me so completely, that I shall be accounted worthy to be called *the light of the world*" (Origen, *Commentary on the Song of Songs* 2.2; cf. John 8:12; 9:5).

110. The context reads: "[Mary Magdalen] turned round and saw Jesus standing

there, but she did not know that it was Jesus. Jesus said to her, 'Woman, why are you weeping? Whom do you seek?' Supposing him to be the gardener, she said to him, 'Sir, if you have carried him away, tell me where you have laid him, and I will take him away.' Jesus said to her, 'Mary.' She turned and said to him in Hebrew, 'Rabboni!' (which means Teacher). Jesus said to her, 'Do not hold me, for I have not yet ascended to the Father . . . '" (John 20:14–17, RSV).

111. Dyer, *White*, p. 17.

112. Snowden, *Before Color Prejudice*, p. 101. What weight should we accord in all of this to Origen's own Egyptian provenance? My colleague Virginia Burrus has proposed a minimal statement of the matter to me that I find persuasive: "Though not himself black, Origen lives in a place in which he regularly comes into contact with blacks ('Ethiopians'), who already come with a culturally charged meaning, to which he adds his own theological gloss" (e-mail correspondence).

113. Delitzsch, *Proverbs, Ecclesiastes, Song of Solomon*, p. 99.

114. The ideal of physical perfection implicitly celebrated in Origen's commentary on the Song finds its antithesis in the rabbinic *Tanḥuma* (fifth or sixth century?), which glosses the "curse of Ham" (Gen. 9:18–27) as follows: "Because Ham's eyes gazed at his father's nakedness, Ham's eyes were reddened. Because his mouth told of it, his lips were made curved. Because he turned his face [to gaze again], his hair and beard became singed" (*Tanḥ.* Noah 13, quoted in Montefiore and Loewe, *Rabbinic Anthology*, p. 56). Cf. the anonymous sixth-century Christian text *Apophthegmata Patrum*, which puts words of self-loathing upon the lips of the Ethiopian ascetic, "Moses the Black": "Rightly have they treated you, ash skin, black one. As you are not a man, why should you come among men?" (quoted in Wimbush, "Ascetic Behavior and Color-ful Language," p. 88).

115. The assumption that the lovers *are* beautiful is near universal, even among critical scholars, supported as it is by such effusions as Song 1:15–16 ("Just look at you, my darling, you're beautiful! Just look at you—beautiful! [*hinnāk yāpâ raʿyātî hinnāk yāpâ*; my translation]"); 2:10, 13; 4:1, 7; 7:7; cf. 7:2. The assumption has been contested of late, however, notably by Athalya Brenner, who argues that the highly lyrical description of the woman's physical aspect in 7:1–7 "may be read as a parody on the [*wasf*] genre—possibly a female parody, put into a male's mouth, and ultimately a critique of male chauvinistic attitudes towards the female object of male desire" ("On Feminist Criticism of the Song of Songs," p. 36, summarizing her "Come Back, Come Back the Shulammite"). *Wasf* is an Arabic term used to denote the stylized physical descriptions found in certain Near Eastern love poems. The Song of Songs contains the only examples in the Hebrew Bible, three in all: 4:1–5 (the first detailed description of the female lover's body, three verses of which are repeated in 6:4–7) and 5:10–16 (the only detailed description of the male lover's body), together with 7:1–10. Brenner reads the latter passage as indicating that the woman is obese ("Your belly is a heap of wheat"), has an outsized nose ("Your nose is like a tower of Lebanon"), and is gener-

ally less than beautiful ("Come Back, Come Back the Shulammite," pp. 247–48, 250). Fiona Black tackles these passages from a related angle, bringing the literary and artistic category of the grotesque to bear on them; see her "Beauty or the Beast?" and "Grotesque Body in the Song of Songs."

116. Parente, "Canticle of Canticles in Mystical Theology," p. 146. Rupert of Deutz's *Commentaria in Canticum Canticorum (de Incarnatione Domini)* (ca. 1125) seems to have been a crucial catalyst in this development (see Salgado, "Considerations mariales de Rupert de Deutz"). The liturgy may have been a more general catalyst. Denys Turner suggests that the Mariological interpretation of the Song was encouraged by the practice, documented as early as the eighth century, of including readings of the Song in the offices of the feast of the Assumption and, later on, the feast of the Nativity of the Virgin (Turner, *Eros and Allegory*, p. 306)—although the argument is somewhat circular since the practice also seems to presuppose the Mariological interpretation. Further on the possible effects of the liturgy on the interpretation of the Song, see Matter, *Voice of My Beloved*, pp. 151–59, 167–70.

117. Denis the Carthusian, *Commentary on the Song of Songs* 2, 49, trans. Denys Turner. Denis's was the first commentary to treat each verse of the Song systematically with reference to the Church, the soul, and the Blessed Virgin in turn, a technique adoped by a number of subsequent expositors.

118. Ibid., 55, 58. Meanwhile, in Jewish kabbalistic interpretation of the Song, specifically in the *Zohar*, Yahwah was engaged in a torrid affair with his own female aspect in the (shapely) form of the *Shekhinah* For details, see Maccoby, "Sex According to the Song of Songs," pp. 55–57.

119. Bernard of Clairvaux, *Sermons on the Song of Songs* 8.1–2, 6. The Holy Spirit has always been notoriously resistant to conventional gender-labeling, nonchalantly switching costumes from blue to pink and even to purple, depending on which language he/she/it happens to find him/her/itself in at any given time: *Hebrew*, in which case she is feminine (*harûaḥ haqqĕdôšâ*); *Latin*, in which case he is masculine (*spiritus sanctus*); or Greek, in which case it is neuter (*to pneuma to hagion*). In and through the Holy Spirit, gender indeterminacy is enshrined within the Godhead itself.

120. Bernard of Clairvaux, *Sermons of the Song of Songs* 8.7. The Fourth Gospel depicts the disciple "whom Jesus loved [*hon ēgapa ho Iēsous*]" "reclining on Jesus' breast [*anakeimenos . . . en tō kolpō tou Iēsou*]" (13:23), just as Jesus himself reclines "on the Father's breast [*eis ton kolpon tou patros*]" in heaven (1:18). For a provocative analysis of the relationship between the Johannine Jesus and his Beloved Disciple in the context of Greco-Roman pederasty, see Tilborg, *Imaginative Love in John*, pp. 77–110, and for a still queerer take on the relationship, Goss, "Beloved Disciple."

121. Bernard of Clairvaux, *Sermons of the Song of Songs* 8.9. What do critical scholars do with the sister/brother epithets in the Song (4:9, 10, 12; 5:1, 2; 8:1–2)? Most attempt to explain them away. Francis Landy and Athalya Brenner refuse to do so, however. Landy reads them as evoking an Edenic state prior to prohibition, in which

everything, even incest, is permissible (*Paradoxes of Paradise*, p. 111), and Brenner takes a similar view (*Intercourse of Knowledge*, pp. 100–101).

122. Classical Jewish exegesis of the Song is more circumspect in this regard, never approaching the recklessness of Bernard—but daring nevertheless to venture statements such as the following: "The yearning of Israel is only toward their father in heaven, as it says, I AM MY BELOVED'S, AND HIS DESIRE IS TOWARD ME" (*Song of Songs Rabbah* 7II § 1).

123. For a book-length application of Bakhtin's concept of the carnivalesque to a biblical text, see Craig, *Reading Esther*.

124. Bakhtin, *Rabelais and His World*, p. 5.

125. Ibid., p. 9.

126. Ibid., p. 10.

127. Ibid., p. 13. An early example of the ecclesiastical carnivalesque was *Coena Cypriani* (Cyprian's Supper), a brazen travesty of the entire Bible. Later came the *parodia sacra*, a cluster of parodic liturgies, litanies, hymns, psalms, prayers (not excluding the Pater Noster and the Ave Maria), gospel stories, and even dominical sayings. "All of it was consecrated by tradition and, to a certain extent, tolerated by the Church. It was created and preserved under the auspices of the 'Paschal laughter,' or of the 'Christmas laughter'; it was in part directly linked, as in the parodies of liturgies and prayers, with the 'feast of fools' and may have been performed during this celebration" (ibid., p. 14).

128. Ibid., p. 9.

129. With no wedding veil in sight and no apparent desire for offspring. For a detailed consideration of these facets of the Song, see Fox, *Song of Songs and the Ancient Egyptian Love Songs*, pp. 229–43, and cf. Brenner, *Intercourse of Knowledge*, pp. 72–78.

130. Bahktin, *Rabelais and His World*, p. 9.

131. It is often assumed that Theodore produced a commentary on the Song, but there is actually no evidence that he did. There are no extant fragments of any such commentary, nor do the catalogues of his titles list one. The Acts of the Council of Constantinople quote an extract from a personal letter from Theodore to a friend, which indicates that he declined to assign any allegorical significance to the Song, preferring to regard it instead as love poetry written by Solomon in defense of his decision to marry an Egyptian princess. Further on Theodore, see Greer, *Theodore of Mopsuestia*, and Zaharopoulos, *Theodore of Mopsuestia on the Bible*.

132. Jerome's broadside was entitled *Adversus Jovinianum* (logically enough).

133. Denis the Carthusian, *Commentary on the Song of Songs* 16, trans. Denys Turner; Chaucer, "The Merchant's Tale," ll. 2132–49, conveniently reprinted in Jasper and Prickett, eds, *Bible and Literature*, pp. 180–202, together with other literary recyclings of the Song, profound as well as profane, ranging from Richard Rolle's *Fire of Love* to Umberto Eco's *Name of the Rose*.

134. J. G. von Herder's *Salomon's Lieder der Liebe, oder die ältesten und schönsten*

*aus Morgenlande* (1778) is often seen as pivotal in this regard, although several isolated voices arguing for a thoroughgoing literal interpretation of the Song preceded Herder's, such as Sebastian Castellio[n]'s *Notae in Canticum Canticorum in Biblia latina* (1547), Hugo Grotius's *Ad Canticum Canticorum* (1644), Jacques-Bénigne Bossuet's *Libri Salomonis, Canticum Canticorum* (1693), and William Whiston's *A supplement to Mr. Whiston's late Essay, towards restoring the true text of the Old Testament, proving that the Canticles is not a sacred book of the Old Testament; nor was originally esteemed as such either by the Jewish or the Christian Church* (1723). Martin Luther stands uncertainly on the fringes of this group; in his *Vorlesung über des Hohelied* (1530–31), he expresses dissatisfaction with the allegorical tradition, but hesitates to go all the way with the literal interpretation. For further particulars on these works, see Pope, *Song of Songs*, pp. 126–32, but esp. Ginsburg, *Song of Songs*, pp. 69–101 (upon whom Pope is largely dependent). Oddly enough, no book-length history of the interpretation of the Song has covered the modern period, as far as I am able to discover. Such histories go only as far as the late medieval period, or the Renaissance at most (for a bibliography, see Murphy, *Song of Songs*, pp. 212–14). For a full-length study of Herder's contributions to Song of Songs scholarship, see Baildam, *Paradisal Love*.

135. Littledale, *Song of Songs from Ancient and Mediaeval Sources*, p. v. He characterizes as "almost exclusively modern" the view that "denies all inner meaning to the poem, save of the most incidental kind, and maintains a literal exposition" (p. xiv).

136. Fowles, *French Lieutenant's Woman*, p. 77.

137. Christian Ginsburg, writing twenty years later, in the 1850s, recalls: "Whilst the battle between the allegorisers and literalists was being waged on the Continent, the few champions who came forward in England to defend the literal interpretation received an important addition to their number in the person of Dr. Pye Smith, who denounced [the allegorical] method of treating Scripture as contrary to all laws of language, and dangerous to real religion" (Ginsburg, *Song of Songs*, p. 94).

138. *Congregational Magazine* 21 (1838): 148–49, quoted in Pope, *Song of Songs*, pp. 135–36. Emphasis in original.

139. And losing his argument with Dr. Pye Smith into the bargain. Ginsburg again: "The controversy between Drs. Pye Smith and Bennett about the Song of Songs produced a salutary effect, inasmuch as it added considerably to the number of those who in this country defended the literal interpretation" (*Song of Songs*, p. 94).

140. See the collection of quotations illustrating the equation, ranging from Roman antiquity to the early twentieth century, in Boyarin, *Unheroic Conduct*, pp. 1–8 (although Boyarin himself is primarily interested in exceptions to this dominant fiction). I have much to say about the Greco-Roman forms of the equation in "Sex and the Single Apostle" below.

141. See further Sanders, *Judaism*, pp. 262–78 (a summary and extension of the influential arguments first set out in his *Paul and Palestinian Judaism*).

142. As David Novak has put it (although with no explicit reference to gender construction), "in the Bible, God alone is autonomous, and God alone can make initiatory choices with impunity. Israel's only choice seems to be to confirm what God has already done to her and for her" (*Election of Israel*, p. 163). But Novak goes on to argue that in rabbinic literature, a realignment of the biblical relationship of God and Israel gradually occurs, so that God is no longer the sole "active initiator" and Israel the "passive recipient" (pp. 163–99). In terms of our elementary gender equation, Israel is thereby accorded a more "masculine" role. This masculinization (Novak himself does not use such terms) can be said to have reached its logical conclusion with Spinoza, who, on Novak's account, fully inverts the traditional relationship between God and Israel, asserting "that in truth it was Israel who elected God and instituted the covenantal relationship with him" (p. 22).

143. The sources surveyed by E. P. Sanders run from "Ben Sira to the Tannaitic rabbis, that is, from 200 B.C.E. to 200 C.E., including the Dead Sea Scrolls, some of the other pietest literature, and the major apocalypses" (*Judaism*, p. 263).

144. In scholarly circles, just as literal readers of the Song had been voices crying in the wilderness in the sixteenth, seventeenth, and eighteenth centuries, allegorical readers increasingly became the isolated voices as the nineteenth century gave way to the twentieth. Just how isolated? Well, two examples are regularly adduced in the scholarly literature: Paul Joüon's 1909 *Le Cantique des Cantiques* and André Robert, Raymond Tournay, and André Feuillet's 1963 *Le Cantique des Cantiques*. Luis Stadelmann's *Love and Politics* (1992) now qualifies as a third, but one would be hard-pressed to extend the list much beyond that. Allegory in the mode of Bernard of Clairvaux or St. John of the Cross is not what we encounter in these commentaries, moreover. All three of the above interpret the Song as an allegory of Israelite history—a far less heady affair than its interpretation as an allegory of the soul's conjugal intimacy with Christ.

145. Littledale, *Song of Songs from Ancient and Mediaeval Sources*, p. xxvii. He has overlooked Johann David Michaelis (d. 1791), who, in his notes to Bishop Robert Lowth's *De Sacra Poesi Hebraeorum Praelectiones* (1753), opined that the Song extols conjugal love, "the attachment of two delicate persons who have been long united in the sacred bond," and asks: "Can we suppose such happiness unworthy of being recommended as a pattern to mankind, and of being celebrated as a subject of gratitude to the great Author of happiness?" (quoted in Ginsburg, *Song of Songs*, p. 87).

146. Delitzsch, *Proverbs, Ecclesiastes, Song of Solomon*, p. 5. The interpretation of the Song as a series of ancient Hebrew wedding songs also made its appearance in the late nineteenth century—in J. G. Wetzstein's appendix to Delitzsch's commentary, for example (see Wetzstein, "Appendix" to Delitzsch, *Proverbs, Ecclesiastes, Song of Solomon*), but particularly in the work of Karl Budde ("Was ist das Hohelied?" and "Das Hohelied erklärt").

147. Rowley, "Interpretation of the Song of Songs," p. 234. But what if "the physi-

cal emotions on which matrimony rests" themselves be objects of suspicion? Let Nicholas of Lyra speak for this earlier view:

> Some have said that the Bridegroom is literally to be taken as Solomon himself but that the Bride is the daughter of Pharaoh, his beloved wife. But this seems not to be true because, granted that this love between Bridegroom and Bride could have been lawful—at any rate if confined within the bounds of marriage . . . —it was of a carnal sort and such love often has something not very fitting and unlawful about it; and so the description of a love of this kind seem inappropriate in canonical books of sacred Scripture, especially as they were written at the dictation of the Holy Spirit. (*The* Postilla Litteralis *on the Song of Songs* 19, trans. Denys Turner)

148. Murphy, *Song of Songs*, p. 100, referring to Barth, *Church Dogmatics*, vol. 3, pt. 1, pp. 288–329; pt. 2, pp. 291–324; and pt. 4, pp. 116–240. Murphy adds: "Barth considers the Song to be a 'second Magna Carta' that develops the view briefly adumbrated in Gen. 2 'although here in a form which is almost terrifyingly strong and unequivocal'" (*Song of Songs*, p. 100, n. 390, quoting Barth, *Church Dogmatics*, vol. 3, pt. 1, p. 312). So alarmed, indeed, is Barth at this spectacle of unfettered heterosexuality that he can barely restrain himself from reaching reflexively for allegory and turning its hose upon the lovers of the Song (pt. 1, p. 312; pt. 2, pp. 294–95).

149. Pope, *Song of Songs*, pp. 192–205.

150. Dempsey, "Interpretation and Use of the Song of Songs," p. 158, quoted in Pope, *Song of Songs*, p. 197.

151. Dempsey, "Interpretation and Use of the Song of Songs," p. 157, quoted in Pope, *Song of Songs*, p. 197.

152. Dempsey, "Interpretation and Use of the Song of Songs," p. 158, quoted in Pope, *Song of Songs*, p. 197.

153. As argued in the Introduction above.

154. Boyarin, *Heroic Conduct*, p. 16.

155. Ibid., pp. 16–17, quoting *Shechter Aboth* 10. Earlier, Boyarin notes: "The 'normal' male in our social formation, and especially the adolescent, is engaged in a constant project of demonstrating to himself that he is not queer, that he does not desire other men." This is quite different from socialization into a culture where it is assumed that men *do* desire other men, but are forbidden to engage in certain acts in response to that desire, "that is, a culture without heterosexuality. There is accordingly a necessary connection between heterosexuality and homophobia." Homophobia is not "an accidental adjunct" of heterosexuality but "its enabling condition" (p. 15).

156. See Pope, *Song of Songs*, pp. 193–205 passim, and Murphy, *Song of Songs*, pp. 40–41. Orthodox Jewish scholars are exceptions to the rule, however. Why should this be? A close reading of Boyarin's *Heroic Conduct* might suggest some answers.

157. As far as I am aware, Cheryl Exum's 1973 article "A Literary and Structural

Analysis of the Song of Songs" was the first published contribution by a woman to critical scholarship on the Song. By now there are many women writing on it—but few of them could be classed as conservative. Their work might be regarded as part of yet another shift in scholarly discourse on the Song, one that has casually set aside the safety net of the older "human love" interpretation—its insistence that the Song is ultimately a validation of marriage. As David Carr has remarked in a related context, "Recent readings of the Song as promoting non-fertility-related erotic love echo the more general shift in industrialized societies toward nonreproductive sexuality" ("Desire in the Song of Songs," p. 235).

More controversially, perhaps, Carr also suggests that such readings unconsciously reproduce "a mini-variant of the myth of repression" postulated by Foucault in the introduction to his *History of Sexuality*, the myth by which we reassure ourselves that we are in a period of unprecedented liberation "from a long process of sexual repression in the Western world" (ibid.). "In place of general sexual repression, we have the specific story of the repression of the original erotic meaning of the Song. In place of more general sexual liberation, we have scholarly recovery of the original erotic meaning of the Song" (ibid.).

158. Cf. the fate of Charles Wesley's well-known hymn "In Temptation," penned shortly after 1738, which begins: "Jesu, Lover of my soul / Let me to thy bosom fly / While the nearer waters roll / While the tempest still is high." Though the popularity of the hymn has, if anything, increased over time, making it a firm hymnbook favorite, more than twenty different variations on the opening lines have appeared. "Lover" has been bowdlerized to "Refuge" or "Savior," for instance, as manly hymn-singers have squirmed uncomfortably at the embarrassing intimacy of the former term, addressed to the male "Jesu"—while heteronormativity and its accomplice homophobia have coalesced all around them. (I owe the fact of the variant readings to Jaroslav Pelikan [*Illustrated Jesus through the Centuries*, p. 131], who, however, doesn't quite seem to know what to do with them.)

And then there is that other hymnbook standard, "Come, O Thou Traveler Unknown," composed by the other Wesley, Charles's brother John, in 1742, and based on Gen. 32:24–32, Jacob's nocturnal wrestling bout with the enigmatic stranger, who, for John and his tradition, is none other than Christ. The hymn runs to fourteen verses, but the following two may suffice to convey the general tenor:

> In vain thou strugglest to get free,
> I never will unloose my hold;
> art thou the man that died for me?
> The secret of thy love unfold;
> wrestling, I will not let thee go
> till I thy name, thy nature know.

And again:

'Tis all in vain to hold thy tongue
or touch the hollow of my thigh;
though every sinew be unstrung,
out of my arms thou shalt not fly;
wrestling I will not let thee go
till I thy name, thy nature know.

(I am grateful to Laurie Zelman for directing my attention to this hymn.)

159. Goulder, *Song of Fourteen Songs*, pp. 7–8.
160. Ibid., p. 51.
161. Ibid., pp. 58–59.
162. Ibid., p. 62.
163. Ibid., p. 79.
164. Ibid., p. 75.
165. Ibid., p. 77; cf. p. 74.
166. Ibid., p. 77.
167. Ibid., p. 78.
168. Pope, *Song of Songs*, pp. 617–18.
169. Ibid., p. 593. Here Pope pulls away from the pack. Pope was not the first commentator to see a vulva in 7:2a, and a flurry of others would follow him (e.g., G. L. Carr, *Song of Solomon*, p. 157; Krinetzki, *Kommentar zum Hohelied*, p. 192; Landy, *Paradoxes of Paradise*, p. 89; Goulder, *Song of Fourteen Songs*, p. 56; Brenner, "Come Back, Come Back the Shulammite," p. 246; Murphy, *Song of Songs*, pp. 182, 185; and Snaith, *Song of Songs*, p. 101). Pope's rendering of 7:8c–d, in contrast, appears to be all his own.
170. Pope, *Song of Songs*, pp. 453, 490–91. H. H. Hirschberg had anticipated Pope in this instance, however, rendering *šĕlāḥayik* less sexily as "your vagina" on the basis of a cognate Arabic word ("Some Additional Arabic Etymologies in OT Lexicography," pp. 379–80). Goulder, for his part, claims to have glimpsed a suspicious bulge in the male lover's anatomy in Song 5:14b, a verse NRSV (innocently?) renders as: "His body is ivory work, / encrusted with sapphires." Pondering alternative meanings for the two problematic Hebrew nouns in the verse (*mēʿāyw* and *sappîrîm*), Goulder arrives at the following question: "So I ask myself, is there a part of the male body, between the hands and the legs [which are described in the lines preceding and succeeding 5:14b respectively], which is heavily veined, and which at all resembles a column of ivory? Indeed, comes the answer, there is" (*Song of Fourteen Songs*, p. 6).
171. Pope, *Song of Songs*, p. 519. G. L. Carr would concur (*Song of Solomon*, pp. 134–35), although Goulder would not (*Song of Fourteen Songs*, pp. 9, 41).
172. Littledale's paraphrase (*Song of Songs from Ancient and Mediaeval Sources*, p. 220).
173. Rupert of Deutz, *In Cantica Canticorum*, PL 168, c 914, trans. Ann Astell.
174. Littledale, *Song of Songs from Ancient and Mediaeval Sources*, p. 220.

175. Pope, *Song of Songs*, p. 519.

176. Although Pope does resist the temptation to ascribe a far kinkier encounter to the two lovers. He translates Song 5:4b as "And my inwards seethed for him" (Hebrew: *ûmēʿay hāmû ʿālayw*), but notes that the King James translators rendered it as "And my bowels were moved for him," "which would not now be considered felicitous," he adds, "although the Rev. Dr. Sibs in 1648, for his sermons on chs. 4–6 of the Canticle, took his title from this passage" (Pope, *Song of Songs*, p. 519). The title in question reads: *Bowels Opened, or, A Discovery of the Neere and Deere Love, Union and Communion betwixt Christ and the Church, and Consequently betwixt Him and Every Beleeving soule*. Pope also notes that the medical library at Yale University contains a copy of this book, the cataloguer apparently assuming that it dealt with cures for constipation (*Song of Songs*, p. 247).

177. Delicacy is not normally one of his failings, but G. L. Carr, in any case, shows how delicately the matter may be stated: "If *yad* does mean the male member here, *hôr* is its female counterpart" (*Song of Solomon*, p. 135).

178. Pope, *Song of Songs*, pp. 514–15. Song 4:16e–f, which Pope translates as "Let my love enter his garden / Let him eat its delectable fruits," similarly elicits the comment that "this is clearly an invitation by the lady to her lover to enjoy to the utmost all her charms which are his preserve" (ibid., p. 499). Pope here enlists the support of Samuel Noah Kramer, who says of 4:12, 16, that "it is not impossible that the 'garden' is a euphemism for the vulva" (*Sacred Marriage Rite*, p. 152, n. 17, quoted in Pope, *Song of Songs*, p. 499). Earlier, Pope himself has remarked on 4:12 (which he translates "A garden locked is my sister bride") that there is "the possibility for erotic interpretation of the garden . . . as with other horticultural terms, fields, furrow, grove, branches, fruit, etc." In fact, "the locked garden denotes virginity" (*Song of Songs*, p. 488).

179. Actually, the Hebrew word *qĕwûṣṣôtay*, which Pope translates as "my locks," can be rendered more simply as "my hair."

180. Pope, *Song of Songs*, p. 515. Snaith also suspects that the feet may be hiding something: "If the beloved's feet here denote her genitals, we have another case of delicate *double entendre*" (*Song of Songs*, p. 73).

181. Pope, *Song of Songs*, p. 515. Snaith similarly suspects the woman of being a tease: "The Heb. word here for 'how' (*ʾeykakah*) is often used in songs of mourning and lamentation: here it may show petulant unwillingness or even teasing" (*Song of Songs*, p. 73). Murphy, also: "Her remonstrations are to be interpreted as a tease, not as a refusal. His reactions in vv 4–5 show this; he attempts to open the door and she rises to let him in. This does not suggest a refusal" (*Song of Songs*, p. 170). The woman says "no," in other words, when she really means "yes" (and the male commentator casually demonstrates his intimate knowledge of the female psyche—doubly impressive when he happens to be a Roman Catholic priest).

182. Pope, *Song of Songs*, p. 680.

183. Eslinger, "Case of an Immodest Lady Wrestler," p. 275.

184. Ibid., p. 276. Eslinger refers us to *Cunningham's Manual of Practical Anatomy*, 2: 211, 219–20.

185. Those in which Israel is sternly instructed to lop off the *kappâ* (traditionally translated "hand") of any woman so depraved as to presume to grab the crotch of a man who is beating the living daylights out of her husband (Deut. 35:11–12). Armed with his reading of Song 5:5, as well as of Gen. 32:26, 33, Eslinger argues that *kappâ* here refers to the external female genitalia.

186. His advent may well be at hand. I refer to Roland Boer, whose hyper-risqué readings of the Song are trickling into print as I write. Boer makes even Pope look like—well, the Pope. See Boer, *Knockin' on Heaven's Door*, pp. 53–70; "Second Coming"; and "King Solomon Meets Annie Sprinkle." The gist of Boer's general take on the Song (although not its midrashic energy or theoretical savvy) may be gleaned from a summary passage in "Second Coming" (pp. 296–97):

> Indeed, the Song spills out a whole vocabulary of sex. In place of the obligatory Hebrew "to know" ($yd^c$), there are pasture a flock (1:7; 2:16; 6:2) or kids (1:8), lie down (1:7), embrace (2:6; 8:20), hold (3:4), hold captive (7:6/5), stir up (2:7; 3:5; 8:4), awaken love (2:7; 3:5; 8:4), ravish (4:9), come (2:8; 4:16; 5:1), come up (3:6; 4:2; 8:5), arise (2:10, 13), lead and bring (8:2), knock (5:2), open (5:2, 6; 7:13/12), bud and bloom (7:13/12), gather lilies (6:2), give forth fragrance (1:12), be sweet to my taste (2:3), feed (2:16; 4:5), eat fruit (4:16; see also 5:1), drink (5:1), pour out (1:3), bathe feet (5:3), and thrust a hand into a hole (5:3).
>
> Apart from this incessant terminology of sex, the whole Song may also be read allegorically as a series of sexual episodes, a poetic porn text: group sex in 1:2–4; a male-female combination with some extras, including shepherds and a bestial phantasy, in 1:5–2:7; animals and humans in 2:8–17; a man with a dildo in 3:1–5; an ode to the phallus and a gay scene in 3:6–11; water sports, especially piss and ejaculate, between two females in 4:1–15; a female-male SM sequence in 4:16–5:9; queer savouring of a grotesque male body in 5:10–16; swinging in 6:1–3; a lesbian sequence in 6:4–12; group female scopophilia in 7:7/6–10/9; and an orgy in 8:1–14. Read this way, the very repetition of a range of sexual acts in this material is a precursor to pornographic literature and film, where all that counts is the sex itself. Everything else is extraneous to this end. . . .

## 2. ON THE FACE AND PHYSIQUE OF THE HISTORICAL JESUS

1. I am not the only one devoutly to desire this consummation—a reaction against the (antiquarian?) obsession with the Bible as an ancient artifact that is the hallmark of traditional biblical scholarship. Diverse attempts to analyze the Bible in contemporary cultural settings can be found in volumes such as these, on the one hand—Boesak, *Comfort and Protest*; Mosala, *Biblical Hermeneutics and Black Theology in South Africa*; Felder, ed., *Stony the Road We Trod*; Smith-Christopher, ed., *Text*

*and Experience*; Kwok, *Discovering the Bible in the Non-Biblical World*; West, *Academy of the Poor*; West, Dube, and Bird, eds., "*Reading With*"; Howard-Brook and Gwyther, *Unveiling Empire*; Segovia, *Decolonizing Biblical Studies* and *Interpreting beyond Borders*; Segovia and Tolbert, eds., *Reading from This Place*; Sugirtharajah, *Bible in the Third World*; and Sugirtharajah, ed., *Voices from the Margins* and *Vernacular Hermeneutics*—and volumes such as these, on the other hand—Hamilton, *Quest for the Post-Historical Jesus*; Jewett, *Saint Paul at the Movies* and *Saint Paul Returns to the Movies*; Kreitzer, *New Testament in Fiction and Film*, *Old Testament in Fiction and Film*, and *Pauline Images in Fiction and Film*; Scott, *Hollywood Dreams and Biblical Stories*; Bach, *Women, Seduction, and Betrayal in Biblical Narrative*; Bach, ed., *Biblical Glamour and Hollywood Glitz*; Exum, *Plotted, Shot, and Painted*; Marsh and Ortiz, eds., *Explorations in Theology and Film*, esp. chs. 4 and 9; Tatum, *Jesus at the Movies*; Exum and Moore, eds., *Biblical Studies / Cultural Studies*; Dowsett, "Theology in the Discography"; Pippin, *Apocalyptic Bodies*; Boer, *Knockin' on Heaven's Door*; Aichele, ed., *Culture, Entertainment, and the Bible*; and Moore, ed., *In Search of the Present*. The cultural studies journal *Biblicon* (now sadly defunct) also belongs with the latter group. Other volumes, such as Porter, Hayes, and Tombs, eds., *Images of Christ*, effortlessly straddle both of my makeshift categories.

2. An ambivalence that has also characterized the field of cultural studies in its assessment of popular culture, fatigue and nausea predominating in the early years, later giving way to increased appreciation, and occasional idealization, of popular culture as a potential site for resistance and subversion. See Strinati, *Introduction to Theories of Popular Culture*; Storey, *Introductory Guide to Cultural Theory and Popular Culture*; and Storey, ed., *Cultural Theory and Popular Culture*.

3. This Latin letter appears to date from the thirteenth or fourteenth century. It is ascribed to one Publius Lentius, a (presumably fictitious) associate of Pontius Pilate's; hence its pen-portrait of Jesus purports to stem from an eyewitness. The translation used above first appeared in the American Millerite broadsheet *The Midnight Cry* in 1843; it is reprinted in Morgan, *Visual Piety*, p. 229, n. 73.

4. *Antichrist* is a medieval Irish text of uncertain date. The translation is Máire Herbert's, from Herbert and McNamara, eds., *Irish Biblical Apocrypha*.

5. Hermann Samuel Reimarus (1694–1768) is generally credited with getting the search under way. David Friedrich Strauss (1808–74) subsequently moved to the head of the search party. Later still, Albert Schweitzer (1875–1965) snatched the torch from Strauss. See Reimarus, *Fragments*; Strauss, *Life of Jesus, Critically Examined*; and Schweitzer, *Quest of the Historical Jesus*.

6. Or so the standard story goes. Schweitzer slammed the brakes on the First Quest in 1906, declaring it to have been on the wrong track all along, after which there was a prolonged pause, interrupted, first by the emergence of a New Quest, centered in postwar Germany, and, more recently, by a Third Quest, centered in the United States, resulting in the following sequence: First Quest, No Quest, New Quest, Third

Quest. This tidy (meta)narrative has recently been ruffled, however; see Marsh, "Quests of the Historical Jesus in New Historicist Perspective," esp. pp. 404–15, 427–28.

7. Handy introductions to the current quest include Borg, *Jesus in Contemporary Scholarship*; Powell, *Jesus as a Figure in History*; and Witherington, *Jesus Quest*. More ambitious in scope, although also introductory, is Theissen and Merz, *Historical Jesus*. More ambitious still, an exhaustive examination of the methods and criteria employed in Jesus research, are Evans and Chilton, eds., *Authenticating the Words of Jesus* and *Authenticating the Acts of Jesus*; and Porter, *Criteria for Authenticity in Historical-Jesus Research*.

8. For which conceit Arius was roundly condemned at Nicaea and exiled to Illyria. For the full story, see Rowan Williams, *Arius*, or, for an abridged version, Aland, *History of Christianity*, 1: 184–98.

9. Because whereas the notion of Jesus' preexistence in heaven with God prior to his incarnation is utterly absent from the Gospels of Matthew, Mark, and Luke, it is emphatically present in the Gospel of John (e.g., 1:1–3, 14; 8:58; 12:41; 17:5). Not surprisingly, therefore, John featured prominently in the Arian controversy. Other Johannine verses that figured in the debate included 3:35; 10:30; 12:27; 14:10; and 17:3, 11.

10. The Seminar's findings have been published as Funk and Hoover, *Five Gospels*. The first leg of its mission completed, the Seminar then set itself the task of scrutinizing Jesus' *actions* as reported in early Christian literature and separating historical wheat from fictional chaff. The results have now been published as Funk, *Acts of Jesus*. Funk has also issued a more personal manifesto, *Honest to Jesus*. For a defense of the Seminar against the barrage of criticism leveled at it, see Miller, *Jesus Seminar and Its Critics*.

11. See Bible and Culture Collective, *Postmodern Bible*.

12. R. E. Brown's *Community of the Beloved Disciple* remains an engaging initiation into these mysteries. For a chatty update by another specialist, see M. D. Smith, "What Have I Learned about the Gospel of John?" For a more exhaustive treatment of these matters, see Painter, *Quest for the Messiah*.

13. Valentinus is the putative author of the *Gospel of Truth*, recovered near Nag Hammadi in Upper Egypt in 1945. Only fragments of his oeuvre otherwise survive, his intricate theological system being known to us mainly through the writings of his opponents.

14. The translation of the fragment is Bentley Layton's (*Gnostic Scriptures*, p. 239).

15. "The Jesus Seminar Spring 1995 Meeting," *The Fourth R* 8 (1995), p. 10. Lüdemann achieved notoriety in Germany with the publication in March 1994 of *Die Auferstehung Jesu*, which sold out overnight and provoked a great public outcry. A publisher's dream come true? Not for Vandenhoeck & Ruprecht, a pillar of scholarly sobriety, which, alarmed by the runaway success of one of its books, refused to reprint it. It is now available in English as *The Resurrection of Jesus*. Also see Lüdemann's ominously titled *What Really Happened to Jesus*.

16. "Jesus Seminar Spring 1995 Meeting," p. 10.

17. Michelet, *Mother Death*, pp. 89–90.

18. Here and in what follows, translations are from Roberts and Donaldson, eds., *Ante-Nicene Fathers*. The apologetic contortions that these unflattering statements induced in certain of the devout editors and translators of the series merit a study in themselves. See, e.g., 2: 272, n. 1, which is appended to the sentence from *The Instructor* quoted above: "But see also Ps. xiv. 2, which was often cited by the ancients to prove the reverse. Both may be reconciled: he was a fair and comely child like his father David; but as 'the man of sorrows,' he became old in looks, and his countenance was marred." "For David's beauty" we are referred to 1 Sam. 16:12, which reads: "Now he was ruddy, and withal of a beautiful countenance, and goodly to look at" (KJV). And for Jesus' "appearance at three and thirty, when the Jews only ventured to credit him with less than fifty years," we are directed to John 8:57: "Then said the Jews unto him, 'Thou art not yet fifty years old, and hast thou seen Abraham?'" Best of all, however, "for our Lord's [beauty] at twelve years of age, when the virgin was seeking her child," we are sent to Song 5:7–16, the physical description of the male lover that extols his whiteness and ruddiness, his bushy raven-black locks, his dovelike eyes, his lips like lilies, his ivory belly, etc.

19. Cf. Tertullian, *Against Marcion* 3.7; Hippolytus, *Treatise on Christ and Antichrist* 44.

20. Cf. Tertullian, *Against Praxeas* 11.

21. In the *Acts of Peter* (ca. 180–90 C.E.), too, we read of Jesus "beauteous, yet appearing among us as poor and ugly," while in the *Acts of John* (late second century?) we read that the polymorphous Jesus "sometimes appeared to [John] as a small man with no good looks" (translations from Schneemelcher, ed., *New Testament Apocrypha*).

22. Origen, *Against Celsus* 6.75; cf. 1.69. Cf. also 1.54; 4.16; 7.16, and id., *Commentary on Matthew* 12.29.

23. Part of Isaiah's famous depiction of the "Suffering Servant," which early Christians took to be a previously unrecognized portrait of Jesus:

> Who has believed what we
>   have heard?
> And to whom has the arm of
>   the LORD been revealed?
> For he grew up before him like a
>   young plant,
> and like a root out of dry
>   ground;
> he had no form or majesty that
>   we should look at him,
> nothing in his appearance that
>   we should desire him.

> He was despised and rejected by
>     others;
> a man of suffering and
>     acquainted with infirmity;
> and as one from whom others
>     hide their faces
> he was despised and we held
>     him of no account.

And so on. David Clines, in the course of noting the striking number of males in the Hebrew Bible who are described as physically beautiful (*Joseph*: Gen. 39:6; *Moses*: Exod. 2:2; *Saul*: 1 Sam. 9:2; 16:12; *David*: 1 Sam. 16:12; 17:42; *Absolom*: 2 Sam. 14:25; *Adonijah*: 1 Kings 1:6), remarks of this passage: "it is implied that ordinarily one would expect a high-ranking 'servant of Yahweh' to be beautiful in form and face..." ("David the Man," p. 222). For more detailed treatments of physical beauty in the Hebrew Bible, see Westermann, "Das Schöne im Altem Testament," pp. 119–37 passim, and Brenner, *Intercourse of Knowledge*, pp. 43–51.

24. The Jewish historian Josephus (37–ca. 100 C.E.) is our principal source for the turbulent period in Jewish history that culminated in the Roman destruction of Jerusalem and its temple in 70 C.E.

25. The latter is quoted as an epigraph to the present section—although there Jesus still retains his good looks.

26. The translation is from Schneemelcher, *New Testament Apocrypha*. The *Acts of Paul and Thecla*, an independently transmitted section of a much longer composition known as the *Acts of Paul*, is usually dated to the late second century. Influenced by this pen-portrait, apparently, the Byzantine author known as Pseudo-Lucian describes Paul as a bald Galilean (!) with a big nose (*Philopatris* 12). The Thecla of the *Acts* is a young woman who falls for Paul in a big way—not for his looks, however, but for his voice. And the "acts" of the title are not sex acts; Thecla's physical involvement with Paul does not go beyond kissing his chains and rolling around on a patch of ground on which his buttocks have recently rested. Yet she refuses to give herself to any other man, which results in her being condemned to death repeatedly—and losing her clothes repeatedly—but only so that she can be divinely delivered from both inconveniences simultaneously: "And there was about her a cloud of fire, so that neither could the beasts touch her nor could she be seen naked" (*Acts of Paul and Thecla* 34). Do I need to add that she is achingly beautiful?

27. Malherbe, "Physical Description of Paul," pp. 170–71.

28. Archilochus, fr. 58. Loeb translation. Robert Grant uses this and other similar descriptions from Greco-Roman sources to argue that the Paul of the *Acts* cuts a dashing military figure and is being presented to us as God's general ("Description of Paul in the Acts of Paul and Thecla").

29. Suetonius, *Augustus* 79.2. Loeb translation.

30. Malherbe, "Physical Description of Paul," p. 174. Bruce Malina and Jerome Neyrey largely concur with Malherbe's conclusion in their own analysis of this description (*Portraits of Paul*, pp. 127–48). János Bollók, however, uses the physiognomic handbooks to resurrect the older argument that the description is of a Paul who is physically unimpressive ("Description of Paul in the *Acta Pauli*").

31. Ford, "Physical Features of the Antichrist" (the quotation is from p. 37); Rosenstiehl, "Portrait de l'Antichrist." Many of Rosenstiehl's Antichrists bear an unmistakable family resemblance to the specimen described in the epigraph to this section.

32. Ford, "Physical Features of the Antichrist," pp. 33, 34, 38.

33. For further details, see Russel, "Byzantine and Romanesque Art and Architecture," p. 28. John's Jesus is broadly in line with the ancient Romans' ideal somatic type, which, as John Clarke notes, "required a man to have tanned skin, wavy brown hair, and brown eyes" ("Hypersexual Black Men in Augustan Baths," p. 188). We do not have to await John of Damascus, however, for verbal assurances of Jesus' good looks. An anonymous, late-sixth-century pilgrim's travelogue, the *Antonini Placentini Itinerarium*, relates how Jesus' footsteps are still clearly visible in the Praetorium in Jerusalem, and that the feet were "well-shaped, small, delicate [*pedem pulchrum, modicum, subtilem*]," from which the writer deduces that Jesus must have been "of an ordinary height, with a handsome face, [and] curly hair"—facts he is already aware of in any case thanks to a picture (*imago*) of Jesus that he has seen, said to have been painted while he was still on earth (*It. Plac.* 23). (My thanks to Virginia Burrus for directing me to this little-known text; for further discussion of it, see Leyerle, "Early Christian Pilgrimage Narratives," pp. 132–37.)

34. Which, no doubt, is why we say that a handsome person is *good-looking*.

35. Tertullian, *Against Marcion* 3.17; cf. id., *Against Praxeas* 11. The Septuagint reads: *anēggeilamen enantion autou hōs paidion*. . . .

36. Tertullian, *Against Marcion* 3.7; id., *On the Flesh of Christ* 9 (and see also 15).

37. Mack does not write Jesus books per se, but a distinctive portrait of the historical Jesus emerges from his work nonetheless; see his *Myth of Innocence*, pp. 53–77, and *Lost Gospel*, pp. 29–39, 105–30. Mack was one of the original "Charter Fellows" of the Jesus Seminar, although he seems to have subsequently dropped out of it (his name is absent from the roster of current Fellows in Funk and Hoover, *Five Gospels*, pp. 533–37). Mack's Jesus, although deliciously witty and undeniably brilliant, is deemed "unattractive" by many of Mack's readers, because he lacks any real sense of mission (in contrast, say, to the socially engaged Jesuses of Richard Horsley and John Dominic Crossan). To Mack's Jesus, too, contrast N. T. Wright's Jesus as depicted in his *Jesus and the Victory of God*, another weighty Jesus tome. According to one reviewer, "The end result of Wright's epistemology and procedural rigor is *to provide a portrait of the Jesus of the Gospels that is wildly attractive*" (Newman, "[W]righting the History of Jesus," p. 139; his emphasis).

38. Mack made this observation in the course of *The Jesus Summit: The Histori-*

*cal Jesus and Contemporary Faith*, a teleconference broadcast by the Episcopal Cathedral Teleconferencing Network on February 19, 1994. In his tongue-in-cheek performance on this video, Mack manages to make John Dominic Crossan seem a thorough traditionalist (no mean feat), and to make Marcus Borg, the third star of the show, look like a schoolboy in short pants. Crossan is co-chair (with Funk) of the Jesus Seminar, and his book *The Historical Jesus* is commonly credited with opening the current chapter of the Jesus quest (an oversimplification, perhaps). Culturally, I feel a profound affinity with Crossan—same rural Irish roots, same rural Irish accent, same abortive affair with a religious order—but Mack's principled skepticism also resonates deeply with me.

39. Not least its founder; see Funk, *Honest to Jesus*, pp. 143–216.

40. Vol. 3 of Meier's *Marginal Jew* has yet to appear as I write.

41. Essentially, this is a digest of Sanders's longer and more "scholarly" *Jesus and Judaism*. Like Crossan, Meier, and Wright, Sanders is seen as a heavy hitter in current Jesus scholarship.

42. The original 1993 edition of *The Historical Figure of Jesus* featured an entirely different jacket design, centered on an image from the Catacombs of Christ as the Good Shepherd. Youthful, short-haired, clean-shaven, and pink-skinned, Jesus looks relaxed and attractive in a revealing shepherd's smock as he addresses an admiring audience of sheep and birds.

43. Just as Sanders's *Historical Figure of Jesus* is a popular digest of *Jesus and Judaism*, so, too, is Crossan's *Jesus: A Revolutionary Biography*, a popular digest of *Historical Jesus* (a "baby Jesus," as he himself has termed it), while *Essential Jesus* is a digest of both books. Then there's Crossan's *Who Killed Jesus?* another spinoff from *Historical Jesus*, and *Birth of Christianity*, his sequel to *Historical Jesus*. Crossan's big Jesus book alone (by no means a bedtime read) sold 55,000 copies in its first eighteen months, apparently. For some trenchant comments on Jesus scholarship as good business, see Marsh, "Quests of the Historical Jesus in New Historicist Perspective," pp. 422–25.

44. Crossan, *Jesus: A Revolutionary Biography*, p. v.

45. The presumption that Jesus was a Jewish Cynic is a pillar of Crossan's work, and also of Mack's. The basis of this hypothesis is a series of alleged parallels between the teachings of Jesus and those of the Greco-Roman Cynic philosophers. The first scholar to set out these parallels in detail, however, was Gerald Downing in *Christ and the Cynics*; also see his *Cynics and Christian Origins*, as well as his recent exchange with a Cynic Jesus skeptic: Eddy, "Jesus as Diogenes?" together with Downing, "Deeper Reflections on the Jewish Cynic Jesus."

46. Then there are the grim Christ Pantocrators whose scowling visages dominate the covers of Borg's *Jesus*, Wright's *Jesus and the Victory of God*, and Witherington's *Jesus Quest*; the less lugubrious Jesus who graces the cover of Johnson's *Real Jesus*; and the cubist Christ who gazes disjointedly at us from the jacket of Borg's

*Meeting Jesus Again for the First Time*, to name but a few. Can these books, too, be judged by their covers?

Of the Christ Pantocrator icons, Jaroslav Pelikan remarks: "By depicting the indissoluble union between the timeless nature of the All-Sovereign and the historical nature of Jesus of Nazareth, this Byzantine icon of Christ Pantocrator succeeded in conceptualizing the one who was the embodiment not only of the True in his teaching and of the Good in his life, but of the Beautiful in his form as 'the fairest of the sons of men' (Ps. 45:2)" (*Jesus through the Centuries*, p. 93).

47. Attributed to him (only) in Mark 6:3 ("Is not this the *tektōn*, the son of Mary . . . ?") and Matt. 13:55 (following Mark). *Tektōn* has, of course, traditionally, if anachronistically, been translated as "carpenter."

48. Meier, *Marginal Jew*, 1: 281.

49. On the latter, see Vance, *Sinews of the Spirit*; Hall, ed., *Muscular Christianity*; and Ladd and Mathisen, *Muscular Christianity*.

50. Bruce Barton, *Man Nobody Knows*, pp. 1–3.

51. Ibid., p. 33.

52. See Sanders, *Jesus and Judaism*, pp. 11, 61–76, and id., *Historical Figure of Jesus*, pp. 10–11, 252–69.

53. See Crossan, *Historical Jesus*, pp. xii, 355–60, and *Jesus: A Revolutionary Biography*, pp. 130–33. What about Meier? We shall have to await his third volume for his definitive pronouncement on the incident. In the meanwhile, see his "Reflections on Jesus-of-History Research Today," pp. 101–2, which suggests that he, too, is convinced that the incident occurred and accords crucial significance to it.

54. The best-known exception being Elisabeth Schüssler Fiorenza, mostly notably in her *Jesus: Miriam's Child, Sophia's Prophet* (although even she does not seem to see herself as participating in the quest per se; see esp. Fiorenza and Bach, "Elisabeth Schüssler Fiorenza: An Interview," pp. 34–36). Paula Fredricksen's *Jesus of Nazareth, King of the Jews* also comes readily to mind. Further reflections on the roles and nonroles of women in historical Jesus scholarship can be found in Schaberg, "Feminist Experience of Historical Jesus Scholarship"; Kwok, "On Color-Coding Jesus," passim; and Marsh, "Quests of the Historical Jesus in New Historicist Perspective," pp. 417–18.

55. See Doss, "Making a 'Virile, Manly Christ,'" pp. 86–89. She also notes that in addition to Bruce Barton's *Man Nobody Knows*, more than two hundred other books featuring a more "masculine" Christ were published in this period, books such as Harry Emerson Fosdick's *Manhood of the Master* (1911), and Charles Francis Stocking and William Wesley Totheroh's *Businessman of Syria* (1923).

56. Recounted in Doss, "Making a 'Virile, Manly Christ,'" pp. 62, 80. Her source is a 1943 issue of the *Evangelical Beacon*.

57. In 1940, based on a charcoal sketch that he had produced for the cover of the *Covenant Companion* in 1924.

58. Quoted in Lundbom, *Master Painter*, p. 152. As Lundbom makes clear, this critic's voice was by no means a lone one (ibid., pp. 151–52). While it lacks analytical finesse, Lundbom's book is the most exhaustive account to date of Sallman's life and art, and a useful companion to Morgan, ed., *Icons of American Protestantism*.

59. A cliché neatly enshrined in an anecdote that I recently came across in the British newspaper *The Guardian* (Jenkins, "Exposed!" p. 24), an anecdote that also hints at the cliché's latent contradictions:

> In the interests of understanding bodily exposure and how it affects social interaction, I have decided to shave my head. "You can't do this! I'm going to cry if you do. Why would you do this to yourself?" Fred is my aerobics student. . . . He has taken my class several times a week for two years. We have never had a personal conversation. . . .
>
> Olivia is a public high-school senior. She and I meet once a week for a tutoring session. "The Bible," Olivia tells me, "is like a book on how to live. It tells us how to act, how to dress, what make-up to wear, everything. Women are not supposed to shave their heads."
>
> "Is it okay for men?" I ask.
>
> "For men, it's okay," she laughs. . . .
>
> "But what if I'm a really good person, I do everything right, except I shave my head?" I say. . . .
>
> "Well, the Bible also tells women not to wear pants, but I don't believe that part of it," she replies. "I believe it's not how you look but what's inside that counts with God."
>
> "I hope so. Because I'm still going to do it."
>
> "I'll pray for you," she tells me.

Still more revealing is Rebecca Mead's "Slim for Him," a profile of the best-selling Christian diet author Gwen Shamblin. Mead notes that "Christian weight-loss programs generally hold that fat is undesirable not because God cares about how you look but because a thin, fit body is a more efficient tool with which to do God's will" (p. 50). Shamblin, too, seems to suggest

> that slenderness is next to godliness, but she is careful to say that God himself doesn't care what you look like. "I think God programmed *you* to care what you look like," she said. God is with her, she says, when she goes shopping for clothes. "Look at the colors in the fall," she told me, gesturing through her office window. "He is so good at colors." Shamblin, who is a former cheerleader, describes herself as having a crush on God. "I think he is fabulously, wonderfully good-looking," she told me. "I think he is a lot more normal than we think. . . . He is so powerful, so rich, so famous. He has got on designer clothes" (p. 51; I am indebted to Helen Tartar for this gem).

60. Or racial identity. In recent theoretical debate, the categories "race" and "ethnicity" have increasingly tended to fade into each other. Introducing a thematic issue of *PMLA* on ethnicity, for example, Sander Gilman is obliged to ask: "Is race the same thing as ethnicity? Is it possible to be of a race and not to be ethnic? to be ethnic as a member of a race?" ("Introduction," p. 24).

61. Cf. Dyer, *White*, p. 68, and Bastide, "Color, Racism, and Christianity," p. 315.

62. Cf. Gölz, "How Ethnic Am I?" p. 47: "In the postdeconstructive context of the 1990s, the practice of elaborating ethnic and other sorts of cultural and group identities has become popular once again. And yet after deconstruction, ethnicity can no longer be a truth. It must be something constructed, potentially multiple, hybridized, and interstitial." See further Sollors, *Invention of Ethnicity*.

63. Cf. Dyer, *White*, pp. 41–81 passim.

64. Walker, *Color Purple*, pp. 165–66. Malcolm X had earlier covered the same terrain as Walker, although less artfully:

> Brothers and sisters, the white man has brainwashed us Black people to fasten our gaze upon a blond-haired, blue-eyed Jesus! We're worshiping a Jesus that doesn't even *look* like us! Now, just think of this. The blond-haired, blue-eyed white man has taught you and me to worship a *white* Jesus, and to shout and sing and pray to this God that's *his* God, the white man's God. The white man has taught us to shout and sing and pray until we *die*, to wait until *death*, for some dreamy heaven-in-the-hereafter, when we're *dead*, while this white man has his milk and honey in the streets paved with golden dollars right here on *this* earth!" (*Autobiography of Malcolm X*, p. 22; emphasis in original)

65. Quoted in Morgan, "Visual Culture of American Protestantism," p. 35.

66. Doss, "Making a 'Virile, Manly Christ,'" p. 88.

67. See pp. 16–17 above.

68. As argued in the previous essay, "The Song of Songs in the History of Sexuality."

69. Quoted in Lundbom, *Master Painter*, pp. 151–52.

70. Howard W. Ellis, *Story of Sallman's "Good Shepherd*," a 1944 promotional pamphlet quoted in Morgan, "Visual Culture of American Protestantism," p. 59.

71. Beginning in 1942, millions of cards featuring the *Head of Christ* were distributed through the USO by the Salvation Army and the YMCA to members of the American armed forces stationed overseas (McDannell, "Marketing Jesus," p. 114).

72. Quoted in Doss, "Making a 'Virile, Manly Christ,'" p. 65.

73. Morgan, "Visual Culture of American Protestantism," p. 27; Doss, "Making a 'Virile, Manly Christ,'" p. 54.

74. Rice, *Memnoch the Devil*, pp. 168–69. Rice's Jesus, physically at least, can count Renan's Jesus among his fine-featured forebears. Of Jesus, Renan wrote: "His amiable character, accompanied doubtless by one of those lovely faces [*une de ces ravissantes*

*figures*] which sometimes appear in the Jewish race, threw around him a fascination from which no one in the midst of these kindly and simple populations could escape" (*Life of Jesus*, p. 63).

75. Hurling is an ancient Irish team sport, not unlike modern-day field hockey, which is still extremely popular in many parts of the country. I was a dismally failed hurler as a boy. At school I stood on the sidelines, or, worse, in goal, vainly attempting to avoid contact with the small hard leather ball that came shooting at me periodically with unnerving velocity.

76. Wallace, *Ben Hur*, p. 118.

77. Ibid., pp. 405–6.

78. Sedgwick, *Epistemology of the Closet*, p. 140. Richard Rambuss, too, has much to say in this vein in his *Closet Devotions* (and he says it superbly).

79. Hopkins, "Sermon for Sunday evening Nov. 23 1879," pp. 137–39.

80. White, *Hopkins*, p. 114. Compare the title character of the film *Priest* (dir. Antonia Bird, 1995), who, to his deep dismay, finds himself looking at the crucified Christ and seeing "a naked man, utterly desirable" (quoted in Rambuss, *Closet Devotions*, p. 5). No less conflicted, although possibly more desperate, is the protagonist of the gay porn movie *More Than a Man* (dir. Jerry Douglas, 1990), which, in the manner of such movies, opens with the leading man on his knees before another, near-naked man and huskily declaring, "You name it, I'll do it"—except that the latter figure happens to be Christ on his cross. For an incisive analysis of this controversial film (once confiscated by the Chicago police in a raid on an adult movie theater), see Rambuss, "Homodevotion." For premodern expressions of anxiety at the prospect of male arousal occasioned by the unclothed Christ, see Trexler, "Gendering Jesus Crucified," esp. p. 116.

81. This theme, sans the beauty angle, is the focus of "Torture: The Divine Butcher," part 1 of my book *God's Gym*.

82. Long, "Sacrality of Male Beauty and Homosex," p. 273.

83. Ibid. (the ellipsis is Long's).

84. Ibid. Hence Long's contention: "A gay theology that has not yet begun to ask what the power of male beauty is and means to a gay man, why sex with a beautiful man—who may or not be an intimate other—is so important, and why it is so important to be found attractive has not yet found its ownmost subject matter" (ibid., p. 281).

85. Long's phrase (ibid., p. 277).

86. *Robo-Jesus?* Well why not? *Robocop* is about death and resurrection, after all. Savagely executed by his enemies, the hero is raised to new life in a now indestructible body.

87. Allen, "Away with the Manger," p. 27. Allen has since published an engaging book-length account of the current Jesus quest entitled *The Human Christ*.

88. Allen, "Away with the Manger," p. 28. Whence the Seminar's concern at Verhoeven's reliance on John? Funk and Hoover's *Five Gospels*, the first full-scale report

of the Seminar's findings, color-coded all the sayings of Jesus in the canonical gospels and *Thomas* (the eponymous "fifth" gospel). Words the historical Jesus "undoubtedly" uttered, "or something very like it," were colored red; words he "probably" uttered were colored pink; words he did not utter, "but the ideas contained in [them] are close to his own," were colored gray; and words he did not utter, but which represent "the perspective or content of a later or different tradition," were colored black (*Five Gospels*, p. 36). So what happened when the Johannine Jesus had his colors done? Red was certainly not his color, as it turned out; black was. In fact, all of his words were shrouded in black in *The Five Gospels*, with the sole exception of 4:43 ("A prophet gets no respect on his own turf"), which provided a small splash of pink for contrast (ibid., p. 412).

89. Allen, "Away with the Manger," p. 28. My friend Stuart Lasine, who was present at the time, jokingly offered to play Jesus in the movie, since he was the only Jew at the meeting. "Jesus wasn't bald!" someone shot back. Stuart asked him how he knew that.

90. "Wallace who?" did you say? Well, you try naming a well-known Hollywood male actor under fifty who is decidedly plain and homely looking (excluding comedians, that is; Jim Carrey as Jesus?). Having hit upon Wallace Shawn, best known for his role in Louis Malle's *My Dinner with André*, I subsequently discovered that John Thompson, similarly casting around for the name of a Hollywood actor who "would be grotesquely miscast as Jesus" (as he puts it), had also settled on Shawn, whose humdrum misfortune it is to be short, bald, and round (to be an average-looking guy, in other words). See Thompson, "Jesus as Moving Image," p. 296.

91. Speaking of accents, the 2000 NBC miniseries *Jesus* took a bold multicultural approach to the problem of ancient Mediterranean English, according American accents to Jesus (played by "newcomer" Jeremy Sisto) and Mary Magdalene (Debra Messing of the sitcom *Will & Grace*), but a French accent to Mary the mother of Jesus (Jacqueline Bisset), a German accent to Joseph (Armin Mueller-Stahl), a Scottish accent to John the Baptist (David O'Hara), an English accent to Pontius Pilate (Gary Oldman), a Dutch accent to Satan (Jeroen Krabbe), and assorted other European, Middle Eastern, and African accents to many of the minor characters.

A recent issue of the *New York Times Magazine* features an illuminating exchange between Sisto and Glenn Carter, who plays the title role in the Broadway revival of *Jesus Christ Superstar*, which opened on April 16, 2000, a month or so before NBC broadcast its *Jesus*. In the course of the dialogue, Sisto opines (apparently straightfaced), "I think I was picked to play Jesus because I'm handsome," to which Carter responds (also without apparent irony), "Yeah. And I have long hair" (Carter and Sisto, "What Would Jesus Do in This Scene?" p. 38).

92. Quoted in Tatum, *Jesus at the Movies*, p. 8.

93. Doss, "Making a 'Virile, Manly Christ,'" pp. 91–92. In addition, David Morgan has remarked how Sallman's "profile of Christ conforms to the standards of popular

commercial portrait photography." In place of the pseudo-Palestinian landscapes favored by other Jesus painters, Sallman employed "a simple screen reminiscent of the studio backdrop used by photographers." His meticulous delineation of Jesus' eyes and lips "resembles retouched photographic portraits designed to present the sitter to best advantage." And the smooth complexion, stylized features, and commercial colors remind us that the painter of the *Head of Christ* had already had a long and successful career in some of Chicago's leading advertising agencies (Morgan, "Warner Sallman and the Visual Culture of American Protestantism," pp. 31–32).

94. Appleyard, "Bloated Victim," p. 1. Further on Elvis and religion, see Rodman, *Elvis after Elvis*, esp. pp. 111–22, and Gottdiener, "Dead Elvis as Other Jesus."

95. Which reads:

Let the same mind be in you that was in Christ Jesus,
who, though he was in the form of God,
did not regard equality with God as something to be exploited,
but emptied himself,
taking the form of a slave,
being born in human likeness.
And being found in human form,
he humbled himself
and became obedient to the point of death—
even death on a cross.
Therefore God also highly exalted him
and gave him the name
that is above every name,
so that at the name of Jesus
every knee should bend,
in heaven and on earth and under the earth,
and every tongue should confess
that Jesus Christ is Lord,
to the glory of God the Father.

The hymn is commonly understood by scholars to be a pre-Pauline fragment, a liturgical snippet that the apostle has slotted into his letter. The classic discussion of it is Ralph Martin's *Carmen Christi*. For a differently focused treatment, see Stephen Fowl's *Story of Christ in the Ethics of Paul*, pp. 49–75.

96. My translation. The Septuagint reads: *ouk estin eidos autō oude doxa; kai eidomen auton, kai ouk eichen eidos oude kallos*. . . .

97. Snapshots such as Rev. 1:13–16 (to which I shall return in "Revolting Revelations" below): "I saw one like the Son of Man, clothed with a long robe and with a golden sash across his chest. His head and his hair were white as white wool, white as snow; his eyes were like a flame of fire, his feet were like burnished bronze, refined as

in a furnace, and his voice was like the sound of many waters. In his right hand he held seven stars, and from his mouth came a sharp, two-edged sword, and his face was like the sun shining with full force."

98. See E. C. Evans, *Physiognomics in the Ancient World*, and id., "Study of Physiognomy in the Second Century A.D."; Armstrong, "Methods of the Greek Physiognomists"; and Gleason, "Semiotics of Gender," as well as much of her *Making Men*. The pervasiveness of physiognomy in the ancient Mediterranean world is suggested, for example, by the fact that at least two physiognomic texts have turned up at Qumran; see Martínez, ed. and trans., *Dead Sea Scrolls Translated*, pp. 456–57 (the texts are 4Q186 and 4Q561). But physiognomy was only the tip of the iceberg, apparently. Dale Martin sums up the situation well: "In popular Greco-Roman culture, bodies were direct expressions of status, usually pictured as a vertical spectrum stretching from inhuman or barbaric ugliness to divine beauty. The gods, of course, were beautiful; and people of aristocratic birth or upper-class origins were expected to manifest their proximity to the divine by possessing a natural beauty and nobility. This cultural common sense recurs repeatedly in novels. In Chariton's *Chareas and Callirhoe*, for example, Callirhoe, the aristocratic heroine, is regularly mistaken for an apparition of Aphrodite. Although it is not as much emphasized in the novels, the converse assumption was also made: people of lower status were expected to be misshapen and ugly" (*The Corinthian Body*, pp. 34–35; see esp. Chariton, *Chareas and Callirhoe* 5.9; also Xenophon of Ephesus, *An Ephesian Tale* 1.1, 2; Heliodorus, *An Ethiopian Story* 1.2, 7, 19–20; 2.19; 7.12, 19; Achilles Tatius, *Leucippe and Clitophon* 1.4). This quotation is from a section of Martin's book entitled "The Beautifully Balanced Body" (pp. 34–38). Further on Greco-Roman ideals of beauty (male beauty especially), see Dover, *Greek Homosexuality*, pp. 15 ff., 111–22; Scroggs, *New Testament and Homosexuality*, pp. 17–28; and Miles, *Plotinus on Body and Beauty*, esp. pp. 33–56. Also relevant is Cohen, "Beauty of Flora and the Beauty of Sarai."

99. Diverse analyses of the ideologies of beauty include Lakoff and Scherr, *Face Value*; Chapkis, *Beauty Secrets*; Wolf, *Beauty Myth*; Bringle, *God of Thinness*; Bordo, *Unbearable Weight*; Jaggar, ed., *Living with Contradictions*, pt. 3 ("Marketing Femininity"); Dutton, *Perfectible Body*; Lambert, *Face of Love*; Cohen, Wilk, and Stoeltje, eds., *Beauty Queens on the Global Stage*; Rooks, *Hair Raising*; Furman, *Facing the Mirror*; Gilman, *Creating Beauty to Cure the Soul* and *Making the Body Beautiful*; Brand, ed., *Beauty Matters*; and cf. Berger, *Ways of Seeing*; Brownmiller, *Femininity*; and Morrison, *Bluest Eye*. Kirwan, *Beauty*, provides a history of the concept of beauty, while Scarry, *On Beauty and Being Just*, provides an apologia for beauty—although one that curiously fails to address the perennial cultural proclivity to equate beauty with virtue, or to engage or even reference any academic analyses of this tendency (such as those listed above). Friday's popularly pitched *Power of Beauty* exhibits still fewer qualms about its title topic.

100. On the global dimensions of the phenomenon, see much of Cohen, Wilk,

and Stoeltje, eds., *Beauty Queens on the Global Stage*, along with Chapkis, *Beauty Secrets*, p. 37, and Furman, *Facing the Mirror*, p. 61.

101. See "Men and Beauty" in Lakoff and Scherr, *Face Value*, pp. 209–44; Bordo, *Male Body*, pp. 168–225; Dutton, *Perfectible Body*; and Edwards, *Men in the Mirror*. While careful not to claim that men in general have been as deeply affected as women in general by contemporary ideologies of beauty (although perhaps not careful enough), Edwards nevertheless notes (p. 130) that

> despite the proliferation of multiple representations of masculinity, from the waifs of Britpop to the muscularity of *Baywatch*, the content of these images and representations remains fixed, divisive and hierarchical, particularly in relation to questions of age, colour and weight. The positive or valorized images of masculinity remain, despite variations, primarily young and white, slim and trim; whilst the vilification of men without muscle tone or flat stomachs has increased. . . .
>
> As a result of all of this, a hierarchy of masculinities is emerging according to image and appearance, where young white men with pumped-up pecs, strong jaw-lines and flat stomachs rule over the rest with a phallocentric intensity. In relation to men's fashion, it is this sense of social division at the level of physical appearance which appears of paramount importance, and which also reinforces wider hierarchies of masculinity according to age, class and race as well as the position to consume. In sum, whilst the white, young, trim and good-looking man with plenty of income and the means to spend it has much to gain from the pleasures and passions of the expansion of fashion in tandem with consumer society, the older, less affluent, less fit or more rurally located man faces an increasing onslaught of negative comments and criticism for his failure to live up to an ideal type.

## 3. SEX AND THE SINGLE APOSTLE

1. Translation from the *Fathers of the Church* series (see Deferrari).
2. *Sappho*, trans. Barnard.
3. Martin, "Heterosexism and the Interpretation of Romans 1:18–32."
4. Ibid., pp. 349–50.
5. Cf. Walters, "No More Than a Boy," p. 21; Moore and Anderson, "Taking It Like a Man," p. 249.
6. Santoro L'Hoir, *Rhetoric of Gender Terms*, p. 1.
7. Ibid, pp. 1–2. The remainder of Santoro L'Hoir's book amounts to a substantiation of this assertion. Her primary witnesses are Cicero, Sallust, Livy, Velleius Paterculus, Tacitus, Pliny the Younger, Suetonius, Petronius, and Apuleius.
8. Especially with regard to females. As Santoro L'Hoir notes, whereas ancient

Greek does have more than one word for "man" and does distinguish between them, "[t]he designation for women is confined to *gyne*, and sometimes *anthropos* with a feminine definite article. There is no counterpart to the noun, *femina*, as an indicator of status, the adjective, *thelus* ['feminine'], being more akin to the poetic *femineus*, which plays no significant part in Latin prose. *Thelus* might be equated to the neutral substantive *femina*, as in *bos femina*, which is usually juxtaposed to *mas*" (*Rhetoric of Gender Terms*, p. 2, n. 4).

9. Even for the elite, however, masculinity was a quicksilver commodity, as we shall see.

10. Walters, "No More Than a Boy," p. 31; see also his "Invading the Roman Body," p. 41. Selected members of these unmanly classes could earn a kind of "honorary" masculinity, however, as we shall also see.

11. In particular, Santoro L'Hoir suggests that the employment of gender terms by orators such as Cicero and his successors seems to presuppose common usage: "Despite the silence of the sources on the subject, the persistent use of *vir* and *femina* with laudatory modifiers, and the employment of *homo* and *mulier* with adjectives of abuse, strongly indicates that such usage was indeed implicit in the language and may well have been tacitly understood to be part of the *arcana* of the effective orator" (*Rhetoric of Gender Terms*, p. 203).

12. In the course of a review of Hallett and Skinner, eds., *Roman Sexualities* (see C. A. Williams, "Online review").

13. What scant evidence there is seems to pertain more to sexuality than to masculinity. Marylin Skinner remarks: "Artifacts such as the clay *lagynos* . . . may offer alternative perspectives on sexuality through images presumably viewed in domestic or menial settings . . . , while inscriptions and graffiti can furnish insight into the attitudes of nonelite and peripheral populations" ("*Quod multo fit aliter in Graecia*," p. 5; on the *lagynos*, see Johns, *Sex or Symbol?* pp. 125–27). Apart from fragments, six brief erotic elegies by the Augustan poet Sulpicia provide the only firsthand evidence for a female slant on Roman sexuality (see further Keith, "*Tandem venit amor*"). To attempt to extrapolate from these and other textual traces would be hazardous at present. As Skinner notes, further research on the sexual ideologies of nonelite Roman populations (slaves and other noncitizens as well as women) is needed ("*Quod multo fit aliter in Graecia*," p. 25). See also C. A. Williams, *Roman Homosexuality*, pp. 153–59 ("Other Voices"), and, for an attempt to reconstruct the sexual subject positions of fifth-century B.C.E. Greek women, Stehle and Day, "Women Looking at Women."

With regard to Roman graffiti, Williams suggests that whereas these, too, would have been produced by and for the literate—and literate males overwhelmingly (*Roman Homosexuality*, p. 20)—we can nevertheless be confident that they were "written by and for a broader cross-section of society than the literary texts, and that they thus constitute a kind of control evidence" (p. 257), especially as so many of them concern sexual behavior. Williams's conclusion, however, is that the preconceptions and prejudices regarding sex and gender detectable in these graffiti, many of which he analyzes in the course of his study, "fall squarely in line with the evidence of the literary texts" (ibid.).

14. Actually, such cultures are not nearly as distant from "ours" as "we" are often disposed to assume. According to Marta Sánchez, "Mexican, Chicano, and Puerto Rican notions of masculinity allow for a man to engage in homosexual acts if he takes the inserter role" ("*La Malinche* at the Intersection," p. 123). See also Almaguer, "Chicano Men," p. 81, and Paz, *Labyrinth of Solitude*, p. 40.

15. Foucault, *History of Sexuality*, 2: 187. See also Dover, *Greek Homosexuality*, p. 1, and esp. C. A. Williams, *Roman Homosexuality*, p. 172.

16. But although the concept of homosexuality, indissolubly bound up as it is with a second uniquely modern concept, that of sexual orientation, was lacking in antiquity (here I am following, inter alia, Halperin, *One Hundred Years of Homosexuality*, pp. 15–53, being ultimately unpersuaded by the counterarguments, as presented most forcibly by Richlin, "Not Before Homosexuality"), there was no shortage of terms for individuals who engaged in homoerotic acts: *kinaidos, hetairistria, tribas, Lesbia, cinaedus, pathicus, impudicus, pedico, fellator, frictrix/fricatrix, virago*....

17. Foucault, *History of Sexuality* 2: 190; see further pp. 187–225. And see also Dover, *Greek Homosexuality*, pp. 4–15, and Cohen, *Law, Sexuality, and Society*, pp. 171–202. Cohen adds nuance to Foucault's generalizations, arguing that even in classical Athens homoeroticism was frequently a source of anxiety.

18. Foucault, *History of Sexuality*, 3: 189. Jewish society was another matter, of course. Sexual relations between men are the object of a stern disqualification in a wide variety of Jewish texts over a long span of time: see Lev. 18.22; 20.13 (on which see Olyan, "And with a Male You Shall Not Lie"); *Testament of Naphtali* 3.4 (on which see Eron, "Early Jewish and Christian Attitudes Toward Male Homosexuality"); Pseudo-Phocylides 3, 190–92, 213–14; *Letter of Aristeas* 152; Wisdom of Solomon 14.26 (?); *Psalms of Solomon* 2:14 ff. (?); Philo, *Special Laws* 1.325; 2:50; 3.37–39; and *Abraham* 135–36; Josephus, *Jewish War* 4.560–63; and *Against Apion* 2.275; *2 Enoch* 10.4; *Sibylline Oracles* 3.185–87, 595–600; 5.386–96; and quite a number of rabbinic texts in addition, e.g., *Genesis Rabbah* 26.6; *Leviticus Rabbah* 23.9; *Sifra Qod.* 9:14 (92b); *b. Hullin* 92b; *b. Niddah* 13b; *b. Shabbat* 65a-b; *b. Yebamot* 76a; *y. Gittin* 8.10, 49c.70–71 (on which see Satlow, "'They Abused Him Like a Woman,'" and id., *Tasting the Dish*, pp. 186–264; and Boyarin, "Are There Any Jews in 'The History of Sexuality'?"). This does not, however, affect the interpretation of Rom. 1:26–27 toward which I am inching.

19. Arthur Hanson's translation (see Apuleius, *Metamorphoses*).

20. Walters, "No More Than a Boy," p. 26. Elsewhere, although not in connection with this passage, Walters argues that the rape and beating of males are, "in Roman terms, structurally equivalent," most of all as punishments for adultery (see esp. Horace, *Satires* 1.2.41 ff.). Each entails symbolic degradation of the adulterer, "who has

asserted his manhood sexually at the expense of another man." The adulterer is thereby emasculated and demoted from *vir* to slave or child ("Invading the Roman Body," p. 39).

21. Walters, "No More Than a Boy," p. 29. Paul uses the label *malakoi* side-by-side with *arsenokoitai* in the vice list of 1 Cor. 6:9-10 (cf. 1 Tim. 1:10). NRSV renders the terms as "male prostitutes" and "sodomites" respectively, although the correct translation/interpretation is a hotly contested issue. See, e.g., Boswell, *Christianity, Social Tolerance, and Homosexuality*, pp. 338-53; Scroggs, *New Testament and Homosexuality*, pp. 62-65, 101-9; Wright, "Homosexuals or Prostitutes?" and id., "Translating ARSENOKOITAI"; Petersen, "Can ARSENOKOITAI Be Translated by 'Homosexuals'?"; Malick, "Condemnation of Homosexuality in 1 Corinthians 6:9"; Martin, "*Arsenokoitēs* and *Malakos*"; and Wold, *Out of Order*, pp. 189-96.

22. Walters, "No More Than a Boy," p. 29. See further Dover, *Greek Homosexuality*, p. 79; Gleason, *Making Men*, pp. 65, 69; C. A. Williams, *Roman Homosexuality*, pp. 127-32; and Davies, "New Testament Ethics and Ours," pp. 316-17.

23. Winkler's book builds on Foucault's *History of Sexuality*, vol. 2. No less representative of the Foucauldian project in classics is Halperin's *One Hundred Years of Homosexuality*, along with his "Historicizing the Subject of Desire"; much of Halperin, Winkler, and Zeitlin, eds., *Before Sexuality*; much of Konstan and Nussbaum, eds., *Sexuality in Greek and Roman Society*; and, to a lesser extent, Gleason, *Making Men*; Downing, *Myths and Mysteries of Same-Sex Love*; and C. A. Williams, *Roman Homosexuality*. For a more critical engagement with Foucault, see Lefkowitz, "Sex and Civilization"; Cohen, *Law, Sexuality, and Society*, pp. 171-202; Cohen and Saller, "Foucault on Sexuality in Greco-Roman Antiquity"; Richlin, "Not Before Homosexuality"; Goidhill, *Foucault's Virginity*; Larmour, Miller, and Platter, eds., *Rethinking Sexuality*, as well as the further critiques listed on p. 265, n. 99, below.

24. Winkler, *Constraints of Desire*, p. 51; cf. Dover, *Greek Homosexuality*, p. 105.

25. If anything, these rules of manhood seem to have solidified further in the Roman period, so that the Roman *vir* emerges as, above all, an "impenetrable penetrator." A male penetrated by another male, therefore, was commonly said to have had "a woman's experience" (*muliebria pati*). See further Walters, "Invading the Roman Body," esp. p. 30, also C. A. Williams, *Roman Homosexuality*, p. 7: "Roman assumptions about masculine identity rested ... on a binary opposition: *men*, the penetrators, as opposed to everyone else, the penetrated" (his emphasis).

26. Walters, "No More Than a Boy," p. 29.

27. Ibid. Apuleius is frequently subtle in his use of gender terms, as Santoro L'Hoir repeatedly demonstrates in her own analysis of the *Metamorphoses* (*Rhetoric of Gender Terms*, pp. 184-96).

28. C. A. Williams, *Roman Homosexuality*, p. 18. In Roman society young male citizens were protected by law from rape or seduction by other males, possibly under the *lex Sca(n)tinia*. See Fantham, "*Stuprum*"; Richlin, *Garden of Priapus*, pp. 220-26;

id., "Not Before Homosexuality," pp. 561–66; C. A. Williams, "Greek Love at Rome," esp. pp. 531–35, and id., *Roman Homosexuality*, pp. 96–124.

29. Williams's terms (*Roman Homosexuality*, p. 18; cf. pp. 132–37).

30. See Finley, *Ancient Slavery and Modern Ideology*, pp. 95–96; Cantarella, *Bisexuality in the Ancient World*, pp. 101–4; and C. A. Williams, *Roman Homosexuality*, pp. 30–38.

31. Walters, "No More Than a Boy," p. 29.

32. Or, alternatively, to cause a Greco-Roman humorist like Martial to double up with mirth (*Epigrams* 2.51; 6.56; 9.47; 11.88).

33. Cf. Aristotle, *Nicomachean Ethics* 1148b26–35; Pseudo-Aristotle, *Problems* 426; Cicero, *On the Orator* 2.277; *Catilinarian Orations* 2.22–24; Quintilian, *Institutions* 5.9.14; and Caelius Aurelianus, *On Chronic Diseases* 4.9.137.

34. The Jewish Philo is here echoing the Levitical prescription (20:13) against males who "lie down" with other males; "they shall certainly be put to death" (Hebrew: *môt yûmātû*; Greek: *thanatō thanatousthōsan*). Paul echoes it too (Rom. 1:32—more on this below). An imperial edict of 390 C.E. later decreed that male prostitutes in Rome (who, of course, would routinely have accepted penetration by other males) should be burned alive. Peter Brown paraphrases the edict thus: "The very thought that males could adopt such practices 'sapped the rude rural vigor of the Roman people'; then, the edict goes on—with a new, Christian certainty—it was unpardonable that a soul allotted in perpetuity to the 'sacrosanct dwelling place' of a recognizable male body should force that body into female poses" ("Bodies and Minds," p. 490, paraphrasing *Mosaicarum et Romanarum Legum Collatio* 5.3).

35. And also of Greek *pais*? According to Donald Wold, *pais*, which normally meant "boy," "child," and "slave," could also denote the passive partner in male-male sexual intercourse (*Out of Order*, p. 191)—although Liddell-Scott-Jones seems to be innocent of this usage, as does Bauer-Arndt-Gingrich-Danker.

36. Walters, "No More Than a Boy," p. 29.

37. Winkler, *Constraints of Desire*, p. 22. See further C. A. Williams, *Roman Homosexuality*, pp. 231–44, appendix on "The Rhetoric of Nature and Same-Sex Practices."

38. Cf. Foucault, *History of Sexuality*, 2: 206.

39. Ibid., pp. 252–53, 250–51; cf. pp. 22–23.

40. Foucault, *History of Sexuality*, 3: 1–36.

41. Ibid., p. 28.

42. More specifically, the first three books of the *Oneirokritika* seem to be addressed to the general public and the last two to Artemidoros's own son.

43. Foucault, *History of Sexuality*, 3: 6.

44. Ibid., p. 9.

45. Ibid., p. 3.

46. Winkler, *Constraints of Desire*, p. 33; cf. pp. 23 ff. There seems to be widespread agreement on this general point (even allowing for a dash of hyperbole in Winkler's formulation of it). See, in addition, for example, Pack, "Artemidoros and His Waking

World," p. 287, and Brooten, *Love Between Women*, pp. 176–78. James Miller mounts a similar argument for Martial and Juvenal: "as humorists they are particularly useful in understanding popular concepts of sexuality near the end of the first century" ("Pederasty and Romans 1:27," p. 861; cf. pp. 861–63).

47. Winkler's translation, here and in what follows. *Oneirokritica* 1.78–80 in translation forms an appendix to his *Constraints of Desire* (pp. 210–16). For a translation of the entire work, see White, ed. and trans., *Interpretation of Dreams*, and for a full-length study of it, see Blum, *Studies in the Dream-Book of Artemidoros*.

48. What makes it all the more relevant is that the appeal to a concept of nature is lacking both in the Levitical (18:22; 20:13) and rabbinic pronouncements on homoeroticism—although Paul's Hellenistic Jewish contemporaries Philo and Pseudo-Phocylides do also have recourse to *physis* in their own statements on homoeroticism (for details, see Brooten, *Love Between Women*, pp. 64, 69–70).

49. Winkler, *Constraints of Desire*, p. 37. One finds a similar admonition in the *summa alû* prescriptions of ancient Mesopotamia: "If a man has intercourse with a [male] slave, care will seize him" (quoted in Greenberg, *Construction of Homosexuality*, who remarks of the prescriptions generally: "What matters are the roles and statuses of the parties" [p. 127]).

50. The reasons are, perhaps, clearest in the case of cunnilingus. As Craig Williams remarks, "in the relentlessly phallocentric sexual ideologies of classical antiquity, this act, not requiring the intervention of a penis, is by its very nature anomalous" ("Online review"; cf. id., *Roman Homosexuality*, pp. 197–203). See further Richlin, *Garden of Priapus*, pp. 25–26, 69.

51. Winkler, *Constraints of Desire*, p. 38. Cf. the quotation from Jorge Luis Borges's "The Analytical Language of John Wilkins" with which Foucault's *Order of Things* opens, which cites a "certain Chinese encyclopaedia," the *Celestial Emporium of Benevolent Knowledge*, for a surreal taxonomy that divides animals into such classes as "belonging to the Emperor," "embalmed," "tame," "sucking pigs," "fabulous," "stray dogs," "drawn with a very fine camelhair brush," "that from a long way off look like flies," and so on, all of which leaves Foucault marveling at "the stark impossibility of thinking *that*" (*Order of Things*, p. xv; his emphasis).

52. Most ancient commentators, however, saw in v. 26b a reference to male-female vaginal sex rendered "unnatural" by reason of the female assuming a "masculine" role (Martin, "Heterosexism and the Interpretation of Romans 1:18–32," p. 348, n. 40; see further Brooten, "Patristic Interpretations of Romans 1:26").

53. Dissident voices include those of James Miller ("Practices of Romans 1:26"), who suggests that "heterosexual" anal or oral sex is envisioned here, and Klaus Haacker ("Exegetische Gesichtspunkte zum Thema Homosexualität"), who suspects that bestiality is the issue.

54. The arguments just presented rely heavily on Brooten's superb treatment of Rom. 1:26b in *Love Between Women*, esp. pp. 241–53.

55. Kellum, "Phallus as Signifier," pp. 172–73. See also Keuls, *Reign of the Phallus*, esp. pp. 65–97 passim, and C. A. Williams, *Roman Homosexuality*, pp. 18, 86–95.

56. Foucault, *History of Sexuality*, 2: 136; cf. p. 129. And see also Halperin, *One Hundred Years of Homosexuality*, p. 30, and Walters, "Invading the Roman Body," p. 30, who notes "the characterization, widespread in the public discourses of the Greco-Roman world, that sex is a one-way street, something that one person does to another."

57. Cf. Winkler, *Constraints of Desire*, p. 40.

58. See further Hallett and Skinner, eds., *Roman Sexualities*, pt. 3, "Gender Slippage in Literary Constructions of the Masculine."

59. On which see Wimbush, *Paul the Worldly Ascetic*, and Deming, *Paul on Marriage and Celibacy*.

60. "( ) signify additional phases of meaning included in the Greek word, phrase or clause" (Siewert, *Amplified New Testament*, p. ix). For the basic translation I am using the RSV rather than my own, lest I be accused of being tendentious.

61. A full 113 pages of Brooten's *Love Between Women* are devoted to the elucidation of Rom. 1:26–27 (with emphasis, as might be expected, on 1:26b), against the panoramic backdrop, moreover, of six chapters on "Female Homoeroticism in the Roman World" that, in effect, prepare for it (although their value far exceeds this function), making it far and away the most exhaustive investigation of these verses ever undertaken. Rom 1:26–27 is the only New Testament text on homoeroticism that Brooten treats in detail (of course, it is the main one; the only other "definite" references to the topic occur in the vice lists of 1 Cor. 6:9–10 and 1 Tim. 1:9–10). The remainder of her book is devoted to "Tortures in Hell: Early Church Fathers on Female Homoeroticism," which section, too, frequently circles back to Rom. 1:26–27.

A 1998 issue of *GLQ* devoted its "forum" section to *Love Between Women*, and featured review articles by David Halperin, Ann Pellegrini, Ken Stone, Natalie Boymel Kampen, and Deirdre Good, with an introduction by Elizabeth Catelli and a response by Brooten herself (see Halperin et al., "Lesbian Historiography Before the Name?"). Halperin and Pellegrini are particularly critical of the book, the former perceiving in it a residual essentialism in its contention that ancient Mediterranean culture "had the concept of an erotic orientation with respect to women" (*Love Between Women*, p. 5), the latter going so far as to claim that Brooten's "conception of sexual love between women and lesbian identity is rooted in contemporary politics, not in the world of ancient Christianity" ("Lesbian Historiography Before the Name?" pp. 582–83), eliciting a vigorous defense from Brooten (pp. 614–26 passim).

62. The term "elite" must be applied with caution to Paul, although it does seem to stick; see Martin, *Corinthian Body*, pp. 51–52.

63. Brooten, *Love Between Women*, p. 240. That Paul should mention female homoeroticism at all "deviates rather strikingly from the standard pattern," as Brendan Byrne observes (*Romans*, p. 76), and as such invites interpretation. Commentators regularly grapple with the problem of sequence: why the women first? Some throw

up their hands in despair, like Douglas Moo: "We cannot know why Paul has mentioned women first" (*Epistle to the Romans*, p. 116, n. 122). Thomas Schreiner flatly states: "no significance should be read from the order" (*Romans*, p. 94, n. 5). Otto Michel argues that Gen. 2-3, in which Eve's sin precedes Adam's, looms in the background (*Brief an die Römer*, p. 105), while James Dunn suggests that "Female homosexual practice is mentioned before male, possibly because the more aggressive character of male sexuality, as indicated in v 27, makes for a better crescendo" (*Romans 1-8*, p. 64; cf. Cranfield, *Epistle to the Romans*, 1: 125, for a similar proposal).

64. Ovid, for example, characterizes female homoeroticism as *prodigiosa*, "monstrous" (*Metamorphoses* 9727), as does Martial (*Epigrams* 1.90.8). John Chrysostom later dubs it *allokoton lyssan*, "monstrous insanity" (*On the Epistle to the Romans* 4.1). And monsters give rise to nightmares, such as Seneca the Younger's vision of a Dildo Monster who, not content with penetrating other females, penetrates males as well (*Moral Epistles* 95.20), or Martial's yet more horrific vision of a Clitoris Monster, one Philaenis, "*tribas* of the very *tribades*," who buggers boys and screws eleven girls each day, "quite fierce with the erection of a husband" (*Epigrams* 7.67.1-3). Even the strap-on dildo (Greek: *olisbos*; Latin: *iuvamen*[?]), which the ancients deemed an indispensable accessory of the woman-loving woman (e.g., Aristophanes, *Lysistrata* 109-10; Seneca the Elder, *Controversiae* 1.2.23; Lucian of Samosata, *Dialogues of the Courtesans* 5.4 §292; b. ʿAboda Zara 44a), is itself a freakish implement in Pseudo-Lucian's *Erōtes* 28, which speaks of "mysterious monstrosities empty of [male] seed [*asporōn terastion ainigma*]."

65. Tamsin Wilton notes how even today female homoeroticism is frequently perceived as "an alien monstrosity prowling around outside the fold of gender conformity" ("Which One's the Man?" p. 126).

66. Judith Hallett has shown how Roman discourse on *female* homoeroticism consistently betrays an anxiety not evident in Roman discourse on *male* homoeroticism ("Female Homoeroticism and the Denial of Roman Reality"). I submit that Paul, too, although a Jew, is culturally predisposed to share this anxiety.

67. On the concept of "limited good," see Malina, *New Testament World*, pp. 81-107.

68. Further on the honor/shame dynamic and its role in gender formation, see Malina and Neyrey, "Honor and Shame in Luke-Acts," pp. 41-46, 61-64; Plevnik, "Honor/Shame," passim; Malina, *Social World of Jesus and the Gospels*, pp. 109-16 and passim; Neyrey, *Honor and Shame in the Gospel of Matthew*, pp. 29-32, 212-14; Malina and Neyrey, *Portraits of Paul*, pp. 176-82; and Stegemann, "Paul and the Sexual Mentality of His World" (which deals with Rom. 1:26-27).

69. As Carlin Barton remarks, "Roman ideas of honor have everything to do with activity, energy, vigor, potency, and expansion. *Virtus*, the word in Latin that comes closest to encompassing the range of notions in our English word *honor*, was the effective energy, the *vis*, or force of the *animus*" ("Savage Miracles," p. 63, n. 16).

70. As Paul is content to do in 1 Cor. 6:9-11; cf. Gal. 5:19-21.

71. Joseph Fitzmyer remarks uncontroversially, with regard to Rom 1:19-23, that whereas the "Hellenistic philosophical notion" of "nature" (*physis*) has "colored Paul's thinking" (cf. pp. 141-42 above), "'nature' also expresses for him the order intended by the Creator, the order that is manifest in God's creation" (*Romans*, p. 286; see also Brooten, *Love Between Women*, pp. 272-75). Indeed, by his unexpected use of the terms *thēlys* ("female") and *arsēn* ("male") in 1:26-27, in place of the more usual *gynē* ("woman") and *anēr* ("man"), Paul may be subtly reminding us that "natural" male-female relations were divinely established at the creation of the cosmos, *thēlys* and *arsēn* arguably evoking the Septuagint translation of Gen. 1:27, *arsen kai thēly epoiēsen autous* ("male and female he made them"; cf. Gal. 3:28; Mark 10:6; Matt. 19:4). As Thomas Schreiner puts it, the use of these terms in Rom. 1:26-27 "emphasize[s] the sexual distinctiveness of male and female, suggesting that sexual relations with the same sex violate the distinctions that God intended in the creation of man and woman" (*Romans*, p. 95)—which all sounds highly edifying until one recalls that the distinctions in question, those between the sexes, were conceived of as being utterly hierarchical in the Greco-Roman world, entailing relations of superordination and subordination, superiority and inferiority, domination and submission. And although many modern exegetes read Gen. 1:26-27 as an egalitarian formulation, an assertion that women no less than men are created in the image of God, Paul himself does not seem to have construed it this way: see 1 Cor. 11:7, "For a man ought not to cover his head since he is the image and glory of God; but women is the glory of man." Paul reads hierarchy in(to) Gen. 1:26-27.

Paul's use of *arsēn* in Rom. 1:27 also evokes Lev. 18:22 (*kai meta arsenos ou koimēthēsē koitēn gynaikos*, "and with a male you shall not lie as with a woman") and 20:13 (*kai hos an koimēthē meta arsenos koitēn gynaikos, bdelygma epoiēsan amphoteroi*, "and should anyone lie with a male as with a woman, both of them have committed an abomination"). Rom. 1:26-32 appears to be extending the Levitical prohibition of same-sex intercourse between males to include homoerotic relations between females, as does Paul's (Alexandrian?) Jewish contemporary Pseudo-Phocylides (*Sentences* 190-92, which also uses *arsēn*), although Paul goes beyond the latter in also extending the Levitical *penalty* for male-male intercourse to females: Rom. 1:32 threatens "unnatural" males and females alike with "God's decree that those who do such things are worthy of death [*axioi thanatou eisin*]" (a threat also sounded in Philo, *Special Laws* 3.38, which, however, adhering more closely to the Levitical script, indicts male homoeroticism only). See further Brooten, *Love Between Women*, pp. 64, 69-70, 282-83, 299. For an attempt to flesh out the shadowy figure of Pseudo-Phocylides, see Horst, ed. and trans., *Sentences of Pseudo-Phocylides*, pp. 81-83.

72. The concept of the female adduced here is not solely a "Greek" or "Roman" one. As Daniel Boyarin notes, "The very word for female, *naqêbâ* in both biblical and talmudic Hebrew, as well as talmudic Aramaic, means 'orifice bearer,' as if male bodies did not possess orifices" ("Are There Any Jews in 'The History of Sexuality'?" p. 345).

73. Paul's debt to Jewish homiletical motifs, not just in Rom. 1:22–23, but throughout 1:18–2:29, has been argued by Sanders, *Paul, the Law, and the Jewish People*, pp. 123–35; see also Bussmann, *Themen der paulinischen Missionspredigt*, pp. 108–22. Related to this are the echoes of certain scriptural passages in these verses (on which see Bassler, *Impartiality of God*, pp. 122, 195–97), notably Ps. 106:20, "They exchanged the glory of God for the image of an ox that eats grass," and Deut. 4:16–18, the proscription of images in "the likeness of male or female, the likeness of any animal that is on the earth, the likeness of any winged bird that flies in the air, the likeness of anything that creeps on the ground." Other "background" texts regularly adduced include Isa. 44:9–20 and Jer. 2:11.

74. F. H. Colson's translation (see Colson, *Philo*). On the centrality of hierarchy to Greco-Roman conceptions of the cosmos, see Martin, *Corinthian Body*, pp. 1–137 passim (esp. p. 34).

75. The author of the Wisdom of Solomon also attributes a tit-for-tat mentality to the deity: "In return for their [the Gentiles'] foolish and wicked thoughts, which led them astray to worship irrational serpents and worthless animals, you sent upon them a multitude of irrational creatures to punish them, that they might learn that one is punished by the very things by which one sins" (11:15–16, NRSV; cf. 12:23, 27; *Testament of Gad* 5:1).

76. And so the punishment (being "given up" [*paradidōmi*] by God to unnatural sex) perfectly fits the crime (idolatry). I shall return to this below.

77. "It has been a main element of much feminist writing that heterosexuality is about the eroticisation of power difference" (Smart, "Collusion, Collaboration and Confession," p. 168). Sheila Jeffreys, in particular, has made this theme her own, and the term "eroticized inequality" is hers. See her *Anticlimax* and *Lesbian Heresy*, as well as her "Heterosexuality and the Desire for Gender."

78. Cf. MacKinnon, *Towards a Feminist Theory of the State*, p. 118, and Jeffreys, "Heterosexuality and the Desire for Gender," p. 77.

79. The near-universal assumption among Hebrew Bible scholars is that Gen. 1–3 contains two originally independent creation accounts, now spliced together, the first extending from 1:1 to 2:4a and the second from 2:4b to 3:24.

80. Brooten, *Love Between Women*, p. 199, extrapolating from Stowers, *Letter Writing in Greco-Roman Antiquity*, pp. 112–14 (cf. pp. 127–28). What interests me about this statement (although Brooten herself doesn't remark on it) is its utterly clichéd, pop-theological character. It could stand as a summary for any number of theological commentaries or homilies on our passage.

81. Elsewhere in Romans we find *hē hypandros gynē* (7:2), the only New Testament occurrence of this telling expression. Elizabeth Castelli notes how contemporary translations of it, such as "a married woman" (e.g., RSV, NAB, NRSV), conceal "the hierarchical formulation of the Greek . . . , literally, 'the woman who is under a man'" ("Romans," p. 283). She adds: "It is perhaps also noteworthy to realize that *hy-*

*pandros* means not only 'under a man, subject to him' but also 'feminine' (see Diodorus Siculus 32.10)" (p. 299, n. 29). As it happens, the term is also used by Artemidoros (*Oneirokritika* 1.78).

82. This eruption of wrath in Rom 1:18 has provoked much reaction (some anxious, some approving) from Pauline scholars over the years. I discuss the matter in *God's Gym*, pp. 15-17.

83. Cf. C. A. Williams, *Roman Homosexuality*, p. 14: "[T]here are certain characteristics of Roman representations of masculine sexual behavior (most outstandingly, a value placed on unusually generous phallic endowments) that are strikingly different from corresponding Greek representations."

84. Cf. Dunn, *Romans 1-8*, p. 284 on Rom. 5:19, "For as by one man's disobedience [*parakoē*] many were made sinners, so by one man's obedience [*hypakoē*] many will be made righteous." He argues persuasively against commentators who see the reference to Christ's "obedience" in this verse "as embracing Christ's whole life"; "almost certainly Paul's thought at this point focuses more or less exclusively on Christ's death," so that "the theme of Christ's 'obedience' refers to his submission to death (Phil. 2:8; Heb. 5:8)." Note that the "obedience" of Rom. 5:19 has as its synonym the "act of righteousness" in 5:18, which in turn has its counterpart in Adam's "trespass": "Then as one man's trespass [*di' henos paraptōmatos*] led to condemnation for all men, so one man's act of righteousness [*di' henos dikaiōmatos*] leads to acquittal and life for all men."

85. An obedience arguably encapsulated in the recurrent Pauline phrase *pistis [Iēsou] Christou*, first used in Romans in 3:22: "But now . . . the righteousness of God has been disclosed, . . . the righteousness of God through *pistis Iēsou Christou*. . . ." If the champions of the so-called "subjective genitive" translation of the phrase are to be credited, it should be rendered as "the faith(fulness) of [Jesus] Christ" rather than "faith in [Jesus] Christ" (the more traditional "objective genitive" translation). Notable blows have been struck for the subjective genitive, e.g., Johnson, "Rom. 3:21–26 and the Faith of Jesus"; Hays, *Faith of Jesus Christ*, esp. pp. 170–74, and id., "PISTIS and Pauline Christology," pp. 35–60; Campbell, *Rhetoric of Righteousness in Romans 3:21-26*, esp. pp. 58–69, and "Romans 1:17"; Martyn, *Galatians*, esp. pp. 263–75.

86. So Crawford, "Female Crucifix," quoted in Ford, "Crucifixion of Women in Antiquity," p. 292. Ford provides details of six recent artistic representations of crucified female Christs, five sculptures and one painting, issuing from Africa, Australia, Canada, Latin America, and the United States (pp. 291–92). Undoubtedly, this list is not exhaustive.

87. Contemporary scholarship is overwhelmingly of the opinion that Ephesians was not composed by Paul. Together with Colossians, 2 Thessalonians, 1 Timothy, 2 Timothy, and Titus, it is one of the six "disputed" Pauline letters, as distinct from the "undisputed" seven: Romans, 1 and 2 Corinthians, Galatians, Philippians, 1 Thessalonians, and Philemon. (But is the authenticity of these seven really beyond dispute? Of

course not. Darrell Doughty, in particular, has mounted some telling arguments for reopening the case; see esp. his "Pauline Paradigms and Pauline Authenticity.")

88. Foucault lists and discusses many of the sources for this topos; see *History of Sexuality*, 2: 75-77, 82-83, and 3: 84-86, 94-95.

89. Gregory Dawes wouldn't agree (at least I think he wouldn't); see his extended, often pained, tussle with this passage in his *Body in Question*.

90. Much of the relevant literature, both primary and secondary, is collected in Moore and Anderson, "Taking It Like a Man."

91. Aside altogether from the Pauline and Deutero-Pauline literature, it is tempting to surmise that Jesus' self-control in the gospel passion narratives would have been construed as a demonstration of his masculinity by Greco-Roman audiences, especially in John's and Luke's passion narratives (arguably, Jesus' "cry of abandonment" in Mark [15:34], Matthew [27:46], and the *Gospel of Peter* [5:19] calls the absoluteness of his self-mastery momentarily into question). Two recent articles come close to asserting this position—Neyrey, "Despising the Shame of the Cross," and Pilch, "Death with Honor"—while Neyrey's *Honor and Shame in the Gospel of Matthew*, pp. 148-51, asserts it more explicitly.

92. So Dunn, *Theology of Paul the Apostle*, p. 111. The disputed Pauline letters are even included in this tally.

93. See esp. Murnaghan, "How a Woman Can Be More Like a Man." The literary and philosophical topos of the subject who is anatomically female but morally masculine is, however, an extremely far-flung one, occurring in ancient Jewish texts (*4 Maccabees* being the most dramatic example) and early Christian texts (ranging from the *Gospel of Thomas* to the *Passion of Perpetua and Felicitas*), and even in early Buddhist texts, not to mention pagan Greek and Roman texts. For bibliography and further examples, see Moore and Anderson, "Taking It Like a Man," pp. 267-69; Cloke, *This Female Man of God*, esp. pp. 213-14; and, above all, Aspegren, *Male Woman*. The topos has acquired a new lease on life in contemporary theory; see esp. Halberstam, *Female Masculinity*. Eve Sedgwick remarks: "[L]ike men, I as a woman am also a producer of masculinities and a performer of them" ("Gosh, Boy George, You Must Be Awfully Secure in Your Masculinity!" p. 13).

94. As with Philo, for instance (who is more up-front about his contempt for the feminine): "For progress [toward virtue] is indeed nothing else than the giving up of the female gender by changing into the male, since the female gender is material, passive, corporeal, and sense-perceptible, while the male is active, rational, incorporeal, and more akin to mind and thought" (*Questions and Answers on Exodus* 18, Colson's trans.; cf. *Questions and Answers on Genesis* 2.12, 49; *The Worse Attacks the Better* 28; *On the Embassy to Gaius* 319). See further Baer, *Philo's Use of the Categories of Male and Female*, esp. pp. 45-49, and Mattila, "Philo's Gender Gradient."

But what of Gal. 3:28: "There is no longer Jew or Greek, there is no longer slave or free, there is no longer male and female [*arsen kai thēlu*], for all of you are one in

Christ Jesus"? An adequate unpacking of this verse, or rather of its immense cultural baggage, would require at least as much effort as Rom. 1:26-27 (the sort of effort Boyarin puts into it in *Radical Jew*, pp. 180-200). But my suspicion in light of our discussion of the Romans passage is that what Gal. 3:28 implicitly proclaims is the replacement of two sexes with one gender—masculinity in the theological trappings of "righteousness," which every believer, regardless of anatomical makeup, is required to put on.

95. We still have not strayed far from Philo, then.

96. Cf. Skinner, "*Quod multo fit aliter in Graecia*," p. 18, quoting Ellen Oliensis: "[A]ny asymmetrical relation between two Roman men is conceivably also a sexual relation." Skinner herself mounts essentially the same argument in her "*Ego Mulier*"; see esp. p. 120: "In the Greco-Roman world . . . power was openly eroticized—so openly and so thoroughly as to undermine biological gender identity." Walters, too, writes of a Roman "concept of manliness which is irreducibly bound up with the holding of power over others, and which is radically incompatible with being the object of power to another," to the extent that Juvenal (*Satire* 2.143 ff.) can imply that a gladiator is even less of a man than a sexually penetrated male (Walters, "Juvenal, Satire 2," p. 152). Also pertinent is Hawley, "Male Body as Spectacle in Attic Drama," pp. 86-87, 97.

97. Brooten, *Love Between Women*, p. 245. The Greek of Rom. 1:27, *homoiōs te kai hoi arsenes aphentes tēn physikēn chrēsin tēs thēleias* . . . , was rendered literally by the King James translators as "likewise also the men, leaving the natural use of the woman. . . . " Most modern translators blanch at this rendering, however, opting for a soft-focus translation instead; KJV's great-grandchild NRSV, for example, has: "in the same way also the men, giving up natural intercourse with women. . . . "

98. Brooten, *Love Between Women*, pp. 245-46.

99. Foucault, *History of Sexuality*, 2: 22. This is one of several such disclaimers that punctuate vols. 2 and 3 of Foucault's *History*. They have not prevented critics such as Amy Richlin from hauling Foucault over the coals—nor should they, since he proceeds to idealize this androcentric ethics anyway. See Richlin, "Foucault's *History of Sexuality*" and "Zeus and Metis"; also DuBois, "Subject in Antiquity after Foucault"; Foxhall, "Pandora Unbound"; Hunt, "Foucault's Subject in *The History of Sexuality*"; MacKinnon, "Does Sexuality Have a History?"; McNay, *Foucault and Feminism*, esp. pp. 75 ff.; and Greene, "Sappho, Foucault, and Women's Erotics."

A more emphatic disclaimer is issued by Foucault in the interview entitled "On the Genealogy of Ethics": "The Greek ethics were linked to a purely virile society with slaves, in which women were underdogs whose pleasure had no importance, whose sexual life had to be oriented toward, determined by, their status as wives. . . . All that is quite disgusting!" (pp. 344, 346). But not disgusting enough, perhaps?

100. Richlin has recently attempted a similar counter-reading of Pliny the Elder's *Natural History* that presents the (dimly glimpsed) women therein as subjects en-

gaged in active self-fashioning. See Richlin, "Pliny's Brassiere," along with her parallel effort in "Foucault's *History of Sexuality*," pp. 152–62.

101. Not that same-sex relations, even between women, are widely conceived in any other terms today. See Richardson, "Heterosexuality and Social Theory," esp. pp. 2–9, and Wilton, "Which One's the Man?" passim, as well as Faderman, *Surpassing the Love of Men*, pp. 31–37 (a chapter entitled "What Do Women Do?").

102. Cf. Skinner, "*Quod multo fit aliter in Graecia*," pp. 5–6: "The caricature of the *tribas*, or mannish female equipped with dildo, must have reassured [Roman] males of their natural physiological advantages." The antics of the *tribas* could be no more "than a sorry endeavor to transcend inescapable female inferiority" (p. 21).

103. Brooten, *Love Between Women*, p. 189. For a full account of the proceedings, Brooten refers us to Faderman, *Scotch Verdict* (itself a book-length version of id., *Surpassing the Love of Men*, pp. 147–54). On consulting Faderman, one is referred in turn to *Miss Marianne Woods and Miss Jane Pirie*, in which the transcripts of the trial are collected. Yet another account of the trial can be found in Roughead, *Bad Companions*.

104. Both from the trial transcripts, as quoted in Faderman, *Surpassing the Love of Men*, p. 149.

105. Lord Meadowbank, quoted in Faderman, *Scotch Verdict*, p. 153. "I detect something inscrutable and disturbing about this child of India," Meadowbank later noted (quoted in ibid., p. 189).

106. Lord Boyle, quoted in Faderman, *Surpassing the Love of Men*, p. 150. What, then, should be the motto of the British missionary to India? Thomas Walker enlightens us in the epigraph to this column: "We Christians of India need to be very 'straight'" (*Epistle to the Philippians*, p. 70). I owe this gem to R. S. Sugirtharajah, who has published an incisive study of the Indian Church Commentaries series of which Walker's volume was a part (Sugirtharajah, "Imperial Critical Commentaries").

107. Loomba, *Colonialism/Postcolonialism*, p. 155, quoting Sandys, *Relation of a Journey*, p. 69. The European orientalization of female homoeroticism finds an interesting parallel in the tendency in ancient Latin literature to dissociate the *tribas* (or woman-penetrating woman) from Rome both geographically and temporally by Hellenizing her and retrojecting her into the past. See Hallett, "Female Homoeroticism and the Denial of Roman Reality," esp. p. 266.

108. Jane Cumming did, however, claim to have heard a sound "like putting one's finger into the neck of a wet bottle" (quoted in Faderman, *Scotch Verdict*, p. 147), a remark that elicited an instructive (if bizarre) exchange:

> "Was it anything like the drawing of a cork?" John Clerk says.
> "No."
> "Was it like a person clapping or patting another on the cheek or shoulders?"
> "No."

"Miss Cumming," Lord Robertson asks, "was it perhaps like a person dabbling their hands in water?"

"It was not quite like that, but more like it I think than rubbing or clapping."

"Miss Cumming," Lord Robertson asks again, "have you ever heard a dairy maid making up butter? Was it anything like a dairy maid patting butter?" (Quoted in ibid., p. 163)

And so on. Faced with the unimaginably "unnatural," language slithers backwards down an analogical slope.

109. John Clerk, quoted in Faderman, *Scotch Verdict*, p. 220. "But it appears quite clear that the practice referred to was that of *sodomy* between a woman and a man," Clerk continues confidently, however (quoted in ibid., pp. 220–21; emphasis in original).

110. Cf. p. 260, n. 64, above.

111. It is not that Brown had no use for the term "heathen." The other great work he bequeathed to posterity, *A Dictionary of the Holy Bible*, contains an illuminating article on "Gentiles, Heathen," which I shall get to in a moment.

112. Would the same have held true for the corresponding terms in other European languages—German *Heiden*, Spanish *paganos*, French *païen* and/or *barbare*, and so on? I assume it would have, although I am not certain, and so shall restrict myself to British usage.

113. In Ireland, for instance, the violent suppression of Roman Catholicism went hand in glove with the violent suppression of the Irish language ("Gaelic," as it is commonly called, although not by the Irish themselves), the eradication of superstition and the imposition of true religion being conjoined with the eradication of a barbaric tongue and the imposition of civilized speech. On language as a colonial instrument, see Fanon, *Black Skin, White Masks*, pp. 17–40, and Thiong'o, *Decolonising the Mind*, pp. 4–33. Specifically on the Irish context, see Kiberd, *Inventing Ireland*, esp. pp. 9–17, 133–54.

114. Sanday and Headlam, *Critical and Exegetical Commentary on the Epistle to the Romans*, "The Church and the Civil Power," pp. 369–73. John Riches has noted the cultural and military triumphalism that animates Headlam's 1923 book, *Life and Teaching of Jesus the Christ*. For instance, Headlam rejoices in the hope that the land that bequeathed Christianity to the world "may never again be brought under the blighting influence of Turkish and Mohammedan rule," thanks to the British Army's conquest of Palestine, a campaign with profound parallels in biblical history (Headlam, *Life and Teaching of Jesus the Christ*, p. vii, quoted in Riches, "Cultural Bias in Biblical Scholarship," p. 440).

115. And over Rom. 1:27 likewise, except for a brief comment on the participle *apolambanontes*, "receiving back/receiving one's due" (Sanday and Headlam, *Critical and Exegetical Commentary on the Epistle to the Romans*, p. 46).

116. See p. 155 above on this cure. Note, too, that the century that witnessed the birth of modern men's team sports and "muscular Christianity" also witnessed the birth of the locker room.

117. Rambuss, *Closet Devotions*, p. 38; his emphasis. He continues: "Accounts that fashion a paradoxically 'female' or a 'bisexual' Jesus often do so at the cost of too quickly effacing the primary maleness of his body and its operations, as well as, perhaps more importantly, the possibilities a male Christ affords for a homoeroticized devotional expression" (ibid.). His remarks are directed to recent interpreters of the devotional verse of the English metaphysical poets (John Donne, George Herbert, Thomas Traherne, and especially Richard Crashaw).

118. Cf. Simpson, *Male Impersonators*, pp. 135 ff. (although his topic is not Greco-Roman sex but gay videoporn).

## 4. REVOLTING REVELATIONS

1. See Kitzberger, ed., *Personal Voice in Biblical Interpretation*—although the essay has had to let out its belt several times since then.

2. "Sweet Jesus, does he really talk like that?" you may idly be asking yourself. To which I can smugly respond in the negative. Ten years at Trinity College, Dublin (founded in 1592 to educate the scions of the Irish colonial aristocracy, its porticos and quadrangles echoing with *faux* English accents even ⟨ ⟩ this day), certainly cured me of dat.

3. But let me numb you with it one more time:

My father was a butcher. As a child, the inner geographical boundaries of my world extended from the massive granite bulk of the Redemptorist church squatting at one end of our street to the butcher shop guarding the other end. Redemption, expiation, sacrifice, slaughter. . . . There was no city abattoir in Limerick in those days; each butcher did his own slaughtering. I recall the hooks, the knives, the cleavers; the terror in the eyes of the victim; my own fear that I was afraid to show; the crude stun-gun slick with grease; the stunned victim collapsing to its knees; the slitting of the throat; the filling of the basins with blood; the skinning and evisceration of the carcass; the wooden barrels overflowing with entrails; the crimson floor littered with hooves.

4. John is obsessed with the number seven, as is well known (although also with the numbers three, four, twelve, and their multiples). See Bauckham, *Climax of Prophecy*, pp. 29-37; Aune, *Revelation 1-5*, pp. 114-17; and Beale, *Book of Revelation*, pp. 58-64.

5. Earlier this year I was forcibly reminded of this forgotten drawer while perusing Jeff Staley's latest adventure in autobiographical criticism. Staley quotes a haiku that he composed when he was nineteen, adding: "This unpublished poem is entitled

*The Artist's Studio* and can be found downstairs in the top drawer of my beige metal file cabinet. I've decided that the only way I will ever get any of my poems published is by putting them in scholarly articles. I have actually written a couple of children's stories, too, but I haven't yet figured out how to insert them into an article like this" ("Narrative Structure [Self-Stricture] in Luke 4:14–9:62," p. 178, n. 13). Staley's *Reading with a Passion* remains the most impressive example of autobiographical or personal criticism in biblical studies. Further on the incipient autobiographical turn in biblical studies, see Anderson and Staley, eds., *Taking It Personally*, which contains Staley's "Narrative Structure (Self-Stricture)," as well as my own survey article, "True Confessions and Weird Obsessions." See also see Kitzberger, ed., *Personal Voice in Biblical Interpretation*, along with the companion volume in classical studies, Hallett and Van Nortwick, eds., *Compromising Traditions*, and certain of the manifestoes for autobiographical criticism issued earlier in literary studies, notably Miller, *Getting Personal*, Freedman, Frey, and Murphy, eds., *Intimate Critique*, and Veeser, ed., *Confessions of the Critics*.

6. The earliest known title of the book, and the one it bears in modern editions of the Greek New Testament, is *Apokalypsis Iōannou*, "Revelation of John." For the historical vicissitudes of the title, see Aune, *Revelation 1–5*, pp. 3–4.

7. Bauckham, *Theology of the Book of Revelation*, pp. 68–69.

8. See Butler, *Gender Trouble*, esp. pp. 134–41; and see also her "Melancholy Gender / Refused Identification," esp. pp. 31–32, and, more generally, Morris, "All Made Up."

9. Washington, "Violence and the Construction of Gender in the Hebrew Bible," pp. 329–30; Cooke, "Wo-man, Retelling the War Myth," p. 177.

10. Clines, "David the Man," pp. 218–19.

11. Bauckham, *Theology of the Book of Revelation*, p. 69.

12. "So he carried me away in the spirit into a wilderness, and I saw a woman sitting on a scarlet beast... and on her forehead was written a name, a mystery: 'Babylon the great, mother of whores and of earth's abominations'" (Rev. 17:3–5). The consensus among critical scholars is that the epithet "Babylon," used six times in Revelation (14:6; 16:19; 17:4; 18:2, 10, 21), is a cipher for imperial Rome (although Mathias Rissi would disagree; see his *Die Hure Babylon und die Verführung der Heiligen*, esp. pp. 55–56). The evidence? Well, the term "Babylon" is used for Rome elsewhere in the New Testament (1 Pet. 5:13) and in Jewish apocalyptic literature, some of it roughly contemporary with Revelation (4 *Ezra* 3:1–2, 31; 28–31; 2 *Baruch* 10:1–3; 11:1; 33:2; 67:7; 79:1; see also *Sibylline Oracles* 5.140–43, 159, 434), as well as in later rabbinic literature (*Leviticus Rabbah* 6.6; *Numbers Rabbah* 7.10; *Midrash Psalms* 137.1; *Song of Songs Rabbah* 1.6 §4). Rome became symbolic Babylon when it destroyed the second Jerusalem temple in 70 C.E., just as historical Babylon had destroyed the first Jerusalem temple in 587 B.C.E. See further Hunzinger, "Babylon als Deckname für Rom."

13. Washington, "Violence and the Construction of Gender in the Hebrew Bible," p. 330.

14. Ibid., quoting Hoffner, "Symbols for Masculinity and Femininity," p. 327.

15. Washington, "Violence and the Construction of Gender in the Hebrew Bible," p. 346. This theme is by no means limited to the Hebrew Bible, of course. The classicist Barbara Kellum ("Phallus as Signifier," p. 171) writes of "the timeworn analogies between the penetration of a woman's body and the breaching of enemy fortresses," referring us to *Iliad* 22.468-70 (cf. 16.100); *Odyssey* 13.388; Euripides, *Hecuba* 536-38; id., *Trojan Women* 308-13; and Ovid, *Amores* 1.9.15-20. See further Paul, "Urbs Capta."

16. Pippin, *Death and Desire*, pp. 57-68, and also her "Revelation to John," p. 120, and *Apocalyptic Bodies*, p. 83. Catherine Keller, too, remarks of 17:16: "In God's name, a powerful, sexual, bejeweled woman is stripped, humiliated, and devoured by hairy and horny beasts. Vision becomes voyeurism: a pious snuff picture unfolds" (*Apocalypse Now and Then*, p. 76). Thus convicted, John stands squarely in the sordid biblical tradition recently dubbed "pornoprophetics." On the latter, see Setel, "Prophets and Pornography"; Carroll, "Desire under the Terebinths"; Exum, *Plotted, Shot, and Painted*, pp. 101-28; and Brenner, *Intercourse of Knowledge*, pp. 153-74. These are all studies of the pornoprophets of the Hebrew Bible (Hosea, Ezekiel, Jeremiah, Nahum, et al.). For attempts to link them to John, see Selvidge, "Reflections on Violence and Pornography," and Kim, "Uncovering Her Wickedness," pp. 61-62, 65-66, 69-74. Also essential reading is "Pornoapocalypse," pp. 92-97 of Pippin's *Apocalyptic Bodies*.

17. Bauckham, *Theology of the Book of Revelation*, pp. 69-70; see also his *Climax of Prophecy*, pp. 229-32.

18. The notorious Rev. 14:4: "It is these who have not defiled themselves with women [*meta gynaikōn ouk emolynthēsan*], for they are virgins; these follow the Lamb wherever he goes" (referring to "the one hundred forty-four thousand who have been redeemed from the earth"). It was Ernst Lohmeyer who first suggested that 14:4 is an allusion to "holy war," which, according to Deut. 23:9-10 (cf. Lev. 15:16; 1 Sam. 21:5; 2 Sam. 11:11; 1QM 7.3-7), requires sexual abstinence of its participants (*Die Offenbarung des Johannes*, p. 120). The suggestion caught on and has been recycled by commentators ever since.

19. The no less infamous Rev. 17:3-6 is the passage stigmatizing the enemy as "Babylon the great, mother of whores [*Babylōn hē megalē, hē mētēr tōn pornōn*]," who holds in her hand "a golden cup full of abominations and the impurities of her fornication" and is "drunk with the blood of the saints and the blood of the witnesses to Jesus."

20. Bauckham, *Theology of the Book of Revelation*, p. 77. The same argument has since been advanced in more detail by P. M. McDonald ("Lion as Slain Lamb").

21. In common with numerous twentieth-century commentators, ranging from Charles to Beale. Charles, *Revelation of St. John*, 2: 135; Beale, *Book of Revelation*, p. 960.

22. Which of the following statements is more accurate? (a) Traditionally, Christian commentators on Revelation have tended to evince profound discomfort in the

face of statements such as 14:9-11. (b) Traditionally, Christian commentators on Revelation have tended to outright cheerfulness in the face of statements such as 14:9-11, so unqualified has their tacit endorsement of Revelation's theology (and ideology) been. If you chose (b) you answered correctly. G. K. Beale's *Book of Revelation*, another victim of commentarial gigantism, weighing in at 1,245 small-printed pages, provides a recent example of this complacency. His noncommittal comments on 14:9-11 run as follows: "That the torment takes place not only 'before the Lamb' but also before 'holy angels' suggests that the angels are not merely present when the judgment occurs but also take part in the execution of it, though their presence may only be intended to call attention to the Lamb. The point is that those who have denied the Lamb will be forced to acknowledge him as they are being punished 'before' him (as in 6:16)" (p. 760). A footnote informs us that "The apocalyptic belief was that the wicked would be punished often by fire, in the presence of the righteous (*1 En.* 48:9; 62:12; 108:14-15; Wis. 5:1-14; *4 Ezra* 7:93; *Targ. Isa.* 33:17) forever (Isa. 66:22-24; *1 En.* 27:2-3; cf. *1 En.* 21)" (ibid., n. 443). Then comes the standard disclaimer: "Even this belief did not underscore gleeful revenge but drew attention to the truth formerly denied by the righteous" (ibid.). What Beale omits to mention, among other things, is that Rev. 14:9-11 was a cornerstone of the ancient and medieval Christian doctrine (championed, inter alia, by Tertullian, Augustine, and Aquinas) that part of the bliss of souls in heaven consists in contemplating the torments of the damned (see further Moore, *God's Gym*, p. 20).

23. Schaberg, "Luke," p. 275: "The Gospel of Luke is an extremely dangerous text, perhaps the most dangerous text in the Bible."

24. Bauckham, *Theology of the Book of Revelation*, pp. 82-83.

25. "I saw one like the Son of Man, clothed with a long robe and with a golden sash across his chest His head and his hair were white as white wool, white as snow; his eyes were like a flame of fire, his feet were like burnished bronze, refined as in a furnace, and his voice was like the sound of many waters. In his right hand he held seven stars, and from his mouth came a sharp, two-edged sword, and his face was like the sun shining with full force" (1:13-16). Most of the details of this portrait are copied from Dan. 10:5-6, where they are used to describe an angelic being (probably Gabriel): "I looked up and saw a man clothed in linen, with a belt of gold from Uphaz around his waist. His body was like beryl, his face like lightning, his eyes like flaming torches, his arms and legs like the gleam of burnished bronze, and the sound of his words like the roar of a multitude." Adela Yarbro Collins notes how "[m]ost Christian readers downplay or ignore the angelic elements" in Rev. 1:12-16 ("The Influence of Daniel on the New Testament," p. 103); she argues that "the 'one like a son of man' in Revelation 1 is an angelic figure" (p. 102). See further her "'Son of Man' Tradition and the Book of Revelation," esp. pp. 548-51; Rowland, "Vision of the Risen Christ in Rev. i.13 ff."; Barker, *Great Angel*, pp. 200-203; and esp. Carrell, *Jesus and the Angels*, pp. 129-74.

Of the expression, "and his face was like the sun shining with full force [*kai hē opsis autou hōs ho hēlios phainei en tē dynamei autou*]," David Aune remarks (*Revelation 1-5*, p. 99) that in ancient Jewish and Christian literature "The face could be compared with the sun as a metaphor for beauty" (Wisdom of Solomon 7:29; *Joseph and Aseneth* 14:9; 18:9), "but more frequently as a metaphor for sanctity, divinity, or transcendence, often in theophanies or angelophanies" (Matt. 17:2; Rev. 10:1; 2 *Enoch* 1:5; 19:2; 4 *Ezra* 7:97, 125; *Apocalypse of Zephaniah* 6:11). Aune's separation of the two sets of passages seems unnecessary, however: beauty itself, epitomized by the radiant face, functions as a metaphor for sanctity, divinity, or transcendence in this tradition. This is especially suggested by two further passages, 2 Maccabees 3:26, 33 and Josephus, *Antiquities* 5.8.2 §277, which depict heavenly beings as exquisitely beautiful youths.

26. In the course of an erudite discussion of the matter, Dale Martin notes: "Even outside the specifically sexual arena, those persons, things, or forces understood as active were construed positively as masculine; those seen to be passive were, negatively, feminine" (*Corinthian Body*, p. 34).

27. That John's target audience has experienced persecution in the recent past is suggested by internal evidence (1:9; 2:3, 9-10, 13; 3:8; 6:9; etc). The puzzle, for scholars, is the extent of the persecution to which John's churches are subject as he writes: is the extensive persecution to which he alludes (see also 7:14; 12:17; 13:7 ff.; 17:6; 18:24; 19:2; 20:4) a present reality or (more likely) a prophetic alert? Recent ruminations on and around the problem include Sweet, *Revelation*, pp. 27-35; Collins, *Crisis and Catharsis*, pp. 84-110; Boring, *Revelation*, pp. 9-23; Thompson, *Book of Revelation*, esp. pp. 15-17, 171-97, 202-10; Aune, *Revelation 1-5*, esp. pp. lxiv-lxix; and Beale, *Book of Revelation*, pp. 5-16.

28. Do you happen to know 4 Maccabees? It is a Jewish martyrological text from the first or early second century C.E. It tells the horatory tale of how one Eleazar, an elderly Jew, and seven unnamed Jewish boys, together with their unnamed mother, inflict moral defeat upon the gentile Syrian tyrant, Antiochus IV Epiphanes, who has subjected them to torture so as to compel them to renounce their religion. Actually, 4 Maccabees contains some of the most sickening accounts of physical torture ever to bleed from a pen (easily eclipsing the *Acts of the Christian Martyrs*, Butler's *Lives of the Saints*, and even pp. 303-6 of Bret Easton Ellis's *American Psycho*). Here's a typical slice of the action:

> Then at [the king's] command the guards brought forward the eldest [of the seven boys], and having torn off his tunic, they bound his hands and arms with thongs on each side. When they had worn themselves out beating him with scourges, without accomplishing anything, they placed him upon the wheel. When the noble youth was stretched out around this, his limbs were dislocated, and every member disjointed.... [T]hey spread fire under him, and while fanning the flames they tightened the wheel further. The wheel was completely smeared with blood, and the heap of coals was being quenched by

the drippings of gore, and pieces of flesh were falling off the axles of the machine. (9:11–14, 19–20, NRSV)

—and so on, *ad nauseam*, through six more chapters and six more boys, their mother all the while forced to look on, seeing "the flesh of her children melting in the fire, and their toes and fingers scattered on the ground, and the flesh of their heads right down to the jaws exposed like masks" (15:15, my translation).

29. As Janice Anderson and I attempt to show in "Taking It Like a Man." See also Young, "Woman with the Soul of Abraham."

30. Shaw, "Body/Power/Identity," pp. 278–79.

31. Ibid., p. 280.

32. Rajak, "Dying for the Law," p. 51.

33. Ibid., pp. 51–52. That the observation might be a gloss does not reduce its interest, as Rajak remarks (p. 52, n. 47).

34. Ibid., p. 55.

35. Carlin Barton, "Savage Miracles," p. 56.

36. Ibid., p. 57.

37. The labeling of a male opponent as feminine was a stock polemical slur in Greco-Roman antiquity; see Kraemer, "Other as Woman."

38. Cf. Keller, *Apocalypse Now and Then*, p. 77: "[W]e may behold the Whore of Babylon as a great 'queen' indeed: imperial patriarchy in drag."

39. Ellis, *American Psycho*, pp. 326–28. The woman forced to watch the video herself later becomes the main course in a further nightmarish repast. This occurs in the chapter entitled "Tries to Cook and Eat Girl." The "tries" applies solely to the cooking, which is not the psycho's forte. He has no trouble eating large uncooked quantities of the woman, however, whom he has hideously tortured to death (with the aid of a very large rat), and whose dismembered and eviscerated corpse has littered his luxurious Manhattan apartment for days or possibly weeks. The novel is narrated by the psycho himself, who is young, rich, and exquisitely handsome (he is regularly taken for a male model). By day he works on Wall Street; by night he dines in chic restaurants with his peers. But day or night, whenever his busy schedule allows it, he kills (or, just conceivably, fantasizes that he kills): small animals (preferably beloved pets), children, homeless men, men in general, and women—especially women—with an insouciant savagery that makes Hannibal Lecter look positively humanitarian (and vegetarian). At its publication, *American Psycho* was the subject of much critical acclaim; it is a literary tour de force. But it outraged other readers who saw it as a virtual "how-to" manual for the serial rape, torture, and murder of women. For a brief but incisive analysis of the book, see Edwards, *Men in the Mirror*, pp. 136–37.

40. Cf. Beale, *Book of Revelation*, p. 883: "The portrayal of the harlot's desolation [in Rev. 17:16] is sketched according to the outlines of the prophecy of apostate Jerusalem's judgment by God in Ezek. 23:25–29, 47: 'your survivors will be *devoured by the fire* . . . they will also *strip you of your clothes* . . . and they will deal with you in

hatred... and leave you *naked and bare*. And the nakedness of your harlotries will be uncovered... they will *burn* their houses *with fire*.' Likewise, Ezek. 16:37–41 prophesies against faithless Israel: 'I will gather together all your lovers with whom you have consorted... they will *break down* your house of harlotry... and they will leave you *naked*... they will *burn* your houses *with fire*'" (Beale's italics). See also Hos. 2:3; Jer. 10:25; 41:22 LXX; Mic. 3:3; Nah. 3:4–5, 15. These and other related passages have drawn much attention from feminist scholars of the Hebrew Bible, as might be imagined; see p. 270, n. 16, above.

41. Cf. "Apocalyptic Horror," pp. 78–99 of Pippin's *Apocalyptic Bodies*.

42. The cattle raid of the title is the invasion of the Irish province of Ulster by the armies of the province of Connaught, along with their allies from the remaining two provinces, Leinster and Munster, in pursuit of the *Donn Cuailnge*, a colossal brown bull that Medb, queen of Connaught, is determined to possess to match the colossal white bull owned by her husband Ailill. The *Táin* (pronounced *Taw*-in) is the centerpiece of the second major cycle of early Irish literature, the first cycle consisting of tales of the *Tuatha Dé Danann* (People of the Goddess Danann), the mythical first inhabitants of Ireland, and the third cycle consisting of tales of Finn and the Fianna, the elite bodyguard of the High King of Ireland. In terms of content, all three cycles are pre-Christian (which, in the Irish context, means pre–fifth century), although the end of the third cycle heralds the arrival of the new religion, the last surviving member of the Fianna, Finn's son Oisín, whose life has been magically preserved for centuries after all his comrades have died, being converted by Saint Patrick before he too expires. Traditionally the *Táin* is said to be set in the time of Christ.

43. Pronounced Coo-*cull*-in

44. One of the three goddesses of war who feature in the *Táin*.

45. Later the narrator will be at pains to stress that, although hideous in combat, Cúchulainn cut a stunningly handsome figure ordinarily: "You would think he had three distinct heads of hair—brown at the base, blood-red in the middle, and a crown of golden yellow. This hair was settled strikingly into three coils on the cleft at the back of his head. Each long loose-flowing strand hung down in shining splendour over his shoulders, deep-gold and beautiful and fine as a thread of gold. A hundred neat red-gold curls shone darkly on his neck, and his head was covered with a hundred crimson threads matted with gems. He had four dimples in each cheek—yellow, green, crimson and blue—and seven bright pupils, eye-jewels, in each kingly eye. Each foot had seven toes and each hand seven fingers, the nails with the grip of a hawk's claw or a gryphon's clench" (Kinsella, *Táin*, pp. 156–58).

46. The boy-troop, together with Cúchulainn himself, still a boy of seventeen, was left to defend Ulster against the invaders after a curse had left all the adult men of Ulster bedridden. Now the boy-troop has been massacred and Cúchulainn has set out to avenge them.

47. Dogs and horses, women and children.... A patriarchal *pièce d'occasion*, to be

sure. Yet the *Táin* does not lack formidable women (by its own lights, at any rate), such as the memorable Queen Medb, distinguished by her greed, her prowess in battle ("Then Medb took up her weapons and hurried into battle. Three times she drove all before her until she was turned back by a wall of javelins . . . "), and her "friendly thighs"; or the woman-warrior Scáthach, "the Shadowy One," from whom the boy Cúchulainn received his training in arms, so that "he could beat any hero in Europe"; or Aife, "the hardest woman warrior in the world," although not quite as hard as the phallic warrior Cúchulainn ("Cúchulainn leaped at her and seized her by the two breasts. He took her on his back like a sack, and brought her back to his own army. He threw her heavily to the ground and held a naked sword over her . . . "); or Cúchulainn's own woman, Emer, who, although not a warrior herself, likes nothing better than to see Cúchulainn strutting his stuff ("'That was a great deed,' Emer said, 'to kill one hundred armed angry men . . . '"). The quotations are from Kinsella, *Táin*, pp. 247, 169, 28, 32, 32–33, and 37 respectively. Further on the ambivalent status of women in ancient Irish mythology, see Bitel, *Land of Women*, and Findon, *Woman's Words*.

48. Kinsella, *Táin*, pp. 150–56. This translation of the *Táin* by the poet Thomas Kinsella is far superior to the one that I read, or had read to me, as a child—Lady Augusta Gregory's *Cuchulain of Muirthemne*. Lady Gregory's translation frequently amounted to a sanitized paraphrase of the *Táin*, as I later discovered. "I left out a good deal I thought you would not care about for one reason or another," she explained to "the people of Kiltartan," the peasant tenants of her Galway estate to whom she dedicated her translation and upon whose dialect she modeled it (*Cuchulain of Muirthemne*, p. 5). As a boy, therefore, I was spared both the excitement and the bafflement that exchanges such as the following would have elicited in me: "Cúchulainn caught sight of the girl's breasts over the top of her dress. 'I see a sweet country,' he said, 'I could rest my weapon there.' Emer answered him by saying: 'No man will travel this country until he has killed a hundred men at every ford from Scenmenn ford on the river Ailbine, to Banchuing . . . where the frothy Brea makes Fedelm leap'" (Kinsella, *Táin*, p. 27).

49. See Bauckham, *Climax of Prophecy*, ch. 8, "The Book of Revelation as a Christian War Scroll."

50. Kinsella, *Táin*, p. 283.

51. The first group of (generally older) scholars has included Laughlin, *Solecisms of the Apocalypse*; Scott, *Original Language of the Apocalypse*; Torry, *Apocalypse of John*; Mussies, *Apocalypse of John*; and Thompson, *Apocalypse and Semitic Syntax*. The latter group (which represents a spectrum of related views) includes Porter, "Language of the Apocalypse in Recent Discussion"; Callahan, "Language of Apocalypse"; MacKenzie, *Author of the Apocalypse*; and Beale, "Solecisms in the Apocalypse."

52. The Dublin GPO is a three-storied early-nineteenth-century edifice with a classical columned portico rising to its roof. It is still the most prominent building on O'Connell Street, Dublin's main thoroughfare.

53. Kinsella, *Táin*, p. 168.

54. Ibid., pp. 193, 196–97.

55. Ibid., pp. 196–97.

56. Ibid., p. 189.

57. McCourt, *Angela's Ashes*, p. 2.

58. Ibid., pp. 54–55.

59. Pearse, "Coming Revolution," p. 99.

60. Kiberd, *Inventing Ireland*, p. 30, in an "Interchapter" entitled "Ireland—England's Unconscious?"

61. Quoted in Kiberd, *Inventing Ireland*, pp. 196–97.

62. Kiberd, *Inventing Ireland*, p. 31.

63. The 1916 rebels were made up mainly of members of the Irish Volunteers under Pearse, who had co-founded the force in 1913, and members of the Irish Citizen Army under the socialist labor leader James Connolly.

64. Kiberd provides a fascinating reading of the uprising as street theater. Pearse was not the only rebel leader in dramatic garb: Éamon Ceannt wore a kilt and played bagpipes, the university don Thomas MacDonagh wore a cloak and carried a swordstick, and the poet Joseph Plunkett was bedecked with Celtic rings and bracelets. And although it proved a disastrous choice militarily for the rebel stand, the GPO, with its imposing Ionic pillars, was the perfect dramatic setting for this "poets' rebellion," as the uprising would derisively be termed in the months and years ahead. Even Michael Collins, who himself fought in the GPO, noted that the entire revolt had "the air of a Greek tragedy." See further Kiberd, *Inventing Ireland*, pp. 203 ff., 223–24. He adds: "So it was fitting that the printing press on which the Proclamation of the Republic was done should have been hidden in the Abbey Theatre" (p. 204).

65. Pearse, "Coming Revolution," p. 99. Earlier in the same speech/essay (which dates from November 1913), we read: "I hold that before we can do any work, any *men's* work, we must first realise ourselves as men. And we of this generation are not in any real sense men, for we suffer things that men do not suffer, and we seek to redress grievances by means which men do not employ. We have, for instance, allowed ourselves to be disarmed; and, now that we have the chance of re-arming, we are not seizing it" (p. 97; his emphasis). How gratified, then, Pearse would have been to know that he and his fellow rebels would be referred to ever after in post-independence Ireland as "the *men* of 1916."

66. Ibid., p. 98.

67. Quoted in Edwards, *Pearse*, pp. 315–16.

68. Quoted in ibid., p. 318.

69. Pearse, "O'Donovan Rossa Graveside Panegyric," pp. 136–37.

70. The Irish Free State was formed in 1922, although it remained a British Dominion and was partitioned from Northern Ireland, which remains part of the United Kingdom to this day. In 1937, the Irish Free State became Eire (the ancient

name for the island), and in 1949, Eire in turn became the Republic of Ireland, only then officially seceding from the British Commonwealth.

71. Pearse would certainly have approved. The uprising had originally been scheduled for Easter Sunday—another fine theatrical gesture—but had to be postponed until Easter Monday due to logistical complications.

72. And one of its *seven* signatories, a touch John would surely have appreciated. Their names were drummed into me at an early age, and I can still rattle them off at will (as effortlessly as the Seven Sacraments). The Easter Rising itself seems to have been a significant seven in the minds of the authors of the Proclamation, which states: "In every generation the Irish people have asserted their right to national freedom and sovereignty; six times during the past three hundred years they have asserted it in arms. Standing on that fundamental right and again asserting it in arms in the face of the world, we hereby proclaim the Irish Republic...." The full text of the Proclamation is available in McLoughlin, ed., *Great Irish Speeches of the Twentieth Century*, pp. 41–43.

73. McCourt, *Angela's Ashes*, pp. 36–37.

74. Ibid, p. 135.

75. It is high time I inserted the conventional caveat, noting that whereas John does repeatedly employ the Greek term *martys* ("witness": 1:5; 2:13; 3:14; 17:6) and its cognates *martyria* ("witness," "testimony": 1:2, 9; 6:9; 11:7; 12:17; 19:10 [twice]; 20:4) and *martyreō* ("bear witness," "testify": 1:2; 22:16, 20), *martys* is not yet the *terminus technicus* it will become in later Christian literature (beginning with the *Martyrdom of Polycarp*, apparently). Yet we are well on the way to such usage—see esp. Rev. 2:13 ("you did not deny my faith even in the days of Antipas my *martys*, my faithful one, who was put to death among you"), 6:9 ("I beheld under the altar the souls of those who had been slain on account of the word of God and their *martyria*"), 17:6 ("And I beheld the woman [Rome], drunk with the blood of the saints and the blood of the *martyres* of Jesus"), and 20:4 ("I also beheld the souls of those who had been beheaded on account of their *martyria* to Jesus")—so that Revelation can aptly be regarded as a proto-martyrological text, at least.

76. Paradoxically, however, the enemies of God in Revelation embrace a course of action that is structurally parallel to Christian martyrdom. Certain Christians refused to curse Christ even under pain of death, as we know from Pliny the Younger's letter to Trajan (*Letters* 10.96–97), composed around 112 C.E., when Pliny was governor of Bithynia, the neighboring province to John's home province of Asia (see further Downing, "Pliny's Prosecutions of Christians"). But the unrepentant in Revelation dare to curse God under pain of death (16:9, 11, 21)—even eternal death by torture (14:9–11), unlike the temporary torment endured by the Christian martyrs—their gesture thereby exceeding that of the latter (at which point John's narrative rhetoric begins to elude his control and conspire behind his back).

77. Assuming that 4 Maccabees is a free expansion of 2 Maccabees 6:12–7:42. So

Dupont-Sommer, *Le Quatrième Livre des Machabées*, pp. 26–32, Hadas, *Third and Fourth Books of Maccabees*, pp. 92–95, and most subsequent commentators, *pace* Freudenthal, *IV Makkabäerbuch*, pp. 72–90, followed by Deissmann, "Das vierte Makkabäerbuch," p. 156, who argued that the authors of 2 and 4 Maccabees each had independent recourse to the (lost) five-volume work of Jason of Cyrene upon which 2 Maccabees purports to be based (2:23).

78. "When he opened the fifth seal, I saw under the altar the souls of those who had been slain for the word of God and for the witness they had borne; they cried out with a loud voice, 'O Sovereign Lord, holy and true, how long before thou wilt judge and avenge [*ekdikeis*] our blood on those who dwell upon the earth?'" (Rev 6:9–10, RSV). Exemplary of the approach to Revelation with which I am implicitly in dialogue here is the "people's commentary" of the Chilean liberationist exegete Pablo Richard (see Richard, *Apocalypse*; also Boesak, *Comfort and Justice*, and Howard-Brook and Gwyther, *Unveiling Empire*)—an approach characterized by a clarion call, not for vengeance, but for justice, I hasten to add. But is it justice or vengeance that is uppermost in Revelation itself?

# BIBLIOGRAPHY

Abelove, Henry, Michele Aina Barale, and David M. Halperin, eds. *The Lesbian and Gay Studies Reader.* New York: Routledge, 1993.

Aichele, George, ed. *Culture, Entertainment, and the Bible. Journal for the Study of the Old Testament* Supplement Series, 309. Sheffield: Sheffield Academic Press, 2000.

Aland, Kurt. *A History of Christianity.* Translated by James L. Schaaf. 2 vols. Philadelphia: Fortress Press, 1985–86. Originally published under the title *Geschichte der Christenheit* (Gütersloh: Gütersloher Verlagshaus Mohn, 1980–82).

Albright, William Foxwell. *Yahweh and the Gods of Canaan: A Historical Analysis of Two Contrasting Faiths.* Jordan Lectures in Comparative Religion, 7. Garden City, N.Y.: Doubleday, 1968. Reprint, Winona Lake, Ind.: Eisenbrauns, 1990.

Alexander, Philip S. "The Song of Songs as Historical Allegory: Notes on the Development of an Exegetical Tradition." In Kevin J. Cathcart and Michael Maher, eds., *Targumic and Cognate Studies: Essays in Honour of Martin McNamara,* pp. 14–29. *Journal for the Study of the Old Testament* Supplement Series, 230. Sheffield: Sheffield Academic Press, 1996.

———. "Textual Criticism and Rabbinic Literature: The Case of the Targum of the Song of Songs." *Bulletin of the John Rylands University Library of Manchester* 75 (1993): 159–73.

———. "Tradition and Originality in the Targum of the Song of Songs." In D. R. G. Beattie and Martin J. McNamara, eds., *The Aramaic Bible: Targums in Their Historical Context,* pp. 318–39. *Journal for the Study of the Old Testament* Supplement Series, 166. Sheffield: JSOT Press, 1994.

Allen, Charlotte. "Away with the Manger: Scholars Tackle the Historical Jesus." *Lingua Franca* (Jan.-Feb. 1995): 27.

———. *The Human Christ: The Search for the Historical Jesus.* New York: Free Press, 1997.

Almaguer, Thomás. "Chicano Men: A Cartography of Homosexual Identity and Behavior." *differences* 3 (1991): 75-100.

Althaus-Reid, Marcella. *Indecent Theology.* New York: Routledge, 2000.

Althusser, Louis. "Ideology and Ideological State Apparatuses (Notes Towards an Investigation)." In idem, *Lenin and Philosophy and Other Essays*, pp. 121-73. Translated by Ben Brewster. London: NLB, 1971.

Anderson, Janice Capel, and Jeffrey L. Staley, eds. *Taking It Personally: Autobiographical Biblical Criticism. Semeia* 72. Atlanta: Scholars Press, 1995.

Appleyard, Bryan. "Bloated Victim." *Sunday Times* (July 13, 1997), sec. 11, p. 1.

Apuleius. *Metamorphoses.* 2 vols. Edited and translated by J. Arthur Hanson. Loeb Classical Library. Cambridge, Mass.: Harvard University Press, 1989.

Armstrong, MacC. A. "The Methods of the Greek Physiognomists." *Greece and Rome* 5 (1958): 52-56.

Aspegren, Kerstin. *The Male Woman: A Feminine Ideal in the Early Church.* Edited by René Kieffer. Stockholm: Almqvist & Wiksell, 1990.

Astell, Ann W. *The Song of Songs in the Middle Ages.* Ithaca, N.Y.: Cornell University Press, 1990.

Attridge, Harold W. "Masculine Fellowship in the Acts of Thomas." In Birger A. Pearson, A. Thomas Kraabel, and George W. E. Nickelsburg, eds., *The Future of Early Christianity: Essays in Honor of Helmut Koester*, pp. 406-13. Minneapolis: Fortress Press, 1991.

Attridge, Harold W., and George W. MacRae, trans. *The Gospel of Truth.* In James M. Robinson, ed., *The Nag Hammadi Library in English*, pp. 38-51. 3d ed. San Francisco: Harper & Row, 1988.

Aune, David E. *Revelation 1-5.* Word Biblical Commentary, 52a. Dallas: Word Books, 1997.

———. *Revelation 6-16.* Word Biblical Commentary, 52b. Nashville, Tenn.: Thomas Nelson, 1998.

———. *Revelation 17-22.* Word Biblical Commentary, 52c. Nashville, Tenn.: Thomas Nelson, 1998.

Bach, Alice. *Women, Seduction, and Betrayal in Biblical Narrative.* Cambridge: Cambridge University Press, 1997.

———, ed. *Biblical Glamour and Hollywood Glitz. Semeia* 74. Atlanta: Scholars Press, 1996.

Baer, R. A., Jr. *Philo's Use of the Categories of Male and Female.* Arbeiten zur Literatur und Geschichte des hellenistischen Judentums, 3. Leiden: E. J. Brill, 1970.

Baildam, John D. *Paradisal Love: Johann Gottfried Herder and the Song of Songs.* Journal for the Study of the Old Testament Supplement Series, 298. Sheffield: Sheffield Academic Press, 1999.

Bailey, Randall C. "Academic Biblical Interpretation among African Americans in the United States." In Vincent L. Wimbush, ed., *African Americans and the Bible: Sacred Texts and Social Textures,* pp. 696–711. New York: Continuum, 2000.

———. "'They Shall Become White as Snow': When Bad Is Turned into Good." *Semeia* 76 (1996): 99–113.

Bakhtin, Mikhail. *Rabelais and His World.* Translated by Hélène Iswolsky. Bloomington: Indiana University Press, 1984. Russian original 1965.

Barker, Margaret. *The Great Angel: A Study of Israel's Second God.* London: SPCK, 1992.

Barth, Karl. *Church Dogmatics.* Vol. 3: *The Doctrine of Creation.* Edited by Geoffrey W. Bromiley and Thomas F. Torrance. Edinburgh: T. & T. Clark, 1958–61.

Barton, Bruce. *The Man Nobody Knows: A Discovery of the Real Jesus.* London: Constable; Indianapolis: Bobbs-Merrill, 1925.

Barton, Carlin A. "All Things Beseem the Victor: Paradoxes of Masculinity in Early Imperial Rome." In Richard C. Trexler, ed., *Gender Rhetorics: Postures of Dominance and Submission in History,* pp. 83–92. Binghamton, N.Y.: Center for Medieval and Early Renaissance Studies, 1994.

———. "Savage Miracles: The Redemption of Lost Honor in Roman Society and the Sacrament of the Gladiator and the Martyr." *Representations* 45 (1994): 41–71.

———. *The Sorrows of the Ancient Romans: The Gladiator and the Monster.* Princeton, N.J.: Princeton University Press, 1992.

Bassler, Jouette M. *The Impartiality of God: Paul's Use of a Theological Axiom.* Chico, Calif.: Scholars Press, 1982.

Bastide, Roger. "Color, Racism, and Christianity." *Daedalus* 96 (1967): 312–27.

Bauckham, Richard. *The Climax of Prophecy: Studies in the Book of Revelation.* Edinburgh: T. & T. Clark, 1993.

———. *The Theology of the Book of Revelation.* New Testament Theology. Cambridge: Cambridge University Press, 1993.

Beale, G. K. *The Book of Revelation.* The New International Greek Testament Commentary. Grand Rapids, Mich.: Eerdmans, 1999.

———. "Solecisms in the Apocalypse as Signals for the Presence of Old Testament Allusions: A Selective Analysis of Revelation 1–22." In *Early Christian Interpretation of the Scriptures of Israel,* ed. C. A. Evans and J. A. Sanders, pp. 421–46. Journal for the Study of the New Testament Supplement Series, 148; Studies in Scripture in Early Judaism and Christianity, 5. Sheffield: Sheffield Academic Press, 1997.

Beemyn, Brett, and Mickey Eliason, eds. *Queer Studies: A Lesbian, Gay, Bisexual, and Transgender Anthology.* New York: New York University Press, 1996.

Berger, John. *Ways of Seeing*. London: British Broadcasting Corporation and Penguin Books, 1972.

Berger, Maurice, Brian Wallis, and Simon Watson, eds. *Constructing Masculinity*. New York: Routledge, 1995.

Berlant, Lauren, and Michael Warner. "What Does Queer Theory Teach Us about X?" *PMLA* 110 (1995): 343–49.

Bernard of Clairvaux. *On the Song of Songs I–IV*. Vols. 2–5 of *The Works of Bernard of Clairvaux*. Edited by M. Basil Pennington. Translated by Kilian Walsh and Irene Edmonds. Kalamazoo, Mich.: Cistercian Publications, 1971–80.

Bible and Culture Collective. *The Postmodern Bible*. New Haven, Conn.: Yale University Press, 1995.

Bitel, Lisa. *Land of Women: Tales of Sex and Gender from Early Ireland*. Ithaca, N.Y.: Cornell University Press, 1997.

Black, Fiona C. "Beauty or the Beast? The Grotesque Body in the Song of Songs." *Biblical Interpretation* 8 (2000): 302–23.

———. "The Grotesque Body in the Song of Songs." Ph.D. diss. University of Sheffield, 1999.

Bloch, Ariel, and Chana Bloch. *The Song of Songs: A New Translation with an Introduction and Commentary*. New York: Random House, 1995.

Blum, Claes. *Studies in the Dream-Book of Artemidoros*. Uppsala: Almqvist & Wiksell, 1936.

Bly, Robert. *Iron John: A Book about Men*. Reading, Mass.: Addison-Wesley, 1990.

Boer, Roland. "King Solomon Meets Annie Sprinkle." *Semeia* 82 (1998): 151–82.

———. *Knockin' on Heaven's Door: The Bible and Popular Culture*. Biblical Limits. New York: Routledge, 1999.

———. "The Second Coming: Repetition and Insatiable Desire in the Song of Songs." *Biblical Interpretation* 8 (2000): 276–301.

Boesak, Allan A. *Comfort and Protest: The Apocalypse from South African Perspective*. Philadelphia: Westminster Press, 1987.

Bollók, János. "The Description of Paul in the *Acta Pauli*." In Jan N. Bremmer, ed., *The Apocryphal Acts of Paul and Thecla*, pp. 1–15. Studies on the Apocryphal Acts of the Apostles, 2. Kampen, Neth.: Kok Pharos, 1996.

Boone, Joseph. "Vacation Cruises; or, the Homoerotics of Orientalism." *PMLA* 110 (1995): 89–107.

Bordo, Susan. *The Male Body: A New Look at Men in Public and in Private*. New York: Farrar, Straus and Giroux, 1999.

———. *Unbearable Weight: Feminism, Western Culture, and the Body*. Berkeley and Los Angeles: University of California Press, 1993.

Borg, Marcus. *Jesus: A New Vision*. San Francisco: Harper & Row, 1987.

———. *Jesus in Contemporary Scholarship* Valley Forge, Pa.: Trinity Press International, 1994.

———. *Meeting Jesus Again for the First Time: The Historical Jesus and the Heart of Contemporary Faith.* San Francisco: HarperSanFrancisco, 1995.

Boring, M. Eugene. *Revelation.* Interpretation: A Bible Commentary for Preaching and Teaching. Louisville, Ky.: John Knox Press, 1989.

Boswell, John. *Christianity, Social Tolerance, and Homosexuality: Gay People in Western Europe from the Beginning of the Christian Era to the Fourteenth Century.* Chicago: University of Chicago Press, 1980.

Boyarin, Daniel. "Are There Any Jews in 'The History of Sexuality'?" *Journal of the History of Sexuality* 5 (1995): 333–55.

———. *Carnal Israel: Reading Sex in Talmudic Culture.* The New Historicism: Studies in Cultural Poetics. Berkeley and Los Angeles: University of California Press, 1993.

———. *Dying for God: Martyrdom and the Making of Christianity and Judaism.* Figurae: Reading Medieval Culture. Stanford, Calif.: Stanford University Press, 1999.

———. *Intertextuality and the Reading of Midrash.* Indiana Studies in Biblical Literature. Bloomington: Indiana University Press, 1990.

———. *A Radical Jew: Paul and the Politics of Identity.* Contraversions: Critical Studies in Jewish Literature, Culture, and Society, 1. Berkeley and Los Angeles: University of California Press, 1994.

———. *Unheroic Conduct: The Rise of Heterosexuality and the Invention of the Jewish Man.* Contraversions: Critical Studies in Jewish Literature, Culture, and Society, 8. Berkeley and Los Angeles: University of California Press, 1997.

Boyd, Stephen B., W. Merle Longwood, and Mark W. Muesse, eds. *Redeeming Men: Religion and Masculinities.* Louisville, Ky.: Westminster John Knox Press, 1996.

Brand, Peg Zeglin, ed. *Beauty Matters.* Bloomington: Indiana University Press, 2000.

Bray, Alan. "Homosexuality and the Signs of Male Friendship in Elizabethan England." In Jonathan Goldberg, ed., *Queering the Renaissance*, pp. 40–61. Durham, N.C.: Duke University Press, 1994.

———. *Homosexuality in Renaissance England.* London: Gay Men's Press, 1982.

Bremmer, Jan, ed. *The Apocryphal Acts of Paul and Thecla.* Studies on the Apocryphal Acts of the Apostles, 2. Kampen, Neth.: Kok Pharos, 1996.

Brenner, Athalya. "An Afterword." In idem, ed., *A Feminist Companion to the Song of Songs*, pp. 279–80. Feminist Companion to the Bible, 1. Sheffield: JSOT Press, 1993.

———. "'Come Back, Come Back the Shulammite' (Song of Songs 7:1–10): A Parody of the *Wasf* Genre." In Brenner, ed., *A Feminist Companion to the Song of Songs*, pp. 234–57.

———. *The Intercourse of Knowledge: On Gendering Desire and "Sexuality" in the Hebrew Bible.* Biblical Interpretation Series, 26. Leiden: E. J. Brill, 1997.

———. "On Feminist Criticism of the Song of Songs." In Brenner, ed., *A Feminist Companion to the Song of Songs*, pp. 28–37.

Bringle, Mary Louise. *The God of Thinness: Gluttony and Other Weighty Matters*. Nashville, Tenn.: Abingdon Press, 1992.

Bristow, Joseph. *Sexuality*. The New Critical Idiom. New York: Routledge, 1997

Brooten, Bernadette J. *Love Between Women: Early Christian Responses to Female Homoeroticism*. Sexuality, History, and Society. Chicago: University of Chicago Press, 1996.

———. "Patristic Interpretations of Romans 1:26." In Elizabeth A. Livingstone, ed., *Studia Patristica XVIII: Papers of the Ninth International Patristics Conference, Oxford 1983*, vol. 1: *Historica-Theologica-Gnostica-Biblica*, pp. 287–91. Kalamazoo, Mich.: Cistercian Publications, 1985.

Brown, John. *The Self-Interpreting Bible, Containing the Old and New Testaments, with References and Illustrations; an Exact Summary of the Several Books; a Paraphrase on the Most Obscure or Important Parts; an Analysis of the Contents of Each Chapter, to Which Are Annexed an Extensive Introduction, Explanatory Notes, Evangelical Reflections, &c.*, 1778. Bungay: Brightly & Childs, 1813.

———. *A Dictionary of the Holy Bible, Corrected and Improved According to the Advanced State of Information at the Present Day, by the Rev. James Smith, A.M.* London: Blackie & Son, 1851.

Brown, Peter. "Bodies and Minds: Sexuality and Renunciation in Early Christianity." In David M. Halperin, John J. Winkler, and Froma I. Zeitlin, eds., *Before Sexuality: Erotic Experience in the Ancient Greek World*, pp. 479–93. Princeton, N.J.: Princeton University Press, 1990.

———. *The Body and Society: Men, Women, and Sexual Renunciation in Early Christianity*. New York: Columbia University Press, 1988.

Brown, Raymond E. *The Community of the Beloved Disciple*. New York: Paulist Press, 1979.

Brownmiller, Susan. *Femininity*. New York: Fawcett Columbine, 1984.

Budde, Karl. "Das Hohelied erklärt." In Karl Budde, Alfred Bertholet, and D. G. Wildeboer, *Die fünf Megillot*, pp. 9–48. Kurzer Hand-Commentar zum Alten Testament, 6. Tübingen: J. C. B. Mohr (Paul Siebeck), 1898.

———. "Was ist das Hohelied?" *Preussische Jahrbücher* 78 (1894): 92–117.

Burrus, Virginia. *"Begotten Not Made": Conceiving Masculinity in Late Antiquity*. Figurae: Reading Medieval Culture. Stanford, Calif.: Stanford University Press, 2000.

Bussmann, Claus. *Themen der paulinischen Missionspredigt auf dem Hintergrund der spätjüdisch-hellenistischen Missionsliteratur*. Europäische Hochschulschriften, ser. 23, Theologie, 3. Frankfurt a./M.: Lang, 1971.

Butler, Judith. "Against Proper Objects." *differences* 6, special issue, *More Gender Trouble: Feminism Meets Queer Theory* (1994): 1–26.

———. *Bodies That Matter: On the Discursive Limits of "Sex."* New York: Routledge, 1993.

———. *Gender Trouble: Feminism and the Subversion of Identity.* 2d ed. New York: Routledge, 1999.

———. "Melancholy Gender / Refused Identification." In Maurice Berger, Brian Wallis, and Simon Watson, eds., *Constructing Masculinity*, pp. 21–36. New York: Routledge, 1995.

Bynum, Caroline Walker. *Fragmentation and Redemption: Essays on Gender and the Human Body.* New York: Zone Books, 1992.

———. *Holy Feast and Holy Fast: The Religious Significance of Food to Medieval Women.* The New Historicism: Studies in Cultural Poetics. Berkeley and Los Angeles: University of California Press, 1987.

———. *Jesus as Mother: Studies in the Spirituality of the High Middle Ages.* Publications of the Center for Medieval and Renaissance Studies, UCLA, 16. Berkeley and Los Angeles: University of California Press, 1982.

Byrne, Brendan. *Romans.* Sacra Pagina, 6. Collegeville, Minn.: Liturgical Press, 1996.

Callahan, Allen D. "The Language of Apocalypse." *Harvard Theological Review* 88 (1995): 453–70.

Campbell, Douglas A. *The Rhetoric of Righteousness in Romans 3:21–26. Journal for the Study of the New Testament* Supplement Series, 65. Sheffield: Sheffield Academic Press, 1992.

———. "Romans 1:17—A *Crux Interpretum* for the ΠΙΣΤΙΣ ΧΡΙΣΤΟΥ Debate." *Journal of Biblical Literature* 113 (1994): 265–85.

Caner, Daniel F. "The Practice and Prohibition of Self-Castration in Early Christianity." *Vigiliae Christianae* 51 (1997): 396–415.

Cantarella, Eva. *Bisexuality in the Ancient World.* Translated by Cormac Ó Couilleanáin. New Haven, Conn.: Yale University Press, 1992. Originally published as *Secondo natura: La bisessualità nel mondo antico* (Rome: Editori riuniti, 1988).

Carr, David. "Gender and the Shaping of Desire in the Song of Songs." *Journal of Biblical Literature* 119 (2000): 233–48.

Carr, G. Lloyd. *The Song of Solomon: An Introduction and Commentary.* Tyndale Old Testament Commentaries. Downers Grove, Ill.: InterVarsity Press, 1984.

Carr, Stephen. "Doing Queer Theology in *The Garden*: Derek Jarman and Christianity." *Theology and Sexuality* 8 (1998): 9–26.

Carrell, Peter R. *Jesus and the Angels: Angelology and the Christology of the Apocalypse of John.* Society for New Testament Studies Monograph Series, 95. Cambridge: Cambridge University Press, 1997.

Carrette, Jeremy R. *Foucault and Religion: Spiritual Corporality and Political Spirituality.* New York: Routledge, 2000.

Carroll, Robert P. "Desire under the Terebinths: On Pornographic Representation in the Prophets—A Response." In Athalya Brenner, ed., *A Feminist Companion to the Latter Prophets*, pp. 275–307. Feminist Companion to the Bible, 8. Sheffield: Sheffield Academic Press, 1995.

Carter, Glenn, and Jeremy Sisto. "What Would Jesus Do in This Scene?" Dialogue moderated by Melanie Rehak. *New York Times Magazine*, Apr. 23, 2000, pp. 36, 38.

Cassian, John. *The Conferences*. Collationes patrum XXIV. Translated and annotated by Boniface Ramsey. Ancient Christian Writers, 57. New York: Paulist Press, 1997.

Castelli, Elizabeth A. *Imitating Paul: A Discourse of Power*. Literary Currents in Biblical Interpretation. Louisville, Ky.: Westminster John Knox Press, 1991.

———. "Romans." In Elisabeth Schüssler Fiorenza, Ann Brock, and Shelly Matthews, eds., *Searching the Scriptures*, vol. 2: *A Feminist Commentary*, pp. 272–300. New York: Crossroad, 1994.

Castle, Terry. *The Apparitional Lesbian*. Gender and Culture. Irvington, N.Y.: Columbia University Press, 1995.

Chadwick, Henry E. *Early Christian Thought and the Classical Tradition*. Oxford: Oxford University Press, 1966.

———. *The Sentences of Sextus*. Text and Studies, 5. Cambridge: Cambridge University Press, 1959.

Chapkis, Wendy. *Beauty Secrets: Women and the Politics of Appearance*. Boston: South End Press, 1986.

Chapman, Rowena, and Jonathan Rutherford, eds. *Male Order: Unwrapping Masculinity*. London: Lawrence & Wishart, 1988.

Charles, R. H. *A Critical and Exegetical Commentary on the Revelation of St. John*. 2 vols. International Critical Commentary. Edinburgh: T. & T. Clark, 1920.

Chauncey, George. *Gay New York: Gender, Urban Culture, and the Making of the Gay Male World, 1890–1940*. New York: Harper Collins, 1994.

Cixous, Hélène. *Stigmata: Escaping Texts*. Translated by Catherine A. F. MacGillivray et al. New York: Routledge, 1998.

Clark, Gillian. "The Old Adam: The Fathers and the Unmaking of Masculinity." In Lin Foxhall and John Salmon, eds., *Thinking Men: Masculinity and Self-Representation in the Classical Tradition*, pp. 83–99. Leicester-Nottingham Studies in Ancient Society, 7. New York: Routledge, 1998.

Clarke, John. "Hypersexual Black Men in Augustan Baths: Ideal Somatypes and Apotropaic Magic." In Natalie Boymel Kampen, ed., *Sexuality in Ancient Art: Near East, Egypt, Greece, and Italy*, pp. 184–98. Cambridge Studies in New Art History and Criticism. Cambridge: Cambridge University Press, 1996.

Clines, David J. A. "David the Man: The Construction of Masculinity in the Hebrew Bible." In idem, *Interested Parties: The Ideology of Writers and Readers of the Hebrew Bible*, pp. 212-43. Gender, Culture, Theory, 1. Sheffield: Sheffield Academic Press, 1995.

———. "Ecce Vir, or, Gendering the Son of Man." In J. Cheryl Exum and Stephen D. Moore, eds., *Biblical Studies/Cultural Studies: The Third Sheffield Colloquium*, pp. 352-75. Journal for the Study of the Old Testament Supplement Series, 266; Gender, Culture, Theory, 7. Sheffield: Sheffield Academic Press, 1998.

———. "Why Is There a Song of Songs and What Does It Do to You If You Read It?" In idem, *Interested Parties*, pp. 94-121.

Cloke, Gillian. *This Female Man of God: Women and Spiritual Power in the Patristic Age*, A.D. *350-450*. New York: Routledge, 1995.

Cohen, Colleen Ballerino, Richard Wilk, and Beverly Stoeltje, eds. *Beauty Queens on the Global Stage: Gender, Contests, and Power*. New York: Routledge, 1996.

Cohen, David. *Law, Sexuality, and Society: The Enforcement of Morals in Classical Athens*. Cambridge: Cambridge University Press, 1991.

Cohen, David, and Richard Saller. "Foucault on Sexuality in Greco-Roman Antiquity." In Jan Goldstein, ed., *Foucault and the Writing of History*, pp. 35-59. Oxford: Basil Blackwell, 1994.

Cohen, Martin Samuel. "The Song of Songs and the *Shiʿur Qomah*." Unpublished paper.

Cohen, Shaye J. D. "The Beauty of Flora and the Beauty of Sarai." *Helios*, n.s., 8 (1981): 41-53.

Collins, Adela Yarbro. *Crisis and Catharsis: The Power of the Apocalypse*. Philadelphia: Westminster Press, 1984.

———. "The Influence of Daniel on the New Testament." In John J. Collins, *Daniel: A Commentary on the Book of Daniel*, pp. 90-112. Hermeneia. Minneapolis: Fortress Press, 1993.

———. "The 'Son of Man' Tradition and the Book of Revelation." In James H. Charlesworth, ed., *The Messiah*, pp. 536-68. Minneapolis: Fortress Press, 1992.

Colson, F. H., ed. and trans. *Philo*. 12 vols. Loeb Classical Library. Cambridge, Mass.: Harvard University Press, 1941.

Combes, Isobel H. "Nursing Mother, Ancient Shepherd, Athletic Coach? Some Images of Christ in the Early Church." In Stanley E. Porter, Michael A. Hayes, and David Tombs, eds., *Images of Christ, Ancient and Modern*, pp. 113-25. Roehampton Institute London Papers, 2. Sheffield: Sheffield Academic Press, 1997.

Comstock, Gary David, and Susan E. Henking, eds. *Que(e)rying Religion: A Critical Anthology*. New York: Continuum, 1997.

Connell, R. W. *Masculinities*. Oxford: Polity Press, 1995.

Cooke, Miriam. "Wo-man, Retelling the War Myth." In idem and A. Woollacott, eds., *Gendering War Talk*, pp. 169-90. Princeton, N.J.: Princeton University Press, 1993.

Copher, Charles B. *Black Biblical Studies: An Anthology of Charles B. Copher.* Biblical and Theological Issues on the Black Presence in the Bible. Chicago: Black Light Fellowship, 1993.

———. "The Black Presence in the Old Testament." In Cain Hope Felder, ed., *Stony the Road We Trod: African American Biblical Interpretation,* pp. 146–64. Minneapolis: Fortress Press, 1991.

———. "Three Thousand Years of Biblical Interpretation with Reference to Black Peoples." In Copher, *Black Biblical Studies,* pp. 95–120.

Cornwall, Andrea, and Nancy Lindisfarne, eds. *Dislocating Masculinity: Comparative Ethnographies.* New York: Routledge, 1994.

Cox, Patricia. *Biography in Late Antiquity: A Quest for the Holy Man.* Berkeley and Los Angeles: University of California Press, 1983.

Craig, Kenneth. *Reading Esther: A Case for the Literary Carnivalesque.* Literary Currents in Biblical Interpretation. Louisville, Ky.: Westminster John Knox Press, 1995.

Cranfield, C. E. B. *A Critical and Exegetical Commentary on the Epistle to the Romans.* 2 vols. International Critical Commentary. Edinburgh: T. & T. Clark, 1975.

Crawford, Bobbie. "A Female Crucifix." *Daughters of Sarah* 14 (Nov.–Dec. 1983): 26.

Crossan, John Dominic. *The Birth of Christianity: What Happened in the Years Immediately after the Execution of Jesus.* San Francisco: HarperSanFrancisco, 1998.

———. *The Essential Jesus.* San Francisco: HarperSanFrancisco, 1994.

———. *The Historical Jesus: The Life of a Mediterranean Jewish Peasant.* San Francisco: HarperSanFrancisco, 1991.

———. *Jesus: A Revolutionary Biography.* San Francisco: HarperSanFrancisco, 1994.

———. *Who Killed Jesus? Exposing the Roots of Anti-Semitism in the Gospel Story of the Death of Jesus.* San Francisco: HarperSanFrancisco, 1995.

Cunningham, D. J. *Cunningham's Manual of Practical Anatomy.* 3 vols. 13th ed. Revised by G. J. Romanes. Oxford: Oxford University Press, 1968.

D'Angelo, Mary Rose. "Women Partners in the New Testament." In Gary David Comstock and Susan E. Henking, eds., *Que(e)rying Religion: A Critical Anthology,* pp. 441–55. New York: Continuum, 1997.

Danby, Herbert, ed. and trans. *The Mishnah.* Oxford: Oxford University Press, 1933.

Davies, Margaret. "New Testament Ethics and Ours: Homosexuality and Sexuality in Romans 1:26–27." *Biblical Interpretation* 3 (1995): 315–31.

Dawes, Gregory W. *Body in Question: Metaphor and Meaning in the Interpretation of Ephesians 5.21–33.* Biblical Interpretation Series, 30. Leiden: E. J. Brill, 1998.

Deferrari, R. J., ed. *Fathers of the Church: A New Translation.* 86 vols. Washington, D.C.: Catholic University of America Press, 1947.

Deissmann, Adolf. "Das vierte Makkabäerbuch." In E. Kautzsch, ed., *Die*

*Apokryphen und Pseudepigraphen des Alten Testaments*, 2: 149–77. Tübingen: J. C. B. Mohr, 1900.

Delitzsch, Franz. *Proverbs, Ecclesiastes, Song of Solomon*. Vol. 6 of Franz Delitzsch and C. F. Keil, *Commentary on the Old Testament in Ten Volumes*. Translated by M. G. Easton. Grand Rapids, Mich.: William B. Eerdmans, 1980. German original 1875.

Deming, Will. "Mark 9.42–10.12, Matthew 5.27–32, and *b. Nid.* 13b: A First-Century Discussion of Male Sexuality." *New Testament Studies* 36 (1990): 130–41.

———. *Paul on Marriage and Celibacy: The Hellenistic Background of 1 Corinthians 7*. Society for New Testament Studies Monograph Series, 83. Cambridge: Cambridge University Press, 1995.

Dempsey, Robert Brinkerhoff. "The Interpretation and Use of the Song of Songs." Ph.D. diss. Boston University School of Theology, 1963.

Dijk-Hemmes, Fokkelien van. "The Imagination of Power and the Power of Imagination." In Athalya Brenner, ed., *A Feminist Companion to the Song of Songs*, pp. 156–70. Feminist Companion to the Bible, 1. Sheffield: JSOT Press, 1993.

Doss, Erika. "Making a 'Virile, Manly Christ': The Cultural Origins and Meanings of Warner Sallman's Religious Imagery." In David Morgan, ed., *Icons of American Protestantism: The Art of Warner Sallman*, pp. 61–94. New Haven, Conn.: Yale University Press, 1996.

Doty, William G. *Myths of Masculinity*. New York: Crossroad, 1993.

Doughty, Darrell J. "Pauline Paradigms and Pauline Authenticity." *Journal of Higher Criticism* 1 (1994): 95–128.

Douglas, Mary. *Purity and Danger: An Analysis of Concepts of Pollution and Taboo*. London: Routledge & Kegan Paul, 1966.

Dover, K. J. *Greek Homosexuality, Updated and with a New Postscript*. Cambridge, Mass.: Harvard University Press, 1989.

Downing, Christine. *Myths and Mysteries of Same-Sex Love*. New York: Continuum, 1991.

Downing, Gerald F. *The Christ and the Cynics*. JSOT Manuals, 4. Sheffield: JSOT Press, 1988.

———. *Cynics and Christian Origins*. Edinburgh: T. & T. Clark, 1992.

———. "Deeper Reflections on the Jewish Cynic Jesus." *Journal of Biblical Literature* 117 (1998): 97–104.

———. "Pliny's Prosecutions of Christians: Revelation and 1 Peter." *Journal for the Study of the New Testament* 34 (1988): 105–23.

Dowsett, Andrew C. "Theology in the Discography: The Bible and Popular Music." Ph.D. diss. University of Sheffield, 1999.

Duberman, Martin, ed. *A Queer World: The Center for Lesbian and Gay Studies Reader*. New York: New York University Press, 1997.

DuBois, Page. "The Subject in Antiquity after Foucault." In David H. J. Larmour, Paul Allen Miller, and Charles Platter, eds., *Rethinking Sexuality: Foucault and Classical Antiquity*, pp. 85–103. Princeton, N.J.: Princeton University Press, 1998.

Dunn, James D. G. *Romans 1–8*. Word Biblical Commentary, 38A. Dallas: Word Books, 1988.

———. *The Theology of Paul the Apostle*. Edinburgh: T. & T. Clark, 1998.

Dupont-Sommer, André. *Le Quatrième Livre des Machabées: Introduction, traduction et notes*. Bibliothèque de l'Ecole des hautes études, IVe section, Sciences historiques et philologiques, 274. Paris: Honoré Champion, 1939.

Dutton, Kenneth R. *The Perfectible Body: The Western Ideal of Physical Development*. London: Cassell, 1995.

Dyer, Richard. *White*. New York: Routledge, 1997.

Eddy, Paul Rhodes. "Jesus as Diogenes? Reflections on the Cynic Jesus Thesis." *Journal of Biblical Literature* 115 (1996): 449–69.

Edwards, Ruth Dudley. *Pearse: The Triumph of Failure*. London: Victor Gollancz, 1977.

Edwards, Tim. *Men in the Mirror: Men's Fashion, Masculinity and Consumer Society*. London: Cassell, 1997.

Eilberg-Schwartz, Howard. *God's Phallus and Other Problems for Men and Monotheism*. Boston: Beacon Press, 1994.

Eisler, Robert. *The Messiah Jesus and John the Baptist According to Flavius Josephus's Recently Rediscovered "Capture of Jerusalem" and the Other Jewish and Christian Sources*. Translated by Alexander Haggerty Krappe. New York: Dial Press, 1931. German original 1929–30.

Ellis, Bret Easton. *American Psycho*. New York: Vintage Books, 1991.

Eron, Lewis John. "Early Jewish and Christian Attitudes Toward Male Homosexuality as Expressed in the Testament of Naphtali." In Michael L. Stemmeler, and J. Michael Clark, eds., *Homophobia and the Judaeo-Christian Tradition*, pp. 25–49. Dallas: Monument, 1990,

Eslinger, Lyle. "The Case of an Immodest Lady Wrestler in Deuteronomy xxv 11–12." *Vetus Testamentum* 31 (1981): 269–81.

Eusebius. *Ecclesiastical History*. 2 vols. Translated by Kirsopp Lake and J. E. L. Oulton. Loeb Classical Library. Cambridge, Mass.: Harvard University Press, 1973–84.

Evans, Craig A. "Images of Christ in the Canonical and Apocryphal Gospels." In Stanley E. Porter, Michael A. Hayes, and David Tombs, eds., *Images of Christ Ancient and Modern*, pp. 34–72. Roehampton Institute London Papers, 2. Sheffield: Sheffield Academic Press, 1997.

Evans, Craig A., and Bruce D. Chilton, eds. *Authenticating the Words of Jesus*. New Testament Tools and Studies, 28/1. Leiden: E. J. Brill, 1999.

———, eds. *Authenticating the Acts of Jesus.* New Testament Tools and Studies, 28/2. Leiden: E. J. Brill, 1999.

Evans, Elizabeth C. *Physiognomics in the Ancient World.* Transactions of the American Philosophical Society, 59/5. Philadelphia: American Philosophical Society, 1969.

———. "The Study of Physiognomy in the Second Century A.D." *Transactions of the American Philological Association* 72 (1941): 96–108.

Evans, G. R. *The Mind of St. Bernard of Clairvaux.* Oxford: Clarendon Press, 1983.

Exum, J. Cheryl. "Asseverative ʾal in Canticles 1.6?" *Biblica* 62 (1981): 416–19.

———. "Developing Strategies of Feminist Criticism / Developing Strategies for Commentating the Song of Songs." In David J. A. Clines and Stephen D. Moore, eds., *Auguries: The Jubilee Volume of the Sheffield Department of Biblical Studies,* pp. 206–49. Journal for the Study of the Old Testament Supplement Series, 269. Sheffield: Sheffield Academic Press, 1998.

———. "A Literary and Structural Analysis of the Song of Songs." *Zeitschrift für die alttestamentliche Wissenschaft* 85 (1973): 47–79.

———. *Plotted, Shot, and Painted: Cultural Representations of Biblical Women.* Gender, Culture, Theory, 3. Sheffield: Sheffield Academic Press, 1996.

Exum, J. Cheryl, and Stephen D. Moore, eds. *Biblical Studies / Cultural Studies: The Third Sheffield Colloquium.* Gender, Culture, Theory, 7. Sheffield: Sheffield Academic Press, 1998.

Faderman, Lillian. *Scotch Verdict: Miss Pirie and Miss Woods v. Dame Cumming Gordon.* New York: William Morrow, 1983.

———. *Surpassing the Love of Men: Romantic Friendship and Love Between Women from the Renaissance to the Present.* New York: William Morrow, 1981.

Falk, Marcia. *The Song of Songs: A New Translation and Interpretation.* San Francisco: HarperSanFrancisco, 1990.

Fanon, Frantz. *Black Skin, White Masks.* Translated by Charles Lam Markmann. New York: Grove Press, 1967. Originally published as *Peau noire, masques blancs* (Paris: Éditions du Seuil, 1952).

Fantham, Elaine. "*Stuprum*: Public Attitudes and Penalties for Sexual Offenses in Republican Rome." *Echos du monde classique / Classical Views* 35 (1991): 267–91.

Felder, Cain Hope. "Race, Racism, and the Biblical Narratives." In idem, ed., *Stony the Road We Trod,* pp. 127–45.

———, ed. *Stony the Road We Trod: African American Biblical Interpretation.* Minneapolis: Fortress Press, 1991.

Féray, Jean-Claude, and Manfred Herzer. "Homosexual Studies and Politics in the Nineteenth Century: Karl Maria Kertbeny." Translated by Glen W. Poppel. *Journal of Homosexuality* 19 (1990): 23–47.

Findon, Joanne. *A Woman's Words: Emer and Female Speech in the Ulster Cycle.* Toronto: University of Toronto Press, 1997.

Finley, Moses I. *Ancient Slavery and Modern Ideology*. New York: Viking Press, 1980.

Fiorenza, Elisabeth Schüssler. *Jesus: Miriam's Child, Sophia's Prophet*. Critical Issues in Feminist Christology. New York: Crossroad, 1994.

Fiorenza, Elisabeth Schüssler, and Alice Bach. "Elisabeth Schüssler Fiorenza: An Interview." *Biblicon* 3 (1998): 27–44.

Fiorenza, Elisabeth Schüssler, Ann Brock, and Shelly Matthews, eds. *Searching the Scriptures*. Vol. 2: *A Feminist Commentary*. New York: Crossroad, 1994.

Fitzmyer, Joseph A. *Romans: A New Translation with Introduction and Commentary*. Anchor Bible, 33. New York: Doubleday, 1992.

Ford, Joan Massyingbaerde. "The Crucifixion of Women in Antiquity." *Journal of Higher Criticism* 3 (1996): 290–309.

———. "The Physical Features of the Antichrist." *Journal for the Study of the Pseudepigrapha* 14 (1996): 23–41.

Forster, E. M. *Maurice: A Novel*. New York: Norton, 1971.

Fosdick, Harry Emerson. *The Manhood of the Master*. New York: Association Press, 1911.

Foucault, Michel. "The Battle for Chastity." Translated by Anthony Forster. In Philippe Ariès and André Béjin, eds., *Western Sexuality: Practice and Precept in Past and Present Times*, pp. 14–25. Oxford: Basil Blackwell, 1985.

———. "The Concern for Truth." In Lawrence D. Kritzman, ed., *Michel Foucault: Politics, Philosophy, Culture. Interviews and Other Writings 1877–1984*, pp. 255–67. New York: Routledge, 1988.

———. "The Confessions of the Flesh." In Colin Gordon, ed., *Power/Knowledge: Selected Interviews and Other Writings 1972–77*, pp. 194–228. Translated by Colin Gordon et al. New York: Pantheon Books, 1980.

———. *Ethics: Subjectivity and Truth*. Vol. 1 of *Essential Works of Foucault, 1954–1984*. Edited by Paul Rabinow. Translated by Robert J. Hurley. New York: New Press, 1998.

———. "Friendship as a Way of Life." In Sylvère Lotringer, ed., *Foucault Live: Interviews 1966–84*, pp. 203–11. Translated by John Johnston. New York: Semiotext(e), 1989.

———. "The History of Sexuality." In Gordon, ed., *Power/Knowledge*, pp. 183–93.

———. *The History of Sexuality*. Translated by Robert Hurley. Vol. 1: *An Introduction*. New York: Random House, Vintage Books, 1978. Vol. 2: *The Use of Pleasure*. New York: Random House, 1985. Vol. 3: *The Care of the Self*. New York: Pantheon Books, 1986. Originally published in 3 vols. as *Histoire de la sexualité* (Paris: Gallimard, 1976–84).

———. "Michel Foucault: An Interview. Sex, Power and the Politics of Identity." In Mark Thompson, ed., *Gay Spirit: Myth and Meaning*, pp. 25–35. New York: St. Martin's Press, 1987.

———. "On the Genealogy of Ethics: An Overview of Work in Progress." In Paul Rabinow, ed., *The Foucault Reader*. New York: Pantheon Books, 1984.
———. *The Order of Things: An Archaeology of the Human Sciences*. New York: Pantheon Books, 1971. Originally published as *Les mots et les choses: Une archéologie des sciences humaines* (Paris: Gallimard, 1966).
———. "Power and Sex." In Kritzman, ed., *Michel Foucault*, pp. 110-24.
———. "The Return of Morality." In Kritzman, ed., *Michel Foucault*, pp. 232-54.
———. "Sexual Choice, Sexual Act: Foucault and Homosexuality." In Kritzman, ed., *Michel Foucault*, pp. 286-303.
———. "Sexuality and Solitude." In Marshall Blonsky, ed., *On Signs*, pp. 365-67. Baltimore: Johns Hopkins University Press, 1985.
———. "Sexual Morality and the Law." In Kritzman, ed., *Michel Foucault*, pp. 271-85.
———. "The Simplest of Pleasures." *Fag Rag* 29 (1979): 3.
———. "The Social Triumph of the Sexual Will: A Conversation with Michel Foucault." *Christopher Street* 64 (May 1982): 36-41.
———. "The West and the Truth of Sex." *Sub/stance* 20 (1978): 83-97.
Fowl, Stephen. *The Story of Christ in the Ethics of Paul: An Analysis of the Function of the Hymnic Material in the Pauline Corpus*. Journal for the Study of the New Testament Supplement Series, 36; Sheffield: JSOT Press, 1992.
Fowles, John. *The French Lieutenant's Woman*. Boston: Little, Brown, 1969.
Fox, Michael. *The Song of Songs and the Ancient Egyptian Love Songs*. Madison: University of Wisconsin Press, 1985.
Foxhall, Lin. "Pandora Unbound: A Feminist Critique of Foucault's *History of Sexuality*." In David H. J. Larmour, Paul Allen Miller, and Charles Platter, eds., *Rethinking Sexuality: Foucault and Classical Antiquity*, pp. 122-37. Princeton, N.J.: Princeton University Press, 1998.
Foxhall, Lin, and John Salmon, eds. *Thinking Men: Masculinity and Its Self-Representation in the Classical Tradition*. Leicester-Nottingham Studies in Ancient Society. New York: Routledge, 1998.
———. *When Men Were Men: Masculinity, Power and Identity in Classical Antiquity*. Leicester-Nottingham Studies in Ancient Society. New York: Routledge, 1999.
Fredriksen, Paula. *Jesus of Nazareth, King of the Jews: A Jewish Life and the Emergence of Christianity*. New York: Knopf, 1999.
Freedman, Diane P., Olivia Frey, and Frances Murphy Zauhar, eds. *The Intimate Critique: Autobiographical Literary Criticism*. Durham, N.C.: Duke University Press, 1993.
Freud, Sigmund. *Moses and Monotheism: Three Essays*. In James Strachey, ed. and trans., with Anna Freud, Alix Strachey, and Alan Tyson, *The Standard Edition of the Complete Psychological Works of Sigmund Freud*, 23: 3-317. London: Hogarth Press, 1955.

Freudenthal, J. *Die Flavius Josephus beigelegte Schrift über die Herrschaft der Vernunft (IV Makkabäerbuch), eine Predigt aus dem ersten nachchristlichen Jahrhundert.* Breslau: Schletter, 1869.

Friday, Nancy. *The Power of Beauty.* London: Hutchinson, 1996.

Frost, Peter. "Attitudes Toward Blacks in the Early Christian Era." *Second Century* 8 (1991): 1-11.

Funk, Robert W. *The Acts of Jesus: What Did Jesus Really Do?* San Francisco: HarperSanFrancisco, 1998.

———. *Honest to Jesus: Jesus for a New Millennium.* San Francisco: HarperSanFrancisco, 1996.

Funk, Robert W., Roy W. Hoover, and the Jesus Seminar. *The Five Gospels: The Search for the Authentic Words of Jesus.* New York: Macmillan, 1993.

Furman, Frida Kerner. *Facing the Mirror: Older Women and Beauty Shop Culture.* New York: Routledge, 1997.

Fuss, Diana. "Inside/Out." In idem, ed., *Inside/Out: Lesbian Theories, Gay Theories*, pp. 1-10. New York: Routledge, 1991.

Garber, Marjorie. *Vested Interests: Cross-Dressing and Cultural Anxiety.* New York: Routledge, 1992.

George, Mark K. "Foucault." In A. K. M. Adam, ed., *Handbook of Postmodern Biblical Interpretation*, pp. 91-98. Saint Louis, Mo.: Chalice Press, 2000.

Giddens, Anthony, et al., eds. *The Polity Reader in Gender Studies.* Oxford: Polity Press, 1994.

Gilman, Sander L. *Creating Beauty to Cure the Soul: Race and Psychology in the Shaping of Aesthetic Surgery.* Durham, N.C.: Duke University Press, 1997.

———. "Introduction: Ethnicity-Ethnicities-Literature-Literatures." *PMLA* 113 (1998): 19-27.

———. *Making the Body Beautiful: A Cultural History of Aesthetic Surgery.* Princeton, N.J.: Princeton University Press, 1999.

Gilmore, David D. *Manhood in the Making: Cultural Concepts of Masculinity.* New Haven, Conn.: Yale University Press, 1990.

Ginsburg, Christian D. *The Song of Songs: Translated from the Original Hebrew, with a Commentary, Historical and Critical.* London: Longman, Brown, Green, Longmans, and Roberts, 1857.

Glancy, Jennifer A. "Unveiling Masculinity: The Construction of Gender in Mark 6:17-29." *Biblical Interpretation* 11 (1994): 34-50.

Gleason, Maud W. *Making Men: Sophists and Self-Presentation in Ancient Rome.* Princeton, N.J.: Princeton University Press, 1995.

———. "The Semiotics of Gender: Physiognomy and Self-Fashioning in the Second Century C.E." In David M. Halperin, John J. Winkler, and Froma I. Zeitlin, eds., *Before Sexuality: Erotic Experience in the Ancient Greek World*, pp. 389-415. Princeton, N.J.: Princeton University Press, 1990.

Goldhill, Simon. *Foucault's Virginity: Ancient Erotic Fiction and the History of Sexuality.* Cambridge: Cambridge University Press, 1995.

Goldin, Judah. *The Song at the Sea, Being a Commentary on a Commentary in Two Parts.* New Haven, Conn.: Yale University Press, 1971.

Goldstein, Laurence, ed. *The Male Body: Features, Destinies, Exposures.* Ann Arbor: University of Michigan Press, 1994.

Gollancz, Hermann. "The Targum to the 'Song of Songs.'" In idem, ed., *The Targum to the "Song of Songs"; The Book of the Apple; The Ten Jewish Martyrs; A Dialogue on Games of Chance*, pp. 1–90. London: Luzac & Co., 1908. Reprinted in Bernard Grossfeld, ed., *The Targum to the Five Megilloth*, pp. 171–252. New York: Hermon Press, 1973.

Gölz, Sabine I. "How Ethnic Am I?" *PMLA* 113 (1998): 46–51.

Goss, Robert E. "The Beloved Disciple: A Queer Bereavement Narrative in a Time of AIDS." In idem and Mona West, eds. *Take Back the Word*, pp. 205–18.

———. *Jesus ACTED UP: A Gay and Lesbian Manifesto.* San Francisco: HarperSanFrancisco, 1993.

Goss, Robert E., and Mona West, eds. *Take Back the Word: A Queer Reading of the Bible.* Cleveland: Pilgrim Press, 2000.

Gottdiener, Mark. "Dead Elvis as Other Jesus." In Vernon Chadwick, ed., *In Search of Elvis: Music, Race, Art, Religion*, pp. 189–200. Boulder, Colo.: Westview Press, 1997.

Goulder, Michael D. *The Song of Fourteen Songs.* Journal for the Study of the Old Testament Supplement Series, 36. Sheffield: JSOT Press, 1986.

Grant, Robert M. "The Description of Paul in the Acts of Paul and Thecla." *Vigiliae Christianae* 36 (1982): 1–4.

Greenberg, David F. *The Construction of Homosexuality.* Chicago: University of Chicago Press, 1988.

Greene, Ellen. "Sappho, Foucault, and Women's Erotics." *Arethusa* 29 (1996): 1–14.

Greer, Rowan A. *Theodore of Mopsuestia: Exegete and Theologian.* London: Faith Press, 1961.

Gregory, Augusta. *Cuchulain of Muirthemne: The Story of the Men of the Red Branch of Ulster Arranged and Put into English by Lady Gregory, with a Preface by W. B. Yeats.* London: John Murray, 1902.

Gregory of Nyssa. *From Glory to Glory: Texts from Gregory of Nyssa's Mystical Writings.* Selected and introduced by Jean Daniélou. Translated and edited by Herbert Musurillo. New York: Scribner, 1961.

Haacker, Klaus. "Exegetische Gesichtspunkte zum Thema Homosexualität." *Theologische Beiträge* 25 (1994): 173–80.

Hadas, Moses. *The Third and Fourth Books of Maccabees.* New York: Harper & Row, 1953.

Haddad, Tony, ed. *Men and Masculinities: A Critical Anthology*. Toronto: Canadian Scholars' Press, 1993.

Haggerty, George E., and Bonnie Zimmerman, eds. *Professions of Desire: Lesbian and Gay Studies in Literature*. New York: Modern Language Association of America, 1995.

Halberstam, Judith. *Female Masculinity*. Durham, N.C.: Duke University Press, 1998.

Hall, Donald, ed. *Muscular Christianity: Embodying the Victorian Age*. Cambridge: Cambridge University Press, 1994.

Hallett, Judith P., and Marilyn B. Skinner, eds. *Roman Sexualities*. Princeton, N.J.: Princeton University Press, 1997.

Hallett, Judith P., and Thomas Van Nortwick, eds. *Compromising Traditions: The Personal Voice in Classical Scholarship*. New York: Routledge, 1997.

Halperin, David M. "Historicizing the Subject of Desire: Sexual Preferences and Erotic Identities in the Pseudo-Lucianic *Erōtes*." In Jan Goldstein, ed., *Foucault and the Writing of History*, pp. 19–34. Oxford: Basil Blackwell, 1994.

———. *One Hundred Years of Homosexuality: And Other Essays on Greek Love*. New Ancient World. New York: Routledge, 1990.

———. *Saint Foucault: Towards a Gay Hagiography*. Oxford: Oxford University Press, 1995.

Halperin, David M., et al. "Lesbian Historiography Before the Name? Commentaries by David M. Halperin, Ann Pellegrini, Ken Stone, Natalie Boymel Kampen, and Deirdre Good, with an introduction by Elizabeth A. Castelli and a response by the author, on *Love Between Women: Early Christian Responses to Female Homoeroticism*, by Bernadette J. Brooten." *GLQ* 4 (1998): 557–630.

Halperin, David M., John J. Winkler, and Froma I. Zeitlin, eds. *Before Sexuality: Erotic Experience in the Ancient Greek World*. Princeton, N.J.: Princeton University Press, 1990.

Hamilton, William. *A Quest for the Post-Historical Jesus*. London: SCM Press, 1993.

Hanson, R. "A Note on Origen's Self-Mutilation." *Vigiliae Christianae* 20 (1966): 81–82.

Hawley, Richard. "The Male Body as Spectacle in Attic Drama." In Lin Foxhall and John Salmon, eds., *Thinking Men: Masculinity and Self-Representation in the Classical Tradition*, pp. 83–99. Leicester–Nottingham Studies in Ancient Society, 7. New York: Routledge, 1998.

Hays, Richard B. *The Faith of Jesus Christ: An Investigation of the Narrative Substructure of Galatians 3:1–4:11*. Society of Biblical Literature Dissertation Series, 56. Chico, Calif.: Scholars Press, 1983.

———. "Pistis and Pauline Christology: What Is At Stake?" In Elizabeth E. Johnson and David M. Hay, eds., *Pauline Theology*, vol. 4: *Looking Back, Pressing On*, pp. 35–60. Symposium Series, 4. Atlanta: Scholars Press, 1997.

Headlam, A. C. *The Life and Teaching of Jesus the Christ.* London: John Murray, 1923.

Herbert, Máire, and Martin McNamara, eds. *Irish Biblical Apocrypha: Selected Texts in Translation.* Edinburgh: T. & T. Clark, 1989.

Heschel, Susannah. "Jesus as Theological Transvestite." In Miriam Peskowitz and Laura Levitt, eds., *Judaism since Gender,* pp. 188–99. New York: Routledge, 1997.

Hirschberg, Harris Hans. "Some Additional Arabic Etymologies in Old Testament Lexicography." *Vetus Testamentum* 11 (1961): 373–85.

Hoffner, Harry A., Jr. "Symbols for Masculinity and Femininity: Their Use in Ancient Near Eastern Sympathetic Magic Rituals." *Journal of Biblical Literature* 85 (1966): 327–32.

Hood, Robert E. *Begrimed and Black: Christian Traditions on Blacks and Blackness.* Minneapolis: Augsburg Fortress, 1994.

Hopkins, Gerard Manley. "Sermon for Sunday Evening Nov. 23 1879 at Bedford Leigh." In *Poems and Prose of Gerard Manley Hopkins,* selected with an introduction and notes by W. H. Gardner, pp. 136–42. Harmondsworth, U.K.: Penguin Books, 1953.

Horst, Pieter W. van der, ed. and trans. *The Sentences of Pseudo-Phocylides.* Studia in Veteris Testamenti pseudepigrapha, 4. Leiden: E. J. Brill, 1978.

Howard-Brook, Wes, and Anthony Gwyther. *Unveiling Empire: Reading Revelation Then and Now.* Bible & Liberation. Maryknoll, N.Y.: Orbis Books, 1999.

Hunt, Lynn. "Foucault's Subject in *The History of Sexuality.*" In Domna Stanton, ed., *Discourses of Sexuality: From Aristotle to AIDS,* pp. 78–93. Ann Arbor: University of Michigan Press, 1992.

Hunzinger, C.-H. "Babylon als Deckname für Rom und die Datierung des I. Petrusbriefes." In H. G. Reventlow, *Gottes Wort und Gottes Land: Hans-Wilhelm Hertzberg zum 70. Geburtstag,* pp. 67–77. Göttingen: Vandenhoeck & Ruprecht, 1965.

Jaggar, Alison M., ed. *Living with Contradictions: Controversies in Feminist Social Ethics.* Boulder, Colo.: Westview Press, 1994.

Jagose, Annamarie. *Queer Theory: An Introduction.* New York: New York University Press, 1996.

Jasper, David, and Stephen Prickett, eds. *The Bible and Literature: A Reader.* Oxford: Blackwell, 1999.

Jeffreys, Sheila. *Anticlimax: A Feminist Perspective on the Sexual Revolution.* London: Women's Press, 1990.

———. "Heterosexuality and the Desire for Gender." In Diane Richardson, ed., *Theorising Heterosexuality: Telling It Straight,* pp. 75–90. London: Taylor & Francis, 1996.

———. *The Lesbian Heresy: A Feminist Perspective on the Lesbian Sexual Revolution.* London: Women's Press, 1994.

Jenkins, Emily. "Exposed!" *Guardian*, Jan. 2, 1999, weekend section, pp. 24–27.

Jerome. *Select Letters of St. Jerome*. Translated by F. A. Wright. Loeb Classical Library. New York: G. P. Putnam's Sons, 1933.

"The Jesus Seminar Spring 1995 Meeting." *The Fourth R* 8 (1995): 10–11.

Jewett, Robert. *Saint Paul at the Movies: The Apostle's Dialogue with American Culture*. Louisville, Ky.: Westminster John Knox Press, 1993.

———. *Saint Paul Returns to the Movies: Triumph over Shame*. Grand Rapids, Mich.: Eerdmans, 1998.

John of the Cross. *The Collected Works of St. John of the Cross*. Translated by Kieran Kavanaugh and Otilio Rodriguez. New York: Doubleday, 1964.

Johns, Catherine. *Sex or Symbol? Erotic Images of Greece and Rome*. Austin: University of Texas Press, 1982.

Johnson, Luke T. *The Real Jesus: The Misguided Quest for the Historical Jesus and the Truth of the Traditional Gospels*. San Francisco: HarperSanFrancisco, 1996.

———. "Rom 3:21–26 and the Faith of Jesus." *Catholic Biblical Quarterly* 44 (1982): 77–90.

Jordan, Mark D. *The Invention of Sodomy in Christian Theology*. Sexuality, History, and Society. Chicago: University of Chicago Press, 1997.

Joüon, Paul, S.J. *Le Cantique des Cantiques: Commentaire philologique et exégétique*. Paris: Beauchesne, 1909.

Kahl, Brigitte. "No Longer Male: Masculinity Struggles behind Galatians 3:28?" *Journal for the Study of the New Testament* 79 (2000): 37–49.

Katz, Jonathan Ned. *The Invention of Heterosexuality*. New York: Penguin Books, 1995.

Keith, Alison. "*Tandem venit amor*: A Roman Woman Speaks of Love." In Judith P. Hallett and Marilyn B. Skinner, eds. *Roman Sexualities*, pp. 295–310. Princeton, N.J.: Princeton University Press, 1997.

Keller, Catherine. *Apocalypse Now and Then: A Feminist Guide to the End of the World*. Boston: Beacon Press, 1996.

Kellum, Barbara. "The Phallus as Signifier: The Forum of Augustus and Rituals of Masculinity." In Natalie Boymel Kampen, ed., *Sexuality in Ancient Art: Near East, Egypt, Greece, and Italy*, pp. 170–83. Cambridge Studies in New Art History and Criticism. Cambridge: Cambridge University Press, 1996.

Keuls, Eva C. *The Reign of the Phallus: Sexual Politics in Ancient Athens*. Berkeley and Los Angeles: University of California Press, 1985.

Kiberd, Declan. *Inventing Ireland*. London: Jonathan Cape, 1995.

Kim, Jean K. "'Uncovering Her Wickedness': An Inter(con)textual Reading of Revelation 17 from a Postcolonial Feminist Perspective." *Journal for the Study of the New Testament* 73 (1999): 61–81.

King, Christopher. "A Love as Fierce as Death: Reclaiming the Song of Songs for

Queer Lovers." In Robert E. Goss and Mona West, eds., *Taking Back the Word: A Queer Reading of the Bible*, pp. 126–42. Cleveland: Pilgrim Press, 2000.

Kimelman, Reuven. "Rabbi Yohanan and Origen on the Song of Songs." *Harvard Theological Review* 73 (1980): 567–95.

Kinsella, Thomas, ed. and trans. *The Táin: Translated from the Irish Epic* Táin Bó Cúailnge *by Thomas Kinsella with Brush Drawings by Louis Le Brocquy*. Mountrath, Ireland: Dolmen Press; Oxford: Oxford University Press, 1970.

Kirwan, James. *Beauty*. Manchester: Manchester University Press, 1999.

Kitzberger, Ingrid Rosa, ed. *The Personal Voice in Biblical Interpretation*. New York: Routledge, 1998.

Konstan, David, and Martha Nussbaum, eds. *Sexuality in Greek and Roman Society. differences* 2.1 (1990).

Kraemer, Ross S. "The Other as Woman: An Aspect of Polemic among Pagans, Jews and Christians in the Greco-Roman World." In L. Silberstein and R. Cohn, eds., *The Other in Jewish Thought and History: Constructions of Jewish Cultural Identity*, pp. 121–44. New York: New York University Press, 1994.

Krahmer, Shawn M. "The Virile Bride of Bernard of Clairvaux." *Church History* 69 (2000): 304–27.

Kramer, Samuel Noah. *The Sacred Marriage Rite: Aspects of Faith, Myth, and Ritual in Ancient Sumer*. Bloomington: Indiana University Press, 1969.

Kreitzer, Larry J. *The New Testament in Fiction and Film: On Reversing the Hermeneutical Flow*. Biblical Seminar, 17. Sheffield: Sheffield Academic Press, 1993.

———. *The Old Testament in Fiction and Film: On Reversing the Hermeneutical Flow*. Biblical Seminar, 24. Sheffield: Sheffield Academic Press, 1994.

———. *Pauline Images in Fiction and Film: On Reversing the Hermeneutical Flow*. Biblical Seminar, 61. Sheffield: Sheffield Academic Press, 1999.

Krinetzki, Leo. *Kommentar zum Hohelied: Bildesprach und Theologische Borschaft*. Beiträge zur evangelischen Theologie, 16. Frankfurt a./M.: Lang, 1981.

Kristeva, Julia. "A Holy Madness: She and He." In idem, *Tales of Love*, pp. 83–100. Translated by Leon S. Roudiez. New York: Columbia University Press, 1987.

Krondorfer, Björn, ed. *Men's Bodies, Men's Gods: Male Identities in a (Post-) Christian Culture*. New York: New York University Press, 1995.

Kwok, Pui-lan. *Discovering the Bible in the Non-Biblical World*. Bible & Liberation. Maryknoll, N.Y.: Orbis Books, 1995.

———. "On Color-Coding Jesus: An Interview with Kwok Pui-lan." In R. S. Sugirtharajah, ed., *The Postcolonial Bible*, pp. 176–88. Bible and Postcolonialism, 1. Sheffield: Sheffield Academic Press, 1998.

LaCocque, André. *Romance, She Wrote: A Hermeneutical Essay on Song of Songs*. Valley Forge, Pa.: Trinity Press International, 1998.

Ladd, Tony, and James A. Mathisen. *Muscular Christianity: Evangelical Protestants and the Development of American Sport*. Grand Rapids, Mich.: Baker Book House, 1999.

Lakoff, Robin Tolmach, and Raquel L. Scherr. *Face Value: The Politics of Beauty*. Boston: Routledge & Kegan Paul, 1984.

Lancaster, Roger N., and Micaela di Leonardo, eds. *The Gender/Sexuality Reader: Culture, History, Political Economy*. New York: Routledge, 1997.

Lambert, Ellen Zetzel. *The Face of Love: Feminism and the Beauty Question*. Boston: Beacon Press, 1995.

Landy, Francis. *Paradoxes of Paradise: Identity and Difference in the Song of Songs*. Bible and Literature. Sheffield: Almond Press, 1983.

Laqueur, Thomas. *Making Sex: Body and Gender from the Greeks to Freud*. Cambridge, Mass.: Harvard University Press, 1990.

Larmour, David H. J., Paul Allen Miller, and Charles Platter, eds. *Rethinking Sexuality: Foucault and Classical Antiquity*. Princeton, N.J.: Princeton University Press, 1998.

———. "Situating *The History of Sexuality*." In idem, eds., *Rethinking Sexuality*, pp. 3–41.

Laughlin, T. C. *The Solecisms of the Apocalypse*. Princeton, N.J.: Princeton University Press, 1902.

Lauretis, Teresa de, ed. *Queer Theory: Lesbian and Gay Sexualities. differences* 3.2 (1991).

Layton, Bentley. *The Gnostic Scriptures: A New Translation with Annotations and Introductions*. Anchor Bible Reference Library. New York: Doubleday, 1987.

Leclercq, Jean. "The Making of a Masterpiece." Translated by Kathleen Waters. In Bernard of Clarivaux, *On the Song of Songs IV*, ed. M. Basil Pennington, pp. ix–xxiv. Cistercian Fathers Series, 40. Kalamazoo, Mich.: Cistercian Publications, 1980.

Lefkowitz, Mary R. "Sex and Civilization." *Partisan Review* 52 (1985): 460–66.

Leiris, Michel. *Manhood: A Journey from Childhood into the Fierce Order of Virility*. Translated by Richard Howard. Chicago: University of Chicago Press, 1992. Originally published as *L'Age d'homme* (Paris: Gallimard, 1946).

Leyerle, Blake. "Landscape as Cartography in Early Christian Pilgrimage Narratives." *Journal of the American Academy of Religion* 64 (1996): 119–43.

Littledale, Richard Frederick. *A Commentary on the Song of Songs from Ancient and Mediaeval Sources*. London: Joseph Masters & Son, 1869.

Loewe, Raphael. "Apologetic Motifs in the Targum to the Song of Songs." In Alexander Altmann, ed., *Biblical Motifs: Origins and Transformations*. Philip W. Lown Institute of Advanced Studies, Brandeis University, Studies and Texts, 3. Cambridge, Mass.: Harvard University Press, 1966.

Lohmeyer, Ernst. *Die Offenbarung des Johannes*. Handbuch zum Neuen Testament, 4/4. Tübingen: J. C. B. Mohr (Paul Siebeck), 1926.

Long, Ronald E. "The Sacrality of Male Beauty and Homosex: A Neglected Factor in the Understanding of Contemporary Gay Reality." In Gary David Comstock and Susan E. Henking, eds., Que(e)rying Religion: A Critical Anthology, pp. 266–81. New York: Continuum, 1997.

Loomba, Ania. Colonialism/Postcolonialism. New Critical Idiom. New York: Routledge, 1998.

Loraux, Nicole. The Experiences of Tiresias: The Feminine and the Greek Man. Princeton, N.J.: Princeton University Press, 1995.

———. "Herakles: The Super-Male and the Feminine." In David M. Halperin, John J. Winkler, and Froma I. Zeitlin, eds., Before Sexuality: Erotic Experience in the Ancient Greek World, pp. 21–52. Princeton, N.J.: Princeton University Press, 1990.

Lüdemann, Gerd. The Resurrection of Jesus: History, Experience, Theology. Translated by John Bowden. Minneapolis: Fortress Press, 1994.

Lüdemann, Gerd, in collaboration with Alf Özen. What Really Happened to Jesus: A Historical Approach to the Resurrection. Translated by John Bowden. Louisville, Ky.: Westminster John Knox Press, 1996.

Lundbom, Jack R. Master Painter: Warner E. Sallman. Macon, Ga.: Mercer University Press, 1999.

Maccoby, Hyam. "Sex According to the Song of Songs." Commentary, June 1979, pp. 53–59.

Mack, Burton. The Lost Gospel: The Book of Q and Christian Origins. San Francisco: HarperSanFrancisco, 1993.

———. A Myth of Innocence: Mark and Christian Origins. Philadelphia: Fortress Press, 1988.

MacKenzie, Robert K. The Author of the Apocalypse: A Review of the Prevailing Hypothesis of Jewish-Christian Authorship. Mellen Biblical Press, 51. Lewiston, N.Y.: Edwin Mellen Press, 1997.

MacKinnon, Catherine. "Does Sexuality Have a History?" In Domna Stanton, ed., Discourses of Sexuality: From Aristotle to AIDS, pp. 117–36. Ann Arbor: University of Michigan Press, 1992.

———. Towards a Feminist Theory of the State. Cambridge, Mass.: Harvard University Press, 1989.

Malcolm X, with Alex Haley. The Autobiography of Malcolm X. New York: Grove Press, 1965.

Malherbe, Abraham J. "A Physical Description of Paul." Harvard Theological Review 79 (1986): 170–75.

Malick, David E. "The Condemnation of Homosexuality in 1 Corinthians 6:9." Bibliotheca Sacra 150 (1993): 479–92.

Malik, Kenan. The Meaning of Race: Race, History and Culture in Western Society. New York: New York University Press, 1996.

Malina, Bruce J. *The New Testament World: Insights from Cultural Anthropology.* 3rd. ed. Atlanta: John Knox Press, 2001.

———. *The Social World of Jesus and the Gospels.* New York: Routledge, 1996.

Malina, Bruce J., and Jerome H. Neyrey. "Honor and Shame in Luke–Acts: Pivotal Values of the Mediterranean World." In Jerome H. Neyrey, ed., *The Social World of Luke-Acts: Models for Interpretation,* pp. 25–66. Peabody, Mass.: Hendrickson, 1991.

———. *Portraits of Paul: An Archaeology of Ancient Personality.* Louisville, Ky.: Westminster John Knox Press, 1996.

Marsh, Clive. "Quests of the Historical Jesus in New Historicist Perspective." *Biblical Interpretation* 4 (1997): 403–37.

Marsh, Clive, and Gaye Ortiz, eds. *Explorations in Theology and Film: An Introduction.* Oxford: Blackwell, 1997.

Martin, Dale B. "*Arsenokoitēs* and *Malakos*: Meaning and Consequences." In Robert L. Brawley, ed., *Biblical Ethics and Homosexuality: Listening to Scripture,* pp. 117–36. Louisville, Ky.: Westminster John Knox Press, 1996.

———. "Contradictions of Masculinity: Ascetic Inseminators and Menstruating Men in Greco-Roman Culture." In Valerie Fanucci and Kevin Brownlee, eds., *Generation and Degeneration: Literature and Tropes of Reproduction.* Durham, N.C.: Duke University Press, forthcoming.

———. *The Corinthian Body.* New Haven, Conn.: Yale University Press, 1995.

———. "Heterosexism and the Interpretation of Romans 1:18–32." *Biblical Interpretation* 3 (1995): 332–55.

Martin, Ralph. *Carmen Christi: Philippians 2:5–11 in Recent Interpretation and in the Setting of Early Christian Worship.* Society of New Testament Studies Monograph Series, 4. Cambridge: Cambridge University Press, 1967. Reprint. Grand Rapids, Mich.: Eerdmans, 1983.

Martínez, Florentino García, ed. and trans. *The Dead Sea Scrolls Translated: The Qumran Texts in English.* English translation by Wilfred G. E. Watson. Leiden: E. J. Brill, 1992.

Martyn, J. Louis. *Galatians: A New Translation with Introduction and Commentary.* Anchor Bible, 33A. New York: Doubleday, 1997.

Matter, E. Ann. *The Voice of My Beloved: The Song of Songs in Western Medieval Christianity.* Middle Ages Series. Philadelphia: University of Pennsylvania Press, 1990.

Mattila, S. L. "Wisdom, Sense Perception, Nature, and Philo's Gender Gradient." *Harvard Theological Review* 89 (1996): 103–29.

Mayerson, Philip. "Anti-Black Sentiment in the *Vitae Patrum.*" *Harvard Theological Review* 71 (1978): 304–11.

McClintock, Anne. *Imperial Leather: Race, Gender and Sexuality in the Colonial Contest.* New York: Routledge, 1995.

McCourt, Frank. *Angela's Ashes: A Memoir of a Childhood*. London: Flamingo, 1997.

McDannell, Colleen. "Marketing Jesus: Warner Press and the Art of Warner Sallman." In David Morgan, ed., *Icons of American Protestantism: The Art of Warner Sallman*, pp. 95–122. New Haven, Conn.: Yale University Press, 1996.

McDonald, P. M. "Lion as Slain Lamb: On Reading Revelation Recursively." *Horizons* 23 (1996): 29–47.

McNay, Lois. *Foucault and Feminism*. Boston: Northeastern University Press, 1992.

Mead, Rebecca. "Slim for Him: God Is Watching What You're Eating." *New Yorker*, Jan. 15, 2001, pp. 48–56.

Mechtilde of Magdeburg. *The Revelations of Mechtilde of Magdeburg, or The Flowing Light of the Godhead*. Edited and translated by Lucy Menzies. London: Longman, Green, 1953.

Meier, John P. *A Marginal Jew: Rethinking the Historical Jesus*. Vol. 1: *The Roots of the Problem and the Person*. Vol. 2: *Mentor, Message, and Miracles*. Anchor Bible Reference Library. New York: Doubleday, 1991–94.

———. "Reflections on Jesus-of-History Research Today." In James H. Charlesworth, ed., *Jesus' Jewishness: Exploring the Place of Jesus in Early Judaism*, pp. 84–107. New York: Crossroad, 1991.

Merck, Mandy, Naomi Segal, and Elizabeth Wright, eds. *Coming Out of Feminism?* Oxford: Blackwell, 1998.

Merton, Thomas. *Elected Silence*. London: Hollis & Carter, 1949. Originally published as *The Seven Storey Mountain* (New York: Harcourt, Brace, 1948).

Michel, Otto. *Der Brief an die Römer*. Kritisch-Exegetischer Kommentar über das Neue Testament, 4. 5th ed. Göttingen: Vandenhoeck & Ruprecht, 1978.

Michelet, Jules. *Mother Death: The Journals of Jules Michelet, 1815–1850*. Edited and translated by Edward K. Kaplan. Amherst: University of Massachusetts Press, 1984.

Miles, Margaret. *Plotinus on Body and Beauty: Society, Philosophy and Religion in Third-Century Rome*. Oxford: Blackwell, 1999.

Milgrom, Jacob. *Leviticus 1–16: A New Translation with Introduction and Commentary*. Anchor Bible, 3. New York: Doubleday, 1991.

Miller, James E. "Pederasty and Romans 1:27: A Response to Mark Smith." *Journal of the American Academy of Religion* 65 (1997): 861–66.

———. "The Practices of Romans 1:26: Homosexual or Heterosexual?" *Novum Testamentum* 37 (1995): 1–11.

Miller, Nancy K. *Getting Personal: Feminist Occasions and Other Autobiographical Acts*. New York: Routledge, 1991.

Miller, Patricia Cox. "'Pleasure of the Text, Text of Pleasure': Eros and Language in Origen's Commentary on the Song of Songs." *Journal of the American Academy of Religion* 54 (1986): 241–53.

Miller, Robert J. *The Jesus Seminar and Its Critics.* Santa Rosa, Calif.: Polebridge Press, 1999.

*Miss Marianne Woods and Miss Jane Pirie against Dame Helen Cumming Gordon.* Trial transcripts. New York: Arno Press, 1975.

Montefiore, C. G., and H. Loewe, eds and trans. *A Rabbinic Anthology.* Cleveland: World Publishing Co.; Philadelphia: Jewish Publication Society of America, 1960.

Moo, Douglas J. *The Epistle to the Romans.* New International Commentary on the New Testament. Grand Rapids, Mich.: Eerdmans, 1996.

Moore, Stephen D. *God's Gym: Divine Male Bodies of the Bible.* New York: Routledge, 1996.

———. *Mark and Luke in Poststructuralist Perspectives: Jesus Begins to Write.* New Haven, Conn.: Yale University Press, 1992.

———. *Poststructuralism and the New Testament: Derrida and Foucault at the Foot of the Cross.* Minneapolis: Fortress Press, 1994.

———. "True Confessions and Weird Obsessions: Autobiographical Interventions in Literary and Biblical Studies." *Semeia* 72 (1995): 19–50.

Moore, Stephen D., ed. *In Search of the Present: The Bible through Cultural Studies.* Semeia 82. Atlanta: Scholars Press, 1998.

Moore, Stephen D., and Janice Capel Anderson. "Taking It Like a Man: Masculinity in 4 Maccabees." *Journal of Biblical Literature* 117 (1998): 249–73.

Morgan, David, ed. *Icons of American Protestantism: The Art of Warner Sallman.* New Haven, Conn.: Yale University Press, 1996.

———. *Visual Piety: A History and Theory of Popular Religious Images.* Berkeley and Los Angeles: University of California Press, 1998.

———. "Warner Sallman and the Visual Culture of American Protestantism." In idem, ed., *Icons of American Protestantism*, pp. 25–60.

Morris, Rosalind C. "All Made Up: Performance Theory and the New Anthropology of Sex and Gender." *Annual Review of Anthropology* 24 (1995): 567–92.

Morrison, Toni. *The Bluest Eye.* New York: Knopf, 1993.

Morton, Donald, ed. *The Material Queer: A LesBiGay Cultural Studies Reader.* Queer Critique. Boulder, Colo.: Westview Press, 1996.

Mosala, Itumeleng J. *Biblical Hermeneutics and Black Theology in South Africa.* Grand Rapids, Mich.: Eerdmans, 1989.

Murnaghan, Sheila. "How a Woman Can Be More Like a Man: The Dialogue Between Ischomachus and His Wife in Xenophon's *Oeconomicus*." *Helios* 15 (1988): 9–22.

Murphy, Roland E. *The Song of Songs: A Commentary on the Book of Canticles or the Song of Songs.* Edited by S. Dean McBride, Jr. Hermeneia. Minneapolis: Fortress Press, 1990.

Mussies, G. *The Morphology of Koine Greek as Used in the Apocalypse of John:*

*A Study in Bilingualism. Novum Testamentum* Supplements, 27. Leiden: E. J. Brill, 1971.

Neusner, Jacob. *The Midrash Compilations of the Sixth and Seventh Centuries: An Introduction to the Rhetorical, Logical, and Topical Program.* Vol. 4: *Song of Songs Rabbah.* Brown Judaic Studies. Atlanta: Scholars Press, 1990.

———. *Introduction to Rabbinic Literature.* Anchor Bible Reference Library. New York: Doubleday, 1994.

Newman, Carey C. "(W)righting the History of Jesus: A Review Essay on *Jesus and the Victory of God.*" *Critical Review of Books in Religion* (1997): 121–44.

Neyrey, Jerome H. "Despising the Shame of the Cross: Honor and Shame in the Johannine Passion Narrative." *Semeia* 68 (1994): 113–37.

———. *Honor and Shame in the Gospel of Matthew.* Louisville, Ky.: Westminster John Knox Press, 1998.

Novak, David. *The Election of Israel: The Idea of the Chosen People.* Cambridge: Cambridge University Press, 1995.

O'Grady, Standish. *History of Ireland.* Vol. 1: *The Heroic Period.* Vol. 2: *Cuculain and His Contemporaries.* 1878–80. Reprint. New York: Lemma, 1970.

Origen. *The Song of Songs: Commentary and Homilies.* Translated by R. P. Lawson. Ancient Christian Writers: The Works of the Fathers in Translation, 26. Westminster, Md.: Newman Press; London: Longmans, Green, 1957.

Pack, Roger. "Artemidoros and His Waking World." *Transactions and Proceedings of the American Philological Association* 86 (1955): 280–90.

Painter, John. *The Quest for the Messiah: The History, Literature and Theology of the Johannine Community.* Edinburgh: T. & T. Clark, 1991.

Pardes, Ilana. *Countertraditions in the Bible: A Feminist Approach.* Cambridge, Mass.: Harvard University Press, 1992.

Parente, Paschal. "The Canticle of Canticles in Mystical Theology." *Catholic Biblical Quarterly* 6 (1944): 142–58.

Parsons, Mikeal C. "Hand in Hand: Autobiographical Reflections on Luke 15." *Semeia* 72 (1995): 125–52.

Paul, G. M. "*Urbs Capta*: Sketch of an Ancient Literary Motif." *Phoenix* (1982): 144–55.

Paz, Octavio. *Labyrinth of Solitude.* Translated by Lysander Kemp. New York: Grove Press, 1961.

Pearse, Padraic H. "The Coming Revolution." In Desmond Ryan, ed., *Collected Works of Padraic H. Pearse*, unnumbered vol.: *Political Writings and Speeches*, pp. 88–99. Dublin: Phoenix, 1924.

———. "O'Donovan Rossa Graveside Panegyric." In *Political Writings and Speeches*, pp. 133–37.

Pelikan, Jaroslav. *The Illustrated Jesus through the Centuries.* New Haven, Conn.: Yale University Press, 1997.

———. *Jesus through the Centuries: His Place in the History of Culture*. New York: Harper & Row, 1985.

Petersen, William L. "Can ARSENOKOITAI Be Translated by 'Homosexuals'? (1 Cor. 6:9; 1 Tim. 1:10)." *Vigiliae Christianae* 40 (1986): 187–91.

Pilch, John J. "Death with Honor: The Mediterranean Style Death of Jesus in Mark." *Biblical Theology Bulletin* 25 (1995): 65–70.

Pippin, Tina. *Apocalyptic Bodies: The Biblical End of the World in Text and Image*. Biblical Limits. New York: Routledge, 1999.

———. *Death and Desire: The Rhetoric of Gender in the Apocalypse of John*. Literary Currents in Biblical Interpretation; Louisville, Ky.: Westminster John Knox Press, 1992.

———. "The Revelation to John." In Elisabeth Schüssler Fiorenza, Ann Brock, and Shelly Matthews, eds. *Searching the Scriptures*, vol. 2: *A Feminist Commentary*, pp. 109–30. New York: Crossroad, 1994.

Plevnik, Joseph. "Honor/Shame." In John J. Pilch and Bruce J. Malina, eds., *Biblical Social Values and Their Meanings: A Handbook*, pp. 95–103. Peabody, Mass.: Hendrickson, 1993.

Polaski, Sandra Hack. *Paul and the Discourse of Power*. Biblical Seminar, 62; Gender, Culture, Theory, 8. Sheffield: Sheffield Academic Press, 1999.

Pope, Marvin H. *Song of Songs: A New Translation with Introduction and Commentary*. Anchor Bible, 7C. Garden City, N.Y.: Doubleday, 1977.

Porter, Stanley E. *The Criteria for Authenticity in Historical-Jesus Research: Previous Discussion and New Proposals*. Journal for the Study of the New Testament Supplement Series, 191. Sheffield: Sheffield Academic Press, 2000.

———. "The Language of the Apocalypse in Recent Discussion." *New Testament Studies* 35 (1989): 582–603.

Porter, Stanley E., Michael A. Hayes, and David Tombs, eds. *Images of Christ: Ancient and Modern*. Roehampton Institute London Papers, 2. Sheffield: Sheffield Academic Press, 1999.

Powell, Mark Allan. *Jesus as a Figure in History: How Modern Historians View the Man from Galilee*. Louisville, Ky.: Westminster John Knox Press, 1998.

"Queer Icons: Jesus Christ." *Pink Paper*, Apr. 10, 1998, p. 39.

Rajak, Tessa. "Dying for the Law: The Martyr's Portrait in Jewish-Greek Literature." In M. J. Edwards and S. Swain, eds., *Portraits: Biographical Representation in the Greek and Latin Literature of the Roman Period*, pp. 39–68. Oxford: Clarendon Press, 1997.

Rambuss, Richard. *Closet Devotions*. Durham, N.C.: Duke University Press, 1998.

———. "Homodevotion." In Sue-Ellen Case, Philip Brett, and Susan Leigh Foster, eds., *Cruising the Performative: Interventions into the Representation of Ethnicity, Nationality, and Sexuality*, pp. 71–89. Bloomington: Indiana University Press, 1995.

Reimarus, Hermann Samuel. *Reimarus: Fragments.* Edited by Charles H. Talbert. Translated by Ralph S. Fraser. Philadelphia: Fortress Press, 1970. German originals 1774–1852.

Renan, Ernest. *The Life of Jesus.* Great Minds Series. Buffalo: Prometheus Books, 1991. Originally published under the title *Vie de Jésus* (Paris: Nelson; Calmann-Lévy, 1863).

Rice, Anne. *Memnoch the Devil: The Vampire Chronicles.* New York: Knopf, 1995.

Richard, Pablo. *Apocalypse: A People's Commentary on the Book of Revelation.* Bible & Liberation. Maryknoll, N.Y.: Orbis Books, 1995.

Richardson, Diane. "Heterosexuality and Social Theory." In idem, ed., *Theorising Heterosexuality: Telling It Straight,* pp. 1–20. London: Taylor & Francis, 1996.

Riches, John. "Cultural Bias in Biblical Scholarship." In Mark Brett, ed., *The Bible and Ethnicity,* pp. 431–48. Biblical Interpretation Series, 19. Leiden: E. J. Brill, 1996.

Richlin, Amy. "Foucault's *History of Sexuality*: A Useful Theory for Women?" In David H. J. Larmour, Paul Allen Miller, and Charles Platter, eds., *Rethinking Sexuality: Foucault and Classical Antiquity,* pp. 138–70. Princeton, N.J.: Princeton University Press, 1998.

———. *The Garden of Priapus: Sexuality and Aggression in Roman Humor.* 2d ed. New York: Routledge, 1992.

———. "Gender and Rhetoric: Producing Manhood in the Schools." In William J. Dominik, ed., *Roman Eloquence: Rhetoric in Society and Literature,* pp. 90–110. New York: Routledge, 1997.

———. "Not Before Homosexuality: The Materiality of the *Cinaedus* and the Roman Law against Love Between Men." *Journal of the History of Sexuality* 3 (1993): 523–73.

———. "Pliny's Brassiere." In Judith P. Hallett and Marilyn B. Skinner, eds., *Roman Sexualities,* pp. 197–220. Princeton, N.J.: Princeton University Press, 1997.

———. "Zeus and Metis: Foucault, Feminism, Classics." *Helios* 18 (1991): 160–80.

Riedlinger, Helmut. *Die Makellosigkeit der Kirche in den Lateinischen Hoheliedkommentaren des Mittelalters.* Beiträge zur Geschichte der Philosophie und Theologie des Mittelalters 38/3. Münster: Aschendorff, 1958.

Rissi, Mathias. *Die Hure Babylon und die Verführung der Heiligen: Eine Studie zur Apokalypse des Johannes.* Beiträge zur Wissenschaft vom Alten und Neuen Testament, 7, Folge, 16. Stuttgart: Kohlhammer, 1995.

Robert, Abbé André, Father Raymond Tournay, and Abbé André Feuillet, trans. and ed. *Le Cantique des cantiques.* Études bibliques. Paris: J. Gabalda, 1963.

Roberts, Alexander, and James Donaldson, eds. *The Ante-Nicene Fathers: Translations of the Writings of the Fathers down to A.D. 325.* 10 vols. Buffalo, N.Y.: Christian Literature Publishing Co., 1885–96.

Robinson, James M., ed. *The Nag Hammadi Library in English.* 3d ed. San Francisco: Harper & Row, 1988.

Rodman, Gilbert B. *Elvis after Elvis: The Posthumous Career of a Living Legend.* New York: Routledge, 1996.

Rogers, Eugene F. *Sexuality and the Christian Body: Their Way into the Triune God.* Challenges in Contemporary Theology. Oxford: Blackwell, 1999.

Rooks, Noliwe M. *Hair Raising: Beauty, Culture, and African American Women.* New Brunswick, N.J.: Rutgers University Press, 1996.

Rosenstiehl, Jean-Marc. "Le Portrait de l'Antichrist." In Marc Philonenko et al., eds., *Pseudépigraphes de l'Ancien Testament et manuscrits de la Mer morte,* pp. 45–60. Cahiers de la Revue d'histoire et de philosophie religieuses, 41. Paris: Presses universitaires de France, 1967.

Roughead, William. *Bad Companions.* New York: Duffield & Green, 1931.

Rowland, Christopher. "The Vision of the Risen Christ in Rev. i.13 ff.: The Debt of an Early Christology to an Aspect of Jewish Angelology." *Journal of Theological Studies,* n.s., 31 (1980): 1–11.

Rowley, H. H. "The Interpretation of the Song of Songs." In idem, *The Servant of the Lord and Other Essays,* pp. 189–234. London: Lutterworth Press, 1952.

Runions, Erin. "Zion is Burning: 'Gender Fuck' in Micah." *Semeia* 82 (1998): 225–46.

Rupert of Deutz. *In Cantica Canticorum de incarnatione domini, commentariorum, libri VII à multis seculis, in hunc usq; diem maximè desyderati, multoq; labore ac sumptu iam tandem excusi.* Cologne: Frans Birckman, 1526. In J.-P. Migne, ed., *Patrologiae Cursus, series Latina* (Turnhout, Belgium, 1956–) [cited in notes as *PL*], 168.

Russel, Cornelius. "Byzantine and Romanesque Art and Architecture." In Gilbert Cope, ed., *Christianity and the Visual Arts,* pp. 24–33. London: Faith Press, 1964.

Salgado, J.-M. "Les Considérations mariales de Rupert de Deutz dans ses *Commentaria in Cantica Canticorum.*" *Divinitas* 32-33 (1988): 692–709.

Sánchez, Marta E. "*La Malinche* at the Intersection: Race and Gender in *Down These Mean Streets.*" *PMLA* 113 (1998): 117–28.

Sanday, William, and Arthur C. Headlam. *A Critical and Exegetical Commentary on the Epistle to the Romans.* International Critical Commentary. Edinburgh: T. & T. Clark, 1895.

Sanders, E. P. *The Historical Figure of Jesus.* London: Allen Lane / Penguin Press, 1993; New York: Penguin Books, 1995.

———. *Jesus and Judaism.* Philadelphia: Fortress Press, 1985.

———. *Judaism: Practice and Belief 63* B.C.E.*–66* C.E. Philadelphia: Trinity Press International, 1992.

———. *Paul and Palestinian Judaism.* Philadelphia: Fortress Press, 1977.

———. *Paul, the Law, and the Jewish People.* Minneapolis: Fortress Press, 1983.

Sandys, George. *A Relation of a Journey Begun An. Dom. 1610: Fovre bookes. Containing a description of the Turkish Empire, of Aegypt, of the Holy Land, of the remote parts of Italy, and ilands adioyning.* 1615. 3d ed. London: Ro. Allot, 1627.

Santoro L'Hoir, Francesca. *The Rhetoric of Gender Terms: "Man," "Woman," and the Portrayal of Character in Latin Prose*. Mnemosyne, bibliotheca classica Batava, supplement 120. New York: E. J. Brill, 1992.

Sappho. *Sappho: A New Translation*. Translated by Mary Barnard. Foreword by Dudley Fitts. Berkeley and Los Angeles: University of California Press, 1958; reprinted 1986.

Satlow, Michael L. *Tasting the Dish: Rabbinic Rhetorics of Sexuality*. Brown Judaic Studies, 303. Atlanta: Scholars Press, 1995.

———. "'They Abused Him Like a Woman': Homoeroticism, Gender Blurring, and the Rabbis in Late Antiquity." *Journal of the History of Sexuality* 5 (1994): 1–25.

Scarry, Elaine. *On Beauty and Being Just*. Princeton, N.J.: Princeton University Press, 1999.

Schaberg, Jane. "A Feminist Experience of Historical Jesus Scholarship." In William E. Arnal and Michel Desjardins, eds., *Whose Historical Jesus?* pp. 146–80. Studies in Christianity and Judaism, 7. Waterloo, Ontario: Wilfred Laurier University Press, 1997.

———. "Luke." In Carol A. Newsom and Sharon H. Ringe, eds., *The Women's Bible Commentary*, pp. 275–92. Louisville, Ky.: Westminster John Knox Press, 1992. Expanded edition 1998.

Schehr, Lawrence R. *Parts of an Andrology: On Representations of Men's Bodies*. Stanford, Calif.: Stanford University Press, 1997.

Schneemelcher, Wilhelm, ed. *New Testament Apocrypha*. Vol. 1: *Gospels and Related Writings*. Vol. 2: *Writings Related to the Apostles; Apocalypses and Related Subjects*. 2d ed. English translation edited by R. McL. Wilson. Louisville, Ky.: Westminster John Knox Press, 1991–92.

Schneider, Laurel C. "Queer Theory." In A. K. M. Adam, ed., *Handbook of Postmodern Biblical Interpretation*, pp. 206–12. Saint Louis, Mo.: Chalice Press, 2000.

Scholem, Gershom. *Jewish Gnosticism, Merkabah Mysticism, and Talmudic Tradition*. New York: Jewish Theological Seminary of America, 1965.

Schor, Naomi A. "Feminist and Gender Studies." In Joseph Gibaldi, ed., *Introduction to Scholarship in Modern Languages and Literatures*, pp. 267–87. 2d ed. New York: Modern Language Association of America, 1992.

Schreiner, Thomas R. *Romans*. Baker Exegetical Commentary on the New Testament, 6. Grand Rapids, Mich.: Baker Book House, 1998.

Schweitzer, Albert. *The Quest of the Historical Jesus: A Critical Study of Its Progress from Reimarus to Wrede*. Translated by W. Montgomery. London: A. & C. Black, 1910. Originally published under the title *Von Reimarus zu Wrede: Eine Geschichte der Leben-Jesu-Forschung* (Tübingen: J. C. B. Mohr [Paul Siebeck], 1906).

Scott, Bernard Brandon. *Hollywood Dreams and Biblical Stories*. Minneapolis: Fortress Press, 1994.

Scott, R. B. Y. *The Original Language of the Apocalypse.* Toronto: University of Toronto Press, 1928.

Scroggs, Robin. *The New Testament and Homosexuality: Contextual Background for Contemporary Debate.* Philadelphia: Fortress Press, 1983.

Sedgwick, Eve Kosofsky. *Between Men: English Literature and Male Homosocial Desire.* 2d ed. New York: Columbia University Press, 1992.

———. *Epistemology of the Closet.* Berkeley and Los Angeles: University of California Press, 1990.

———. "Gender Criticism." In Stephen Greenblatt and Giles Gunn, eds., *Redrawing the Boundaries: The Transformation of English and American Literary Studies,* pp. 271–302. New York: Modern Language Association of America, 1992.

———. "Gosh, Boy George, You Must Be Awfully Secure in Your Masculinity!" In Maurice Berger, Brian Wallis, and Simon Watson, eds., *Constructing Masculinity,* pp. 11–20. New York: Routledge, 1995.

———. *Tendencies.* Durham, N.C.: Duke University Press, 1993.

———, ed. *Novel Gazing: Queer Readings in Fiction.* Series Q. Durham, N.C.: Duke University Press, 1997.

Segovia, Fernando F. *Decolonizing Biblical Studies: A View from the Margins.* Maryknoll, N.Y.: Orbis Books, 2000.

———. *Interpreting beyond Borders.* Bible and Postcolonialism, 3. Sheffield: Sheffield Academic Press, 2000.

———, ed. *"What Is John?"* Vol. 2: *Literary and Social Readings of the Fourth Gospel,* Biblical Literature Symposium Series, 7. Atlanta: Scholars Press, 1998.

Segovia, Fernando F., and Mary Ann Tolbert, eds. *Reading from This Place.* Vol. 1: *Social Location and Biblical Interpretation in the United States.* Vol. 2: *Social Location and Biblical Interpretation in Global Perspective.* Minneapolis: Fortress Press, 1995.

Selvidge, Marla J. "Reflections on Violence and Pornography: Misogyny in the Apocalypse and Ancient Hebrew Prophecy." In Athalya Brenner, ed., *A Feminist Companion to the Hebrew Bible in the New Testament,* pp. 274–85. Feminist Companion to the Bible, 10. Sheffield: Sheffield Academic Press, 1996.

Setel, T. Drorah. "Prophets and Pornography: Female Sexual Imagery in Hosea." In Letty M. Russell, ed., *Feminist Interpretation of the Bible,* pp. 86–95. Philadelphia: Westminster Press, 1985.

Shaw, Brent D. "Body/Power/Identity: Passions of the Martyrs." *Journal of Early Christian Studies* 4 (1996): 269–312.

Siewert, Frances E., ed. *Amplified New Testament.* Grand Rapids, Mich.: Zondervan, 1958.

Silverman, Kaja. *Male Subjectivity at the Margins.* New York: Routledge, 1992.

Simon Maurice, trans. *Esther and Song of Songs.* Vol. 9 of E. H. Freedman and Maurice Simon, eds., *Midrash Rabbah.* London: Soncino Press, 1939.

Simpson, Mark. *Male Impersonators: Men Performing Masculinity*. New York: Routledge, 1994.

Skinner, Marilyn B. "*Ego Mulier*: The Construction of Male Sexuality in Catullus." *Helios* 20 (1993): 107–30. Reprinted in Judith P. Hallett and Marilyn B. Skinner, eds., *Roman Sexualities* (Princeton, N.J.: Princeton University Press, 1997), pp. 129–50.

———. "*Quod multo fit aliter in Graecia*." In Judith P. Hallett and Marilyn B. Skinner, eds., *Roman Sexualities*, pp. 1–25.

Smart, Carol. "Collusion, Collaboration and Confession: On Moving beyond the Heterosexuality Debate." In Diane Richardson, ed., *Theorising Heterosexuality: Telling It Straight*, pp. 161–77. London: Taylor & Francis, 1996.

Smith, Bruce R. "Premodern Sexualities." *PMLA* 115 (2000): 318–29.

Smith, Moody D. "What Have I Learned about the Gospel of John?" In Fernando F. Segovia, ed., *"What Is John?" Readers and Readings of the Fourth Gospel*, pp. 217–35. Society of Biblical Literature Symposium Series, 3. Atlanta: Scholars Press, 1996.

Smith-Christopher, Daniel, ed. *Text and Experience: Towards a Cultural Exegesis of the Bible*. Biblical Seminar, 35. Sheffield: Sheffield Academic Press, 1995.

Snaith, John G. *The Song of Songs*. New Century Bible Commentary. Grand Rapids, Mich.: William B. Eerdmans, 1993.

Snowden, Frank M., Jr. *Before Color Prejudice: The Ancient View of Blacks*. Cambridge, Mass.: Harvard University Press, 1983.

———. *Blacks in Antiquity: Ethiopians in the Greco-Roman Experience*. Cambridge, Mass.: Belknap Press of Harvard University Press, 1970.

Sollors, Werner. *The Invention of Ethnicity*. Oxford: Oxford University Press, 1989.

Solomos, John, and Les Back, eds. *Theories of Race and Racism: A Reader*. New York: Routledge, 1999.

Spargo, Tamsin. *Foucault and Queer Theory*. New York: Totem Books, 1999.

Sparks, Kenton L. *Ethnicity and Identity in Ancient Israel: Prolegomena to the Study of Ethnic Sentiments and Their Expression in the Hebrew Bible*. Winona Lake, Ind.: Eisenbrauns, 1998.

*Das St. Trudperter Hohelied: Eine Lehre der liebenden Gotteserkenntnis*. Edited by Friedrich Ohly and Nicola Kleine. Bibliothek des Mittelalters, 2. Frankfurt a./M.: Deutscher Klassiker Verlag, 1998.

Stadelmann, Luis. *Love and Politics: A New Commentary on the Song of Songs*. Mahwah, N.J.: Paulist Press, 1992.

Staley, Jeffrey L. "Narrative Structure (Self-Stricture) in Luke 4:14–9:62: The United States of Luke's Story World." *Semeia* 72 (1995): 173–213.

———. *Reading with a Passion: Rhetoric, Autobiography, and the American West in the Gospel of John*. New York: Continuum, 1995.

Stecopoulos, Harry, and Michael Uebel, eds. *Race and the Subject of Masculinities*. Durham, N.C.: Duke University Press, 1997.

Stegemann, Wolfgang. "Paul and the Sexual Mentality of His World." *Biblical Theology Bulletin* 23 (1993): 162–66.

Stehle, Eva, and Amy Day. "Women Looking at Women: Women's Ritual and Temple Sculpture." In Natalie Boymel Kampen, ed., *Sexuality in Ancient Art: Near East, Egypt, Greece, and Italy*, pp. 101–16. Cambridge Studies in New Art History and Criticism. Cambridge: Cambridge University Press, 1996.

Stein, Edward, ed. *Forms of Desire: Sexual Orientation and the Social Constructionist Controversy.* New York: Routledge, 1992.

Stocking, Charles Francis, and William Wesley Totheroh. *The Businessman of Syria.* Chicago: Maestro Company, 1923.

Stone, Ken. "Biblical Interpretation as a Technology of the Self: Gay Men and the Ethics of Reading." *Semeia* 77 (1997): 139–55.

———. "Sexuality." In A. K. M. Adam, ed., *Handbook of Postmodern Biblical Interpretation*, pp. 233–38. Saint Louis, Mo.: Chalice Press, 2000.

Storey, John. "Cultural Studies: An Introduction." In idem, ed., *What Is Cultural Studies? A Reader*, pp. 1–13. London: Arnold, 1996.

———. *An Introductory Guide to Cultural Theory and Popular Culture.* Athens: University of Georgia Press, 1993. 2d ed. Englewood Cliffs, N.J.: Prentice-Hall, 1998.

———, ed. *Cultural Theory and Popular Culture: A Reader.* New York: Harvester Wheatsheaf, 1994. 2d ed. Englewood Cliffs, N.J.: Prentice-Hall, 1998.

Stowers, Stanley K. *Letter Writing in Greco-Roman Antiquity.* Philadelphia: Westminster Press, 1986.

———. *A Rereading of Romans: Justice, Jews, and Gentiles.* New Haven, Conn.: Yale University Press, 1994.

Strauss, David Friedrich. *The Life of Jesus, Critically Examined.* Edited by Peter C. Hodgson. Translated by George Eliot (Marian Evans). 1846. Philadelphia: Fortress Press, 1973. Originally published in 2 vols. under the title *Das Leben Jesu* (Tübingen: C. F. Osiander, 1835–36).

Strinati, Dominic. *An Introduction to Theories of Popular Culture.* New York: Routledge, 1995.

Sugirtharajah, R. S. *Asian Biblical Hermeneutics and Postcolonialism: Contesting the Interpretations.* Maryknoll, N.Y.: Orbis Books, 1998.

———. *The Bible in the Third World: Precolonial, Colonial and Postcolonial Encounters.* Cambridge: Cambridge University Press, forthcoming.

———. "Imperial Critical Commentaries: Christian Discourse and Commentarial Writings in Colonial India." *Journal for the Study of the New Testament* 73 (1999): 83–112.

———. *Vernacular Hermeneutics.* Bible and Postcolonialism, 2. Sheffield: Sheffield Academic Press, 1999.

———, ed. *Voices from the Margin: Interpreting the Bible in the Third World.* Maryknoll, N.Y.: Orbis Books, 1991.

Sweet, J. P. M. *Revelation.* Westminster Pelican Commentaries. Philadelphia: Westminster Press, 1979.

Tatum, W. Barnes. *Jesus at the Movies: A Guide to the First Hundred Years.* Santa Rosa, Calif.: Polebridge Press, 1997.

Taylor, Peter. *Provos: The IRA and Sinn Fein.* London: Bloomsbury, 1997.

Teresa of Avila. *The Complete Works of Saint Teresa of Jesus.* 3 vols. Edited and translated by E. Allison Peers. London: Sheed & Ward, 1946.

Theissen, Gerd, and Annette Merz. *The Historical Jesus: A Comprehensive Guide.* Translated by John Bowden. London: SCM Press; Minneapolis: Fortress Press, 1998.

Thiong'o, Ngugi wa. *Decolonising the Mind: The Politics of Language in African Literature.* London: James Curry; Portsmouth, N.H.: Heinemann, 1986.

Thompson, John O. "Jesus as Moving Image: The Question of Movement." In Stanley E. Porter, Michael A. Hayes, and David Tombs, eds., *Images of Christ Ancient and Modern*, pp. 290-305. Roehampton Institute London Papers, 2. Sheffield: Sheffield Academic Press, 1997.

Thompson, Leonard L. *The Book of Revelation: Apocalypse and Empire.* Oxford: Oxford University Press, 1990.

Thompson, Lloyd A. *Romans and Blacks.* Norman: University of Oklahoma Press, 1989.

Thompson, Steven. *The Apocalypse and Semitic Syntax.* SNTS Monograph Series, 52. Cambridge: Cambridge University Press, 1985.

Thornton, Bruce. "Constructionism and Ancient Greek Sex." *Helios* 18 (1991): 181-93.

Tilborg, Sjef van. *Imaginative Love in John.* Biblical Interpretation Series, 2. Leiden: E. J. Brill, 1993.

Torry, C. C. *The Apocalypse of John.* New Haven, Conn.: Yale University Press, 1958.

Trexler, Richard. "Gendering Jesus Crucified." In Brendan Cassidy, ed., *Iconography at the Crossroads*, pp. 107-19. Princeton, N.J.: Department of Art and Archaeology, Princeton University, 1993.

Trible, Phyllis. "Love's Lyrics Redeemed." In idem, *God and the Rhetoric of Sexuality*, pp. 144-65. Overtures to Biblical Theology, 2. Philadelphia: Fortress Press, 1978.

Trigg, Joseph Wilson. *Origen: The Bible and Philosophy in the Third-Century Church.* Atlanta: John Knox Press, 1983.

Turner, Denys. *Eros and Allegory: Medieval Exegesis of the Song of Songs.* Cistercian Studies, 156. Kalamazoo, Mich.: Cistercian Publications, 1995.

Urbach, Ephraim E. "The Homiletical Interpretation of the Sages and the Expositions of Origen on Canticles, and the Jewish-Christian Disputation." *Scripta Hierosolymitana* 22 (1971): 248-75.

Vance, C. S. "Social Construction Theory and Sexuality." In Maurice Berger, Brian Wallis, and Simon Watson, eds., *Constructing Masculinity*, pp. 37–48. New York: Routledge, 1995.

Vance, Norman. *The Sinews of the Spirit: The Ideal of Christian Manliness in Victorian Literature and Religious Thought*. Cambridge: Cambridge University Press, 1985.

Veeser, H. Aram, ed. *Confessions of the Critics*. New York: Routledge, 1996.

Vercoutter, Jean, et al. *The Image of the Black in Western Art*. Vol. 1. New York: Morrow, 1976.

Walker, Alice. *The Color Purple*. New York: Harcourt Brace Jovanovich, 1983.

Walker, Thomas. *The Epistle to the Philippians*. Indian Church Commentaries. Madras: SPCK Depository, 1906.

Wallace, Lew. *Ben Hur*. 1880. London: Collins, 1954.

Walters, Jonathan. "Invading the Roman Body: Manliness and Impenetrability in Roman Thought." In Judith P. Hallett and Marilyn B. Skinner, eds. *Roman Sexualities*, pp. 29–43. Princeton, N.J.: Princeton University Press, 1997.

——. "Juvenal, *Satire* 2: Putting Male Sexual Deviants on Show." In Lin Foxhall and John Salmon, eds., *Thinking Men: Masculinity and Self-Representation in the Classical Tradition*, pp. 148–54. Leicester-Nottingham Studies in Ancient Society, 7. New York: Routledge, 1998.

——. "'No More Than a Boy': The Shifting Construction of Masculinity from Ancient Greece to the Middle Ages." *Gender & History* 5 (1991): 20–33.

Ward, Graham. "The Displaced Body of Jesus Christ." In John Milbank, Catherine Pickstock, and Graham Ward, eds., *Radical Orthodoxy: A New Theology*, pp. 163–81. New York: Routledge, 1999.

Warner, Michael. "Introduction." In idem, ed., *Fear of a Queer Planet*, pp. vii–xxxi.

——, ed. *Fear of a Queer Planet: Queer Politics and Social Theory*. Minneapolis: University of Minnesota Press, 1993.

——. *The Trouble with Normal: Sex, Politics and the Ethics of Queer Life*. New York: Free Press, 1999.

Washington, Harold C. "Violence and the Construction of Gender in the Hebrew Bible: A New Historicist Approach." *Biblical Interpretation* 5 (1997): 324–63.

Webster, Alison. "Queer to Be Religious: Lesbian Adventures beyond the Christian/ Post-Christian Dichotomy." *Theology and Sexuality* 8 (1998): 27–39.

Weed, Elizabeth, and Naomi Schor, eds. *Feminism Meets Queer Theory*. Bloomington: Indiana University Press, 1997.

Weems, Renita J. "Song of Songs." In Carol A. Newsom and Sharon H. Ringe, eds., *The Women's Bible Commentary*, pp. 156–60. Louisville, Ky.: Westminster/John Knox Press, 1992. Expanded edition 1998.

——. "Song of Songs." In Leander E. Keck et al., eds., *The New Interpreter's Bible*, vol. 5: *Introduction to Wisdom Literature; Proverbs; Ecclesiastes; Song of Songs; Wisdom; Sirach*, pp. 361–434. Nashville, Tenn.: Abingdon Press, 1997.

West, Gerald O. *The Academy of the Poor: Towards a Dialogical Reading of the Bible.* Interventions, 2. Sheffield: Sheffield Academic Press, 1999.

West, Gerald, Musa Dube, and Phyllis A. Bird, eds. *"Reading With": An Exploration of the Interface Between Critical and Ordinary Readings of the Bible. African Overtures. Semeia* 73. Atlanta: Scholars Press, 1996.

Westermann, Claus. "Das Schöne im Altem Testament." In idem, *Erträge der Forschung am Alten Testament: Gesammalte Studien III*, pp. 119–37. Munich: Chr. Kaiser Verlag, 1984.

Westphal, Karl Friedrich Otto. "Die conträre Sexualempfindung." *Archiv für Psychiatrie und Nervenkrankheiten* 2 (1869): 73–108.

White, Norman. *Hopkins: A Literary Biography.* Oxford: Oxford University Press, 1992.

White, Robert J., ed. and trans. *The Interpretation of Dreams:* Oneirocritica *by Artemidoros*. Park Ridge, N.J.: Noyes, 1975.

William of St. Thierry et al. *St. Bernard of Clairvaux: The Story of His Life as Recorded in the* Vita Prima Bernardi *by Certain of His Contemporaries, William of St. Thierry, Arnold of Bonnevaux, Geoffrey and Philip of Clairvaux, and Odo of Deuil.* Translated by Geoffrey Webb and Adrian Walker. London: A. R. Mowbray & Co., 1960.

Williams, Craig A. "Greek Love at Rome." *Classical Quarterly* 45 (1995): 517–39.

———. Online review of Judith P. Hallett and Marilyn B. Skinner, eds., *Roman Sexualities. Bryn Mawr Classics Review* 98.10.16. bmr-1@brynmawr.edu.

———. *Roman Homosexuality: Ideologies of Masculinity in Classical Antiquity.* Ideologies of Desire. Oxford: Oxford University Press, 1999.

Williams, Rowan. *Arius: Heresy and Tradition.* London: Darton, Longman & Todd, 1987.

Wilson, Nancy L. *Our Tribe: Queer Folks, God, Jesus, and the Bible.* San Francisco: HarperSanFrancisco, 1995.

Wilton, Tamsin. "Which One's the Man? The Heterosexualisation of Lesbian Sex." In Diane Richardson, ed., *Theorising Heterosexuality: Telling It Straight*, pp. 125–42. London: Taylor & Francis, 1996.

Wimbush, Vincent L. "Ascetic Behavior and Color-ful Language: Stories about Ethiopian Moses." *Semeia* 58 (1992): 81–92.

———. *Paul the Worldly Ascetic: Response to the World and Self-Understanding According to 1 Corinthians 7.* Macon, Ga.: Mercer University Press, 1987.

Winkler, John J. *The Constraints of Desire: The Anthropology of Sex and Gender in Ancient Greece.* New York: Routledge, 1990.

Witherington, Ben, III. *The Jesus Quest: The Third Search for the Jew of Nazareth.* Downers Grove, Ill.: InterVarsity Press, 1995.

Wold, Donald J. *Out of Order: Homosexuality in the Bible and the Ancient Near East.* Grand Rapids, Mich.: Baker Books, 1998.

Wolf, Naomi. *The Beauty Myth: How Images of Beauty Are Used against Women.* London: Chatto & Windus, 1990.

Wright, David F. "Homosexuals or Prostitutes? The Meaning of ARSENOKOITAI (1 Cor. 6:9; 1 Tim. 1:10)." *Vigiliae Christianae* 38 (1984): 125–53.

———. "Translating ARSENOKOITAI (1 Cor. 6:9; 1 Tim. 1:10)." *Vigiliae Christianae* 41 (1987): 396–98.

Wright, N. T. *Jesus and the Victory of God.* Minneapolis: Fortress Press, 1997.

Young, Robin Darling. "The 'Woman with the Soul of Abraham': Traditions about the Mother of the Maccabean Martyrs." In Amy-Jill Levine, ed., *"Women Like This": New Perspectives on Jewish Women in the Greco-Roman World*, pp. 67–81. Society of Biblical Literature: Early Judaism and Its Literature, 1. Atlanta: Scholars Press, 1991.

Young, Steve. "Being a Man: The Pursuit of Manliness in *The Shepherd of Hermas.*" *Journal of Early Christian Studies* 2 (1994): 237–55.

Zaharopoulos, Dimitri Z. *Theodore of Mopsuestia on the Bible: A Study of His Old Testament Exegesis.* Mahwah, N.J.: Paulist Press, 1989.

# GENERAL INDEX

4 Maccabees: and 2 Maccabees, 197–98, 277n77; horror of, 6, 193–94, 197–98, 272n28; martyrdom in, 6, 191–95, 197–98, 217n22; masculinity in, 6, 191–95, 264n93; and Revelation, 6, 191–96, 198–99; self-mastery in, 192, 197
Aaron, 32–33, 51, 225n87
Abdimelech, 61
Abelove, Henry, 208n10, 210n13
Abraham, 34, 225n87, 242n18
Absolom, 243n23
Adam, 4, 121, 127–28, 263n84
Adonijah, 243n23
Aichele, George, 240n1
Aife, 275n47
Ailill, 274n42
Akiba, Rabbi, 29–31, 75, 216n15, 217n22
Alan of Lille, 67–68
Aland, Kurt, 241n8
Albright, William Foxwell, 52, 224n78
Alexander, Philip S., 216n15, 217n23, 218n25
Allen, Charlotte, 249–50nn87–89
Almaguer, Thomás, 255n14
Althaus-Reid, Marcella, 208n10
Althusser, Louis, 220n41
Ambrose of Milan, 67, 220n42

Anderson, Janice Capel, 209n12, 253n5, 264n90, 264n93, 269n5, 273n29
Antiochus IV Epiphanes, 192, 196, 199, 272n28
Aponius, 43, 51
Appleyard, Brian, 251n94
Apuleius, 135, 137–40, 253n7, 256n27
Aquinas, Thomas, 271n22
Aristophanes, 260n64
Aristotle, 141
Arius, 93, 241nn8–9
Armstrong, MacC. A., 252n98
Artemidoros, 141–45, 146, 257n42, 263n81
Aspegren, Kerstin, 264n93
Astell, Ann W., 213n7, 214n11
Attridge, Harold W., 209n12
Augustine, 58, 64, 78, 96, 98, 228n107, 271n22
Aune, David E., 268n4, 269n6, 272n25, 272n27
Autobiographical criticism, 2, 268n5

Bach, Alice, 240n1, 246n54
Back, Les, 220n40
Baer, R. A., Jr., 264n94
Baildam, John D., 233n134
Bailey, Randall C., 227n100, 227n104

Bakhtin, Mikhail, 72–74, 232nn123–28, 232n130
Barale, Michele Aina, 208n10, 210n13
Barker, Margaret, 271n25
Barth, Karl, 80, 235n148
Barthes, Roland, 222n55
Barton, Bruce, 105, 106–7, 246nn50–51, 246n55
Barton, Carlin, 195, 209n12, 260n69, 273nn35–36
Bassler, Jouette M., 262n73
Bastide, Roger, 248n61
Bauckham, Richard, 176–77, 178, 180–81, 184–85, 186, 189, 268n4, 269n7, 269n11, 270n17, 270n20, 271n24, 275n49
Beale, G. K., 268n4, 270nn21–22, 272n27, 273n40, 275n51
Beauty, 2; and class, 252n98, 253n101; contemporary cult of, 128, 247n59, 253n101; critical literature on, 252–53nn99–101; of Cúchulainn, 274n45; as divine reflection, 55–77, 110, 247n59, 252n98, 272n25; and ethnicity, 4, 38–39, 58–65, 108, 110–11, 127, 227n94, 227n100, 228nn106–7, 229n110, 230n114, 253n101; and global entertainment industry, 4, 92, 127–28; Greco-Roman concepts of, 98, 127, 244n33, 252n98; in Hebrew Bible, 219n29, 230n115, 243n23; and heterosexuality, 4, 127; and holiness, 37–39, 65–66, 220n37, 272n25; ideology of, 4, 39, 128, 253n101; male, 122–23, 127–28, 243n23, 249n84, 253n101; and physiognomy, 127–28, 252n98; and racism, 39, 65; and radiance, 272n25; sacrality of, 123; and violence, 122; and virtue, 4, 38, 57–58, 62, 65–66, 99, 128, 252n99; and worth, 57, 127. See also Bernard of Clairvaux; God; Jesus
Beemyn, Brett, 208n10
Beloved Disciple, 91, 129, 231n120
Bennett, James, 75–77, 233n139
Berger, John, 252n99
Berger, Maurice, 209n12
Berlant, Lauren, 208n6, 208n9
Bernard, Mary, 253n2
Bernard of Clairvaux: counter-epistemology of, 45; lustful temptations of, 48–49; and Origen, 224n66; physical beauty of, 224n70; on Song of Songs, 23–24, 44, 45, 54, 56, 63–64, 66, 69–72, 224n66, 224n70, 225nn85–86, 227n94, 228n107
Bestiality, 143, 149, 166
Bible and Culture Collective, 207n1, 210n16, 241n11
Bird, Antonia, 249n80
Bird, Phyllis A., 240n1
Bisset, Jacqueline, 250n91
Bitel, Lisa, 275n47
Black, Fiona C., 231n115
Bloch, Ariel, 222n50
Bloch, Chana, 222n50
Blum, Claes, 258n47
Boer, Roland, 209n10, 239n186, 240n1
Boesak, Allan A., 239n1, 278n78
Bollok, János, 244n30
Boobs, Betty, 53
Boone, Joseph, 211n20
Bordo, Susan, 252n99, 253n101
Borg, Marcus, 241n7, 245n38, 245n46
Borges, Jorge Luis, 258n51
Boring, M. Eugene, 272n27
Bossuet, Jacques-Bénigne, 233n134
Boswell, John, 211n20, 256n21
Boyarin, Daniel, 31, 37, 46, 48, 81, 208n10, 209n12, 217n22, 220n36, 221n47, 223n60, 233n140, 235nn154–55, 255n18, 261n72, 265n94
Boyd, Stephen B., 209n12
Brand, Peg Zeglin, 252n99
Bray, Alan, 15, 211n22
Brenner, Athalya, 214n10, 219n29, 231n121, 230n115, 232n129, 237n169, 243n23, 270n16
Brett, Mark, 227n104
Bringle, Mary Louise, 252n99
Bristow, Joseph, 211n24
Brooten, Bernadette J., 147–49, 151–52, 159, 165–67, 258n46, 258n48, 258n52, 258n54, 259n61, 259n63, 261n71, 262n80, 265nn97–98, 266n102
Brown, John, 156–61, 267n111
Brown, Peter, 41–42, 221n49, 257n34
Brown, Raymond E., 241n12

Brownmiller, Susan, 252n99
Budde, Karl, 234n146
Burrus, Virginia, 209n12, 230n112, 244n33
Bussmann, Claus, 262n73
Butler, Judith, 13, 210n13, 224n72, 269n8
Bynum, Caroline Walker, 222n54
Byrne, Brendan, 259n63

Callahan, Allen D., 275n51
Campbell, Douglas A., 263n85
Caner, Daniel F., 221n46
Cantacuzene, Matthew, 86
Cantarella, Eve, 257n30
Carr, David, 236n157
Carr, G. Lloyd, 222n50, 237n169, 237n171, 238n177
Carr, Stephen, 208n10
Carrell, Peter R., 271n25
Carrette, Jeremy R., 211n16
Carrey, Jim, 250n90
Carroll, Robert P., 270n16
Carter, Glenn, 250n91
Cassian, John, 212n2
Castelli, Elizabeth A., 210n16, 259n61, 262n81
Castellio[n], Sebastian, 233n134
Castle, Terry, 211n21
Ceannt, Eamon, 276n64
Celsus, 96–97, 99
Chadwick, Henry, 221n46
Chapkis, Wendy, 252nn99–100
Chapman, Rowena, 209n12
Charles, R. H., 270n21
Chaucer, Geoffrey, 74–75, 232n133
Chauncey, George, 211n21
Chilton, Bruce, 241n7
Cicero, 135, 253n7, 254n11
Clark, Gillian, 223n62
Clarke, John, 244n33
Clement of Alexandria, 95, 96, 142, 143
Clerk, John, 154–55, 267n109
Clines, David J. A., 178–79, 209n12, 225n83, 243n23, 269n10
Cloke, Gillian, 264n93
Clooney, George, 128
Cohen, Colleen Ballerino, 252nn99–100
Cohen, David, 255n17, 256n23

Cohen, Martin S., 217n17
Cohen, Shaye J. D., 252n98
Collins, Adela Yarbro, 271n25, 272n27
Collins, Michael, 276n64
Colonialism: British, 158–65, 168–69, 184–85, 187–96, 198, 267nn113–14, 276n70; and female homoeroticism, 151–54, 168–69, 266n107; and "heathenism," 158–63, 267n112, 267n114; and Ireland, 198, 184–85, 187–96, 198, 267n113, 268n2, 276nn63–65, 276–77nn70–72; and language, 267n113, 268n2; and martyrdom, 6, 193–96
Colson, F. H., 262n74, 264n94
Combes, Isobel H., 222n50
Comstock, Gary David, 208n10
Connell, R. W., 209n12
Connolly, James, 276n63
Constantine, 196–97
Cooke, Miriam, 178, 269n9
Copher, Charles B., 227n102, 229n107
Cornwall, Andrea, 209n12
Cox, Patricia, 221n46
Craig, Kenneth, 232n123
Cranfield, C. E. B., 260n63
Crashaw, Richard, 268n117
Crawford, Bobbie, 263n86
Crossan, John Dominic, 100, 105, 107, 244–45nn37–38, 245n41, 245nn43–45, 246n53
Cross-dressing, 26, 47, 49, 67, 196, 224n72, 273n38
Cruise, Tom, 128
Cúchulainn, 6, 176–81, 184–91, 274n43, 274–75nn45–48
Cultural studies, 2, 92, 239–40nn1–2
Cumming, Jane, 149, 151, 266n105, 266n108
Cunnilingus, 258n50
Cunningham, D. J., 239n184
Cyprian, 96

Dafoe, Willem, 125
Danby, Herbert, 216n16
D'Angelo, Mary Rose, 209n10
David, 45, 176–80, 242n18, 243n23
Davies, Margaret, 256n22
Dawes, Gregory, 264n89

Day, Amy, 254n13
*Dead Man Walking*, 124
Deconstruction, 9, 248n62
Deferrari, R. J., 253n1
Deissmann, Adolf, 278n77
Delitzsch, Franz, 30, 65, 79, 217nn19–20, 230n113, 234n146
Deming, Will, 209n12, 259n59
Dempsey, Robert Brinkerhoff, 80, 235nn150–52
Denis the Carthusian, 25–27, 28, 46, 51, 67, 68–69, 74, 86, 226n90, 231n117
DiCaprio, Leonardo, 128
Dijk-Hemmes, Fokkelien van, 214n10
Dio Chrysostom, 140
Diocletian, 196
Dionysius of Alexandria, 183
Donaldson, James, 242n18
Donne, John, 268n117
Dorotheos of Sidon, 143
Doss, Erica, 125, 246n55, 246n56, 248n66, 248nn72–73, 250n93,
Doty, William G., 209n12
Doughty, Darrell J., 264n87
Douglas, Jerry, 249n80
Douglas, Mary, 220n37
Dover, K. J., 252n98, 255n17, 256n22, 256n24
Downing, Christine, 256n23
Downing, Gerald F., 245n45, 277n76
Dowsett, Andrew C., 240n1
Dube, Musa, 240n1
Duberman, Martin, 208n10
DuBois, Page, 265n99
Dunn, James D. G., 260n63, 263n84, 264n92
Dupont-Sommer, André, 278n77
Dutton, Kenneth, 252n99, 253n101
Dyer, Richard, 64–65, 230n111, 248n61, 248n63

Eco, Umberto, 232n133
Eddy, Paul Rhodes, 245n45
Edwards, Ruth Dudley, 276nn67–68
Edwards, Tim, 253n101, 273n39
Eilberg-Schwartz, Howard, 209n12
Eisler, Robert, 97–98
Eleazar, 272n28
Eliason, Mickey, 208n10

Ellis, Bret Easton, 196–98, 272n28, 273n39
Ellis, Howard W., 248n70
Emer, 275nn47–48
Ephesians, Letter to the, 158–59
Ephraem, 67
Epiphanius, 53, 67
Eron, Lewis John, 255n18
Eslinger, Lyle, 88–89, 238–39nn183–85
Esther, 224n76
Eusebius, 40–41, 221n46, 221n49
Evans, Craig A., 8, 207n2, 241n7
Evans, E. C., 252n98
Eve, 4, 121, 127
Exum, J. Cheryl, 59, 214n10, 227nn97–99, 235n157, 240n1, 270n16
Ezekiel, 270n16

Faderman, Lillian, 150, 211n21, 266n101, 266nn103–6, 266–67nn108–9
Fairbanks, Douglas, 125
Falk, Marcia, 214n10
Fantham, Elaine, 256n28
Felder, Cain Hope, 220n40, 227n104, 228n105, 239n1
Femininity: and ancient Irish mythology, 274n47; and Christianity, 78; equated with passivity, 77–78, 142, 150, 166–67, 169, 191, 233n140, 262n81, 272n26; Greco-Roman vocabulary of, 135, 253n8, 254n11, 262n81; as object of male aggression, 6, 155, 158, 168–69, 182–84, 186, 196–98, 202, 264n94, 270n16, 273nn39–40; as sinfulness, 5, 163; subsumed in masculinity, 264nn93–94. *See also* Gender; Israel; Jesus
Feminist studies: and gender studies, 12, 209n11, 210n14; and Greco-Roman gender constructs, 169–70; and Hebrew prophets, 274n40; and masculinity studies, 12–13; and Michel Foucault, 17, 211n19, 265n99; and queer theory, 13, 210n13; and Song of Songs, 214n10, 235n157
Féray, Jean-Claude, 211n24
Ferdia, 185–87
Feuillet, André, 234n144
Findon, Joanne, 275n47

Finley, Moses I., 257n30
Finn, 274n42
Fiorenza, Elisabeth Schüssler, 246n54
Fitzmyer, Joseph A., 261n71
Ford, Joan Massingbaerde, 99, 244nn31–32, 263n86
Form criticism, 207n2
Forster, E. M., 166–67
Fosdick, Harry Emerson, 246n55
Foucault, Michel, 211n18, 211n23, 255n15, 255nn17–18, 257nn38–41, 257nn43–45, 258n51, 259n56, 264n88; and biblical studies, 210n16; and classical studies, 256n23; feminist critiques of, 211n19, 265n99; on Greco-Roman sex, 136–37, 141, 142, 145–46; *History of Sexuality*, 14, 17, 18, 210n16, 236n157; on homosexuality, 14–16, 136–37, 211n20; postfeminist appropriation of, 17; and queer theory, 14, 17, 210n16; and religious studies, 211n16; on technologies of the self, 141, 167–68
Fowl, Stephen, 251n95
Fowles, John, 75, 233n136
Fox, Michael, 232n129
Foxhall, Lin, 209n12, 265n99
Fredricksen, Paula, 246n54
Freeman, Diane P., 269n5
Freud, Sigmund, 14, 16–17, 181, 219n32
Freudenthal, J., 278n77
Frey, Olivia, 269n5
Friday, Nancy, 252n99
Frost, Peter, 228n107
*Full Metal Jacket*, 182
Funk, Robert W., 94, 241n10, 244n37, 245nn38–39, 249n88
Furman, Frida Kerner, 252nn99–100
Fuss, Diana, 212n27

Gallus, Thomas, 226n90
Garber, Marjorie, 47–48, 223nn63–65
Gender: crisis in American Protestantism, 108, 113; defined, 13; as divinely ordained, 151–54, 171–72, 261n71; and feminist studies, 13; of God, 203; Greco-Roman equations of, 169, 233n140, 272n26; indeterminate, 43, 47–48, 50, 71, 115, 158, 225n85, 231n119; and masculinity studies, 13; monstrous, 77, 149, 153–54, 166, 169, 260n64; as performative, 177–78; in rabbinic Judaism, 37, 78, 81, 223n60; and sex, 13–14, 50, 72, 136, 153–54, 171; and social status, 136, 139–41, 142, 143, 145–46; and soteriology, 78; third, 46–48. *See also* Femininity; Masculinity
Gender studies: defined, 12–13; and feminist studies, 12–13, 209n11, 210n14; and queer theory, 12–13
George, Mark K., 210n16
Gerson, John, 74
Giddens, Anthony, 209n11
Gilman, Sander L., 248n60, 252n99
Gilmore, David D., 209n12
Ginsburg, Christian D., 218nn23–24, 223n58, 233n134, 233n137, 233n139, 234n145
Glancy, Jennifer A., 209n12
Gleason, Maud W., 209n12, 252n98, 256nn22–23
God: beauty of, 29–30, 36, 55, 66, 216n17, 226n91, 247n59; beauty parlor of, 1, 55–57; body of, 216n15; as Bottomless Top, 172; and dieting, 247n59; and ethnicity, 108, 110–11, 248n64; and homophobia, 201–2; as Impenetrable Penetrator, 169; incestuousness of, 69–72, 202–3; masculinity of, 77–78, 161, 169, 190, 199, 202–3; as military commander, 184, 189–90; as scholar, 36–37, 220n34; as sexual subject, 4, 32–36, 69–72, 151, 155, 168–69, 170, 171–72, 184, 202–3; vengeance of, 198–99; wrath of, 5, 155, 188, 263n82. *See also* Trinity, Holy
Goldhill, Simon, 256n23
Goldin, Judah, 216n17
Goldstein, Laurence, 209n12
Gollancz, Hermann, 38, 218n25, 248n62
Good, Deirdre, 259n61
Goss, Robert E., 209n10, 231n120
Goulder, Michael D., 60, 82–84, 227nn103–4, 237nn159–71
Grant, Robert, 343n28
Greenberg, David F., 211n17, 258n49
Greene, Ellen, 265n99

Greer, Rowan A., 232n131
Gregory, Lady Augusta, 275n48
Gregory of Elvira, 43
Gregory of Nyssa, 51, 55, 58, 224n71, 226n89
Gregory the Great, 40, 51, 53, 222n56, 229n107
Grotius, Hugo, 233n134
Gwyther, Anthony, 240n1, 278n78

Haacker, Klaus, 258n53
Hadas, Moses, 278n77
Haddad, Tony, 209n12
Haggerty, George E., 208n6
Halberstam, Judith, 264n93
Hall, Donald, 246n49
Hallett, Judith P., 209n12, 259n58, 260n66, 266n107, 269n5
Halperin, David M., 142, 166–67, 208n10, 210n13, 210nn15–16, 211n20, 211n24, 212n25, 255n16, 259n56, 259n61
Hamilton, William, 240n1
Hanson, Arthur, 255n19
Hanson, R., 221n46
Hawley, Richard, 265n96
Hayes, Michael A., 240n1
Hays, Richard B., 263n85
Headlam, Arthur C., 158–59, 163–66, 168, 267nn114–15
Henking, Susan E., 208n10
Herbert, George, 268n117
Herbert, Máire, 240n4
Herder, J. G. von, 232n134
Herzer, Manfred, 211n24
Heschel, Susannah, 209n10
Heteronormativity, 17, 170–71, 236n158
Heterosexuality: compulsory, 17, 170–71; as eroticized inequality, 262n77; and homophobia, 81–82, 235n155; and homosexuality, 14, 16–17, 211n24, 212n27; as ideology, 17; invention of, 4, 16–17, 80–82, 113, 211n24; as perversion, 16–17, 211–12n25; and Song of Songs, 79–82, 215n14, 235n148. *See also* Heteronormativity; Sex; Sexuality
Hippolytus, 39–40, 51, 96, 242n19
Hirschberg, H. H., 237n170
Hitler, Adolf, 128

Hoffner, Harry A., Jr., 181–82, 270n14
Holy Spirit, 69–70, 121, 203, 231n119, 235n147
Homer, 227n105
Homoeroticism, female, 1, 266n101; in eighteenth- and nineteenth-century Britain, 148-58, 165–66, 168–69, 266–67nn103–9; in the Greco-Roman world, 2, 143–45, 147–53, 155, 159, 165–69, 171, 172, 255n16, 259n61, 259n63, 260n66, 266n102; as monstrous, 154, 166, 168, 260nn64–65; and orientalism, 151–54, 165–66, 168–69, 266n107; as unthinkable, 147–48, 149–51, 153–54, 171. *See also* Homophobia; Homosexuality; Lesbianism; Queer; Queer theory; Romans, Letter to the; Sex; Sexuality
Homoeroticism, male, 1, 77, 78, 81–82, 113, 115, 119–23, 166–67, 174–75, 249n80, 249n84, 255n14, 256n21, 258n49, 260n66, 265n96; in ancient Jewish literature, 255n18; and the Fathers and Doctors of the Church, 3–4, 22–28, 39–50, 54–58, 69–74, 213n7, 224n70; in the Greco-Roman world, 2, 136–40, 142, 147–53, 156, 157, 164–65, 170–72, 255n16, 257n34; and the Rabbis, 3–4, 29–37, 81, 255n18. *See also* Homophobia; Homosexuality; Queer; Queer theory; Romans, Letter to the; Song of Songs; Sex; Sexuality
Homophobia, 81–82, 113, 115, 120, 201–2, 235n155. *See also* Homosexuality
Homosexuality: and Christianity, 120; Greco-Roman tolerance of, 136–37; and heterosexuality, 14, 16–17, 211n24, 212n27; invention of, 14–16, 211n21, 211n24, 255n16; monolithic concept of, 211n10; and Paul, 134–35; and sodomy, 15; Western concept of, 211n20. *See also* Cross-dressing; Homophobia; Homoeroticism, female; Homoeroticism, male; Lesbian and gay studies; Lesbianism; Queer; Queer theory; Romans, Letter to the; Sex; Sexuality; Song of Songs
Hood, Robert E., 228n107
Hook, Richard, 111, 113
Hoover, Roy W., 241n10, 244n37, 249n88

Hopkins, Gerard Manley, 121–23, 249nn79–80
Horsley, Richard, 244n37
Horst, Pieter W. van der, 261n71
Hosea, 270n16
Howard-Brook, Wes, 240n1, 278n78
Hughes, Thomas, 105
Hunt, Lynn, 265n99
Hunzinger, C.-H., 269n12

Ibn Ezra, 222n58
Irenaeus, 96
Israel: blackness of, 38; as Cinderella, 30; as beautiful woman, 30, 32–33, 34–35, 37, 66, 218n26, 219nn29–30; as bride, 3, 31, 33, 35, 36, 54; femininity of, 77, 234n142; masculinity of, 78, 234n142; as princess, 30; self-infatuation of, 37; submissiveness of, 35–36, 234n142

Jacob, 236n158
Jaggar, Alison, 252n99
Jagose, Annamarie, 16, 208n10, 211n24
Jambor, Louis, 111, 113
Jason of Cyrene, 278n77
Jeffreys, Sheila, 262nn77–78
Jenkins, Emily, 247n59
Jeremiah, 45, 61, 270n16
Jerome, 40, 55, 58, 74, 86, 221n44, 223n59, 226n88, 228nn106–7, 229n108, 232n132
Jesus: as angel, 190, 271n25; artistic representations of, 100–105, 107–8, 111–17, 156–57, 251n93, 263n86; as beautician, 55–57, 158; as book, 90–92; breasts of, 40, 42–43, 44, 57, 68, 221n43, 221n50; cinematic representations of, 92, 123–25, 128, 249n80; "cleansing the temple," 106–7; corpse of, 95, 128; crucifixion of, 91–92, 120, 121, 122, 127, 156–57, 159–60, 163–64, 186, 190, 191, 192, 202, 263n86; as Cynic philosopher, 105, 245n45; as Davidic Messiah, 176–77, 180–81, 184–88; and Elvis, 126; and ethnicity, 62–63, 65, 108, 110–11, 124–25, 227n94, 248n64; as fantasy object, 50, 122, 164–65; femininity of, 5, 42–3, 44, 106, 108, 113, 115, 120, 158, 163–64, 169, 202, 268n117; incandescence of, 115, 117, 128, 272n25; incestuousness of, 68–72, 202–3; made over, 4, 128; masculinity of, 5, 43–44, 78, 105, 107, 108, 111, 113, 115, 123, 158, 159–64, 180–81, 190, 203, 246n55, 264n91; as movie star, 125; muscularity of, 106, 111; as phallic warrior, 181, 184; physical attractiveness of, 2, 4, 23, 55–57, 62–64, 66, 69, 71, 92, 99, 100, 108, 111, 117–22, 123, 124, 125, 126, 128, 129, 226n90, 226n94, 242n18, 244n33, 245n42, 246n46, 248n74, 250n91, 272n25; physical descriptions of, 97, 117, 118–19, 121, 242n18, 242n23, 244n33, 251n97, 271n25; pre-existence of, 127, 241n9; as queer icon, 113, 120; quest for historical, 4, 93–95, 99–105, 107, 123–24, 128, 240–41nn5–7, 246n54, 249–50nn87–88; resurrected body of, 63–64, 90–92, 95, 127; submissiveness of, 5, 156, 158, 159, 163–65, 169–70, 172, 263n84; ugliness of, 4, 96–99, 100–1, 126–28, 226n94, 242n18, 242n23; whiteness of, 108, 110. See also Jesus Seminar; John, Gospel of; Romans, Letter to the
*Jesus of Nazareth*, 125
Jesus Seminar, 93–95, 99–100, 123–24, 128, 241n10, 244n37, 245nn38–39, 250nn88–89
Jewett, Robert, 240n1
John, Gospel of, 199, 264n91: as basis for screenplay, 124; Christology of, 93, 94–95, 99, 115, 117, 124, 126–27, 128; and christological orthodoxy, 93; as Gospel of the Incandescent Christ, 115, 117, 128; midrash on, 90–91, 129; and quest for historical Jesus, 93, 94–95, 99, 123–24, 250n88
John, the apostle, 45, 70
John Chrysostom, 143, 148, 260n64
John of Damascus, 99, 244n33
John of Patmos. *See* Revelation, Book of
John of the Cross, 27, 44, 56–57, 213n8, 234n144
John the Baptist, 250n91
Johns, Catherine, 254n13
Johnson, Luke T., 245n46, 263n85
Jordan, Mark D., 208n10, 211n21
Joseph (father of Jesus), 250n91
Joseph (son of Jacob), 243n23

Josephus, 97–98, 243n24
Joüon, Paul, 234n144
Jovinian, 74
Justin Martyr, 96
Juvenal, 150, 265n96, 257n46

Kahl, Brigitte, 209n12
Kampen, Natalie Boymel, 259n61
Katz, Jonathan Ned, 16–17, 211nn24–25, 212n26
Keith, Alison, 254n13
Keller, Catherine, 270n16, 273n38
Kellum, Barbara, 209n12, 259n55, 270n15
Kertbeny, Karl Maria, 16, 211n24
Keuls, Eva C., 259n55
Kiberd, Declan, 189, 190, 276nn60–62, 276n64
Kim, Jean K., 270n16
Kimelman, Reuven, 221n45
King, Christopher, 215n14, 227n104
Kinsella, Thomas, 274n45, 275nn47–48, 275n50, 276nn53–56
Kirwan, James, 252n99
Kitzberger, Ingrid Rosa, 268n1, 269n5
Konstan, David, 256n23
Krabbe, Jeroen, 250n91
Kraemer, Ross S., 273n37
Krahmer, Shawn M., 225n85
Kramer, Samuel Noah, 238n178
Kreitzer, Larry J., 240n1
Krinetzski, Leo, 237n169
Kristeva, Julia, 214n10
Krondorfer, Björn, 209n12
Kwok, Pui-lan, 240n1, 246n54

LaCocque, André, 214n10
Lactantius, 96
Ladd, Tony, 246n49
Lakoff, Robin Tolmach, 252n99, 253n101
Lambert, Ellen Zetzel, 252n99
Lancaster, Roger N., 210n15
Landy, Francis, 215n15, 221n48, 231n121, 237n169
Laqueur, Thomas, 210n15
Larmour, David H., 211n24, 256n23
Lasine, Stuart, 250n89
*Last Temptation of Christ*, 125

Lauretis, Teresa de, 208n10
Layton, Bentley, 241n14
Leclercq, Jean, 225n86
Lecter, Hannibal, 273n39
Lefkowitz, Mary R., 256n23
Leiris, Michel, 209n12
Leonardo, Micaela di, 210n15
Lesbian and gay studies, 12, 17, 210n13. *See also* Queer theory
Lesbianism, 152, 171, 211n19, 211n21, 259n61. *See also* Homoeroticism, female
Leyerle, Blake, 244n33
Lindisfarne, Nancy, 209n12
Littledale, Richard Frederick, 51, 53, 75, 79, 87, 215n12, 222n52, 224n75, 225n81, 225n84, 233n135, 234n145, 237n172, 237n174
Livy, 253n7
Loewe, H., 230n114
Loewe, Raphael, 218n23
Lohmeyer, Ernst, 270n18
Long, Roland E., 123, 249nn82–85
Longwood, W. Merle, 209n12
Loomba, Ania, 152–53, 266n107
Loraux, Nicole, 209n12
Lowth, Robert, 234n145
Lucas, Abbot of Mount St. Cornelius, 43
Lucian of Samosata, 150, 260n64
Lüdemann, Gerd, 95, 241n15
Luke, Gospel of, 188–89, 264n91, 271n23
Lundbom, Jack, 247n58
Luther, Martin, 58, 78, 84, 233n134

Maccoby, Hyam, 223n58, 231n118
MacDonagh, Tomas, 276n64
Mack, Burton, 99–100, 244nn37–38, 245n45
MacKenzie, Robert K., 275n51
MacKinnon, Catherine, 262n78, 265n99
Malherbe, Abraham J., 98, 243n27, 244n20
Malick, David E., 256n21
Malik, Kenan, 220n40
Malina, Bruce J., 244n30, 260nn67–68
Malle, Louis, 250n90
Manetho, 143
Marcus Aurelius, 194
Mark, Gospel of, 91–92, 264n91

Marsh, Clive, 240n1, 241n6, 245n43, 245n54
Martial, 143, 150, 257n32, 257n46, 260n64
Martin, Dale B., 134–35, 209n12, 252n98, 253nn3–4, 256n21, 258n52, 262n74
Martin, Ralph, 251n95
Martinez, Florentino Garcia, 252n98
Martyn, J. Louis, 263n85
Mary, mother of Jesus, 25, 26, 65, 67–69, 86, 192, 203, 242n18, 250n91
Mary Magdalen, 63–64, 129, 229n110, 250n91
Masculinity, 1, 12; and anatomy, 162, 170, 264nn93–94, 265n96; ancient vs. modern, 135; contemporary stereotypes of, 136; critical literature on, 209n12; deessentialized, 177–78; equated with activity, 77–78, 139–40, 142, 150, 166–67, 169, 191, 192–95, 233n140, 234n142, 272n26; and eunuchs, 42; as female performance, 149–50, 264n93; Greco-Roman rules of, 135–46, 159–64, 170, 192–95, 255n20, 256n25, 256n28, 257n34, 263n83, 265n96; Greco-Roman vocabulary of, 135–36, 138–40, 253n8, 254n11; in the Hebrew Bible, 178–79, 181–83; hegemonic, 17, 140, 142, 159, 169, 190; of the Holy Trinity, 202–3; hypostatized, 162; and Irish nationalism, 189–91, 276n65; and martyrdom, 191–95; and self-mastery, 5, 159–64, 192–95, 197, 264n91; and warfare, 3, 5–6, 139, 163, 177–86, 189–92. *See also* Gender; God; Israel; Jesus; Masculinity studies; Muscular Christianity; Revelation, Book of; Romans, Letter to the
Masculinity studies, 2; as biblical studies, 209n12; as classical studies, 209n12; and feminist studies, 12–13; and gender studies, 12. *See also* Masculinity
Mathisen, James A., 246n49
Matter, E. Ann, 212n4, 221n45, 222n53, 231n116
Matthew, Gospel of, 264n91
Mattila, S. L., 264n94
Mayerson, Philip, 228n107
McClintock, Anne, 152
McCourt, Frank, 187–89, 194–96, 276nn57–58, 277nn73–74
McDannell, Colleen, 248n71

McDonald, P. M., 270n20
McNamara, Martin, 240n4
McNay, Lois, 265n99
Mead, Rebecca, 247n59
Mechtilde of Magdeburg, 213n9
Medb, Queen, 274n42, 275n47
Meier, John P., 100, 105, 115, 245nn40–42, 246n48, 246n53
Melons, Honey, 53
Merck, Mandy, 210n13
Merton, Thomas, 24–25, 213n6
Merz, Annette, 241n7
Messing, Debra, 250n91
Meyers, Carol, 214n10, 221n48
Michaelis, Johann David, 234n145
Michel, Otto, 260n63
Michelet, Jules, 95, 242n17
Miles, Margaret, 252n98
Milgrom, Jacob, 220n37
Miller, James, 258n46, 258n53
Miller, Nancy K., 269n5
Miller, Patricia Cox, 222n55,
Miller, Paul Allen, 211n24, 256n23
Miller, Robert J., 241n10
Modern Language Association, 7–12, 207n1
Montefiore, C. G., 230n114
Moo, Douglas J., 260n63
Moore, Stephen D., 209n12, 210n16, 222n57, 240n1, 249n81, 253n5, 263n82, 264n90, 264n93, 269n5, 271n22, 273n29
Morgan, David, 240n3, 248n65, 248n73, 250n93
Morris, Rosalind C., 269n8
Morrison, Toni, 252n99
Morton, Donald, 208n10
Mosala, Itumeleng J., 239n1
Moses, 32–33, 44, 45, 51, 60, 225n87, 243n23
Moses the Black, 230n114
Mount Melleray Abbey, 24–25
Muesse, Mark W., 209n12
Murnaghan, Sheila, 264n93
Murphy, James M., 157
Murphy, Roland E., 59, 79–80, 222n50, 223n61, 227n101, 233n134, 235n148, 235n156, 237n169, 238n181
Murphy Zauhar, Frances, 269n5

Muscular Christianity, 105, 108, 268n116
Mussies, G., 275n51

Nahum, 270n16
Narratology, 9, 207n4
Necrophilia, 149
Neusner, Jacob, 216n15, 218n24
Newman, Carey C., 244n37
Neyrey, Jerome H., 209n12, 244n30, 260n68, 264n91
Nicholas of Lyra, 229n107, 235n147
Nietzsche, Friedrich, 203
Nigidius, 67
Nortwick, Thomas Van, 269n5
Novak, David, 234n142
Novatian, 96
Nussbaum, Martha, 256n23

O'Donovan Rossa, Diarmuid, 193
O'Grady, Standish, 189, 190
O'Hara, David, 250n91
Oisín, 274n42
Oldman, Gary, 250n91
Oliensis, Ellen, 265n96
Olyan, Saul, 208n10, 255n18
Origen, 66, 89: alleged self-castration of, 40–41, 47, 221n46; and Bernard of Clairvaux, 224n66; on Jesus' physical appearance, 96–97, 99, 242n22; on Song of Songs, 23, 27–28, 40–46, 49–50, 54–58, 60–62, 64–65, 214n11, 219n31, 221n44, 222n51, 222n55, 224n66, 224n73, 226n88, 226n92, 226n94, 228–29nn106–9, 230n115; and "whitening" of Christianity, 65
Ortiz, Gaye, 240n1
Ovid, 143, 150, 260n64

Pack, Roger, 257n46
Painter, John, 241n12
Pardes, Ilana, 214n10
Parente, Paschal, 67, 231n116
Parsons, Mikeal C., 209n12
Patrick, Saint, 274n42
Paul, 45, 70–71, 256n21, 259n62, 260n70, 262n73: celibacy of, 5, 146; disputed and undisputed letters of, 263n87; gender theory of, 153–54; physical description of, 98, 243n28, 244n30; sexual soteriology of, 156, 158, 172, 202; and Thecla, 243n26. *See also* Romans, Letter to the
Paul, G. M., 270n15
Paz, Octavio, 255n14
Pearse, Padraic, 189–94, 276n59, 276nn63–69
Pelikan, Jaroslav, 223n62, 236n158, 246n46
Pellegrini, Ann, 259n61
Penn, Sean, 124
Perez, 224n74
Peter, 91, 129
Peter Chrysologus, 67
Petersen, William L., 256n21
Petronius, 253n7
Phaedrus, 150
Philo of Alexandria, 140, 151–52, 194, 257n34, 258n48, 261n71, 264n94, 265n95
Philo of Carpasia, 40, 53
Pilch, John J., 264n91
Pippin, Tina, 183, 209n10, 240n1, 270n16, 274n41
Pirie, Jane, 149, 150
Pitt, Brad, 128
Plato, 141, 143
Platter, Charles, 211n24, 256n23
Plevnik, Joseph, 260n68
Pliny the Elder, 265n100
Pliny the Younger, 253n7, 277n76
Plunkett, Joseph, 276n64
Plutarch, 140
Polaski, Donald, 225n83
Polaski, Sandra Hack, 210n16
Polycarp, 217n22
Pontius Pilate, 250n91
Pope, Marvin H., 33–34, 52, 59, 80, 82, 84–89, 218n23, 218n25, 218n28, 220n34, 222n50, 222n58, 224n77, 227nn95–96, 227n100, 233n134, 233n138, 235nn149–52, 235n156, 237nn166–71, 238nn175–82, 239n186
Porter, Stanley E., 240n1, 275n51
Postcolonial studies, 2. *See also* Colonialism
Powell, Mark Allan, 241n7
Powell, Robert, 125,
Presley, Elvis, 126, 251n94
Psellus, 51

Pseudo-Lucian, 243n26, 264n64
Pseudo-Phocylides, 143, 145, 258n48, 261n71
Ptolemy, 143

Queer: book titles, 11–12, 208n8; Christianity, 120; defined, 18; gender identity, 48, 123; Holy Trinity, 202–3, 231n119; Jesus, 113, 115, 120, 164, 202, 231n120, 249n80, 268n117; journals, 208n8; Mariology, 67; MLA paper titles, 10–11; MLA session titles, 11–12, 208n7; Paul, 164–65; spirituality, 3–4, 120, 123, 221n46, 268n117; subject positions, 3. *See also* Queer theory
Queer theory, 2, 210n13; and ancient Mediterranean culture, 17–18; and biblical studies, 208n10; charter document of, 14; as commentary, 12; and feminist studies, 13, 210n13; and gender studies, 12–13; and heteronormativity, 17, 170–71; as inaccurate label, 12; introductions to, 208n10; and masculinity studies, 13; and Michel Foucault, 14; and the New Testament, 18; and normality, 18, 212n28; obituary for, 208n7; public debut of, 12; and Pauline theology, 164, 169–72; and religious studies, 208n10; and sex and sexuality, 13, 17; and social constructionism, 17. *See also* Heterosexuality; Homosexuality; Lesbian and gay studies; Queer; Sex; Sexuality

Rajak, Tessa, 193–95, 273nn32–34
Rambuss, Richard, 170, 208n10, 249n78, 249n80, 268n117
Reader-response criticism, 9, 207n3
Redaction criticism, 207n2
Reimarus, Hermann Samuel, 240n5
Renan, Ernest, 248n74
Revelation, Book of: and 4 Maccabees, 6, 191–96, 198–99; and *American Psycho*, 196–98; as apologia for passive resistance, 192–95; Babylon in, 181, 183–84, 196, 269n12, 270n19, 273n38, 273n40; cannibalism in, 183, 196–97; as Christian war scroll, 6, 182; and Ezekiel, 196, 197–98; first-person narrator of, 173; holy war in, 270n18; and Irish nationalism, 6, 196–97; language of, 183; and martyrdom, 6, 186–87, 191–99, 277nn75–76; masculinity in, 3, 5–6, 177–86, 190–98, 199; and mass death, 6, 187–89; messianic war in, 3, 5–6, 175–90; millenium in, 197; numbers in, 268n4; Parousia in, 187–88; and persecution, 272n27; plot précis of, 185–86; and pornoprophetics, 270n16, 273n40; seductiveness of, 183; and *Táin Bó Cuailnge*, 6, 176, 181–82, 198; title of, 175, 269n6; torture in, 188, 199, 270n22, 277n76; vengeance in, 198–99, 278n78
Rice, Anne, 117, 248–49n74
Richard, Pablo, 278n78
Richard of Saint Victor, 51
Richardson, Diane, 266n101
Riches, John, 267n114
Richlin, Amy, 209n12, 255n16, 256n23, 256n28, 258n50, 265nn99–100
Riedlinger, 214n9, 220n42
Rissi, Mathias, 269n12
Robert, André, 234n144
Roberts, Alexander, 242n18
Rogers, Eugene F., 208n10
Rolle, Richard, 232n133
Romans, Letter to the: crime and punishment in, 147–53; defamiliarization of, 135; as discourse on self-mastery, 159–64; on homoeroticism, 5, 134–5, 141–44, 146–57, 161–62, 165–69, 171, 202, 203, 257n34, 258n48, 259n63, 261n71, 265n97, 267n115; on idolatry, 150–53, 262n73, 262nn75–76; logics of sexuality of, 134–35; masculinity in, 159–64; and *pistis Christou* debate, 263n85; on righteousness, 5, 163; on sin, 5, 162–63. *See also* Paul
Rooks, Noliwe M., 252n99
Rosenstiehl, J. M., 99
Rowland, Christopher, 271n25
Rowley, H. H., 79, 234n147
Rufinus, 40, 58, 221n44, 224n73, 228n106
Runions, Erin, 209n10
Rupert of Deutz, 67, 68, 86–87, 226n90, 231n116
Russel, Cornelius, 244n33

Russell, George, 190
Rutherford, Jonathan, 209n12

Sadomasochism, 31, 35–36, 122, 154, 239n186
Salgado, J.-M., 231n116
Saller, Richard, 256n23
Sallman, Warner, 107–8, 111–17, 125, 246–47nn57–58, 250n93
Sallust, 253n7
Salmon, John, 209n12
Sánchez, Marta, 255n14
Sanday, William, 158–59, 163–66, 168, 267nn114–15
Sanders, E. P., 100, 107, 233n141, 234n143, 245nn41–43, 246n52, 262n73
Sandys, Edwina, 156–57
Sandys, George, 266n107
Santoro L'Hoir, Francesca, 135–36, 253–54nn6–8, 254n11, 256n27
Sappho, 76
Sarah, 34
Satan, 250n91
Satlow, Michael L., 255n18
Saul, 243n23
Scarry, Elaine, 252n99
Scáthach, 275n47
Schaberg, Jane, 188, 246n54, 271n23
Schehr, Lawrence R., 209n12
Scherr, Raquel L., 252n99, 253n101
Schneider, Laurel C., 209n10
Scholem, Gershom, 215n15
Schor, Naomi A., 17, 209n11, 210n13, 212n27
Schreiner, Thomas R., 260n63, 261n71
Schweitzer, Albert, 240nn5–6
Scott, Bernard Brandon, 240n1
Scott, R. B. Y., 275n51
Scroggs, Robin, 252n98, 256n21
Sedgwick, Eve Kosofsky, 8, 13–14, 120, 208n10, 210nn14–15, 211n20, 211n24, 249n78, 264n93
Segal, Naomi, 210n13
Segovia, Fernando F., 240n1
Selvidge, Marla J., 270n16
Seneca the Elder, 143, 193, 260n64
Seneca the Younger, 260n64
Setel, T. Drorah, 270n16

Sex: cultural contingency of, 210n15; defined, 13; as eroticized inequality, 153–54, 262n77; and gender, 13–14, 50, 72, 136, 153–54, 171; Greco-Roman conceptions of, 2, 136–72, 254n13, 259n56; Greco-Roman vocabulary of, 166–67, 255n16, 257n35; and honor vs. shame, 140, 146, 147, 150, 260nn68–69; and nature, 140, 141–43, 145, 147, 148, 152–53, 258n48, 258n52, 261n71; phallocentric conception of, 145–46, 258n50; and queer theory, 13; and social status, 136, 139–41, 142, 143, 145–46, 147, 166, 167; in Song of Songs, 82–89; third, 48, 223n65; and violence, 31, 35–36, 122. See also Bestiality; Cunnilingus; Heterosexuality; Homoeroticism, female; Homoeroticism, male; Homosexuality; Necrophilia; Sadomasochism; Sexuality
Sexuality, 167, 210n13: and culture, 14; defined, 13–14, 210n15; in Greco-Roman world, 254n13, 258n46; masculine, 181; and nature, 14; and Paul, 134–35, 156; and social constructionism, 15, 17, 211n20, 212n25. See also Heterosexuality; Homoeroticism, female; Homoeroticism, male; Homosexuality; Sex
Shamblin, Gwen, 247n59
Shaw, Brent D., 192–93, 273nn30–31
Shawn, Wallace, 250n90
Siewert, Frances E., 259n60
Silverman, Kaja, 209n12
Simon, John, 125
Simon, Maurice, 38, 217n18
Simpson, Mark, 209n12, 268n118
Sisto, Jeremy, 250n91
Skinner, Marilyn B., 209n12, 254n13, 259n58, 265n96, 266n102
Smart, Carol, 262n77
Smith, Bruce, 212n2
Smith, J. Pye, 75–76, 233n137, 233n139
Smith, Moody D., 241n12
Smith-Christopher, Daniel, 239n1
Snaith, John G., 237n169, 238nn180–81
Snowden, Frank M., Jr., 65, 228n105, 228n107, 230n112
Sollors, Werner, 248n62

Solomon, 77, 216n15, 226n94, 228n106, 232n131, 235n147
Solomon, Immanuel ben, 222n58
Solomos, John, 220n40
Song of Songs: as book for celibates, 45–49; allegorical interpretation of, 3–4, 22–89 passim, 113; and the carnivalesque, 72–74, 77; censorship of, 75; early female commentators on, 213n9; and ethnicity, 38–39, 52, 58–65, 84, 215n14, 227n102, 228–29nn106–9; female voice in, 214n10; and feminist studies, 214n10, 236n157; and Genesis creation accounts, 79–80, 235n148; incest in, 228n106, 231n121; and invention of heterosexuality, 79–82, 113; Jewish vs. Christian interpretation of, 50–55, 66; kabbalistic interpretation of, 231n118; literal interpretation of, 3, 22, 27, 46, 49–50, 74–89, 212n1, 216n15, 232–33nn131–35, 233n137, 233n139, 234nn144–46, 235–39nn157–86; and male sexual fantasy, 53; Mariological interpretation of, 25, 67–69, 231nn116–17; and marriage, 79–80, 232n129, 234–35nn145–47; as occasion of sin, 45–46; and pornography, 53, 84, 89, 225n83, 239n186; and queer spirituality, 123, 221n46; and sadomasochism, 31, 35–36, 239n186; sex in, 82–89; *wasf* genre in, 230n115
Source criticism, 207n2
Spargo, Tamsin, 210n16
Sparks, Kenton L., 227n104
Stadelmann, Luis, 234n144
Staley, Jeffrey L., 268n5
Stecopoulos, Harry, 209n12
Stegemann, Wolfgang, 260n68
Stehle, Eva, 254n13
Stein, Edward, 211n20
Stocking, Charles Francis, 246n55
Stoeltje, Beverly, 252nn99–100
Stone, Ken, 209n10, 259n61
Stone, Sharon, 85
Storey, John, 240n2
Stowers, Stanley K., 148, 160–63, 262n80
Strauss, David Friedrich, 240n5
Strinati, Dominic, 240n2

Studiorum Novi Testamenti Societas, 8, 9, 193–94
Suetonius, 98, 253n7
Sugirtharajah, R. S., 162, 240n1, 266n106
Sweet, J. P. M., 272n27

Tacitus, 253n7
*Táin Bó Cuailnge*, 6, 176–82, 185–88, 190, 191, 197, 198, 274–75nn42–48, 276nn53–56
Tatum, W. Barnes, 240n1, 250n92
Teresa of Avila, 213n9
Tertullian, 96, 99, 143, 242nn19–20, 244nn35–36, 271n22
Thecla, 243n26
Theissen, Gerd, 241n7
Theodore of Mopsuestia, 74, 232n131
Theodoret of Cyrus, 40
Thompson, John, 250n90
Thompson, Leonard L., 272n27
Thompson, Lloyd, 228n107
Thompson, Steven, 275n51
Thornton, Bruce, 211n20
Tilborg, Sjef van, 231n120
Tolbert, Mary Ann, 240n1
Tombs, David, 240n1
Torry, C. C., 275n51
Totheroh, William Wesley, 246n55
Tournay, Raymond, 234n144
Traherne, Thomas, 268n117
Trexler, Richard, 249n80
Trible, Phyllis, 214n10
Trigg, Joseph Wilson, 221n46
Trinity, Holy, 70, 203–4
Trinity College, Dublin, 268n2
Turner, Denys, 213n7, 231n116

Uebel, Michael, 209n12
Ulrichs, Karl Heinrich, 16
Urbach, Ephraim E., 217n21, 221n45

Valentino, Rudolph, 125
Valentinus, 95, 241n13
Vance, Norman, 211n20, 246n49
Veeser, H. Aram, 269n5
Velleius Paterculus, 253n7
Vercoutter, Jean, 228n107

Verhoeven, Paul, 124, 249n88

Walker, Alice, 110–11, 248n64
Walker, Thomas, 266n106
Wallace, Lew, 108, 118–20, 249nn76–77
Wallis, Brian, 209n12
Walters, Jonathan, 136, 138, 139–40, 253n5, 254n10, 255–56nn20–22, 256nn25–27, 257n36, 259n56, 265n96
Ward, Graham, 209n12
Warner, Michael, 208n6, 208n9, 208n10, 212n28
Washington, Harold C., 178, 181–83, 209n12, 269n9, 269–70nn13–15
Waters, Muddy, 177
Watson, Simon, 209n12
Weapons, Letha, 53
Webster, Alison, 208n10
Weed, Elizabeth, 210n13
Weems, Renita J., 52, 59–60, 214n10, 224n79, 227nn102–4
Wesley, Charles, 236n158
Wesley, John, 236n158
West, Gerald O., 240n1
West, Mona, 209n10
Westermann, Claus, 243n23
Westphal, Karl Friedrich Otto, 14, 211n18
Wetzstein, J. G., 234n146
Whiston, William, 233n134
White, Norman, 122, 249n80
White, Robert J., 258n47
Whoppers, Wendy, 53
Wilk, Richard, 252nn99–100

William of Saint Thierry, 48–49, 52, 224nn67–70, 224n76, 226n93
Williams, Craig A., 136, 139, 209n12, 254nn12–13, 255n15, 256nn22–23, 256n25, 256–57nn28–30, 257n37, 258n50, 259n55, 263n83
Williams, Rowan, 241n8
Willis, Bruce, 128
Wilson, Nancy L., 209n10
Wilton, Tamsin, 260n65, 266n101
Wimbush, Vincent L., 228n107, 230n114, 259n59
Winkler, John J., 139, 140, 141, 142, 143, 144, 145, 210n15, 256nn23–24, 257n37, 257–58nn46–47, 258n49, 258n51, 259n57
Witherington, Ben, III, 241n7, 245n46
Wold, Donald J., 256n21, 257n35
Wolf, Naomi, 252n99
Woods, Marianne, 149, 150
Wright, David F., 256n21
Wright, Elizabeth, 210n13
Wright, N. T., 244n37, 245n41, 245n46

Xenophon, 141

York, Michael, 125
Young, Robin Darling, 273n29

Zaharopoulos, Dimitri Z., 232n131
Zeffirelli, Franco, 125
Zeitlin, Froma I., 210n15, 256n23
Zerach, 224n74
Zimmerman, Bonnie, 208n6

# INDEX OF ANCIENT AND MEDIEVAL SOURCES

## I. JEWISH SOURCES

### Hebrew Bible

GENESIS
| | |
|---|---|
| 1:1 | 262n79 |
| 1:26–27 | 261n71 |
| 1:26–31 | 79–80 |
| 1:27 | 153, 261n71 |
| 2:4a | 262n79 |
| 2:4b | 262n79 |
| 2:18–25 | 80 |
| 3:16 | 34, 153–54 |
| 3:24 | 262n79 |
| 32:26 | 239n185 |
| 32:33 | 239n185 |
| 39:6 | 243n23 |
| 49:9 | 176 |

EXODUS
| | |
|---|---|
| 2:2 | 243n23 |
| 24:7 | 37 |
| 33:21–23 | 44 |

LEVITICUS
| | |
|---|---|
| 15:16 | 270n18 |
| 18:6 | 72 |
| 18:22 | 72, 255n18, 258n48, 261n71 |
| 20:13 | 255n18, 257n34, 258n48, 261n71 |

NUMBERS
| | |
|---|---|
| 5:2 | 37 |
| 24:17 | 176 |
| 24:17–19 | 176 |

DEUTERONOMY
| | |
|---|---|
| 4:16–18 | 262n73 |
| 20:10–20 | 182–83 |
| 20:10 | 183 |
| 20:11 | 183 |
| 20:19 | 183 |
| 22:5 | 39 |
| 22:28 | 183 |
| 23:9–10 | 270n18 |
| 35:11–12 | 239n185 |

1 SAMUEL
| | |
|---|---|
| 4:9 | 179 |
| 9:2 | 243n23 |
| 16:12 | 242n18, 243n23 |
| 17:42 | 243n23 |
| 21:5 | 270n18 |

## 2 SAMUEL
| | |
|---|---|
| 7:23 | 54 |
| 11:11 | 270n18 |
| 14:25 | 243n23 |

## 1 KINGS
| | |
|---|---|
| 1:6 | 243n23 |

## ISAIAH
| | |
|---|---|
| 1:18 | 227n100 |
| 11:4 | 177 |
| 37:22 | 183 |
| 44:9–20 | 262n73 |
| 47:1–4 | 183 |
| 47:8 | 183 |
| 47:9 | 183 |
| 49:2 | 177 |
| 53:1–12 | 127 |
| 53:2 | 99, 226n94 |
| 53:2–3 | 96–97, 127, 242n23 |
| 54:4 | 183 |
| 57:8–10 | 86 |
| 59:17 | 219n33 |
| 62:3 | 183 |
| 62:5 | 183 |
| 63:1 | 219n33 |
| 66:8–13 | 182 |
| 66:22–24 | 271n22 |

## JEREMIAH
| | |
|---|---|
| 2:11 | 262n73 |
| 6:1–8 | 183 |
| 10:25 | 274n40 |
| 13:22 | 183 |
| 41:22 | 274n40 |

## EZEKIEL
| | |
|---|---|
| 1:4–12 | 216n17 |
| 16:37–41 | 274n40 |
| 23:1–49 | 197–98 |
| 23:25–29 | 273n40 |
| 23:47 | 273n40 |
| 33:24 | 225n87 |

## HOSEA
| | |
|---|---|
| 2:3 | 274n40 |

## MICAH
| | |
|---|---|
| 3:3 | 274n40 |

## NAHUM
| | |
|---|---|
| 2:5 | 36 |
| 3:4–5 | 274n40 |
| 3:5–6 | 183 |
| 3:15 | 274n40 |

## PSALMS
| | |
|---|---|
| 2:1–2 | 180 |
| 2:8 | 180 |
| 2:9 | 180 |
| 8:4 | 135 |
| 8:6 | 63 |
| 14:2 | 242n18 |
| 21:7 | 227n94 |
| 44:3 | 19, 63 |
| 44:23 | 29 |
| 44:12 | 19 |
| 45:2 | 121, 246n46 |
| 64:7 | 64 |
| 92:1 | 19 |
| 93:1 | 219n33 |
| 97:2 | 170 |
| 103:2 | 64 |
| 104:1 | 219n33 |
| 106:20 | 262n73 |

## SONG OF SONGS
| | |
|---|---|
| 1:2 | 23–24, 26, 68–71, 224n70 |
| 1:2 | 40, 42–43, 68–69, 221n50 |
| 1:2–4 | 239n186 |
| 1:3 | 29, 31, 239n186 |
| 1:3–4 | 45 |
| 1:4 | 228n107 |
| 1:4e | 30–31 |
| 1:5 | 38, 58–61, 65–66, 215n14, 220n38, 229–30nn107–8 |
| 1:5–2:7 | 239n186 |
| 1:6 | 61–62, 225n83 |
| 1:6a | 59–60 |
| 1:7 | 239n186, 239n186 |
| 1:8 | 55, 239n186 |
| 1:9 | 83 |
| 1:10 | 43, 55–56, 218n26, 219n31 |
| 1:12 | 239n186 |
| 1:15 | 32 |
| 1:15–16 | 230n115 |
| 1:16 | 219n29 |
| 2:1 | 63, 226n94 |

| | | | |
|---|---|---|---|
| 2:3 | 239n186 | 5:7–16 | 242n18 |
| 2:6 | 23, 28, 49–50, 239n186 | 5:8 | 36 |
| 2:7 | 239n186 | 5:8–16 | 22 |
| 2:8 | 239n186 | 5:9 | 29, 31 |
| 2:8–17 | 239n186 | 5:9–16 | 216n15 |
| 2:10 | 230n115, 239n186 | 5:10 | 63 |
| 2:13 | 230n115, 239n186 | 5:10ff. | 29 |
| 2:13b–14 | 44 | 5:10–16 | 41, 216n15, 230n115, 239n186 |
| 2:14 | 33, 57–58 | 5:11 | 35, 36, 88 |
| 2:15 | 224n66 | 5:13 | 33 |
| 2:16 | 29, 45, 54, 239n186 | 5:14b | 237n170 |
| 3:1–5 | 239n186 | 6:1 | 29 |
| 3:4 | 239n186 | 6:1–3 | 239n186 |
| 3:5 | 239n186 | 6:2 | 239n186 |
| 3:6 | 239n186 | 6:3 | 29 |
| 3:6–11 | 239n186 | 6:4 | 226n87 |
| 3:8 | 220n42 | 6:4–7 | 230n115 |
| 4:1 | 32, 219n30, 230n115 | 6:4–12 | 239n186 |
| 4:1–5 | 230n115 | 6:9 | 54, 225n87, 226n89 |
| 4:1–15 | 239n186 | 6:10 | 30 |
| 4:2 | 239n186 | 6:12 | 30, 83 |
| 4:4 | 41 | 6:13 | 215n13 |
| 4:5 | 32, 51–52, 224n74, 225n87, 239n186 | 7:1 | 60 |
| 4:7 | 37, 225n87, 230n115 | 7:1–7 | 230n115 |
| 4:9 | 226n87, 231n121, 239n186 | 7:1–10 | 230n115 |
| 4:10 | 231n121 | 7:2 | 53, 60, 220n35, 230n115 |
| 4:10a | 52–53 | 7:2a | 84, 237n169 |
| 4:11 | 33 | 7:3 | 35, 51–52, 218n26 |
| 4:12 | 231n121, 238n178 | 7:3a | 84 |
| 4:13a | 85 | 7:5 | 239n186 |
| 4:16 | 238n178, 239n186 | 7:6 | 239n186 |
| 4:16e–f | 238n178 | 7:7 | 230n115 |
| 4:16–5:9 | 239n186 | 7:7–10 | 239n186 |
| 5:1 | 71, 231n121, 239n186 | 7:8c–d | 85 |
| 5:2 | 231n121, 239n186 | 7:9 | 224n74 |
| 5:2c | 87–88 | 7:9c–d | 85, 237n169 |
| 5:2–5 | 89 | 7:10b | 83 |
| 5:2–6 | 85–89 | 7:11 | 232n122 |
| 5:3 | 239n186 | 7:12 | 239n186 |
| 5:4a | 86–87 | 7:13 | 239n186 |
| 5:4b | 238n176 | 8:1–2 | 231n121 |
| 5:4–5 | 238n181 | 8:1–14 | 239n186 |
| 5:5 | 239n185 | 8:2 | 83, 239n186 |
| 5:5d | 89 | 8:3 | 83 |
| 5:6 | 239n186 | 8:4 | 239n186 |
| 5:7 | 225n83 | 8:5 | 61, 62, 239n186 |
| | | 8:5b | 82–83 |

| | |
|---|---|
| 8:8 | 52 |
| 8:8–9 | 88–89 |
| 8:10 | 43 |
| 8:20 | 239n186 |

## LAMENTATIONS
| | |
|---|---|
| 1:1 | 183 |
| 4:7ff. | 59 |

## ESTHER
| | |
|---|---|
| 2:12 | 36 |

## DANIEL
| | |
|---|---|
| 5:24 | 201 |
| 7:10 | 63 |
| 10:5–6 | 271n25 |

## Apocrypha, Pseudepigrapha, and Related Sources

### APOCALYPSE OF ZEPHANIAH
| | |
|---|---|
| 6:11 | 272n25 |

### 2 BARUCH
| | |
|---|---|
| 10:1–3 | 269n12 |
| 11:1 | 269n12 |
| 33:2 | 269n12 |
| 67:7 | 269n12 |
| 79:1 | 269n12 |

### 1 ENOCH
| | |
|---|---|
| 21:1–10 | 271n22 |
| 27:2–3 | 271n22 |
| 48:9 | 271n22 |
| 62:12 | 271n22 |
| 108:14–15 | 271n22 |

### 2 ENOCH
| | |
|---|---|
| 1:5 | 272n25 |
| 10.4 | 255n18 |
| 19:2 | 272n25 |

### 2 ESDRAS
| | |
|---|---|
| 5:24–36 | 216n15 |
| 7:26 | 216n15 |

### 4 EZRA
| | |
|---|---|
| 3:1–2 | 269n12 |
| 3:31 | 269n12 |

| | |
|---|---|
| 7:93 | 271n22 |
| 7:97 | 272n25 |
| 7:125 | 272n25 |
| 12:31–32 | 176 |

### JOSEPH AND ASENETH
| | |
|---|---|
| 14:9 | 272n25 |

### LETTER OF ARISTEAS
| | |
|---|---|
| 152 | 255n18 |

### 2 MACCABEES
| | |
|---|---|
| 2:23 | 278n77 |
| 3:26 | 272n25 |
| 3:33 | 272n25 |
| 6:12–7:42 | 277n76 |
| 7:3 | 199 |
| 7:3–5 | 197–98 |

### 4 MACCABEES
| | |
|---|---|
| 9:11–14 | 272n28 |
| 9:19–20 | 272n28 |
| 12:11–12 | 199 |
| 15:15 | 273n28 |
| 17:11–17 | 194 |

### PSALMS OF SOLOMON
| | |
|---|---|
| 2:14ff. | 255n18 |

### SENTENCES OF PSEUDO-PHOCYLIDES
| | |
|---|---|
| 3 | 255n18 |
| 190–92 | 255n18, 261n71 |
| 192 | 145 |
| 213–14 | 255n18 |

### SIBYLLINE ORACLES
| | |
|---|---|
| 3.185–87 | 255n18 |
| 3.595–600 | 255n18 |
| 5.140–43 | 269n12 |
| 5.159 | 269n12 |
| 5.386–96 | 255n18 |
| 5.434 | 269n12 |

### SIRACH
| | |
|---|---|
| 47:14–17 | 216n15 |

### TESTAMENT OF GAD
| | |
|---|---|
| 5:1 | 262n75 |

TESTAMENT OF NAPHTALI
3:4                         255n18

WISDOM OF SOLOMON
8:2                         216n15
5:1–14                      271n22
7:29                        272n25
11:15–16                    262n75
12:23                       262n75
12:27                       262n75
14:26                       255n18

DEAD SEA SCROLLS
1QM (*War Scroll*)
7:3–7                       270n18

1QS (*Rule of the Community*)
7:13                        86

4Q186 (*Horoscope*)
                            252n98

4Q561 (*Aramaic Horoscope*)
                            252n98

PHILO AND JOSEPHUS
Philo
   *Abraham*
135–36                      255n18
   *On the Contemplative Life*
8–9                         152
   *On the Embassy to Gaius*
215                         194
319                         264n94
   *Questions and Answers on Exodus*
18                          264n94
   *Questions and Answers on Genesis*
2.12                        264n94
   *Special Laws*
1.325                       255n18
2.50                        255n18
3.37–39                     255n18
3.38                        140, 261n71
   *The Worse Attacks the Better*
28                          264n94

Josephus
   *Against Apion*
1.8                         216n15
2.275                       255n18
   *Antiquities of the Jews*
5.8.2 §277                  272n25
18.3.3 §63                  97
   *Jewish War*
4.560–63                    255n18

## Rabbinic and Related Sources

B. ʿABODA ZARA
44a                         260n64

B. HULLIN
92b                         255n18

B. NIDDAH
13b                         255n18

B. SANHEDRIN
12.10                       75
100a                        36
101a                        75
108b                        220n39

B. SHABBAT
65a–b                       255n18

B. YEBAMOT
76a                         255n18

GENESIS RABBAH
22.5–6                      220n39
26.6                        255n18
36.7–8                      220n39

HEKHALOT RABBATI
13.4                        216n17
167                         216n15

IBN EZRA
   *Commentary on the Song of Songs*
   Introduction to the Second Gloss
                            222n58

## LEVITICUS RABBAH
| | |
|---|---|
| 6.6 | 269n12 |
| 23.9 | 255n18 |

## MIDRASH ON PSALMS
| | |
|---|---|
| 137.1 | 269n12 |

## NUMBERS RABBAH
| | |
|---|---|
| 7.10 | 269n12 |

## MEKILTA DE RABBI ISHMAEL
Shirata 3.49–63   29

## M. YADAIM
| | |
|---|---|
| 3.5 | 29 |

## RASHI
Commentary on the Song of Songs
  Prologue   21

## SHECHTER ABOTH
| | |
|---|---|
| 10 | 235n155 |

## SIFRA QODASIN
| | |
|---|---|
| 9.14 (92b) | 255n18 |

## SONG OF SONGS RABBAH
| | |
|---|---|
| 1.5 §1 | 38 |
| 1.6 §3 | 38 |
| 1.6 §4 | 269n12 |
| 1.10 §2 | 218n26 |
| 1.15 §2 | 32 |
| 1.16 §1 | 219n29 |
| 2.14 §5 | 33 |
| 2.14 §8 | 35 |
| 2.16 §1 | 54 |
| 4.1 §1 | 219n30 |
| 4.1 §3 | 32 |
| 4.5 §1 | 33, 51, 225n87 |
| 4.6 §1 | 34 |
| 4.7 §1 | 37, 225n87 |
| 4.8 §1 | 36 |
| 4.9 §1 | 225n87 |
| 4.10 §1 | 218n27, 219n33 |
| 4.11 §1 | 34, 220n33 |
| 4.11 §2 | 33 |
| 5.11 §1 | 35 |
| 5.11 §5 | 36 |
| 5.13 §1 | 33 |
| 5.14 §2 | 35 |
| 6.4 §1 | 226n87 |
| 6.9 §1 | 225n87 |
| 6.9 §5 | 54 |
| 6.12 §1 | 30 |
| 7.2 §3 | 220n35 |
| 7.3 §1 | 218n26 |
| 7.3 §2 | 35 |
| 7.7 §1 | 219n30 |
| 7.9 §1 | 224n74 |
| 7.11 §1 | 232n122 |

## TARGUM OF ISAIAH
| | |
|---|---|
| 33:17 | 271n22 |

## TARGUM OF THE SONG OF SONGS
| | |
|---|---|
| 1:5 | 38 |
| 1:15 | 35 |
| 1:16 | 36 |
| 4:1 | 32 |
| 4:2 | 33 |
| 4:5 | 51 |
| 4:7 | 35 |
| 4:8 | 33 |
| 4:9 | 33 |
| 4:10 | 33 |
| 4:11 | 33 |
| 5:8 | 36 |
| 5:9 | 34 |
| 5:10 | 36, 220n34 |
| 5:12 | 32 |
| 5:13 | 33 |
| 5:16 | 33 |
| 6:4 | 35 |
| 6:9 | 35 |
| 6:12 | 35 |
| 7:7 | 36 |
| 7:14ff. | 220n34 |

## TANHUMA
| | |
|---|---|
| Noah 13 | 230n114 |

## Y. GITTIN
| | |
|---|---|
| 8.10 | 255n18 |
| 49c | 255n18 |

## II. PAGAN SOURCES

### Achilles Tatius
*LEUCIPPE AND CLITOPHON*
1.4　　　　　　252n98

### Apuleius
*METAMORPHOSES/THE GOLDEN ASS*
9.27–28　　　　138
9.28　　　　　　138–39

### Archilochus
Fr. 58　　　　　98

### Aristophanes
*LYSISTRATA*
109–10　　　　260n64

### Aristotle
*NICOMACHEAN ETHICS*
1148b26–35　　257n33

### Artemidoros
*ONEIROKRITIKA*
1.45　　　　　144–45
1.78　　　　　141–42, 263n81
1.78–79　　　142
1.78–80　　　258n47
1.80　　　　　142–43

### Caelius Aurelianus
*ON CHRONIC DISEASES*
4.9.137　　　　257n33

### Chariton
*CHAREAS AND CALLIRHOE*
5.9　　　　　　252n98

### Cicero
*CATILINARIAN ORATIONS*
2.22–24　　　　257n33

*ON THE ORATOR*
2.277　　　　　257n33

### Claudius Mamertinus
*PANEGYRICI LATINI*
11.19.4　　　　221n49

### Dio Chrysostom
*ORATION*
7.151　　　　　140

### Diodorus Siculus
32.10　　　　　263n81

### Euripides
*HECUBA*
536–38　　　　270n15

*TROJAN WOMEN*
308–13　　　　270n15

### Heliodoros
*ETHIOPIAN STORY*
1.2　　　　　　252n98
1.7　　　　　　252n98
1.19–20　　　　252n98
2.19　　　　　　252n98
7.12　　　　　　252n98
7.19　　　　　　252n98

### Homer
*ILIAD*
16.100　　　　270n15
22.468–70　　　270n15

*ODYSSEY*
13.388　　　　270n15
19.246ff.　　　228n105

### Horace
*SATIRES*
1.2.41ff.　　　255n20

## Juvenal

*SATIRES*

2.143ff.          265n96

## Lucian of Samosata

*DIALOGUES OF THE COURTESANS*

5.4 §292          260n64

## Martial

*EPIGRAMS*

1.90          260n64
2.51          257n32
6.56          257n32
7.67.1–3          260n64
9.47          257n32
11.88          257n32

*MOSAICARUM ET ROMANARUM LEGUM COLLATIO*

5.3          257n34

## Ovid

*AMORES*

1.9.15–20          270n15

*METAMORPHOSES*

9727          260n63

## Pliny the Younger

*LETTERS*

10.96–97          277n76

## Plutarch

*DIALOGUE ON LOVE*

768a          140

## Pseudo-Aristotle

*PROBLEMS*

426          257n33

## Pseudo-Lucian

*EROTES*

28          260n64

## Quintilian

*INSTITUTIONS*

5.9.14          257n33

## Sappho

Fr. 126          134

## Seneca the Elder

*CONTROVERSIAE*

1.2.23          260n64

## Seneca the Younger

*MORAL EPISTLES*

95.20          260n64

## Suetonius

*LIVES OF THE CAESARS*

*Augustus*

79.2          243n29

## Xenophon of Ephesus

*EPHESIAN TALE*

1.1–2          252n98

## III. CHRISTIAN SOURCES

### New Testament

MATTHEW

8:17          127
11:27          44
11:29–30          219n31
13:55          246n47
17:2          272n25
18:8–9          41
19:4          261n71

| | | | |
|---|---|---|---|
| 19:12 | 40–41 | 17:3 | 241n9 |
| 26:63a | 127 | 17:5 | 241n9 |
| 27:46 | 264n91 | 17:11 | 241n9 |
| | | 19:28 | 95 |

## MARK

| | | | |
|---|---|---|---|
| 1:1 | 91 | 19:34 | 95 |
| 6:3 | 246n47 | 20:14–17 | 229n110 |
| 9:12 | 127 | 20:16 | 129 |
| 10:6 | 261n71 | 20:17 | 63 |
| 15:28 | 127 | 20:25 | 95 |
| 15:34 | 264n91 | 20:27 | 95 |
| 15:39 | 91 | | |

## ACTS OF THE APOSTLES

| | |
|---|---|
| 8:32–33 | 127 |

## LUKE

| | |
|---|---|
| 1:31 | 68 |
| 1:35 | 68 |
| 2:52 | 121 |
| 22:37 | 121 |

## ROMANS

| | |
|---|---|
| 1:18 | 155, 263n82 |
| 1:18–23 | 151, 153 |
| 1:18–27 | 152, 152–53 |
| 1:18–32 | 133–34, 135, 147, 154–55, 158–59, 162, 166, 168, 171 |
| 1:18–2:29 | 262n73 |
| 1:18–3:20 | 156 |
| 1:18–3:31 | 5 |
| 1:19–23 | 261n71 |
| 1:21 | 150 |
| 1:22 | 161 |
| 1:22–23 | 151, 262n73 |
| 1:24 | 143 |
| 1:24–26 | 168–69 |
| 1:24–27 | 151, 157–58 |
| 1:25 | 161 |
| 1:26b | 143–44, 150, 159, 165, 166, 259n61, 267n109 |
| 1:26 | 155, 166 |
| 1:26–27 | 5, 134–35, 141–42, 143, 146–49, 154, 161, 165, 201, 259n61, 261n71, 265n94 |
| 1:26–32 | 261n71 |
| 1:27 | 143, 149, 260n63, 261n71, 265n97, 267n115 |
| 1:29–31 | 150 |
| 1:32 | 257n34 |
| 2:6 | 152 |
| 3:22 | 263n85 |
| 3:23 | 156 |
| 3:24 | 156 |

## JOHN

| | |
|---|---|
| 1:1–3 | 241n9 |
| 1:1–4 | 91 |
| 1:4 | 115 |
| 1:14 | 241n9 |
| 1:18 | 70, 231n120 |
| 3:29 | 70 |
| 3:35 | 241n9 |
| 4:6 | 95 |
| 4:7 | 95 |
| 4:43 | 250n88 |
| 7:37–38 | 70 |
| 8:12 | 115, 126, 229n108 |
| 8:44 | 229n108 |
| 8:57 | 242n18 |
| 8:58 | 241n9 |
| 9:5 | 115, 126, 229n108 |
| 10:30 | 70, 71, 241n9 |
| 12:27 | 241n9 |
| 12:35 | 115 |
| 12:38 | 127 |
| 12:41 | 241n9 |
| 13:23 | 70, 231n120 |
| 14:2 | 1 |
| 14:6 | 126 |
| 14:10 | 70, 241n9 |
| 14:31 | 69 |

| | |
|---|---|
| 5:18 | 263n84 |
| 5:19 | 156, 263n84 |
| 6:1–7:6 | 162–63 |
| 6:3–6 | 164 |
| 6:5 | 64 |
| 6:16–23 | 165 |
| 7:2 | 262n81 |
| 7:14 | 163 |
| 8:29–30 | 165 |
| 10:16 | 127 |
| 13:1–7 | 165 |

1 CORINTHIANS

| | |
|---|---|
| 3:1–3 | 226n88 |
| 4:16 | 164 |
| 6:9–10 | 256n21, 259n61 |
| 6:9–11 | 260n70 |
| 7:7–8 | 146, 165 |
| 9:5 | 146, 165 |
| 9:15 | 146, 165 |
| 11:1 | 164 |
| 11:7 | 261n71 |
| 15:3 | 127 |
| 15:24–28 | 165 |
| 15:48–49 | 165 |

2 CORINTHIANS

| | |
|---|---|
| 3:18 | 57 |
| 12:2 | 71 |

GALATIANS

| | |
|---|---|
| 1:10 | 165 |
| 1:12 | 164 |
| 2:19–20 | 164 |
| 3:28 | 50, 261n71, 264n94 |
| 5:19–21 | 260n70 |

EPHESIANS

| | |
|---|---|
| 5:21–33 | 157–59 |
| 5:21–6:9 | 159 |
| 5:24 | 158 |
| 5:25b | 159 |
| 5:27 | 56, 58, 158 |
| 6:5–6 | 159 |

PHILIPPIANS

| | |
|---|---|
| 2:5–8 | 156 |
| 2:6 | 71 |
| 2:6–11 | 127, 251n95 |
| 2:7 | 63, 229n107 |
| 2:8 | 263n84 |

COLOSSIANS

| | |
|---|---|
| 3:10 | 58 |

1 THESSALONIANS

| | |
|---|---|
| 1:6 | 164 |

2 THESSALONIANS

| | |
|---|---|
| 3:7 | 164 |
| 3:9 | 164 |

1 TIMOTHY

| | |
|---|---|
| 1:9–10 | 259n61 |
| 1:10 | 256n21 |

HEBREWS

| | |
|---|---|
| 1:4 | 63 |
| 5:8 | 263n84 |
| 15:12–14 | 226n88 |

1 Peter

| | |
|---|---|
| 2:2–3 | 226n88 |
| 2:22–24 | 127 |
| 5:13 | 269n12 |

1 JOHN

| | |
|---|---|
| 1:5 | 115 |
| 3:5 | 127 |
| 3:8 | 229n108 |

REVELATION

| | |
|---|---|
| 1:2 | 277n75 |
| 1:5 | 277n75 |
| 1:9 | 173, 272n27, 277n75 |
| 1:12–16 | 271n25 |
| 1:13–14 | 126–27 |
| 1:13–16 | 251n97, 271n25 |
| 1:16 | 177 |
| 2:3 | 272n27 |
| 2:7 | 184 |
| 2:9–10 | 272n27 |
| 2:11 | 184 |
| 2:12 | 177 |
| 2:13 | 272n27, 277n75 |
| 2:16 | 177 |
| 2:17 | 184 |
| 2:18 | 181 |

| | | | |
|---|---|---|---|
| 2:26-28 | 181 | 16:19 | 269n12 |
| 2:28 | 184 | 16:21 | 277n76 |
| 3:5 | 184 | 17:3-5 | 269n12 |
| 3:8 | 272n27 | 17:3-6 | 186, 270n19 |
| 3:12 | 184 | 17:4 | 269n12 |
| 3:14 | 277n75 | 17:5 | 181 |
| 3:30 | 216n15 | 17:6 | 272n27, 277n75 |
| 3:21 | 184, 185 | 17:14 | 184, 185, 187 |
| 5:5 | 176, 184, 185 | 17:16 | 183, 196-97, 270n16, 273n40 |
| 5:5-6 | 186 | 17:17 | 184 |
| 6:8 | 189 | 18:2 | 269n12 |
| 6:9 | 272n27, 277n75 | 18:10 | 269n12 |
| 6:9-10 | 278n78 | 18:21 | 269n12 |
| 6:9-11 | 198-99 | 18:24 | 272n27 |
| 6:16 | 271n22 | 19:2 | 272n27 |
| 7:4-14 | 186 | 19:10 | 277n75 |
| 7:14 | 272n27 | 19:11 | 177, 185 |
| 8:1 | 174 | 19:14 | 187 |
| 8:7-12 | 189 | 19:15 | 177, 181 |
| 9:15 | 189 | 19:19 | 185 |
| 9:18 | 189 | 19:19-21 | 181-82 |
| 10:1 | 272n25 | 19:21 | 177, 187 |
| 10:4 | 70, 174 | 20:4 | 272n27, 277n75 |
| 10:7 | 189 | 20:4-6 | 197 |
| 11:7 | 185, 277n75 | 20:7-10 | 182 |
| 11:15 | 181 | 21:7 | 184 |
| 11:18 | 181 | 22:8 | 173 |
| 12:5 | 181 | 22:16 | 176, 277n75 |
| 12:7-8 | 185 | 22:18 | 182 |
| 12:9 | 78 | 22:20 | 277n75 |
| 12:10 | 181 | | |
| 12:11 | 184, 185 | | |
| 12:17 | 185, 272n27, 277n75 | | |
| 13:7 | 185 | | |
| 13:7ff. | 272n27 | | |
| 14:1 | 181 | | |
| 14:4 | 186, 270n18 | | |
| 14:6 | 269n12 | | |
| 14:9-11 | 188, 199, 271n22, 277n76 | | |
| 15:1 | 189 | | |
| 15:2 | 184, 185 | | |
| 16:2-21 | 189 | | |
| 16:9 | 277n76 | | |
| 16:11 | 277n76 | | |
| 16:14 | 176, 181, 185 | | |
| 16:16 | 181 | | |

## Apocryphal Gospels and Acts

*ACTS OF JOHN*

| | |
|---|---|
| 89 | 272n21 |

*ACTS OF PAUL AND THECLA*

| | |
|---|---|
| 3.2 | 98 |
| 3.4 | 243n26 |

*ACTS OF PETER*

| | |
|---|---|
| 7.104 | 242n21 |

*GOSPEL OF PETER*

| | |
|---|---|
| 5.19 | 264n91 |

*GOSPEL OF TRUTH*

| | |
|---|---|
| 20.24-25 | 90 |

## Patristic, Medieval, and Related Sources

### ALAN OF LILLE

*In Cantica Canticorum*

| | |
|---|---|
| 2–4 | 68 |
| 8 | 68 |

*Antichrist* 92

*Antonini Placentini Itinerarium*

| | |
|---|---|
| 23 | 244n33 |

*Apophthegmata Patrum*

230n114

### AUGUSTINE

*Exposition of Psalm 127*

| | |
|---|---|
| 8 | 96 |

### BERNARD OF CLAIRVAUX

*Sermons on the Song of Songs*

| | |
|---|---|
| 2.2 | 23 |
| 3.5 | 69, 224n70 |
| 4.1 | 224n70 |
| 7.2 | 66 |
| 8.1–2 | 69 |
| 8.6 | 69 |
| 8.7 | 70 |
| 8:8 | 71 |
| 8.9 | 71 |
| 9.2 | 24 |
| 9.7 | 24 |
| 25.3 | 228n107 |
| 25.7 | 226n91 |
| 25.9 | 227n94 |
| 25–28 | 228n107 |
| 28.2 | 229n107 |
| 28.10 | 63, 229n107 |
| 61.2 | 44 |
| 67.4–5 | 45 |
| 67.7 | 45 |
| 75.8 | 64 |
| 83.1 | 226n91 |
| 82.7 | 56 |
| 85.10 | 19 |

### CLEMENT OF ALEXANDRIA

*Instructor*

| | |
|---|---|
| 3.1 | 96 |
| 3.19.2 | 142 |

*Miscellanies*

| | |
|---|---|
| 2.5 | 96 |
| 3.59.3 | 95 |

### CYPRIAN

*To Donatus*

| | |
|---|---|
| 9 | 134 |

*Treatises*

| | |
|---|---|
| 12.2.13 | 96 |

### DENIS THE CARTHUSIAN

*Commentary on the Song of Songs*

| | |
|---|---|
| 2 | 67 |
| 5 | 51 |
| 16 | 74 |
| 17 | 46 |
| 20 | 226n90 |
| 42 | 28 |
| 43–45 | 25–26 |
| 49 | 67 |
| 55 | 68 |
| 58 | 68–69 |

### EUSEBIUS

*Ecclesiastical History*

| | |
|---|---|
| 6.8.1–3 | 40–41 |
| 7.25.26–27 | 183 |

### GREGORY OF ELVIRA

*Tractatus de epithalamio*

| | |
|---|---|
| 19 | 43 |

### GREGORY THE GREAT

*Exposition of the Song of Songs*

| | |
|---|---|
| 19 | 222n56 |
| 39 | 229n107 |

### HIPPOLYTUS

*Treatise on Christ and Antichrist*

| | |
|---|---|
| 44 | 242n19 |

IRENAEUS

*Against Heresies*

| 2.22.4 | 96 |
| 3.19.2 | 96 |
| 4.33.12 | 96 |

JEROME

*Letters*

| 22.1 | 228n106, 229n108 |
| 22.25 | 86 |
| 107.12 | 223n59 |
| 96.5–6 | 221n44 |
| 612 | 221n44 |

JOHN CASSIAN

*Collationes*

| 14.8 | 212n2 |

JOHN CHRYSOSTOM

*On the Epistle to the Romans*

| Homily 4.1 | 148, 260n64 |

JOHN OF THE CROSS

*Spiritual Canticle*

| 27 | 27 |
| 36.5 | 57 |
| 37.5 | 44 |

JUSTIN MARTYR

*First Apology*

| 50 | 96 |
| 291–92 | 221n46 |

LACTANTIUS

*Divine Institutes*

| 4.16 | 96 |

*Letter of Lentulus* 92

NICHOLAS OF LYRA

*Postilla Litteralis* on the Song of Songs

| 19 | 235n147 |
| 36 | 229n107 |
| 62–63 | 28 |

NOVATIAN

*Concerning the Trinity*

| 9 | 96 |

ORIGEN

*Against Celsus*

| 1.54 | 242n22 |
| 1.69 | 242n22 |
| 4.16 | 242n22 |
| 6.75 | 96–97, 99 |
| 6.76 | 99 |
| 7.16 | 242n22 |

*Commentary on Matthew*

| 12.29 | 242n22 |

*Commentary on the Song of Songs*

| Prologue 1 | 46, 226n88 |
| Prologue 2 | 55 |
| Prologue 3 | 55 |
| Prologue 4 | 42, 44 |
| 1.1 | 54, 55 |
| 1.2 | 42–43, 55 |
| 1.4 | 42, 44–45, 222n51, 44 |
| 2.1 | 58, 60–61 |
| 2.2 | 62, 229n108, 229n109 |
| 2.5 | 55 |
| 2.7 | 43, 219n31, 55–56 |
| 3.1 | 55 |
| 3.2 | 55, 56, 226n94 |
| 3.4 | 226n94 |
| 3.9 | 28, 49–50 |
| 3.14 | 58 |
| 3.15 | 43–44, 57–58 |

*Homilies on the Song of Songs*

| 1.2 | 28 |
| 1.2–3 | 23 |
| 1.5 | 222n55, 226n92 |
| 1.6 | 228n106, 229n108 |
| 1.8 | 28 |
| 1.10 | 56 |

PSEUDO-LUCIAN

*Philopatris*

| 12 | 243n26 |

RUPERT OF DEUTZ

*In Cantica Canticorum*
PL 168, c 914        86–87
PL 168, c 929–30    226n90

TERTULLIAN

*Against Marcion*
3.7                  99, 242n19
3.17                 99

*Against Praxeas*
11                   242n20, 244n35

*Answer to the Jews*
14                   96

*On the Flesh of Christ*
9                    244n36
15                   233n36

*On Idolatry*
18                   96

THOMAS GALLUS

*Explanation of the Song of Songs*
12                   226n90

WILLIAM OF SAINT THIERRY

*Brevis Commentatio*
17                   224n76
18                   50, 52

**CONTRAVERSIONS**

**JEWS AND OTHER DIFFERENCES**

---

Stephen D. Moore, *God's Beauty Parlor: And Other Queer Spaces In and Around the Bible*

Rela Mazali, *Else Where: Maps of Women's Goings and Stayings*

Shelly Matthews, *First Converts: Rich Pagan Women and the Rhetoric of Mission in Early Judaism and Christianity*

Menachem Lorberbaum, *Politics and the Limits of Law: Secularizing the Political in Medieval Jewish Thought*

Gabriella Safran, *Rewriting the Jew: Assimilation Narratives in the Russian Empire*

Galit Hasan-Rokem, *Web of Life: Folklore in Rabbinic Literature*

Charlotte Elisheva Fonrobert, *Menstrual Purity: Rabbinic and Christian Reconstructions of Biblical Gender*

James A. Matisoff, *Blessings, Curses, Hopes, and Fears: Psycho-Ostensive Expressions in Yiddish*, second edition

Benjamin Harshav, *The Meaning of Yiddish*

Benjamin Harshav, *Language in Time of Revolution*

Amir Sumaka'i Fink and Jacob Press, *Independence Park: The Lives of Gay Men in Israel*

Alon Goshen-Gottstein, *The Sinner and the Amnesiac: The Rabbinic Invention of Elisha ben Abuya and Eleazar ben Arach*

Bryan Cheyette and Laura Marcus, eds., *Modernity, Culture, and 'the Jew'*

Benjamin D. Sommer, *A Prophet Reads Scripture: Allusion in Isaiah 40–66*

Marilyn Reizbaum, *James Joyce's Judaic Other*

The authorized representative in the EU for product safety and compliance is:
Mare Nostrum Group
B.V Doelen 72
4831 GR Breda
The Netherlands

www.ingramcontent.com/pod-product-compliance
Lightning Source LLC
Chambersburg PA
CBHW020120240426
43673CB00038B/545